'Dr Kokkinis' book reminds us of the importance to critically question the shareholder primacy model in corporate governance especially when certain public interests are at stake in how important corporations are governed. It is very much aligned with UK financial regulators' view that senior managers should be made more responsible for public interest objectives, charting a unique path away from religious adherence to shareholder primacy.'

Dr Iris H Chiu
Professor of Corporate Law and Financial Regulation at UCL

'For too long, corporate and banking law have remained mutually distinct subject areas. This was illustrated by the markedly differing academic and policy discourses in these fields following the financial crisis. In this ground-breaking and thought-provoking work, an author who is equally well-versed in both specialisms provides a lucid, compelling and conceptually sophisticated exposition of why prudential bank regulation is incapable of resolving financial stability concerns in the absence of supportive corporate law reforms. Kokkinis' polemic is at once both radical and common-sense. Above all, it calls on academics and policymakers to recognise the potential of corporate law to act as a powerful public policy mechanism in the financial domain.'

Dr Marc Moore
Reader in Law at Cambridge University

Corporate Law and Financial Instability

Virtually all large banks and other financial institutions in the UK and internationally are public limited liability companies whose shares are listed on one or several stock exchanges. As such, their corporate governance and, in particular, the incentives faced by their directors and senior managers are to a significant extent determined by corporate and securities law rules such as directors' duties, directors' liability in insolvency, takeover regulation, disclosure obligations, shareholder rights and rules on executive remuneration. At the same time, systemically important financial institutions in the UK are licensed, regulated and supervised by the Prudential Regulation Authority (PRA).

This book explores the relationship between, on the one hand, the broader corporate law, corporate governance and securities law framework and, on the other, the prudential regulatory framework. Although the book's main focus is on UK law, much of the policy argumentation is relevant globally and therefore appropriate international comparisons are drawn, and analysis of EU law and regulation is included. The book argues that the corporate law regime, which focuses on shareholder empowerment and profit maximisation, operates as an antithesis to prudential regulatory objectives thus undermining the safety and soundness of banks and other financial institutions by encouraging risky behaviour that may be in the best interests of their shareholders, but is clearly not in the public interest.

Andreas Kokkinis is Assistant Professor at the School of Law of the University of Warwick, UK.

Routledge Research in Corporate Law

Available titles in this series include:

Rethinking Corporate Governance in Financial Institutions
Demetra Arsalidou

Board Accountability in Corporate Governance
Andrew Keay

Piercing the Corporate Veil in Latin American Jurisprudence
A Comparison with the Anglo-American Method
Jose Maria Lezcano

Legal Approaches and Corporate Social Responsibility
Towards a Llewellyn's Law-Jobs Approach
Adaeze Okoye

Disqualification of Company Directors
A Comparative Analysis of the Law in the UK, Australia, South Africa, the US and Germany
Jean Jacques du Plessis and Jeanne Nel de Koker

Beyond Shareholder Wealth Maximisation
Towards a More Suitable Corporate Objective for Chinese Companies
Min Yan

Corporate Law and Financial Instability
Andreas Kokkinis

Forthcoming titles in this series include:

Behavioural Risks in Corporate Governance
Regulatory Intervention as a Risk Management Mechanism
Ngozi Vivian Okoye

Regulation and Inequality at Work
Isolation and Inequality Beyond the Regulation of Labour
Vanisha Sukdeo

Corporate Law and Financial Instability

Andreas Kokkinis

Routledge
Taylor & Francis Group
LONDON AND NEW YORK

First published 2018 by Routledge

2 Park Square, Milton Park, Abingdon, Oxfordshire OX14 4RN
52 Vanderbilt Avenue, New York, NY 10017

Routledge is an imprint of the Taylor & Francis Group, an informa business

First issued in paperback 2019

British Library Cataloguing in Publication Data
A catalogue record for this book is available from the British Library

Library of Congress Cataloging in Publication Data
Names: Kokkinis, Andreas, author.
Title: Corporate law and financial instability / Andreas Kokkinis.
Description: Abingdon, Oxon [UK] ; New York : Routledge, 2017. |
Series: Routledge research in corporate law | Includes bibliographical references and index.
Identifiers: LCCN 2017028448 | ISBN 9781138289130 (hardback) |
ISBN 9781315267340 (ebook)
Subjects: LCSH: Corporation law—Great Britain. | Stockholders—Legal status, laws, etc.—Great Britain. | Private companies—Great Britain. | Corporations—Finance—Law and legislation—Great Britain. | Corporation law.
Classification: LCC KD2079 .K65 2017 | DDC 346.41/066—dc23
LC record available at https://lccn.loc.gov/2017028448

ISBN: 978-1-138-28913-0 (hbk)
ISBN: 978-0-367-88641-7 (pbk)

Typeset in Galliard
by Taylor & Francis Books

Dedicated to my late uncle, Sotirios, and to the study of the Greek social security system that he never had time to write due to his untimely demise.

Contents

Tables

Cases

England and Wales

Scotland

European Court of Justice

European Court of Human Rights

United States

Canada

Australia

Legislation

UK statutes

Bank of England Act 1998
Banking Act 1979
Banking Act 1987
Banking Act 2009
Building Societies Act 1986
Companies Act 1862
Companies Act 2006
Company Directors Disqualification Act 1986
Criminal Justice Act 1993
Enterprise and Regulatory Reform Act 2013
Financial Services and Markets Act 2000
Financial Services Act 2010
Financial Services Act 2012
Financial Services (Banking Reform) Act 2013
Health and Safety at Work etc. Act 1974
Human Rights Act 1998
Insolvency Act 1986
Small Business, Enterprise and Employment Act 2015
Tribunals, Courts and Enforcement Act 2007

UK statutory instruments

Banking Coordination (Second Council Directive) Regulations (SI 1992/3218)
Banks and Building Societies (Depositor Preference and Priorities) Order 2014 (SI 2014/3486)
Company (Model Articles) Regulations (SI 2008/3229)
Financial Services (Banking Reform) Act 2013 (Commencement No. 1) Order 2014 (SI 2014/377)
Financial Services (Banking Reform) Act 2013 (Commencement No. 9) Order 2015 (SI 2015/490)

Financial Services (Banking Reform) Act 2013 (Commencement No. 10) Order 2016 (SI 2016/512)
Financial Services and Markets Act 2000 (PRA-regulated Activities) Order 2013 (SI 2013/556)
Small Business, Enterprise and Employment Act 2015 (Commencement No. 2 and Transitional Provisions) Regulations 2015 (SI 2015/1689)
Transfer of Tribunal Functions Order 2010 (SI 2010/22)

EU treaties, directives and regulations

Acquisition Directive 2007/44/EC [2007] OJ L247/1
Agreement between the European Economic Community and the Swiss Confederation of 26 July 1989 on direct insurance other than life insurance [1991] OJ L205/3
Agreement on the European Economic Area [1994] OJ L1/3
Bank Recovery and Resolution Directive 2014/59/EU [2014] OJ L173/190
Banking Union Regulation (EU) No 1024/2013 [2013] OJ L287/63
Capital Requirements (CRD III) Directive 2010/76/EU [2010] OJ L329/3
Capital Requirements (CRD IV) Directive 2013/36/EU [2013] OJ L176/338
Capital Requirements Directive 2006/49/EC [2006] OJ L177/201
Capital Requirements Regulation (CRR) (EU) No 575/2013 [2013] OJ L176/1
Consolidated version of the Treaty on European Union and the Treaty on the Functioning of the European Union [2012] OJ C326/1
Deposit-Guarantee Schemes Directive 2009/14/EC [2009] OJ L68/3
EEC Switzerland Free Trade Agreement [1972] OJ L300/189
European Banking Authority Regulation (EU) No 1093/2010 [2010] OJ L331/12
European Banking Authority II Regulation (EU) No 1022/2013 [2013] OJ L287/5
European Insurance and Occupational Pensions Authority Regulation (EU) No 1094/2010 [2010] OJ L331/48
European Securities and Market Authority Regulation (EU) No 1095/2010 [2010] OJ L331/84
European Systemic Risk Board Regulation (EU) No 1092/2010 [2010] OJ L331/1
Financial Conglomerates Directive 2002/87/EC [2003] OJ L35/1
Insider Dealing Directive 89/592/EEC [1989] OJ L334/30
Market Abuse Directive 2003/6/EC [2003] OJ L96/16
OTC Derivatives Regulation (EU) No 648/2012 [2012] OJ L201/1
Shareholder Rights Directive 2007/36/EC [2007] OJ L184/17
Single Resolution Mechanism Regulation (EU) No 806/2014 [2014] OJ L225/1
Solvency II Directive 2009/138/EC [2009] OJ L335/1
Treaty of Lisbon [2007] OJ C306/1

Foreign statutes

US statutes

Banking Act 1933
Financial Services Modernization Act 1999
Internal Revenue Code 1993
Wall Street Reform and Consumer Protection Act 2010 (Dodd-Frank Act)

German statutes

Co-determination Act (*Mitbestimmungsgesetz*) 1976

Swiss statutes

Federal Constitution of the Swiss Confederation of 18 April 1999

Preface and acknowledgements

This book is based on my doctoral research and therefore its inception goes back to 2009 when I first started contemplating pursuing a PhD. Its core idea, to look at corporate law as applying to financial institutions in view of the prudential regulation framework, was generated then as a response to the ongoing pubic debates surrounding the financial crisis which was still at its height. Since then, my views and assumptions have no doubt changed a lot, not least during the nearly three years that elapsed between being awarded my PhD and publishing this book. Equally, prudential regulation has undergone dramatic changes in the UK and internationally, and has expanded into areas previously considered as within the exclusive scope of private law. Despite this, there is still no 'special corporate law' for financial institutions, and the dichotomy between private (corporate) law and public (regulatory) law stands largely unscathed. The aim of this book is to challenge this dichotomy and to argue that a special corporate law regime is needed for financial institutions if we want to ensure that prudential regulation is effective.

As is true for all projects of this type, this book would not have been possible without the help, advice and support of many individuals who I would like to acknowledge. First of all, I would like to thank all the people with whom I have worked at Routledge, the book's publisher, and especially Ms Katie Carpenter and Ms Olivia Manley for their great support. Special thanks are also due to the anonymous reviewers of my book proposal, the helpful insights of whom greatly contributed to the present structure and development of the book. Finishing the manuscript on time would not have been possible without the excellent support of my research assistant Miss Julie Mansuy whose professionalism and skill left me impressed.

I also wish to thank all my colleagues at the University of Warwick School of Law for their support and help, which has contributed to an excellent research environment. In particular, I am indebted to Professor Fiona Smith, my mentor, for her feedback on my book proposal, as well as Professors Dalvinder Singh and Lorraine Talbot, and Dr John Snape and Stephen Connelly for their valuable suggestions and the conversations we have had. I also wish to thank all my students over the past six years for their stimulating questions and seminar discussions.

As this is a monograph that is based on my doctoral research at University College London (UCL), special thanks are due to my primary PhD supervisor,

Dr Marc Moore, for his continuous support and guidance over a period of four years and beyond, even after the end of my doctoral studies. His dedication, patience, experience and expertise have provided me with valuable academic advice, criticism and help, and have kept me on track for all this period of time. I am especially grateful to Marc for his willingness to engage in long and enthusiastic conversations on the theoretical problems raised by my research, which have been extremely helpful and fascinating, and for his detailed review of my work, which has helped me develop my 'authorial voice' and writing style.

Equally, I am indebted to my second PhD supervisor, Dr Iris Chiu, who kindly accepted to act as such at the beginning of my second year despite her other commitments, and has since then provided valuable advice and constructive criticism of my work. I therefore wish to thank Iris for her precious help, especially in the parts of my thesis focusing on banking regulation, and for her overall contribution to honing my arguments and ensuring the consistency and coherence of my central *thesis* throughout the thesis. In parallel, I wish to thank my initial second supervisor, who also acted as my primary supervisor for the second term of my first year, Professor Philip Rawlings.

I am, of course, equally indebted to my PhD examiners, Professor Andrew Keay and Professor Dan Prentice, for agreeing to examine my thesis, and for the valuable comments and insights that they provided. In parallel, I would like to thank the two funding bodies that sponsored me during my doctoral studies, the Greek State Scholarships Foundation and the Alexander Onassis Public Benefit Foundation, for their generous support.

Apart from the outstanding level of formal supervision that I received, I am grateful to the University College London Faculty of Laws as a whole for providing a vibrant and engaging research environment and for making PhD candidates feel fully integrated into the Faculty's research community. I am particularly indebted to many members of staff for their guidance and support of my research and teaching at UCL: Professor John Lowry, Professor Alison Diduck, Professor Dan Prentice, Professor Edward Walker Arnott, Professor Valentine Korah, Dr Arad Reisberg, Dr Fiona Smith, Dr Jane Holder, Dr Douglas Guilfoyle, Dr Florian Wagner-von Papp, Dr Prince Saprai and many more. Equally important has been the contribution of the PhD student community at UCL, which has been a constant source of constructive academic conversations and personal support. I am especially indebted to Dr Joseph Spooner, Dr Bolanle Adebola, Dr Danae Azaria, Dr Deni Mantzari, Dr Carrie Bradshaw, Dr Bas Leeuw, Dr Anna Donovan, Dr Oisin Suttle, Dr Claire Lougarre, and Dr Azi Chalabi.

Lastly, I would like to thank my family and friends for their sustained support and intelligent conversations that helped me maintain my enthusiasm throughout the long life of this project.

Dr Andreas Kokkinis, May 2017

Abbreviations

ABI	Association of British Insurers
ABS	asset-backed securities
AFBD	Association of Futures Brokers and Dealers
AGM	Annual General Meeting
APER	Approved Persons Regime
BCCI	Bank of Credit and Commerce International
BIS	Bank for International Settlements
BOFIs	banks and other financial institutions
BRRD	Bank Recovery and Resolution Directive
CDDA	Company Directors Disqualification Act
CEO	chief executive officer
CET1	Common Equity Tier 1
CFO	chief finance officer
CG Code	Corporate Governance Code
CRD-IV	Capital Requirements Directive IV
CRO	chief risk officer
CRR	Capital Requirements Regulation
EBA	European Banking Authority
ECAI	External Credit Assessment Institution
ECB	European Central Bank
ECHR	European Convention on Human Rights
ECMH	efficient capital markets hypothesis
EEA	European Economic Area
EEC	European Economic Community
EFTA	European Free Trade Association
EIOPA	European Insurance and Occupational Pensions Authority
ELA	Emergency Liquidity Assistance
EMS	Entity Maximisation and Sustainability
EPS	earnings per share
ESAs	European Supervisory Authorities
ESFS	European System of Financial Supervision
ESMA	European Securities and Markets Authority
ESRB	European Systemic Risk Board

ESV	enlightened shareholder value
EU	European Union
FCA	Financial Conduct Authority
FIMBRA	Financial Intermediaries, Managers and Brokers Regulatory Association
FPC	Financial Policy Committee
FSA	Financial Services Authority
FSB	Financial Stability Board
FSMA 2000	Financial Services and Markets Act
G-SIB	global systemically important bank
G-SII	global systemically important institution
GDP	gross domestic product
HBOS	Halifax Bank of Scotland
HFC	HSBC Finance Corporation
ILO	International Labour Organisation
IMF	International Monetary Fund
IMRO	Investment Management Regulatory Organisation
IRB Approach	Internal Ratings-Based Approach
LAUTRO	Life Assurance and Unit Trust Regulatory Organisation
LIBOR	London Interbank Offered Rate
LTIP	long-term incentive plan
MAD	Market Abuse Directive
NED	non-executive director
NGO	non-governmental organisation
NSFR	net stable funding ratio
OECD	Organisation for Economic Co-operation and Development
O-SII	other systemically important institution
PIA	Personal Investment Authority
PRA	Prudential Regulation Authority
RBS	Royal Bank of Scotland
ROE	return on equity
RoRWA	return on risk-weighted assets
SFA	Securities and Futures Authority
SIB	Securities and Investment Board
SIV	structured investment vehicle
SPV	special purpose vehicle
SRM	Single Resolution Mechanism
SRO	self-regulating organisation
SSM	Single Supervisory Mechanism
SYSC	Systems and Controls
TEU	Treaty on European Union
TFEU	Treaty for the Functioning of the European Union
TSA	The Securities Association
TSR	total shareholder return

Introduction

> Though the principles of the banking trade may appear somewhat abstruse, the practice is capable of being reduced to strict rules. To depart upon any occasion from these rules, in consequence of some flattering speculation of extraordinary gain, is almost always extremely dangerous, and frequently fatal to the banking company which attempts it.
>
> Adam Smith, *The Wealth of Nations*[1]

I. Corporate law and the 2007–2009 financial crisis

The images of desperate depositors queuing outside the branches of Northern Rock on Friday 14 September 2007 and the cataclysmic events that followed, including the partial nationalisation of the Royal Bank of Scotland (RBS) and Lloyds Banking Group,[2] have left a lingering legacy of distrust to the UK financial system.[3] A decade later and after the implementation of a series of legislative and regulatory reforms at the UK, European Union (EU) and international levels, academic debate continues on the causes of the crisis and the adequacy of the post-crisis reforms. This book is intended to contribute to this debate by exploring ways to create appropriate personal financial incentives for senior managers in the financial industry – both via the corporate law and corporate governance framework and the prudential banking regulation framework.

Banks and other financial institutions have traditionally played a distinctive role in the economy of Britain. Since the establishment of the Bank of England in 1694 and the Bank of Scotland in 1695, banking has grown steadily in tandem with industrial capitalism. Initially, all private sector banks operated as partnerships. However, from 1826 English banks started to adopt the legal form of a

1 Adam Smith, *An Inquiry into the Nature and Causes of the Wealth of Nations* (Strahan and Cadell, 1776), Book V, 820.

2 Immediately after injecting public funds in 2009, the government owned approximately 82% of the share capital of RBS and 43% of the share capital of Lloyds. See Emma Dunkley, 'Lloyds Back in Private Ownership After Government Sells Out', *Financial Times* (London, 17 May 2017).

3 For a succinct discussion of the five main banking failures in the UK during the 2007–2009 crisis, see Edward Walker-Arnott, 'Company Law, Corporate Governance and the Banking Crisis' (2010) 7 *International Corporate Rescue* 19, 19–20, and 24–26.

joint stock company, and from 1858 the form of registered limited liability companies under the relevant statutory provisions, which had been nearly universally adopted by the end of the 19th century. It was only during the 1980s that investment banks completed the same process of adopting the corporate form, or being acquired by retail banks.

At the same time, most of the UK's building societies, which are co-operative banks functioning as mutual institutions, transformed to public companies or merged with banking corporations. As a result, since the 1990s the greatest part of retail and investment banking activity has been carried out by financial conglomerates, which are structured as groups of companies ultimately owned by a parent public company which has its shares listed on the London Stock Exchange. The deregulation of the 1980s culminating in the Big Bang of 1986 allowed banks to engage in securities trading, and generally to adopt risky business strategies of their own choice under the generally liberal supervision of the relevant authorities: the Bank of England until 1998, the Financial Services Authority (FSA) from 1998 until 2013, and currently the Prudential Regulation Authority (PRA) and Financial Conduct Authority (FCA).[4] Deregulation led to an unprecedented increase in financial sector activities, which up until the recent financial crisis grew at a significantly faster pace than the rest of the economy. Indeed, financial intermediation contributed 9% of the UK's gross domestic product (GDP) in 2008[5] and the assets of the banking sector amounted to more than 500% of GDP in 2006.[6]

Given the prominence of the banking sector it is of no surprise that the UK felt the consequences of the 2007–2009 global financial crisis more severely than most continental European countries, and that its economy consequently entered a protracted recession. During the years that followed the financial crisis of 2007–2009, several UK banks have faced serious scandals and regulatory scrutiny of their actions. Most notably, in 2012 Barclays was fined by the FSA, the Commodity Futures Trading Commission and the US Department of Justice for manipulation of the London Interbank Offered Rate (LIBOR).[7] In 2013 Barclays and RBS were amongst the six global financial institutions fined by the European Commission, and the Co-operative Bank faced serious losses and was recapitalised partially via bailing in bondholders whose bonds were converted to equity.[8]

4 For a concise account of the evolution of financial regulation in the UK, see Chapter 3, section II.

5 See Stephen Burgess, 'Measuring Financial Sector Output and its Contribution to UK GDP' (2011) *Bank of England Quarterly Bulletin* 234, 234–235.

6 The data are taken from a conference speech given by Mr Haldane, Bank of England Executive Director for Financial Stability. See Andrew Haldane, 'The Contribution of the Financial Sector: Miracle or Mirage?' (Future of Finance conference, London, 14 July 2010), 14–15 www.bis.org/review/r100716g.pdf accessed 1 May 2017.

7 As this is a conduct of business issue, it will not be discussed in this book. For an overview of the relevant events and a discussion of regulatory lessons learnt from them, see David Hou and David R Skeie, 'LIBOR: Origins, Economics, Crisis, Scandal, and Reform' (2014) Federal Reserve Bank of New York Staff Report 667 https://papers.ssrn.com/sol3/papers.cfm?abstract_id=2423387 accessed 1 May 2017.

8 On this, see Chapter 5, section IV (a).

Finally, several major UK banks – amongst other large companies – attracted widespread opposition to their executive remuneration policies from their institutional shareholders in 2014 and 2015, a phenomenon described by the financial press as the shareholder spring.[9]

Indeed, bank corporate governance owes its elevation to an independent field of study to the 2007–2009 financial crisis, as the crisis led to an increasing awareness of the significance of bank corporate governance internationally. For instance, the Organisation for Economic Co-operation and Development (OECD) Steering Group on Corporate Governance concluded that: 'the financial crisis can be to an important extent attributed to failures and weaknesses in corporate governance arrangements which did not serve their purpose to safeguard against excessive risk taking in a number of financial services companies.'[10] The report identified three problematic areas of governance, namely qualified board oversight and risk management, executive remuneration, and accounting standards. At the EU level, a consultation held in 2009 led to the publication of a Green Paper in 2010 on the corporate governance of financial institutions. The core normative finding of the Paper is the suggestion that '[i]n the financial services sector, corporate governance should take account of the interests of other stakeholders (...), as well as the stability of the financial system, due to the systemic nature of many players'.[11] At the same time the Paper rejected the notion of regulatory-driven governance of financial institutions, and insisted that it should be the board of directors under the supervision of the shareholders which defines a financial firm's strategy and risk appetite.

In the UK, the report of the Commission on Banking Standards painted a grim picture of bank governance practices: '[t]he corporate governance of large banks was characterised by the creation of Potemkin villages to give the appearance of effective control and oversight, without the reality. In particular, many non-executive directors – in many cases experienced, eminent and highly-regarded individuals – failed to act as an effective check on, and challenge to, executive managers.'[12] A number of the Commission's recommendations were implemented by the Financial Services (Banking Reform) Act 2013 (also referred to as the Banking Reform Act 2013), but the identified misalignment between the company law duties of bank directors and prudential requirements has not so far been remedied.

In view of the potential economic and social significance of addressing the complex corporate governance problems faced by banks and other financial institutions, a considerable amount of scholarly work has been undertaken, and further work is currently in progress, on the topic. The interdisciplinary nature of the

9 On this, see Chapter 7, n 77 and accompanying text.

10 Grant Kirkpatrick, 'The Corporate Governance Lessons from the Financial Crisis' (2009) *OECD Journal: Financial Market Trends* 61, 61.

11 See Commission, 'Corporate Governance in Financial Institutions and Remuneration Policies' COM (2010) 284 final, 2.

12 Parliamentary Commission on Banking Standards, *Changing Banking for Good* (2013–14, HL 27-I, HC 175-I), para 119.

subject explains the wide range of academics that have shown an interest in the area, including lawyers, economists and other social scientists.[13]

II. The objectives of the book

The purpose of this book is to explore the relationship between, on the one hand, the broader corporate law, corporate governance and securities law framework and, on the other, the prudential regulatory framework. Essentially, it attempts to answer the following normative question: *does the public interest in financial stability, and the ensuing need to regulate financial institutions prudentially, necessitate the adoption of a regulatory approach to the corporate law framework applying to financial institutions?* In parallel, this book seeks to analyse the impact that post-crisis legislative and regulatory reforms are having on financial institution corporate governance to ascertain the extent to which the area has been transformed towards a regulatory direction. This second task of doctrinal legal analysis informs and supports the normative discussion by clarifying the contours of the topic, identifying the range of possible available solutions, and helping to formulate workable reform proposals that take into account the broader institutional context within which any such reforms would have to operate.

A regulatory approach to the corporate law framework applying to financial institutions would entail the state legislatively intervening in the internal organisation of financial institutions and making decisions on fundamental aspects of their governance, such as their corporate objective. Such intervention would have been extremely controversial until the recent financial crisis, and is still only occurring in some specific areas, predominantly in executive remuneration and the approval of proposed directors and senior managers by prudential regulators. At the same time, corporate law scholarship has not explicitly addressed the issue of corporate governance in the financial sector. Generic corporate theory remains dominated by the contractarian view of the company, which explains company law as a fundamentally facilitative area of law and defends this approach normatively on grounds of economic efficiency. As a result, the prudential regulatory discourse

13 Some of the post-crisis monographs and edited volumes which devote a substantial part of their analysis to bank corporate governance are the following: Iris Hse-Yu Chiu (ed), *The Legal Framework for Corporate Governance in Banks and Financial Institutions in the UK* (Edward Elgar, 2015); Wolf-Georg Ringe and Peter Huber (eds), *Legal Challenges in the Global Financial Crisis* (Hart Publishing, 2014); James Barth, Chen Lin and Clas Wihlborg (eds), *Research Handbook on International Banking and Governance* (Edward Elgar, 2012); Eddy Wymeersch, Klaus Hopt and Guido Ferrarini (eds), *Financial Regulation and Supervision: A post-crisis analysis* (OUP, 2012); William Sun, Jim Stewart and David Pollard (eds), *Corporate Governance and the Global Financial Crisis: International Perspectives* (CUP, 2011); Sol Picciotto, *Regulating Global Corporate Capitalism* (CUP, 2011); Marc Goergen and others, *Corporate Governance and Complexity Theory* (Edward Elgar, 2010); Iain McNeil and Justin O'Brien, *The Future of Financial Regulation* (Hart Publishing, 2010). For a pre-crisis discussion, see Benton Gup (ed), *Corporate Governance in Banking: A Global Perspective* (Edward Elgar Publishing, 2007).

and the company law and corporate theory discourse remain disjointed, thus creating the following conceptual confusion. Is a financial institution, which has the legal form of a body corporate, fundamentally a private association that should be free to pursue whatever goals its members choose within the limits of the law and regulation, or rather a public-interest entity[14] whose governance must be conducive to the protection of the public interest, and therefore should only promote the benefit of its members insofar as this is consistent with the public interest?

The following chapters will seek to demonstrate that the public interest in financial stability can only be sufficiently protected if the corporate law regime for financial institutions becomes complementary to prudential regulation; and that this outcome is consistent with the normative implications of the neo-classical economic analysis of law, and of corporate law in particular, given the specific characteristics of the financial sector. The book thus seeks to provide a theoretical justification for adopting a regulatory approach to financial institutions corporate governance as a necessary step to safeguard financial stability. To do so, the book reviews the other main aspects of prudential regulation (structural regulation, capital adequacy and liquidity requirements, and crisis management) to establish that a supportive corporate law framework is indispensable for the successful operation of prudential regulation. Having done so, the book will explore potential ways to reform the corporate law framework. The proposed reforms will be underpinned by the findings of relevant empirical economic research, which will be contextualised within the existing UK legal framework, and used to develop concrete proposals that would be likely to promote the long-term stability of the UK financial system.

To sum up, the main argument is that the 'corporate' regime, which focuses on shareholder empowerment and profit maximisation, operates as an antithesis to prudential regulatory objectives, thus undermining the safety and soundness of banks and other financial institutions by encouraging risky behaviour which may

14 The issue of whether financial institutions and indeed companies in general ought to be run in the public interest or not is logically separate from the way in which corporations are conceptualised – i.e. as autonomous entities (real entity theory), creations of state power (concession theory), or as fictional aggregations of private relations (nexus of contracts theory). Parkinson succinctly illustrates the distinction between the ontological description of companies as a social phenomenon and the determination of the normative question of whether they should be regulated in the public interest or not: '[The concession] theory and its antithesis, the contract theory, share a common assumption that *whether or not society has a right to demand that companies serve the public interest depends on whether the state can be depicted as playing some special role in corporate existence*, different in kind from its role in sustaining unincorporated businesses. [...] If the assumption is false, then the contract theory, while currently popular in some quarters, cannot in itself immunize the company from public-interest demands, nor explain why the state may not intervene in companies' "internal affairs" in order to enforce those demands.' See John Parkinson, *Corporate Power and Responsibility: Issues in the Theory of Company Law* (Clarendon Press, 1993), 25 (emphasis added).

be in the best interests of their shareholders (or not depending on the extent of agency costs), but is clearly not in the public interest due to the negative externalities caused by risk-taking by financial institutions.[15] It is argued that this problem has been addressed only partially by the series of regulatory reforms that have been implemented since the recent financial crisis, which the book explores in depth with a particular emphasis on regulatory enforcement cases and the new Senior Persons Regime. A rethink of core corporate law doctrines – to the extent that they apply to financial institutions – and of the way in which legal scholars who follow the economic analysis of law method conceptualise the nature and purpose of corporate law is therefore necessary. Such a rethink will give effect to the admonition of the Parliamentary Commission on Banking Standards to the government to review the duty of loyalty and corporate objective as applying to banks with a view to prioritising financial stability over profit maximisation.[16]

III. The scope of the present work

As this book is about the impact of the current corporate law framework on the governance of financial institutions, and hence on financial stability, it is necessary to define the terms 'financial institutions' and 'corporate law framework'. As the book is concerned with financial institutions whose business strategies, distress and failure can affect financial stability, it is evident that only systemically important financial institutions fall within its scope, although for the sake of brevity they will be referred to simply as financial institutions. As such, the book covers all financial institutions that are regulated by the Prudential Regulation Authority – that is, systemically important deposit-taking institutions, investment firms and insurance firms.[17] Still, as many of the regulatory rules apply only to banks – both retail and investment[18] – and much of the empirical research refers to banks, some parts of the discussion will focus on banks. Indeed, given the particular systemic significance of large banks which are listed on the stock exchange, much of the discussion will draw on the governance practices and characteristics of these banks. A further restriction to the scope of the book is that it only covers financial institutions that have the legal form of a limited liability company. So, the discussion does not extend to building societies and other mutual institutions, unless it allows light to be shed on the issues in question.

15 A detailed examination of the concept of negative externalities and public goods can be found in Richard Cornes and Todd Sandler, *The Theory of Externalities, Public Goods and Club Goods* (2nd edn, CUP, 1996) 39–67.

16 Parliamentary Commission on Banking Standards (above n 12), para 124.

17 A detailed examination of the firms and activities regulated by the PRA can be found in Chapter 3, section II.

18 An overview of the distinction between retail (or commercial) banking activities and investment (or merchant) banking activities can be found in Peter Ellinger, Eva Lomnicka and Christopher Hare, *Ellinger's Modern Banking Law* (5th edn, OUP, 2011), 5–18.

With regard to the term 'corporate law framework', it was chosen rather than the term 'corporate governance' because the latter is used to denote various different concepts, and different scholarly disciplines take a diverging approach with regard to its definition. Corporate governance can be defined as the nexus of relationships between boards, managers, shareholders and other stakeholders.[19] This notion of corporate governance is naturally multi-disciplinary as it includes all possible factors that determine the shape and dynamics of these relationships: formal contracts, informal understandings and expectations, norms of behaviour, mandatory rules of law (and regulation), default/enabling rules of law, and codes of best practice. More frequently, the term corporate governance is used to refer to the internal procedures by which power is distributed within companies amongst directors, managers, shareholders and – possibly – other stakeholders.[20]

This is also reflected on the traditional definition of corporate governance proposed by Cadbury.[21] Given the heavy reliance of the modern corporate governance movement on voluntary codes of best practice, corporate governance has reached to signify the particular technique of using soft-law rules and the 'comply-or-explain' method of enforcement, as opposed to using formal legal rules to influence the behaviour of companies and those involved in them. In that latter sense of a body of self-enforcing extra-legal norms, which are promulgated by specialist industry bodies rather than by Parliament and the courts,[22] corporate governance is often contrasted with corporate law (or company law),[23] which

19 See e.g. Stephen Bloomfield, *Theory and Practice of Corporate Governance: An Integrated Approach* (CUP, 2013), 19–20.

20 For instance, according to Demb and Neubauer, 'Corporate Governance is the process by which corporations are made responsive to the rights and wishes of stakeholders'. See Ada Demb and Franz-Freidrich Neubauer, *The Corporate Board: Confronting the Paradoxes* (OUP, 1992) 1. According to the OECD, corporate governance comprises the 'procedures and processes according to which an organisation is directed and controlled. The corporate governance structure specifies the distribution of rights and responsibilities among the different participants in the organisation – such as the board, managers, shareholders and other stakeholders – and lays down the rules and procedures for decision-making'. See Organisation for Economic Co-operation and Development Glossary, http://stats.oecd.org/glossary/detail.asp?ID=6778 accessed 1 May 2017.

21 Sir Adrian Cadbury, the pioneer of the corporate governance movement in the UK, defined corporate governance as 'the system by which companies are directed and controlled'. See Adrian Cadbury, *Report of the Committee on the Financial Aspects of Corporate Governance* (Gee Professional Publishing, 1992), para 2.5. This definition is included in the latest edition of the Corporate Governance Code. See Financial Reporting Council, 'UK Corporate Governance Code' (2016), 1. From now on, the Code will be abbreviated as the 'CG Code'.

22 Self-regulation (as a market-orientated approach to legal policy) should not be confused with reflexive regulation as the latter need not comply with the deregulation political agenda. On this see Gunther Teubner, *Law as an Autopoietic System*, Anne Bankowska and Ruth Adler trs, Zenon Bankowski ed (Blackwell, 1993), 68.

23 The terms 'company law' and 'corporate law' are frequently used interchangeably, although it tends to be the case that UK scholars prefer the former, while US scholars prefer the latter. In this book, the term company law will be used when referring to UK

encompasses the statutory, common law and equitable rules and principles that govern companies. This book does not adopt this distinction between corporate governance and company law, but rather defines the corporate law framework as the field of law that deals with the distribution of powers and duties among different interested parties to a corporation and determines the overall objective of the corporation.

That being said, there is no consensus regarding the logical boundaries between the corporate law framework and other areas of law. In the broadest possible sense, the framework comprises company law, securities regulation and labour law which, combined together, determine the boundaries between the corporation, capital markets and the labour market.[24] However, the generally accepted notion of corporate law in the Anglo-American context excludes labour law from its scope,[25] and tends to focus mostly on the rules of law that govern the relationship between directors/managers and equity providers.[26] It is submitted that the scope of the corporate law framework depends on the policy choices made by each legal system so that where employees are given decision-making rights within companies, labour law forms part of the corporate law framework of that given country,[27] but this is evidently not the case as far as the UK is concerned.[28] Given the purpose of the book, its main focus will be on rules that determine the powers,

company law doctrine whereas the term corporate law will be used when discussing policy issues and when alluding to the corporate law framework applicable to financial institutions. On the historical significance of using the term 'corporation' in the US rather than the term 'company', as evidence of adherence to the concession theory of the firm, see William Bratton, 'The New Economic Theory of the Firm: Critical Perspectives from History' (1989) 41 *Stanford Law Review* 1471, 1483–1485.

24 See John Cioffi, *Public Law and Private Power; Corporate Governance Reform in the Age of Finance Capitalism* (Cornell University Press, 2010), 38–43.

25 For an in-depth explanation of the position of employees in the Anglo-American context and of the usage of collective adversarialism as a substitute for direct empowerment of the employees within the company, see Marc T Moore, *Corporate Governance in the Shadow of the State* (Hart Publishing, 2013), 44–57. However, the definition of corporate governance proposed by Moore, as 'an enquiry into the cause and consequences of the allocation of power within large economic organisations' anticipates the potential inclusion of broader stakeholder groups within the corporate governance discourse, so far as they are subjected to the discretionary administrative power exercised by corporate managers. Ibid., 13.

26 An example of the focus of corporate governance on the protection of shareholder interests is the definition given by Shleifer and Vishny according to which 'corporate governance deals with the ways in which suppliers of finance to corporations assure themselves of getting a return on their investment'. See Andrei Shleifer and Robert Vishny, 'A Survey of Corporate Governance' (1997) 52 *The Journal of Finance* 737, 737.

27 A manifestation of this is the German system of co-determination whereby employee and trade union representatives elect half of the members of the supervisory boards of large companies, while the shareholders elect the other half. This is a mandatory rule for companies with at least 2,000 employees, introduced by the Co-determination Act (*Mitbestimmungsgesetz*) 1976.

28 At least insofar as companies are solvent. When the solvency of a company is dubious or threatened, directors' duties shift towards creditors, as will be seen in further detail in Chapter 2, section IV.

rights and duties of company directors and shareholders, as well as any other areas of law that influence these rights and duties and the exercise of corporate power, mainly capital markets regulation.

From a jurisdictional perspective, this book focuses on the United Kingdom. The corporate law reforms envisaged herein are thus tailored to the needs of UK financial institutions, taking into account the existing institutional framework of UK company law and prudential regulation. As such, it is not directly relevant to institutions incorporated in other jurisdictions. However, given the significant and expanding degree of harmonisation of financial regulation across the EU, and the inevitable focus of the discussion on rules deriving from EU law, the book will also be of interest for corporate law and financial regulation scholars and practitioners from other EU member states. The normative insights and links drawn between available empirical economic evidence and the need for legal reform are relevant globally, irrespective of legal jurisdiction, and even more so with respect to common law jurisdictions whose corporate governance systems share many of the characteristics of the UK system, such as the United States, Canada, Australia, New Zealand, Singapore and Hong Kong.

IV. An overview of the discussion per chapter

The main body of this monograph consists of seven chapters, followed by a brief conclusion.[29]

Chapter 1 challenges the conventional and still widely accepted position that doing business in a 'safe and sound' manner is in the best interests of shareholders and hence that conventionally understood good corporate governance is likely to enhance bank and other financial institution stability. The chapter demonstrates the inherent misalignment between, on the one hand, the private interests of the shareholders of banks and other financial institutions, and on the other, the public interest in financial stability given the prevalence of systemic risk. Then the discussion brings together empirical economic evidence which suggests that: (a) greater shareholder power is positively correlated with higher insolvency risk in financial institutions; and (b) the ability of current and potential equity and debt investors to restrain inefficient risk-taking and other forms of opportunistic behaviour by financial institution managers is limited compared to most other companies. This is due to the inherent opacity of financial institution assets. The latter finding demonstrates that the widespread problem of shareholder short-termism is very acute in financial institutions and therefore shareholders are likely to encourage managers to take unsustainably high levels of risk. Therefore, relying on market discipline as a regulatory tool to foster a resilient financial system is misconceived and likely to fail to deliver its intended outcomes.

Chapter 2 demonstrates how key UK corporate law doctrines and corporate governance principles achieve what financial regulation strives to prevent: the facilitation of risk-taking by financial institution managers by shielding them from

29 The law as stated in this book is correct as of 1 May 2017.

the financial consequences of these risks. In particular, it is shown that modern corporate law and governance seek to align the risk appetite of (generally) risk-averse senior managers with that of risk-neutral shareholders by setting strong incentives for executive directors and managers to maximise the market price of a company's (and thus a bank's or other financial institution's) shares in the short term in order to earn higher remuneration and secure their position. At the same time, company law and insolvency law, through the doctrines of separate corporate personality and limited liability, shield financial institution directors and senior managers from the consequences of risky decisions that turn out badly insofar as they acted in good faith and followed a reasonable decision-making process, as was demonstrated in the aftermath of the 2007–2009 financial crisis.

In Chapter 3 it is demonstrated that there is now a widely recognised public interest in maintaining the stability of the financial markets and that the economic characteristics of banks and other financial institutions make it necessary that they are regulated and supervised to the effect of protecting financial stability. It will also be argued that having in place a prudential regulation framework (formal or informal) is necessary as soon as banks and other major financial firms adopt limited liability in view of the incentives the latter creates. The structure of such regulatory arrangements will be shown to depend largely on political impetus generated by perceived regulatory failures, and therefore to be susceptible to relatively frequent change. UK regulatory architecture will also be shown to have been influenced by developments in EU law, which poses the question of the likely impact of the UK's withdrawal from the EU on the country's prudential regulation framework. Finally, the discussion will seek to provide an overview of regulatory techniques and strategies, with a particular emphasis on reflexive regulation and meta-regulation.

The aim of Chapters 4 and 5 is to review the financial regulation reforms that have been implemented, or are on course to be implemented, with a view to assessing whether they are likely to resolve the problems identified in the previous chapters. To this effect, Chapter 4 focuses on rules that seek to regulate the corporate and capital structure of banks and other financial institutions. These include the new capital adequacy and liquidity framework which impacts on institutions' needs to raise share capital, the so-called ring-fencing of retail UK banks, the introduction of convertible debt that can be used to bail-in an ailing bank, and the new banking resolution framework. It is argued that even the most apparently radical of these reforms, such as the capital requirements and the ring-fencing of retail banks, are limited in scope and heavily reliant on the wholehearted support of institutions' senior management who have considerable ability to comply with them in letter only and not in spirit. It thus becomes evident that in order for these reforms to be effective a supporting incentive structure should be in place for financial institutions' directors and senior management.

The purpose of Chapter 5 is to explore the post-crisis regulatory reforms that have addressed directly the behaviour of financial institutions' leaders. Such rules include the regulatory approval process for senior persons, requirements on the composition and role of boards of directors and senior management, limits on the ratio of fixed and variable executive remuneration and accountability mechanisms in case of regulatory breaches. The discussion will particularly explore reported cases of enforcement action by financial regulators against individuals since the beginning of the 2007–2009 financial crisis. It will be argued that although apparently radical, the rules in question are fraught with difficulties, especially the so-called bonus cap, which may lead to adverse unintended consequences and thus undermine rather than enhance financial stability. In any case, it will be demonstrated that the resulting framework remains heavily influenced by the traditional corporate law emphasis on shareholder empowerment and shareholder value maximisation, and therefore that the incipient transformation of the corporate law framework for financial institutions remains unfinished.

Chapter 6 introduces the financial stability-focused approach to financial institutions' corporate law and governance framework that is proposed in the present monograph. Given the causal relationship between the safety and soundness of individual institutions and the stability of the financial system as a whole, it is submitted that the appropriate corporate objective for banks and other financial institutions would be to safeguard their financial sustainability in the long term. Such a reform would complement existing prudential regulatory tools and would enhance the effectiveness of reflexive regulatory techniques by fine-tuning the corporate objective of financial institutions with the statutory objectives of the PRA. The new corporate objective would incorporate the pursuit of sustainable profitability by optimising operational efficiency, but would preclude taking an overall level of risk that threatens the institution's viability even if this level of risk maximises its expected net value (and thus maximises shareholder wealth). Counter-intuitively perhaps, the new paradigm would be entirely consistent with economic analysis of law as it is based on economic efficiency grounds, albeit challenging the conventional way in which economic analysis is used by corporate law scholars.

Chapter 7, the final substantive chapter of the volume, operationalises the principles proposed in the previous chapter by making a series of concrete law reform proposals. A new legal provision is thus proposed which would effectively implement the new corporate objective and ensure that financial institution directors and senior managers face powerful financial incentives to refrain from taking decisions that increase the insolvency risk of their institution. The new provision would be in line with the spirit of the recommendations of the Parliamentary Commission on Banking Standards, and would respond to the inadequacy of the present regulatory regime. It is also envisaged that the duty of loyalty owed by financial institution directors and wrongful trading and disqualification rules should be reformed to reflect the corporate objective proposed herein. Several other additional reforms are also proposed with a view to fostering appropriate incentives: further improving the performance metrics used in connection with variable executive remuneration; limiting the financial dependence of independent directors on any single financial institution; and requiring chief risk officers to sit on financial institution boards.

The volume's concluding chapter provides an overview of the key findings, arguments and law reform proposals put forward. It also briefly examines the political environment that is necessary for the proposed reforms to be accepted by policy-makers and suggests that, failing this, the conceptual framework developed in the book could influence the way courts develop the law on directors' duties in the context of banks and other financial institutions.

1 Shareholder power as a major cause of excessive risk-taking in banks and other financial institutions

The principal aim of this chapter is to illustrate that the standard UK corporate law and governance framework – which applied to banks and other financial institutions nearly unmodified, until the introduction of a series of reforms after the 2007–2009 financial crisis – is prone to undermine financial stability.[1] Indeed, it will be shown that the pursuit of profit maximisation inevitably entails taking a level of risk that, even if it is totally desirable from the point of view of diversified financial institution shareholders, tends to be excessive from the perspective of society as a whole, due to the systemic consequences of the failure or distress of any major financial institution. This claim will be further supported by exploring available empirical evidence on the relationship between shareholder power and risk-taking in financial institutions. Thus, a level of risk that is optimal for financial institution shareholders is likely to be excessive from the perspective of the public interest. For the purposes of this chapter, it is assumed that financial stability is a public good and that increasing the insolvency risk of one financial institution undermines financial stability, while further analysis on this matter will be deferred to Chapter 3, which sets out the development of the prudential regulation framework in the UK.

The second aim of the chapter is to demonstrate that the externalities problem described above is materially exacerbated by the limited potential of market discipline – both by the equity and debt capital markets – to curb excessive risk-taking by financial institutions. Of course, the less-than-perfect operation of market-based governance mechanisms is not a phenomenon exclusive to the financial sector and many of the problems identified in this chapter affect all large

1 Of course, it is by no means claimed that shareholder power and the nature of the corporate law framework were the only or even the dominant factors leading to the financial crisis. No doubt various factors contributed to the 2007–2009 crisis both at the macro- and micro-economic levels. On this, see Markus K Brunnermeier, 'Deciphering the Liquidity and Credit Crunch 2007–2008' (2009) 23 *Journal of Economic Perspectives* 77; and James K Galbraith, *Inequality and Instability: A Study of the World Economy Just Before the Great Crisis* (OUP, 2012). A concise but competent overview of the causes of the crisis can be found in Howard Davies, *The Financial Crisis: Who is to Blame?* (Polity Press, 2010).

public companies.[2] However, the opacity of financial assets and the acute information asymmetries involved, combined with the moral hazard effect of expected state intervention in case of systemic institution failures, make these problems far more serious in the case of the financial sector. The outcome of this is that financial institution senior managers are – in the standard case – free to take even more risk than perfectly informed shareholders and creditors would allow, to their detriment and to the additional detriment of financial stability.

The chapter is structured as follows. Section I illustrates that – theoretically – rational diversified shareholders often stand to gain from an increase in the investee company's insolvency risk and thus that on certain occasions the private interests of financial institution shareholders will clash with the public interest in financial stability. Section II complements the above finding by reviewing empirical evidence that confirms the existence of a positive correlation between shareholder power and insolvency risk in banks and other financial institutions and identifies the ways in which shareholder preferences are channelled into executive decision-making via the design of remuneration contracts. Then, section III demonstrates that shareholder monitoring of risk-taking in the financial sector tends to be ineffective, thus allowing senior managers to take even more risk than fully informed shareholders would accept. Section IV engages with evidence regarding risk monitoring by financial institution creditors, that is depositors and bondholders, and reaches a similar conclusion. Section V concludes by bringing together the two strands of the discussion in this chapter, arguing that reduced market discipline exacerbates the inherent misalignment between the optimal level of risk for diversified financial institution shareholders and the level of risk that is acceptable in the public interest.

I. The divergence between the optimal level of risk in the interests of rational diversified financial institution shareholders, and in the public interest

This section demonstrates the inevitable misalignment between, on the one hand, the collective private interests of diversified shareholders, and on the other, the public interest in financial stability.[3] As a preliminary point, it is necessary to

2 In particular, concerns that the function of the equity market is characterised by shareholder short-termism, which leads to excessive risk-taking by corporate managers and inhibits the sustainable growth of the economy, led to the publication of the influential Kay Review. See Department of Business, Innovations and Skills, 'A Long-Term Focus for Corporate Britain – A Call for Evidence' BIS/10/1225 (2010) www.gov.uk/government/consultations/a-long-term-focus-for-corporate-britain-a-call-for-evidence accessed 1 May 2017; and John Kay, 'The Kay Review of UK Equity Markets and Long-Term Decision Making – Final Report' BIS/12/917 (2012) www.gov.uk/government/consultations/the-kay-review-of-uk-equity-markets-and-long-term-decision-making accessed 1 May 2017.

3 Market-driven corporate governance mechanisms and the financialisation of corporate governance since the 1980s deregulation have been identified by several scholars as two of the major causes of the recent financial crisis. See e.g. Thomas Clarke,

explain the concept of risk, as used in the present discussion. Economists draw a clear distinction between risk and uncertainty.[4] There is risk when the future is unknown, but the probability distribution of possible outcomes is known. The best example of that is a fair dice or casino gambling. Conversely, there is uncertainty when we do not know the future and when the probability distribution of possible outcomes is unknown. Almost all business activities entail a degree of uncertainty. Take the example of a bank advancing a personal loan to a customer. It is not known whether the customer will repay the loan, nor what the probability is that he will repay the loan in full and in time. Of course, the bank in question will estimate the probability of the loan being duly repaid based on historical data and on certain assumptions about the type of customer. However, this estimation is a subjective opinion on the probability of repayment, and is not necessarily correct, as the true probability of repayment is – strictly speaking – unknown. It follows that whenever there is uncertainty there is also potential for divergence of opinions between different parties with regard to the probability of a future event.[5] In the above example, there is no single definitive way for banks to calculate the probability of loan default, different models leading to different results.[6] It is evident thus that financial institutions, as other businesses, face uncertainties rather than (known) risks and therefore that using the term risk is somewhat inaccurate. However, given the conventional usage of the term risk to include uncertainty in legal and regulatory literature, I will use the term risk in this manner, although what is meant is really uncertainty.

The attitude of different persons to risk is different. In the case of a known probability distribution, we can define as risk-neutral any individual who is indifferent to the risk and makes decisions based on the expected value of the outcome. Using the dice example, a risk-neutral person will be indifferent between being given £10 or having the chance to win £60 if he correctly predicts the outcome of a fair dice. A risk-averse person will prefer being given £10, and will demand more than £60 to take the chance. How much more a person would demand to choose a risky outcome instead of a risk-free one depends on one's degree of risk aversion. On the contrary, a risk-preferring person will prefer to be given the chance to win £60 rather than to be given £10. A risk-preferring individual may actually accept to bet even if the possible gain was less than £60, depending on his risk appetite. Of course, the same person may be in some contexts risk-averse and in others risk-preferring. However, empirical evidence shows that individuals are generally

'Corporate Governance Causes of the Global Financial Crisis' in William Sun, Jim Stewart and David Pollard (eds), *Corporate Governance and the Global Financial Crisis: International Perspectives* (CUP, 2011).

4 See e.g. Frank Knight, *Risk, Uncertainty and Profit* (Houghton Mifflin Harcourt Publishing, 1967, first printed in 1921), chapter 11.

5 On this, see Edward Miller, 'Risk, Uncertainty and Divergence of Opinion' (1977) 32 *The Journal of Finance* 1151, esp 1151–1155.

6 The FCA Handbook BIPRU 7.10.3–7.10.5 emphasises that the choice of risk calculation model is the responsibility of each firm, and that regulators do not endorse any particular method of computing.

risk-averse,[7] while the degree of risk aversion varies dependent on demographic characteristics.[8]

Generally, rational dispersed shareholders prefer the corporate strategy with the highest risk-adjusted return, even if it engenders a risk to the company's survival, as they tend to be risk-neutral. This is because the vast majority of shareholders in the UK are institutional investors[9] with fully diversified portfolios.[10] In other words, they have no financial interest in the preservation of any particular company as a goal in itself, but rather view investee companies as vehicles to maximise the economic returns on their investment. Table 1.1 provides an illustration of the

Table 1.1 Shareholders' incentives (disregarding systemic risk)

	Financial institution value at point A	*Financial institution value at point B*			*Expected profit (exp. value at B - value at A)*
		Good scenario (99%)	*Bad scenario (1%)*	*Expected value at B*	
Strategy 1	100	102	101	101.99	1.99
Strategy 2	100	104	0	102.96	2.96

7 Psychological experimental research indicates that the uncertainty effect on individuals is significant and widespread. For instance, Simonsohn asked the participants to value certain pairs of gift vouchers independently and then to value a ticket to a lottery whereby they would win either the one voucher or the other at a 50:50 chance (but they would certainly win one of the two). Most individuals (80%) were willing to pay for the lottery ticket less than they were willing to pay for the less valuable voucher. So, they valued a lottery ticket at less than its worst possible outcome as a result of risk aversion. See Uri Simonsohn, 'Direct Risk Aversion: Evidence From Risky Projects Valued Below Their Worst Outcome' (2009) 20 *Psychological Science* 686.

8 Empirical data on actual investor choices of a sample of American investors show that relative risk aversion decreases as a person's income and wealth increase, and falls sharply for individuals of very high (top 10%) wealth. The data also suggest that risk aversion decreases mildly with age until the age of 65 when it increases again. See William Riley and Victor Chow, 'Asset Allocation and Individual Risk Aversion' (1992) 48 *Financial Analysts Journal* 32.

9 It was estimated that at the end of 2014 only 11.9% of UK quoted shares were owned by individuals who were resident in the UK, while 28.2% of shares were held by UK-based institutional investors, including financial institutions, and 6.1% of shares were held by the public sector, charities and non-financial private sector companies. Crucially, 53.8% of shares were held by investors from outside the UK, most of whom are institutional investors. See 'Ownership of UK Quoted Shares: 2014' (Office for National Statistics, September 2015) www.ons.gov.uk/economy/investmentspensionsandtrusts/bulletins/ownershipofukquotedshares/2015-09-02 accessed 1 May 2017.

10 According to Bhattacharya and Galpin, the popularity of portfolio diversification is growing globally; UK investors are the second most diversified amongst 46 countries, and investors in developed economies are more likely to diversify than investors in developing economies. See Utpal Bhattacharya and Neal Galpin, 'The Global Rise of the Value-Weighted Portfolio' (2011) 46 *Journal of Financial and Quantitative Analysis* 737. See also Edwin Elton and others, *Modern Portfolio Theory and*

point that in some cases it is efficient for rational shareholders of a financial institution to prefer a business strategy with a high net risk-adjusted value, which, however, may lead to the failure of the institution. All figures are hypothetical. They show a financial institution's expected financial value, after two alternative strategic options (a conservative and an aggressive one) have been implemented at point B in time. The initial value of the financial institution is 100 (at point A in time). In both cases, there is a good scenario (99% probability of happening) and a bad scenario (1% probability of happening).

The expected value of the financial institution at point B is the average of the risk-adjusted values in the good and bad scenarios. For strategy 1, this is (99% x 102) + (1% x 101), which equals 100.98 + 1.01 = 101.99. The expected profit is 101.99 – 100 = 1.99. For Strategy 2, this is (99% x 104) + (1% x 0), which equals 102.96 + 0 = 102.96. Therefore, the expected profit is 102.96 – 100 = 2.96. This example illustrates the evident point that limited liability combined with risk neutrality means that it is in the interest of fully diversified shareholders to follow corporate strategies that are likely to lead to very high profits but carry a small risk of causing the institution to fail. Of course, this is the case in all companies with dispersed shareholders,[11] and not only in financial institutions. What is special in the case of financial institutions is that, given the far-reaching consequences of their failure on the financial system and the economy as a whole, questions of public interest arise.

So far, the discussion analysed shareholders' incentives ignoring systemic risk. The following discussion takes systemic risk into account. Suppose that there are five systemic financial institutions with a value of 100 each and that all of them can follow either the prudent Strategy 1 or the risky Strategy 2, with the same expected returns as in Table 1.1. As before, there is a good scenario and a bad scenario. The difference is that if any of the five financial institutions fails, the others will suffer a decrease of their value by 40% (hypothetical figure).[12] If no other institution fails, the expected value of each institution is as in Table 1.1. Table 1.2 illustrates the incentives of the shareholders of one of the five systemic institutions

Investment Analysis (8th edn, John Wiley & Sons Inc, 2010). The first scholar to analyse the benefits of portfolio diversification was Harry Markowitz. See Harry Markowitz, 'Portfolio Selection' (1952) 7 *The Journal of Finance* 77.

11 This is due to limited liability. A detailed explanation of how limited liability encourages risk-taking can be found in Stephen M Bainbridge and M Todd Henderson, *Limited Liability: A Legal and Economic Analysis* (Edward Elgar Publishing, 2016), 47–51.

12 Although all figures are hypothetical, they are not unrealistic. Evidence from the 2007–2009 financial crisis shows that the destruction of shareholder value amounted to 60% of market value for UK major banks and other financial institutions (BOFIs). According to the analysis by Nestor Advisors of the share price performance of FTSE 100 BOFIs for the six years ended 31 March 2009, UK BOFIs lost approximately 60% of their market value. See David Walker, 'A Review of Corporate Governance in UK Banks and Other Financial Industry Entities: Final Recommendations' (2009), para 1.7 www.icaew.com/en/library/subject-gateways/corporate-governance/codes-and-reports/walker-report accessed 1 May 2017.

Table 1.2 Shareholders' incentives (factoring systemic risk)

(Bank B1)	*Value at A*	*Value at B if no bank fails*		*Value at B if one bank fails*		*Expected value at B*	*Exp. profit*
Strategy 1: 96.05% no bank fails; 3.95% one other bank fails	100	Good scenario 99%: 102	Bad scenario 1%: 101	60		100.33	0.33
Strategy 2: 95.1% no bank fails; 3.9% another bank fails, 1% bank B1 fails	100	104		Another bank fails: 60	Bank B1 fails: 0	101.24	1.24

(Bank B1) if they assume that all other institutions will follow the risky strategy and thus that each other bank has a 1% chance of failure within the relevant time period. If any other institution fails, the value of Bank B1 will be 60 irrespective of the strategy it followed, unless B1 itself fails. If, however, no other institution fails the value of Bank B1 will depend on which strategy it followed and on whether it was successful or not (i.e. whether the good or the bad scenario materialises).

If bank B1 follows the safe strategy, there is no risk that it may fail. As we assumed that the other four institutions will follow the risky strategy, each of them has a 1% chance of failure. Thus, the chance that any of the four will fail is 3.95%. This includes the very unlikely cases (less than 1 in 10,000) that more than one institution will fail, but these cases are excluded from the table. It follows that there is a 96.05% chance that no bank will fail, if B1 follows the prudent strategy. If Strategy 1 is followed, and no other institution fails, then the probability distribution and outcomes are the same as in Table 1.1. If Bank B1 follows the risky strategy there is a higher chance that one of the five institutions may fail, as there is a 1% probability that B1 may fail. Then, the chance that at least one of the five institutions fails during the relevant time is 4.9% (3.9% another institution fails + 1% B1 fails). It follows that the chance that no institution fails is (under Strategy 2) 95.1%.

The expected value of B1 at point B is calculated as follows. For Strategy 1, it is the sum of the case where no other institution fails and the case that one other institution fails. If no institution fails, the expected value of B1 is (99% x 102) + (1% x 101), which amounts to 101.99. If one other institution fails, the expected value of B1 is 60. The total expected value of B1 is therefore (96.05% x 101.99) + (3.95% x 60), which is equal to 97.96 + 2.37 = 100.33. For Strategy 2, it is the sum of three cases: the case that no institution fails, the case that one other institution fails and the case that B1 itself fails. If no institution fails, the expected value of B1 is: 95.1% x 104 = 98.9. If one other fails, it is: 3.9% x 60 = 2.34. If B1 fails, it is 0. Overall, the expected value of B1 under Strategy 2 is: 98.9 + 2.34 + 0 = 101.24.

We observe that once the consideration that all other institutions will take a similarly high level of risk and hence another institution may fail is taken into account, the shareholders of bank B1 face an even stronger incentive to take the risky option than under Table 1.2, where we calculated their incentives in isolation of the rest of the financial system. In isolation, the risky strategy is approximately 50% more profitable than the prudent strategy. However, once the risk that another systemic institution may fail during the following year is taken into account, the risky strategy leads to an expected profit of 1.24, while the prudent only to 0.33, i.e. the risky strategy is four times more rewarding. This is due to the fact that the risk that another institution fails is not dependent on whether bank B1 follows the risky or the prudent strategy. In other words, financial stability is a public good, in the sense that no individual institution has an incentive to 'produce' it, as will be discussed in Chapter 3.

Finally, Table 1.3 illustrates how the aforementioned incentive structure can destroy value in the financial sector by comparing the total value of the five institutions in our hypothetical financial system in two cases: first, the case that all follow Strategy 1; and second, the case that all follow Strategy 2. All figures come from Tables 1.1 and 1.2.[13] If all institutions follow the prudent strategy there is no risk that any institution will fail and the expected value of the system at point B is the sum of the expected values of each institution (from Table 1.1), that is 509.95. If all institutions follow the risky strategy, then in the case that no institution fails (95.1%) the value of the system is 520, but in the case that one fails (4.9%) the value of the system is only 240 (4 institutions x 60). It follows that the expected value of the system under Strategy 2 is: (95.1% x 520) + (4.9% x 240), which equals 494.52 + 11.76 = 506.28.

Table 1.3 illustrates that due to systemic risk, the attempt of each individual institution to maximise its profits can lead to all institutions suffering losses in the case that at least one of them fails (or, in real life, in the case that one institution faces serious difficulties). This is a classic example of a prisoner's dilemma situation. If all the shareholders of all systemic institutions were able to negotiate collectively and decide the policies followed by all institutions, they would not sanction a level of risk-taking that is value decreasing for the financial sector as a whole, such as the one in Table 1.3. However, in the real world, this degree of

Table 1.3 The value-decreasing effect of profit-seeking by individual financial institutions

	Value at A	*Expected value of the system at point B*		
All institutions follow Strategy 1	500	509.95		
All institutions follow Strategy 2	500	No failure: 520	One failure: 240	Expected value: 506.28

13 Due to transaction costs, bank shareholders fail to co-operate despite the fact that this would be in their best interests. The limited potential of shareholder co-ordination will be further explored below in Chapter 5. This phenomenon resembles a prisoner's dilemma situation analysed by game theory. The concept of prisoner's dilemma was introduced by Merrill Flood, Melvin Dresher and Albert Tucker in 1950. They did not make a formal publication presenting their research.

formal co-ordination between the shareholders of all major financial institutions is not feasible – at least in the UK – due to prohibitive transaction costs resulting from the high level of share ownership fragmentation.[14] Indeed, international empirical evidence on the effect of ownership structure on financial stability supports the claim that concentrated ownership is generally conducive to lower levels of risk-taking.[15]

It follows that the current corporate law framework does not necessarily maximise the aggregate wealth of the shareholders of all systemic financial institutions, as the attempt of each institution to maximise its profits decreases the overall expected value of the system. This is not to say that any strategy that would be optimal for the shareholders of all systemic institutions would necessarily be compatible with the public interest, as the problem of negative externalities would persist. Rather, it means that financial stability is a public good both for society and for the shareholders of systemic institutions as a whole, although the interests of the latter would favour taking more risk than is in society's interest. Of course, the public interest, under utilitarian assumptions, is not to avoid financial crises at all costs. If the only way to operate a modern financial system was to allow crises to happen, it would then be in the public interest to allow that. If, however, there are ways to reduce the likelihood of the occurrence of financial crises, while preserving the function of the system (but at the cost of lower profits), the latter option would appear to be in the public interest.

Overall, the above over-simplified examples illustrate than where risk appetite is concerned, financial regulators (representing the public interest) and shareholders are markedly different. Therefore, the prevalent norm of shareholder value

14 The best available evidence on UK banks' ownership structure can be found in Parliamentary Commission on Banking Standards, *Changing Banking for Good* (2013–14, HL 27-II, HC 175-II), Annex 5. The highest shareholdings were in 2013: an 18% stake in Standard Chartered by Temasek, a 7% stake in HSBC by JP Morgan, and a 7% stake in Barclays by Blackrock. Other than UK Financial Investments Ltd's large holdings in RBS and Lloyds, the top 20 shareholders in each major UK bank own approximately 52% of Standard Chartered and Barclays, 40% of HSBC, 25% of Lloyds and 14% of RBS. However, out of the top 20 shareholders, the percentage of shares owned by active domestic institutions was only 15% in Standard Chartered, 8% in HSBC, 7% in RBS, 4% in Lloyds and 3% in Barclays. The rest were global investors, UK index funds, sovereign wealth funds and other investors. The Annex also emphasises that the average holding period for bank shares fell from three years in 1998 to three months in 2008.

15 Empirical research comparing the ownership structure and financial performance of 11,888 banks worldwide concludes that banks with a controlling shareholder (block holder) perform better, especially in times of crisis. This finding is consistent with the claim that dispersed ownership leads to higher risk-taking. See Iftekhar Hasan and Liang Song, 'Bank Ownership and Performance: A Global Perspective' in James Barth, Chen Lin and Clas Wihlborg (eds), *Research Handbook on International Banking and Governance* (Edward Elgar Publishing, 2012). An empirical study on smaller US banks also confirms that when managers own a substantial stake in a bank they are likely to manage risks more effectively. See Kenneth Spong and Richard Sullivan, 'Bank Ownership and Risk Taking: Improving Corporate Governance in Banking After the Crisis' in the same volume.

maximisation, expressed in section 172 (1) of the Companies Act 2006[16] and enforced in practice via performance-based remuneration and shareholder activism, leads to financial institutions adopting a risk profile that may be (or appears to be) optimal for their shareholders, but is in fact detrimental to financial stability.[17] It follows that the core governance problem in financial institutions must be reconceptualised to include the public interest, rather than focusing only on shareholder agency costs.[18]

II. More powerful shareholders lead to higher insolvency risk in banks and other financial institutions: influencing managers and boards to take on more risk

The previous section offered a theoretical illustration of the argument that business strategies, which can lead to a company's insolvency if they fail, but which are optimal regarding expected profit, are indeed in the best interests of rational dispersed financial institution shareholders; and that the presence of systemic risk exacerbates rather than alleviates this phenomenon. This section reviews empirical evidence which suggests that strong shareholders are associated with higher insolvency risk in banks and other financial institutions.

Indeed, the causal link between shareholder empowerment and bank distress at times of crisis has recently been empirically confirmed. A major study by Erkens *et al* assessed the impact of ownership structure on the performance of financial institutions during the recent financial crisis. The study examined the impact of the percentage of shares owned by institutional investors on the stock returns of 296 financial firms (primarily banks) from 30 countries during the 2007–2008 period.[19] It found that firms with a higher percentage of institutional ownership experienced worse stock returns during the crisis. To further explore this finding the authors tested whether higher institutional ownership led to higher risk-taking and concluded that firms with a higher percentage of institutional ownership took higher risk before the crisis, which evidently caused them to perform worse during the crisis.

This study is highly relevant from our point of view since the percentage of a bank's shares that are held by institutional shareholders is a good proxy for overall shareholder involvement in the context of widely held banks, as are all major UK

16 A detailed examination of the duty of loyalty can be found in Chapter 2, section IV.

17 In that sense, it has been argued that it was not the failure but the *success* of (conventional) corporate governance that led to the recent crisis. See Nicholas Howson, 'When "Good" Corporate Governance makes "Bad" (Financial) Firms: The Global Crisis and the Limits of Private Law' (2009) 108 *Michigan Law Review (First Impressions)* 44, 49–50.

18 This view has been expressed by several scholars including Penny Ciancanelli and Jose Antonio Reyes-Gonzalez, 'Corporate Governance in Banking: A Conceptual Framework' (European Financial Management Association conference, Athens, June 2000) http://ssrn.com/abstract=253714 accessed 1 May 2017.

19 See David Erkens, Mingyi Hung and Pedro Matos, 'Corporate Governance in the 2007–2008 Financial Crisis: Evidence from Financial Institutions Worldwide' (2012) 18 *Journal of Corporate Finance* 389, 389–392.

banks. The findings of the study imply that institutional shareholder activism and engagement is destabilising for banks as the negative consequences of increased risk-taking seem to outbalance the positive aspects (lower agency costs). Although the study does not focus exclusively on the UK, there is no apparent reason why these findings should not hold strong in the case of UK banks.[20]

There are several examples of shareholder activism in UK banks that opposed measures intended to strengthen the capital base of the bank concerned.[21] The most notable case of such shareholder behaviour was the campaign of Knight Vinke[22] against the board of HSBC. In 2008 Knight Vinke, a private fund manager, akin to a hedge fund, publicly opposed HSBC's decision to increase its share capital by 20% in order to cope with the financial crisis. They argued that the capital increase would harm the interests of current shareholders. As an alternative strategy, they proposed that HSBC allow HSBC Finance Corporation (HFC),[23] one of its US subsidiaries, to seek Chapter 11 protection.[24] Such a course of action would have been detrimental to HSBC bondholders and would probably have led to the withdrawal of HSBC's authorisation to engage in banking in the US. Furthermore, it would have severely affected HSBC's global reputation. HSBC's board successfully resisted the pressure, and proceeded with the capital increase.

Activist shareholder pressure has also been experienced by Barclays under similar circumstances.[25] Indeed, in 2008 Barclays decided to increase its equity capital by £7.3 billion to cope with the financial crisis. It rejected an offer from the UK

20 A recent empirical study also confirms that banks in which managers were insulated from shareholder pressures were less likely to fail during the 2007–2009 crisis. The explanation suggested is that bank shareholders tend to push banks to take a level of risk that is excessive from society's point of view. See Daniel Ferreira and others, 'Measuring Management Insulation from Shareholder Pressure' (2013) ECGI Finance Working Paper No 345/2013 http://papers.ssrn.com/sol3/papers.cfm?abstract_id=2170392## accessed 1 May 2017.

21 Of course, in financial services – as in other sectors – shareholder activism is an exception as most shareholders tend to behave as passive investors or traders rather than as owners. On this, see Robert Monks, 'A Review of Corporate Governance in UK Banks and Other Financial Industry Entities: The Role of Institutional Shareholders' in William Sun, Jim Stewart and David Pollard (eds), *Corporate Governance and the Global Financial Crisis: International Perspectives* (CUP, 2011). See also Roger Barker, 'Ownership Structure and Shareholder Engagement: Reflections on the Role of Institutional Shareholders in the Financial Crisis' in the same volume.

22 Knight Vinke Asset Management LLC is an institutional asset manager headquartered in New York. It specialises in the energy and financial services industries and targets large companies that are unlikely to become the target of a hostile takeover.

23 Household International was a US financial company acquired in 2003 by HSBC and renamed HFC. It was heavily exposed to the US sub-prime mortgage market.

24 For a brief overview of their main argument, see Knight Vinke, 'Briefing Note for Shareholders on HFC and its Impact on HSBC Valuation, Capital Requirements and Image' (Knight Vinke, 2008) www.knightvinke.com/includes/documents/2009/a/article_14_20080229_briefing.pdf accessed 1 June 2014.

25 See Investment Management Association, 'Adherence to the FRC's Stewardship Code: At 30 September 2010' (2011) 20–21 www.investmentfunds.org.uk/research/stewardship-survey/ accessed 1 June 2014.

government for assistance, and instead sought to raise equity capital from private investors. Several shareholders protested that this course of action was more costly to Barclays' current shareholders than accepting the government aid. As a result, the whole board put itself up for re-election at the next annual meeting in 2009. The board argued successfully that accepting government aid – and hence public intervention – would not be in the long-term interest of Barclays and its shareholders.

The common factor in the aforementioned cases was that shareholder pressure was targeted against a decision to increase share capital that was in the short term value-decreasing for current shareholders.[26] Conversely, shareholders of UK banks consistently welcomed any strategies that increased the leverage and hence the riskiness of banks, often to the detriment of banks' long-term sustainability. For instance, the shareholders of RBS overwhelmingly supported the catastrophic acquisition of ABN AMRO and the shareholders of Northern Rock did not object to the exponential debt-financed growth of the latter.[27] Also, there is evidence that the shareholders of RBS continuously pressed for (unsustainable) levels of return and encouraged an extremely leveraged business model, which turned out to be fatal for the bank.[28] Indeed, evidence given by major UK banks in Parliament demonstrates that in the years leading up to the 2007 crisis most activist bank shareholders enthusiastically supported further increases in leverage and balance sheet restructurings to increase short-term profits.[29]

This is contrary to conventional wisdom in corporate governance which assumes that institutional shareholder involvement is a potentially powerful tool to ensure good governance and to reduce managerial agency costs.[30] However, shareholder engagement has also been criticised as conducive to leading corporate managers to take more risks,[31] and focus more strongly on short-term

26 On that, see Anat Admati and others, 'Debt Overhang and Capital Regulation' (2012) Stanford University Rock Center for Corporate Governance Working Paper No 114, 8–11 http://ssrn.com/abstract=2031204 accessed 1 May 2017.

27 See Kay Review (above n 2) para 1.29. This is why the review stresses that it is the quality and not the quantity of shareholder engagement that matters. Ibid., para 1.30. See also Roman Tomasic, 'Corporate Rescue, Governance and Risk Taking in Northern Rock: Part 2' (2008) 29 (11) *The Company Lawyer* 330.

28 Evidence provided by Mr Douglas Flint in *Changing Banking for Good* (above n 14), para 174.

29 Ibid., paras 326–327.

30 A discussion of the increasing power of activist shareholders and non-executive directors in the US can be found in Marcel Kahan and Edward Rock, 'Embattled CEOs' (2010) 88 *Texas Law Review* 987. Assuming that shareholder engagement can potentially reduce agency costs, Bebchuk advocated increasing shareholder access to the proxy mechanism of US companies. See Lucian Bebchuk, 'Private Ordering and the Proxy Access Debate' (2010) 65 *Business Lawyer* 329. For a generally positive account of hedge fund activism, see Brian Cheffins and John Armour, 'The Rise and Fall (?) of Shareholder Activism by Hedge Funds' (2012) 14 *Journal of Alternative Investments* 17.

31 On this, see William Lazonick, 'From Innovation to Financialization: How Shareholder Value Ideology is Destroying the US Economy' in Martin H Wolfson and Gerald A Epstein (eds), *The Handbook of the Political Economy of Financial Crises* (OUP, 2013).

profitability. Thus, it is not surprising that shareholder short-termism has caused serious concerns in recent years.[32] Whatever the gravity of this problem may be for generic companies, in the special case of financial institutions it is arguably a serious one, as increased risk-taking can lead to financial crises. Still, the empirical finding of a correlation between shareholder strength and risk-taking begs the question of how exactly shareholder pressure is channelled into the incentives faced by senior managers in the financial sector. In short, the answer is via the design of executive remuneration. As will be explained in the following chapter, the major mechanism that aligns the risk appetite of senior managers of public companies with the appetite of dispersed shareholders is performance-based remuneration. This structure incentivises managers to seek to maximise the price of the company's shares in two ways: (a) the performance of the company's shares compared to a group of similar companies is one of the most significant criteria to assess performance and determine the award of bonuses and long-term incentive plan (LTIP) shares; and (b) paying part of a manager's salary in shares rather than in cash incentivises him or her to seek to maximise the value of the shares.[33]

That being said, it has been argued that financial incentives set by the structure of executive remuneration did not play any material role in risk-taking by executives during the recent financial crisis, and are not to blame for short-termism or excessive risk-taking. The argument goes as follows. Financial institution managers face no financial incentives to take risks that threaten their viability, as when financial institutions fail or need state aid, their managers lose their jobs and most of their personal wealth, as a substantial portion of their wealth is typically invested in shares of the financial institution for which they work. It follows that excessive risk-taking was not a consequence of remuneration structures and hence the recent crisis builds no case for a radical reform of executive pay.[34] However,

32 Moore and Walker-Arnott provide an in-depth analysis of managerial and shareholder short-termism in Marc T Moore and Edward Walker-Arnott, 'A Fresh Look at Stock Market Short-termism' (2014) 41 *Journal of Law and Society* 416. They argue that short-termism is unlikely to be a self-correcting phenomenon and put forward the notion of information centricity to explain listed companies' constant urge to produce news items. See also Mark J Roe, 'Corporate Short-termism – In the Boardroom and in the Courtroom' (2013) 68 *Business Lawyer* 981. Of course, there are opposite views in the literature. For instance, Reisberg remains unconvinced that short-termism is generally a bad thing. See Arad Reisberg, 'The Role of Institutional Shareholders: Stewardship and the Long-/ Short-term Debate' in Iris H-Y Chiu (ed), *The Law on Corporate Governance in Banks* (Edward Elgar Publishing, 2015), 124–127.

33 The potential perverse incentive to take excessive risk exists insofar as managers are left free to dispose of their shares at any time. This allows them to time the sale of the shares to benefit from short-term improvements of the share price and protects them against possible corporate under-performance in the future. Requiring managers to retain their performance shares until retirement has been proposed as a way to tackle this problem. See Kay Review (above n 2), paras 11.13–11.16.

34 There is empirical research from the United States indicating that the executives of failed financial institutions did not anticipate the collapse of their firms, as they did not choose to sell their shares in these companies before the crisis erupted. In addition, the top executives of failed banks suffered tremendous personal financial losses of at least

the same study found that banks in which CEOs' incentives were more tightly aligned with the interests of the shareholders performed worse than other banks during the crisis. This supports the view that aligning the interests of managers with those of the shareholders undermines the safety and soundness of financial institutions. The finding that financial institution executives did not anticipate the recent crisis early enough to sell their shares before prices collapsed does not undermine the argument that appropriate *ex ante* incentives should be in place. Indeed, what really matters is whether financial institution managers had incentives to take decisions which they knew posed a risk (probably a low-probability risk) that at some point in the future financial institutions would face significant problems and possibly even collapse. This is perfectly consistent with the lack of appreciation of the exact timing of the occurrence of the recent crisis.

Indeed, Bebchuk *et al* demonstrate that a proper interpretation of available empirical evidence supports the claim that financial incentives were (at least partly) to blame for excessive risk-taking by bank managers.[35] After reviewing the overall gains and losses of the executives of Lehman Brothers and Bear Stearns from 2000 to 2008, Bebchuk *et al* conclude that the management teams of these firms earned in total more than $1 billion in variable compensation. This sum greatly exceeds their losses when the two banks failed. It follows that it may well be possible that bank executives faced perverse incentives to take excessive risk. According to Bebchuk *et al*, the evidence suggests that the risks executives took before the credit crisis were excessive even from the point of view of bank shareholders, let alone from the point of view of bank creditors and taxpayers. There is also empirical evidence from American retail banks that in the years leading up to the financial crisis the remuneration of bank CEOs was made more responsive to bank performance so as to create stronger incentives for CEOs to exploit new (risky) opportunities, and that CEOs responded positively to these incentives by taking more risks.[36] Moreover, evidence from European banks suggests that large LTIP rewards for CEOs are positively correlated with an increased likelihood of failure.[37] This evidence is consistent with the view that increased risk-taking was at least one of the causes of financial institution failures.

$30 million on average. See Rudiger Fahlenbrach and Rene Stulz, 'Bank CEO Incentives and the Credit Crisis' (2010) Dice Center Working Paper 2009–2013 www.ssrn.com/abstract=1439859 accessed 1 May 2017. See also Douglas O Edwards, 'An Unfortunate "Tail": Reconsidering Risk Management Incentives after the Financial Crisis of 2007–2009' (2010) 81 *University of Colorado Law Review* 247.

35 Lucian Bebchuk, Alma Cohen and Holger Spamann, 'The Wages of Failure: Executive Compensation at Bear Sterns and Lehman 2000–2008' (2010) 27 *Yale Journal on Regulation* 257.

36 Robert DeYoung, Emma Peng and Meng Yan, 'Executive Compensation and Business Policy Choices at U.S. Commercial Banks' (2013) 48 *Journal of Financial and Quantitative Analysis* 165.

37 See Rym Ayadi, Emrah Arbak and Willem Pieter De Groen, 'Executive Compensation and Risk-taking in European Banking' in James Barth, Chen Lin and Clas Wihlborg (eds), *Research Handbook on International Banking and Governance* (Edward Elgar Publishing, 2012).

III. The limited benefits of shareholder monitoring in financial institutions[38]

The two preceding sections established that the level of risk that is optimal for financial institution shareholders is excessive for society as a whole and that shareholders have in the past accepted or encouraged such excessive risk-taking. However, this is not to say that financial institutions' actual level of risk may not be even higher than what would be optimal for their shareholders. In theory, the incorporation of long-term prospects into the market price of shares and enhanced monitoring of corporate performance by – at least some – institutional shareholders[39] should ensure that the level of risk taken by a listed company is consistent with the risk appetite of diversified shareholders.[40] In parallel, monitoring by the main providers of debt capital to companies such as bondholders and major creditors also operates as a check on excessive risk-taking, especially given the starkly different risk appetite of creditors vis-à-vis the shareholders. Therefore, assuming perfectly efficient capital markets, monitoring by financial institution shareholders and creditors should preclude the assumption of a level of risk that is not in the private interests of these groups, as such risk-taking ought to be fully reflected in the market price of a company's shares and bonds and in the interest rate paid by the company.[41] It is worth noting that most of the available studies in this area are focusing particularly on banks and thus the forthcoming analysis will revolve mostly around banks, but the insights gained are – arguably – at least partially relevant to other systemically important financial institutions.

This section argues that risk monitoring by shareholders is unlikely to be effective in the case of financial firms, whose business, assets, capital structure, and regulatory framework are distinct. By saying so, I do not purport to imply that, in the case of non-financial public companies, markets work perfectly efficiently and the level of risk taken is aligned with the interests of all their private constituencies. There is a widespread concern that UK equity markets are permeated by short-termism and investor myopia. This phenomenon is believed to lead to underinvestment in sound long-term projects, an excessive emphasis on corporate

38 This and the next part of this chapter are based on section 3 of the chapter I published in 2015 with Edward Elgar. See Andreas Kokkinis, 'A Primer on Corporate Governance in Banks and Financial Institutions – Are Banks Special?' in Iris H-Y Chiu (ed), *The Law on Corporate Governance in Banks* (Edward Elgar Publishing, 2015), 18–30.

39 I refer to institutional investors who manage their portfolio actively rather than passive index funds which invest across the market.

40 This would be the implication of the strong form of the efficient markets hypothesis according to which the rate at which shares trade reflects all knowable information about the shares. See Eugene F Fama, 'Efficient Capital Markets: A Review of Theory and Empirical Work' (1970) 25 *The Journal of Finance* 383; Eugene F Fama, 'Market Efficiency, Long-Run Returns, and Behavioral Finance' (1998) 49 *Journal of Financial Economics* 283.

41 In addition, in a perfect market all private constituencies would protect themselves against risk-taking by a company. For instance, employees would bargain for a higher salary to compensate themselves for the increased risk of the company failing and them being dismissed, suppliers would charge higher prices when supplying on credit and so on.

restructurings and portfolio management, and the fostering of regulatory breaches.[42] The argument here is that financial institutions face essentially the same problems in this regard as all major public companies but that due to the special nature of the financial sector, these problems are generally more severe in financial institutions than in generic companies. I proceed by first explaining the limits of risk monitoring by shareholders, then by bondholders and finally by depositors, who provide the greatest part of bank debt capital.

To appreciate the limitations of shareholder monitoring of risk-taking by financial institutions it is necessary to return to the efficient market hypothesis and provide some background on the specific nature of financial institutions' business and assets, namely the phenomenon of asset opacity. There is some confusion in this area due to the misleading way that the efficient market hypothesis is often interpreted.[43] The efficient market hypothesis is a model that purports to provide a generally plausible abstraction of reality and merely claims (in its semi-strong form) that the prices of shares and other securities reflect publicly available information. The theory does not claim that market prices reflect the fundamental or inherent value of securities.

As there is no way to observe the intrinsic value of a security (or of any other form of property), we can only conclude *ex post facto* that at some point in time a security was overvalued. An example of this is the shares of a company that engages in fraudulent accounting practices (e.g. Enron)[44] until the fraud is discovered. Furthermore, there is nothing in the efficient markets hypothesis that implies that past returns on a security will be repeated in the future. The unprecedented movements in share prices during the recent financial crisis do not undermine the validity of the efficient markets hypothesis, but rather suggest that risk in financial markets is non-stationary.[45] Therefore, the extent to which the market price of securities reflects their fundamental value depends on the quality of available information and on the costs investors face to acquire (these are low) and process (these can be high) information.

The argument here is that in the financial sector relevant information is more difficult to process than in other sectors. This affects both financial institutions when preparing their financial disclosures to the market, and investors and analysts when they make investment decisions subsequent to such disclosures. If this is the

42 Indeed, the Kay Review (above n 2), paras 13.1–13.18, acknowledges the need to focus on relationships of trust between market players rather than on a trading culture.

43 On the frequent misinterpretation of the hypothesis, see the insightful analysis of Ray Ball, 'The Global Financial Crisis and the Efficient Markets Hypothesis: What Have We Learned?' (2009) 21 *Journal of Applied Corporate Finance* 8. See also Burton G Malkiel, 'The Efficient Market Hypothesis and its Critics' (2003) 17 *The Journal of Economic Perspectives* 59.

44 An academic analysis of the Enron scandal focusing on the limited independence of auditors can be found in David Kershaw, 'Waiting for Enron: The Unstable Equilibrium of Auditor Independence Regulation' (2006) 33 *Journal of Law and Society* 388.

45 A non-stationary process is a stochastic process whose joint probability distribution is not constant when shifted in time. There is a rich body of relevant mathematical literature, but its examination falls outside the scope of this study.

case, we may infer that the shares of financial institutions will be more volatile than other shares for a considerable period after a financial crisis,[46] and that there will be scope for senior managers to influence share prices in normal economic conditions until the misunderstood information becomes apparent to the market. In the following paragraphs, I seek to explain why information processing with respect to the financial performance of financial institutions is particularly difficult.

There is a considerable body of financial literature that focuses on banks and questions whether banks are specific in their market behaviour and governance problems.[47] Recent work highlights the specificity of banks, especially with regard to the opacity (or opaqueness) of their assets and heavy regulation.[48] The reason why banks are more opaque than other companies is that their assets consist primarily of claims against borrowers, and financial instruments.[49] A loan portfolio is far more difficult to value than other assets, such as manufacturing plants, machinery and intellectual property. Of course, some loans are secured by mortgages or charges so that the bank's claim can be satisfied by selling the collateral in the case of a borrower's default. Still, security does not eliminate the risky nature of loans, since the value of the collateral may not be sufficient to cover the whole claim, especially if there are sharp changes in the relevant market, such as the real estate market, or if accrued interest has significantly increased the amount of the claim. It is thus very difficult for an external investor to assess the quality of loans

46 Indeed, the volatility of bank shares has increased sharply since 2008 and has remained at high levels compared to the shares of non-financial companies since then. See Andrew Atkeson and William Simon, 'The Rising Fear in Bank Stock Prices', *The Wall Street Journal* (New York, 28 November 2011) http://online.wsj.com/news/articles/SB10001424052970204531404577052493270860130 accessed 1 May 2017.

47 Early American economic literature on the subject generally viewed banks as not posing any special governance problems. See e.g. Anthony Saunders, Elizabeth Strock and Nickolaos Travlos, 'Ownership Structure, Deregulation and Bank Risk Taking' (1990) 45 *The Journal of Finance* 643; Linda Allen and Sinan Cebenoyan, 'Bank Acquisitions and Ownership Structure: Theory and Evidence' (1991) 15 *Journal of Banking and Finance* 425; Stephen Prowse, 'Alternative Methods of Corporate Control in Commercial Banks' (1995) *Federal Reserve Bank of Dallas Economic and Financial Policy Review* (Third Quarter) 24; Anthony Crawford, John Ezzell and James Miles, 'Bank CEO Pay-Performance Regulations and the Effects of Deregulation' (1995) 68 *Journal of Business* 231.

48 See e.g. Dirk Heremans, 'Corporate Governance Issues for Banks. A Financial Stability Perspective' (2007) University of Leuven Working Paper http://ssrn.com/abstract=1024693 accessed 1 May 2017; Peter O Mulbert, 'Corporate Governance of Banks after the Financial Crisis – Theory, Evidence, Reforms' (2010) ECGI Working Paper No 151/2010 http://papers.ssrn.com/sol3/papers.cfm?abstract_id=1448118 accessed 1 May 2017; Andrea Polo, 'The Corporate Governance of Banks: The Current State of the Debate' (2007) http://ssrn.com/abstract=958796 accessed 1 May 2017; and Maria Cristina Ungureanu, 'Banks: Regulation and Corporate Governance Framework' (2008) 5 *Corporate Ownership and Control* 449.

49 On this, see Ross Levine, 'The Corporate Governance of Banks: A Concise Discussion of Concepts and Evidence' (2004), 7–9. World Bank Policy Research Working Paper 3404 http://elibrary.worldbank.org/doi/book/10.1596/1813-9450-3404 accessed 1 May 2017.

and to predict the rate of defaults, as this depends on the creditworthiness of individual (personal, corporate or sovereign) borrowers.

Take the example of a borrower who faces serious difficulties in repaying a loan. The bank may either: accelerate the loan and seek to enforce its claim against the debtor immediately; or keep the loan facility running and possibly refinance it at a higher rate of interest. The latter option is generally more risky than immediate enforcement, as the delay is likely to lead to a deterioration of the bank's losses as the value of the assets of the debtor may continue to decrease, and the bank may be 'throwing good money after bad'. In the first case, the accelerated non-serviced loan will appear in the bank's accounts as an impairment, while in the second case the bank will appear to be as profitable as before (or more – if a higher interest rate is charged). As a result, a bank following the first approach will suffer a decrease in the value of its assets and hence its profits and share price will fall, whereas a bank following the second approach will face no such problems.

Securitisation of loans and investment banking activities such as proprietary trading in various securities[50] on behalf of banks and other financial institutions further exacerbates asset opacity. The process of securitisation which became extremely popular until the recent crisis involves a bank selling a number of loans to a special purpose vehicle (SPV, a separate company) which then issues debt instruments to investors on the collateral of the income stream from the loans. For instance, asset-backed securities (ABS) are debt instruments serviced by the cash flows of a discrete pool of fixed or revolving assets, e.g. mortgages, credit card receivables, and student loans. Collateralised debt obligations are structured ABSs, divided into different risk tranches. Senior tranches are to be serviced first so they are in theory safe even if the underlying loans are given to borrowers with low creditworthiness. The complex nature of the securitisation process due to packaging together loans of different nature and risk, and the uncertainty with regard to the continuing liability of the originating bank in case of default of the SPV, exacerbates asset opacity as investors are likely to disagree about the value of such instruments. Indeed, Cheng *et al* found in 2008 that US banks which engaged in securitisation were more opaque than those that did not, and that opacity increased in tandem with the size of securitised assets.[51]

If this is the case, we can expect that in times of financial turmoil, when a substantial number of borrowers default, financial institutions' opacity deteriorates as they face a strong incentive to conceal their losses by tolerating or refinancing troubled loans rather than calling off the facilities and reporting them as non-serviced loans. Given that financial institutions with low-quality assets tend not to disclose fully the extent of their losses, the market is unlikely to be able to distinguish

50 These include several types of securities such as derivatives and options. Credit default swaps, for instance, are contracts whereby the protection buyer makes a series of payments to the protection seller in exchange for a pay-off in the event that the underlying credit instrument, bond or loan, defaults.

51 The study was conducted before the 2007–2009 financial crisis. See Mei Cheng, Dan Dhaliwal and Monica Neamtiu, 'Asset Securitization, Securitization Recourse, and Information Uncertainty' (2011) 86 *The Accounting Review* 541.

between 'good' and 'bad' institutions, and thus it is likely that market confidence in the whole financial sector will suffer. This is an example of a market for lemons problem whereby the inability of market players to distinguish between high- and low-quality goods or services leads them to assume that all goods are of poor quality.[52] The outcome of this is that buyers are only happy to pay a uniform low price for the goods, which gives a competitive advantage to the producers of the worst goods, as their cost of production is lower. In our context, the inability of investors to distinguish between institutions gives a competitive advantage to riskier institutions which tend to be more profitable in times of economic growth.

Indeed, the hypothesis that asset opacity increases sharply in times of crisis as institutions avoid disclosing relevant information on their assets has found strong empirical support in a recent study. Flannery *et al* examined bank opacity over a 20-year period and confirmed that during the recent financial crisis the opacity of bank assets increased to a level that is unique to the banking sector.[53] This evidence provides formal support for the widespread view that the distrust among banks about the quality of their assets during the crisis indicates that 'even banks themselves find it difficult to assess the riskiness of other banks accurately'.[54] Although it is uncontroversial to say that banks are generally much more opaque than generic companies in times of crisis, whether banks are always particularly opaque is an empirical question that has yet to be settled. A number of studies have failed to find any significant difference between banks and other companies in normal economic conditions.[55] However, other recent studies confirm that bank opacity is a pervasive feature of the sector at all times and not only in times of crisis.[56] Each study uses a different methodology to measure asset opacity which

52 See George Akerlof, 'The Market for "Lemons": Quality Uncertainty and the Market Mechanism' (1970) 84 *The Quarterly Journal of Economics* 488.

53 See Mark Flannery, Simon Kwan and Mahendrarajah Nimalendran, 'The 2007–09 Financial Crisis and Bank Opaqueness' (2010) Federal Reserve Bank of San Francisco Working Paper 2010–27 www.frbsf.org/economic-research/files/wp10-27bk.pdf accessed 1 May 2017.

54 See Mulbert (above n 48), 11.

55 See e.g. Mark Flannery, Simon Kwan and Mahendrarajah Nimalendran, 'Market Evidence on the Opaqueness of Banking Firms' Assets' (2004) 71 *Journal of Financial Economics* 419; Flannery et al (above n 53).

56 Morgan found that credit rating agencies were more likely to disagree on the rating of bonds issued by banks than by other companies between 1983 and 1993. See Donald Morgan, 'Rating Banks: Risk and Uncertainty in an Opaque Industry' (2002) 92 *American Economic Review* 874. The same was found with respect to European banks in the period 1993–2003 by Iannotta. See Giuliano Iannotta, 'Testing for Opaqueness in the European Banking Industry: Evidence from Bond Credit Ratings' (2006) 30 *Journal of Financial Services Research* 287. In addition, Iannotta and Navone found that between 1990 and 2000 US banks were more likely to suffer abrupt negative changes in their share prices (crashes) than other companies. See Giuliano Iannotta and Marco Navone, 'Crashes and Bank Opaqueness' (2009) Universita Luigi Bocconi CAREFIN Research Paper No 20/09 http://papers.ssrn.com/sol3/papers.cfm?abstract_id=1600190 accessed 1 May 2017. Consistent with the hypothesis that banks are more opaque than other companies are the findings of Haggard and Howe that the shares of banks incorporate less firm-specific information than other companies of

cannot be observed directly such as the disagreement amongst credit rating agencies on the rating of bonds issued by banks,[57] the bid-ask spread, and the likelihood of analysts' forecasts errors.

On balance, the opacity of financial assets is widely accepted by the relevant literature[58] as one of the main components of financial institution specificity. From the perspective of the argument here, it is sufficient that all available evidence supports the proposition that financial assets are intrinsically opaque. It may be true that in good times market confidence[59] reduces the degree of disagreement between market players about the value of financial institutions' assets, and hence reduces observable opacity, but the dramatic exacerbation of opacity in times of crisis shows that financial assets are intrinsically difficult to value.

The opacity of financial assets neutralises the effect of market discipline on risk-taking for the following reasons. Since equity investors are not capable of assessing the real value of the assets in financial institutions' balance sheets based on available information, the price at which financial institutions' shares trade does not reflect this information but rather only reflects the profits made and the dividends paid. Indeed, there is evidence that in the years leading up to the recent financial crisis, investors did not appreciate that the increased returns on financial institution shares were achieved by increasing leverage and taking on more risk.[60] It follows that financial institutions did not face a higher cost of capital as a result of increased risk-taking.[61] In other words, increasing leverage and engaging in risky activities were virtually costless. It is evident that in such conditions, the senior

similar characteristics. See Stephen Haggard and John Howe, 'Are Banks Opaque?' (2007) University of Southern Mississippi Working Paper www.scribd.com/doc/156507098/Haggard-Stephen-K-John-S-Howe-2007-Are-Banks-Opaque-Jan-11-41-Pp accessed 1 May 2017.

57 The use of split credit ratings as a proxy for asset opacity has been criticised by Hauck and Neyer. See Achim Hauck and Ulrike Neyer, 'Are Rating Splits a Useful Indicator for the Opacity of an Industry?' (2008) Heinrich-Heine University of Düsseldorf Economics, Finance, and Taxation Discussion Paper No 3/2008 http://papers.ssrn.com/sol3/papers.cfm?abstract_id=2103169 accessed 1 May 2017.

58 See Mulbert (above n 48), Levine (above n 49), Heremans (above note 48), Polo (above n 48) and Ungureanu (above n 48). The failure of equity markets to restrain excessive risk-taking is also supported by the findings of Apanard Prabha, Clas Wihlborg and Thomas Willett, 'Market Discipline for Financial Institutions and Markets for Information' in James Barth, Chen Lin and Clas Wihlborg (eds), *Research Handbook on International Banking and Governance* (Edward Elgar Publishing, 2012).

59 Before the recent crisis, market confidence in banks was also supported by the implied government support that large systemic institutions enjoyed.

60 From 2002 to 2007 large global banks raised their dividends on average by 15% per annum. At the same time investors did not price correctly the greater risks taken by banks until the crisis began. On this, see Michael King, 'The Cost of Equity for Global Banks: A CAPM Perspective from 1990 to 2009' (2009) *BIS Quarterly Review* (September) 56, 70–71.

61 Empirical evidence confirms that banks with shareholder-friendly boards and higher stock returns before the crisis performed significantly worse during the 2007–2008 crisis. See Andrea Beltratti and René Stulz, 'The Credit Crisis Around the Globe: Why Did Some Banks Perform Better?' (2012) 105 *Journal of Financial Economics* 1.

managers of large financial institutions faced a powerful incentive to take on more risk so as to achieve the highest possible performance-based remuneration. Far from acting as a constraint on risk-taking, the capital market facilitated excessive risk-taking,[62] which fully informed investors would not have sanctioned without demanding an appropriate risk premium.[63]

A connected problem is that since the assets of financial institutions cannot be accurately valued by investors, senior managers can easily manipulate financial results and hence manage share prices. This frequently enables them to reach the targets set by their remuneration contracts and entrench themselves in their positions. At this point it is essential to clarify that this claim does not imply that senior managers of UK financial institutions have been engaging in unlawful market abuse, which carries criminal and civil penalties.[64] Rather, the argument is that, given the opacity of financial assets discussed above, senior managers generally face a strong incentive to engage in borderline practices of managing financial announcements and strategically forming corporate policy in order to influence the share price. Indeed, there is considerable empirical evidence that in the years leading up to the crisis banks (and other financial institutions) resorted to securitisation at carefully selected points in time when their earnings were low to prevent a fall in their share prices.[65] There is also strong evidence that banks can

62 One additional way in which banks can take excessive risk is by expanding their assets via irresponsible lending. This was particularly easy in the early to mid-2000s in part due to the favourable general market conditions and low interest rates. Relaxed lending policies were also encouraged by the UK government. There is anecdotal evidence that any attempt by UK regulators (the then FSA) to constrain the banking euphoria was met by an implied threat that the banks would complain to a government minister and ensure that the regulator would not interfere. A discussion of the principal limits to regulatory effectiveness can be found in Chapter 7, section I (d).

63 Jones and others observed a feedback effect in the share prices of banks between 2000 and 2006. This means that risky banks were rewarded with higher equity values and hence other banks were encouraged to invest in risky and more opaque assets. See Jeffrey Jones, Wayne Lee and Timothy Yeager, 'Valuation and Systemic Risk Consequences of Bank Opacity' (2013) 37 *Journal of Banking & Finance* 693.

64 The UK regime is based on EU law. Sections 52 and 53 of the Criminal Justice Act 1993 implemented the Insider Dealing Directive. See Council Directive 89/592/EEC of 13 November 1989 co-ordinating regulations on insider dealing [1989] OJ L334/30. Further amendments to the UK regulatory framework were introduced in compliance with the Market Abuse Directive (MAD), including the new section 118 of the Financial Services and Market Act (FSMA 2000), which identifies seven types of prohibited behaviour. See Directive 2003/6/EC of the European Parliament and of the Council of 28 January 2003 on insider dealing and market manipulation (market abuse) [2003] OJ L96/16. There are several English and European cases clarifying the test to be used. See e.g. *Winterflood Securities Ltd v The Financial Services Authority* [2010] EWCA Civ 423; Case C-45/08 *Spector Photo Group NV and Chris Van Raemdonck v Commissie voor het Bank, -Financie-en Assurantiewezen (CBFA)* [2009] ECR I-12073. On the effect of MAD, see Jesper Lau Hansen, 'Insider Dealing after the Market Abuse Directive' in Dan Prentice and Arad Reisberg (eds) *Corporate Finance in the UK and EU* (OUP, 2011).

65 On this, see Patricia Dechow and Catherine Shakespeare, 'Do Managers Time Securitization Transactions to Obtain Accounting Benefits?' (2006) http://papers.ssrn.

manage the information content of their periodic financial disclosures and hence influence share prices without being noticed by investors and analysts.[66]

Overall, the preceding discussion establishes that equity market discipline on risk-taking by financial institutions is severely limited as potential equity investors cannot accurately value their assets and assess their level of risk. This allows senior managers to take excessive risks and manage their share price by appropriately tailoring financial disclosures and balance sheet restructurings. It is therefore argued that in financial institutions shareholder agency costs are higher than in non-financial companies. Taking into account asset opacity, it is evident that it is more difficult for financial institution shareholders to monitor senior management and protect themselves against excessive risk-taking. The significance of this finding from the point of view of the negative externalities caused by risk-taking will be further explored in the concluding section of this chapter, after the examination of the limitations of risk monitoring by the principal creditors of financial institutions, namely bondholders and depositors.

IV. The limited potential of financial institution creditors (bondholders and depositors) to monitor management and constrain excessive risk-taking

Creditor governance is generally an additional check on risk-taking by companies, as creditors demand higher interest rates to advance credit to companies that take higher risks. Covenants in loan facilities also serve a governance function in generic companies with regard to their business activities and risk profile.[67] In the context of banks, it is necessary to distinguish between two types of creditors, namely depositors and bondholders. Bonds are debt securities issued by banks and other financial institutions that are traded on regulated markets. Depositors are the beneficiaries of bank accounts and their potential role will be explored in the following section. In other financial institutions there are, of course, no depositors but such institutions are active on the bond market. It is worth noting that in the UK all deposits that are covered by deposit insurance[68] have the status of ordinary

com/sol3/papers.cfm?abstract_id=928741 accessed 1 May 2017. In addition, the same authors found that CEO pay sensitivity to securitisations is high thus allowing for a perverse incentive to manage the timing of the transactions. See Patricia Dechow, Linda Myers and Catherine Shakespeare, 'Fair Value Accounting and Gains from Asset Securitizations: A Convenient Earnings Management Tool with Compensation Side-benefits' (2010) 49 *Journal of Accounting and Economics* 2.

66 In particular, a US study found that quarterly disclosure of impaired loans was only meaningful in quarters when banks were examined by regulators. See Adam Ashcraft and Hoyt Bleakley, 'On the Market Discipline of Informationally Opaque Firms: Evidence from Bank Borrowers in the Federal Funds Market' (2006) FRBNY Staff Report 257 www.newyorkfed.org/research/staff_reports/sr257.html accessed 1 May 2017.

67 In term loans and syndicated loans agreed between banks and commercial companies it is typical to include covenants that restrict the freedom of the borrower to change its business or enter into substantial transactions without the approval of the bank.

68 On deposit protection coverage, see below n 80 and accompanying text.

preferential debts, while non-covered deposits have the status of secondary preferential debts, thus ranking after ordinary preferential debts but before ordinary debts such as obligations under bonds.[69]

Bondholders have a rational incentive to monitor risk-taking by financial institutions and to demand higher interest rates as compensation for increased risk-taking.[70] Indeed, bondholders' attitude to risk is markedly different from that of the shareholders, as creditors stand to lose their investment in the event of failure and have nothing to gain if a financial institution does exceptionally well. Faith in bondholder governance is reinforced by the fact that investors in bonds are usually professional funds with a reasonable level of expertise and a substantial investment size that allows for monitoring expenditure. Indeed, in recent years banks have been encouraged to use subordinated debt (bonds) as an additional tier of capital and it has been contemplated that market discipline would complement supervision by public authorities.[71] In particular, if risk-taking by financial institutions was accurately reflected in the interest rates they pay on their bonds (and on the prices at which bonds trade on the secondary market) then financial institutions would be incentivised to curtail excessive risk, and a clear signal would be given to regulators that an institution is perceived by the market as highly risky.[72]

However, the opacity of financial institutions' assets limits the potential of the capital market to price accurately the bonds issued by banks and other financial institutions, and thus exposes bondholders to the risk of managerial opportunism. The preceding analysis on asset opacity and the evidence examined in the previous section is also relevant from the perspective of bondholders. If the market cannot distinguish between more and less risky banks and other financial institutions, then both shareholders and bondholders are unable to assess the riskiness of their investment and the return they demand will not reflect the level of risk taken by the issuing institution. In particular, empirical studies on bank opacity confirm that in the case of bonds issued by banks, credit rating agencies are more likely to disagree on their ratings than in bond issues by other companies.[73] Of course, it is not argued that bond market discipline is totally obsolete in the case of financial institutions. The bond market – as indeed the equity market – provides a degree of

69 See Insolvency Act 1986, Schedule 6, para 15B, inserted by Banking Reform Act 2013, s 13; and paras 15BA – 15BB, inserted by The Banks and Building Societies (Depositor Preference and Priorities) Order 2014 (SI 2014/3486), s 11.

70 On the role of bondholders, see also Klaus Hopt, 'Corporate Governance of Banks after the Financial Crisis' in Eddy Wymeersch, Klaus Hopt and Guido Ferranini (eds), *Financial Regulation and Supervision: A Post-crisis Analysis* (OUP, 2012).

71 The emphasis on market discipline until the crisis was reflected in Basel II. See Basel Committee on Banking Supervision, 'International Convergence of Capital Measurement and Capital Standards: A Revised Framework – Comprehensive Version' (Bank for International Settlements Publications, 2006) Part 4: The Third Pillar www.bis.org/publ/bcbs128.htm accessed 1 May 2017.

72 This is an example of enrolling private parties to perform regulatory functions as part of modern reflexive regulatory techniques. On this, see Chapter 3, section IV.

73 See Morgan (above n 56). See also Donald Morgan and Kevin Stiroh, 'Bond Market Discipline of Banks: The Asset Test' (2001) 20 *Journal of Financial Services Research* 195.

discipline and partly reflects available information on financial institutions' riskiness.[74] That being said, information on the quality of financial assets is more difficult to process and verify, and financial institutions tend to withhold relevant information in times of crisis.

Furthermore, risk monitoring by bondholders is also weakened as a result of the perception of an implied government guarantee in the case of bonds issued by large banks. Although bonds are not protected by deposit insurance schemes, the market may perceive very big banks as 'too big to fail', and thus expect that they will be rescued by the government if they face financial difficulties. Indeed, in the UK the government recapitalised and rescued the Royal Bank of Scotland and Lloyds Banking Group at a very high cost to UK taxpayers, but – unlike their shareholders – their bondholders did not lose their investments. A further concern with market discipline by bondholders is its cyclical nature. There is evidence from European banks that market discipline has been effective since the economic downturn in 2008, but was not particularly effective in the years of economic expansion that preceded the crisis.[75] During that period, prospective bondholders did not demand significantly higher returns to invest in riskier or less efficient banks. This finding suggests that market discipline is a weak tool to prevent financial crises, which tend to occur after a long period of euphoria, as it relaxes during exactly the period when it is needed to constrain the excesses that lead to a crisis.[76] Overall, the preceding analysis demonstrates that bondholders are not fully capable of monitoring risk-taking by financial institutions, as they are not in a good position to access and process relevant information due to financial asset opacity. Therefore, it follows that the interest rates paid by financial institutions on their bonds do not generally fully reflect their risk profile.[77]

In the following paragraphs, it is explained that the depositors of UK banks cannot be relied on to perform an effective risk-monitoring function because of the combined effect of three factors. First, depositors lack the necessary expertise to process relevant information on the level of risk taken by banks. In the previous

74 See Neil Esho and others, 'Market Discipline and Subordinated Debt of Australian Banks' (2005) Australian Prudential Regulation Authority Working Paper https://pdfs.semanticscholar.org/cc95/2d0f4b0dbe0289991d33f2fbfa0c65798cb2.pdf accessed 1 May 2017.

75 Casteuble, Nus and Rous found – on a sample of 67 European listed banks issuing bonds between 2002 and 2011 – that banks with more capable managers benefited from lower cost of debt throughout the relevant period, while the probability of default only affected the cost of debt after 2008. See Cecile Casteuble, Emmanuelle Nus and Philippe Rous, 'Do Bank Bondholders Price Banks' Ability to Manage Risk/Return?' (2015) http://papers.ssrn.com/sol3/papers.cfm?abstract_id=2232889 accessed 1 May 2017.

76 Of course, the same problem affects banking supervision by regulatory authorities, as will be explained in Chapter 7, nn 46–48 and accompanying text.

77 Bank creditors can thus be said to have incomplete contracts, like shareholders. The concept of incomplete contracts was introduced by Williamson. See Oliver Williamson, *Markets and Hierarchies: Analysis and Antitrust Implications: A Study in the Economics of Internal Organization* (Collier-Macmillan Publishers, 1975).

two sections, it was argued that even shareholders and bondholders who have much higher expertise than average depositors failed to assess appropriately the risks that banks took in the euphoric period until the recent crisis. Retail depositors are in a far worse position to process relevant information as most of them are unsophisticated individuals who lack an adequate understanding of the sector and of financial reporting.[78] Second, depositors are in a relatively weak bargaining position vis-à-vis banks and therefore it is difficult for them to demand a higher interest rate if they think that a bank is more risky. The retail banking market in the UK is oligopolistic and despite fierce competition to attract depositors, the practical difficulties and costs of moving one's accounts from one bank to another, combined with the feeling of loyalty that many depositors have for their banks, raises an additional obstacle to the operation of market discipline.[79]

The third and most important factor that neutralises depositor monitoring is the existence of deposit insurance. Bank depositors are to a large extent immune to bank failures, due to deposit insurance offered by the UK Financial Services Compensation Scheme.[80] It follows that their incentives to monitor banks are very weak, even more so after the recent financial crisis,[81] especially if it is taken into account that processing relevant information is costly and time consuming. Depositors who hold large deposits can still structure their portfolio so as to be fully covered, as the maximum limit of £85,000 applies to accounts held with each separately licensed banking group.[82] Given that depositors need not worry about

78 A review of the literature on the inability of depositors to monitor banks and its implications can be found in Joao Santos, 'Bank Capital Regulation in Contemporary Banking Theory: A Review of the Literature' (2001) 10 *Financial Markets, Institutions & Instruments* 41, 46–52.

79 On this, see Treasury Committee, *Competition and Choice in Retail Banking* (HC 2010–2011, 612-I). The report finds that the retail banking market is particularly concentrated as more than 90% of current accounts are held with the five largest banks (para 47). Although market concentration does not necessarily indicate limited competition, the committee considered that – on the balance of evidence – competition in the retail banking market is limited (paras 49–50).

80 Since 31 December 2010, the coverage limit has been raised to the equivalent in pounds of €100,000, currently £85,000, as specified by the PRA Rulebook, CRR Firms, Depositor Protection 4.2. See Directive 2009/14/EC of the European Parliament and of the Council of 11 March 2009 amending Directive 94/19/EC on deposit-guarantee schemes as regards the coverage level and the pay-out delay [2009] OJ L68/3, art 1. The amount is payable in full for each account (or set of accounts) or other eligible non-equity investment in a separately licensed bank to natural persons and small companies. On this, see John Raymond LaBrosse and David K Walker, 'The Role of Deposit Insurance Post Implementation of the EU Recovery, Resolution and Deposit Guarantee Directives' in Jens-Hinrich Binder and Dalvinder Singh (eds), *Bank Resolution: The European Regime* (OUP, 2016).

81 Until December 2010 the coverage limit was £50,000 and until October 2008 it was £35,000. It is worth noting that until October 2007 depositors could only claim 90% of the sum between £2,000 and £35,000 so the maximum payoff could reach £31,700.

82 To the extent that they are covered by the Financial Services Compensation Scheme, depositors' claims now enjoy preferential status. This will in the future enable the

the creditworthiness of banks, they face a perverse incentive to place their funds with riskier banks which can pay a higher interest rate, as they generally tend to have a higher income.[83] It follows that far from acting as a constraint on risk-taking, market pressures in this context actually encourage risk-taking in order to attract deposits.

The inability of depositors to monitor risk-taking by banks would seem to support the finding that they are susceptible to suffering managerial agency costs, similarly to bondholders. However, a caveat is necessary here. Deposit protection and government intervention insulates (most) depositors from managerial agency costs and transfers these costs to the public. The same happened during the recent crisis with regard to the bondholders of major UK banks that faced severe difficulties, but it is unlikely to be repeated in the future. It follows that while bondholders stand to bear the costs of managerial opportunism directly, depositors are protected from bank failures and instead it is the public as taxpayers who stand to suffer from excessive risk-taking in the financial sector.

V. Conclusions: the impact of limited market discipline on the problem of excessive risk-taking by financial institutions

Bringing together the two strands of discussion in the present chapter, it must be emphasised that the argument advanced in sections I and II stands irrespective of the finding of sections III and IV that banks and other financial institutions are more opaque than most other large companies, and hence that shareholder and creditor governance is likely to be less effective in the case of financial institutions. However, the phenomenon of financial institution opacity and the ensuing severe limitations of effective risk monitoring by market players is connected to the core problem of misaligned risk appetite in several ways.

First, the finding that risk monitoring by financial institution shareholders and creditors is ineffective, demonstrates that the misalignment identified in section III is a very serious one. Of course, even if market discipline ensured that equity and debt providers were fully compensated *ex ante* for the level of risk assumed by financial institutions, the existence of systemic risk[84] would still mean that failures cause negative externalities on the shareholders and creditors of other institutions. However, the limited ability of shareholders and creditors to restrain risk-taking by financial institution managers, combined with the incentives the latter face to take excessive risks, means that financial institutions are likely to take even more risk

Scheme manager to recover a larger part of the relevant deposits and therefore will reduce the likelihood that a loss is incurred by the Treasury. See Financial Services (Banking Reform) Act 2013, s 13, which will insert ss 15B and 15C into Schedule 6 of the Insolvency Act 1986.

83 For instance, a risky bank may have a higher income because it is more highly leveraged than another bank, or because the funds of the depositors are lent out to debtors of low creditworthiness who pay higher interest rates.

84 It should be kept in mind that opacity is not the only cause of systemic risk and hence it would exist even in the absence of any opacity.

than fully informed investors would accept. It follows that the profit maximisation norm leads to the assumption of a level of risk that is excessive even from the perspective of institutions' shareholders and creditors, and is thus far higher than the level of risk that is socially desirable. In this sense, the opacity argument strengthens the finding of sections I and II that the current corporate governance regime undermines financial stability.[85]

Second, the deep-rooted causes of financial institution opacity that go beyond the availability of information and include the inability of investors to process the relevant information, suggest that the misalignment between the current corporate governance paradigm and financial stability is unlikely to be tackled effectively merely by reinforcing market discipline. The previous analysis shows that the introduction of further regulatory requirements to disclose more information would be unlikely to increase the risk-monitoring potential of financial institution shareholders[86] and bondholders materially, while it would be prone to lead to undesirable unintended consequences.[87] It follows that reliance on market discipline to alleviate the financial stability consequences of risk-taking and profit seeking by financial sector firms is misguided and unlikely to achieve its purpose.[88] This argument supports the view that it is necessary to take a more directly interventionist approach to remedy this problem.

85 On this, see Emilios Avgouleas and Jay Cullen, 'Market Discipline and EU Corporate Governance Reform in the Banking Sector: Merits, Fallacies, and Cognitive Boundaries' (2014) 41 *Journal of Law and Society* 28.

86 An additional reason to be sceptical about the potential of shareholders to monitor risk effectively is the presence of conflicts of interest. It has to be kept in mind that financial institutions are a major category of institutional investors and that there are dense business relationships between banks, insurance firms and investment firms. On the general obstacles to meaningful shareholder involvement with companies, see Andreas Kokkinis, 'Shareholder Short-Termism in the UK: The Kay Review and the Potential Role of Corporate Law' (2014) 11 *Corporate Ownership and Control* 166.

87 Disclosing sensitive information about a systemic financial institution to the market can lead to panic and thus reduce the chances of survival of the relevant institution. Indeed, Chiu observed that: 'Reporting to regulators is being refined [...] for the purposes of micro and macro-prudential supervision, but not all such forms of reporting may be suitable for capital markets as there may be implications for stock prices and cost of capital.' See Iris H-Y Chiu, 'Corporate Reporting and the Accountability of Banks and Financial Institutions' in Iris H-Y Chiu (ed), *The Law on Corporate Governance in Banks* (Edward Elgar Publishing, 2015), 204.

88 On the failure of disclosure as a regulatory technique in the financial sector, see Emilios Avgouleas, 'The Global Financial Crisis and the Disclosure Paradigm in European Financial Regulation: The Case for Reform' (2009) 6 *European Company and Financial Law Review* 440. See also Emilios Avgouleas, 'What Future for Disclosure as a Regulatory Technique? Lessons from Behavioural Decision Theory and the Global Financial Crisis' in Iain MacNeil and Justin O'Brien (eds), *The Future of Financial Regulation* (Hart Publishing, 2010). Similarly, Schwarcz argues that the complexity of the financial sector undermines the effectiveness of disclosure as a regulatory tool to remedy asymmetry of information problems. See Steven Schwarcz, 'Information Asymmetry and Information Failure: Disclosure Problems in Complex Financial Markets' in William Sun, Jim Stewart and David Pollard (eds), *Corporate Governance and the Global Financial Crisis: International Perspectives* (CUP, 2011).

Third, the discussion demonstrated that the current regime – although apparently focused on shareholder value maximisation – does not necessarily lead to this outcome, as it allows a level of risk-taking that is often excessive even from the viewpoint of financial institution shareholders. This finding further supports the case for regulating risk-taking in the financial sector, as it undermines the potential objection that regulation is necessarily value-decreasing for shareholders. In other words, regulating risk-taking by financial institutions would partly benefit their shareholders by preventing senior managers from taking risks that are excessive from the shareholders' point of view. Of course, restricting risk-taking to the extent required by the public interest would come at the cost of leading to a level of risk that is lower than the optimal level of risk for shareholders, thus partly decreasing their wealth. Whether on balance such a regime would be more value-increasing for financial institution shareholders than the current regime is of course an empirical question, and one which it is very difficult to answer. However, at any rate, the discussion here illustrates that shareholders would at least partially benefit from an interventionist approach to risk-taking by financial institutions.

Before examining how prudential regulation has historically sought to remedy the problem described in this chapter and the steps taken in this direction after the 2007–2009 financial crisis, Chapter 2 will analyse which particular company law doctrines and which aspects of the UK corporate governance system are conducive to the problem of excessive risk-taking by financial institutions. This is necessary in order to evaluate the adequacy of the regulatory measures that will be analysed in subsequent chapters, and also serves as necessary background to the legal reform recommendations made in the latter chapters of this volume.

2 The UK corporate law and governance framework as a mechanism to facilitate risk-taking by corporate managers and shareholders

Having examined conceptual arguments and empirical evidence demonstrating that the interests of equity investors in financial institutions and of the public are diverging with regard to risk-taking, this chapter seeks to identify the corporate law doctrines that make this possible. In particular, it is shown that modern corporate law and governance seek to align the risk appetite of risk-averse senior managers with that of risk-neutral shareholders by setting strong incentives for executive directors and managers to maximise the market price of a company's (and thus a bank's or other financial institution's) shares in the short term in order to maximise their remuneration and secure their positions. At the same time, UK company and insolvency laws shield financial institution directors and senior managers from the negative consequences of risky decisions insofar as they acted in good faith and followed a reasonable decision-making process, as was demonstrated in the aftermath of the 2007–2009 global financial crisis.

This chapter is structured as follows. Section I reviews the broadly accepted conceptual framework of agency theory as it applies to corporate law, emphasising the issue of aligning the interests of managers with those of shareholders. Section II explains how limited liability banking arose and argues that limited liability is a necessary precondition for the separation of ownership from control and portfolio diversification. Sections III and IV then analyse the legal and soft-law mechanisms which seek to align the risk appetite of corporate managers with that of diversified shareholders. Turning to the issue of shielding managers from the risks of failure, section V explains how the legal formulation of the duty of care owed by directors to companies insulates the directors of financial institutions from liability in case of failure due to excessive risk-taking. Section VI proceeds to explain how the modern corporate governance framework has attempted to mitigate the problem of excessive risk-taking and discusses the limitations of such attempts. Section VII concludes with an overall assessment of the legal framework.

I. Agency costs and the role of corporate law

The need for corporate law and corporate governance[1] to devise mechanisms to protect and empower the shareholders vis-à-vis the directors and managers is

1 Tackling the agency problem has been the *raison d'être* of the corporate governance movement since its inception. See Daniel R Fischel, 'The Corporate Governance Movement' (1982) 35 *Vanderbilt Law Review* 1259.

grounded on agency theory. A principal-agent relationship is a concept frequently used in economics and political science to describe a situation in which one person appoints another to act on his behalf and in his best interests, occasionally in exchange for remuneration.[2] In this sense, the relationship between voters and members of Parliament, patients and doctors, and shareholders and managers in a company are all examples of a principal-agent relationship. It is worth noting that this concept of agency is broader than the legal notion of agency[3] and includes all fiduciary relationships and other relationships. An agency relationship gives rise to a principal-agent problem when the agent does not have the same interests as the principal, and there is information asymmetry between the two. In other words, this occurs when the agent is in possession of relevant information which is not available to – or cannot be properly understood by – the principal. In such cases, the principal cannot *prima facie* ensure that the agent will use his powers in the principal's best interests. Assuming that the agent is a rational actor who seeks to maximise his own utility, it can be expected that the agent will shirk his duties and may even transfer wealth from the principal to himself when a conflict exists between the interests of the principal on the one hand, and those of the agent on the other.

In companies, it is the separation of ownership and control – first empirically observed by Berle and Means[4] – which gives rise to an agency relationship between the shareholders, who are the principals, and the directors and senior managers,[5] who are their agents. The separation of ownership and control occurs when the ownership of shares is so dispersed that no shareholder – or small group of shareholders – holds a majority of shares, or even a stake that would guarantee effective control of the company. This means that no individual shareholder (or small group) acting alone can usually determine the outcome of a shareholder vote.[6] On these conditions, the costs faced by shareholders who wish to influence

2 Joseph Stiglitz, 'Principal and Agent' in Eatwell J, Milgate M and Newmann P (eds), *The New Palgrave Dictionary of Economics*, Vol. 3 (Macmillan, 1987). See also Sanford J Grossman and Oliver D Hart, 'An Analysis of the Principal-Agent Problem' (1983) 51 *Econometrica* 7; and Frank H Easterbrook, 'Managers' Discretion and Investors' Welfare: Theories and Evidence' (1984) 9 *Delaware Journal of Corporate Law* 540.

3 In law, an agent is a person who is given the power (the authority) to alter the legal position of another person (the principal), especially by entering into contracts on behalf of the principal. An agent's authority can be actual, which is conferred by agreement between the principal and the agent, or apparent.

4 Berle and Means's empirical work confirmed that 44% of the 200 largest US corporations were managerially controlled, i.e. no single shareholder owned more than 5% of shares. See Adolf Berle and Gardiner Means, *The Modern Corporation and Private Property* (rev edn, Harcourt, Brace & World, 1967), 108–109.

5 Although the terms are often used interchangeably in economic literature, is should be kept in mind that they are clearly distinct. Directors are the members of the board, formally elected by the shareholders, and owing fiduciary duties to the company. Executive directors are full-time managers as well, while non-executive directors are not. Managers are those responsible for the day-to-day running of the business of the company and the implementation of the board's strategies.

6 See Bernard Black, 'Agents Watching Agents: The Promise of Institutional Investor Voice' (1991–1992) 39 *UCLA Law Review* 811, 821–822.

corporate decision-making are significant. First, they have to invest time and resources in analysing relevant information to form an opinion. Second, they have to try to put together and maintain a coalition of shareholders. Third, they need to communicate with the board, and possibly pay legal and other professional fees. At the same time, the potential benefit from activism is relatively small, as it is by no means certain that the coalition will be successful in winning the vote against the board. Moreover, even if the activist shareholders are successful, any benefits will be equally spread among all shareholders. As a result, each shareholder is tempted to remain passive and wait for someone else to engage, a phenomenon described as the rational apathy of the shareholders.[7] The outcome of this is that the recommendations of the board are nearly invariably approved by the shareholders, as the latter either do not use their voting rights at all, or tend to vote in favour of the board. This includes the election of directors itself, and thus the board becomes a self-perpetuating organ, except for the most exceptional occasions of poor performance.[8]

The separation of ownership from control, which since the late 1960s is prevalent in the UK nearly as much as in the US, is argued to give rise to agency costs, which are imposed by senior managers on shareholders. These costs are of two types: (a) lack of optimal effort and diligence by senior managers in discharging their duties; and (b) the risk that senior managers may pursue objectives other than the maximisation of shareholder wealth, such as the advancement of their own financial interests. This can be achieved (*inter alia*) by self-dealing, exploiting corporate opportunities, misappropriating corporate assets and receiving excessive remuneration.[9] Additionally, or alternatively, managers may pursue non-value-maximising objectives to serve their non-financial interests. An example of that is corporate 'empire-building', i.e. the creation of inefficiently large corporate groups with a view to enhance senior managers' personal power, prestige and security of office.[10]

In order to reduce primary agency costs, shareholders have to engage in monitoring managers by keeping informed on the performance of companies and getting involved when necessary. In parallel, senior managers also wish to signal to potential investors that agency costs will be held in tight control in order to encourage investment in the company's shares. To do so, senior managers put in place majority independent boards which have the power to monitor their performance and replace them. Of course, monitoring by shareholders and using

7 For a modern explanation of the dynamics of shareholder voting and the rational apathy of the shareholders from a US perspective, see Christopher Gulinello, 'The Retail Investor Vote: Mobilizing Rationally Apathetic Shareholders to Preserve or Challenge the Board's Presumption of Authority' (2010) *Utah Law Review* 547, 573–576.

8 Berle and Means were the first scholars who observed the collective action problems faced by dispersed shareholders. See Berle and Means (above n 4), 76–82 and 129–131.

9 On this, see Andrew Keay, 'Company Directors Behaving Poorly: Disciplinary Options for Shareholders' (2007) *Journal of Business Law* 656.

10 Large corporations owning diverse businesses and operating in various markets are less susceptible to insolvency and hostile takeovers.

bonding devices by managers are costly activities in their own right, so they can be seen as types of agency costs themselves. This explains why Jensen and Meckling classify agency costs into three categories, namely monitoring costs, bonding costs and residual agency costs.[11]

Monitoring by the shareholders and the emergence of independent boards are processes that evolved in the UK through market practice and are now positively encouraged by soft-law codes.[12] Still, high transaction costs have made it necessary for company law to devise further default rules that seek to minimise agency costs which are argued to be similar to what the relevant parties (i.e. shareholders and senior managers) would have agreed to. In this sense, contractarian theory analyses and rationalises most company law doctrines as an attempt to minimise the agency costs borne by the shareholders.[13] There are various ways to achieve this objective. The authors of the influential comparative law monograph, *The Anatomy of Corporate Law*,[14] identify five alternative strategies, namely: decision-making, appointment, trusteeship, reward, and affiliation. I will briefly outline the usage of these strategies by UK company law in order to demonstrate the explanatory power of the agency costs analysis in this context.

The decision-making strategy empowers directly the principal so that he can monitor the agent. In the UK, it is manifested *inter alia* by shareholder approval of amendments to the company's articles of association[15] and major transactions,[16] as well as by the power of the shareholders to initiate constitutional amendments[17] and call General Meetings.[18]

11 See Michael C Jensen and William H Meckling, 'Theory of the Firm: Managerial Behavior, Agency Costs and Ownership Structure' (1976) 3 *Journal of Financial Economics* 305, 308–310.

12 Mainly the UK Corporate Governance Code and the UK Stewardship Code, which are both promulgated by the Financial Reporting Council.

13 A major exception to this includes those doctrines that seek to protect the creditors of companies from the effects of limited liability, such as the capital maintenance doctrine and the wrongful trading provision applying when a company has no reasonable prospect of avoiding insolvent liquidation (s 214 of the Insolvency Act 1986).

14 Reinier Kraakman and others, *The Anatomy of Corporate Law: A Comparative and Functional Approach* (3rd edn, OUP, 2017).

15 According to Companies Act 2006, s 21, a company may amend its articles by special resolution. However, the power of the majority to amend the articles must be exercised *bona fide* for the benefit of the company as a whole. See *Allen v Gold Reefs of West Africa Ltd* [1990] 1 Ch 656 (CA).

16 The UK Listing Rule 10 requires shareholder approval for Class 1 transactions, i.e. transactions that amount to 25% of the value of the company. It applies only to listed public companies.

17 Companies Act 2006, s 338 enables shareholders representing 5% of the total voting rights – or 100 shareholders who have paid up for their shares £100 on average – to require the circulation of a resolution in a General Meeting. Shareholders may thus initiate a change in the company's constitution or any other decision, although it is usually the directors who set the agenda of General Meetings.

18 Companies Act 2006, s 303, as amended in compliance with the EU Shareholder Rights Directive (Directive 2007/36/EC), enables shareholders representing 5% of the voting rights to convene a General Meeting at the company's expense.

The second strategy enables the principal to appoint and remove freely the agent. Section 168 (1) of the Companies Act 2006, for instance, enables shareholders to remove any director at any time without contractual cause by passing an ordinary resolution.[19] In addition, the default rule for UK public companies is that directors are elected or re-elected by an ordinary resolution of the company in a General Meeting.[20]

The trusteeship strategy aims at extinguishing the 'selfishness' of the agent. One example of its use in the UK is the fiduciary duties of directors, who are expected to put the interests of the company ahead of their personal interests. Directors who thus owe a duty of loyalty to the company,[21] must exercise their powers for the purposes they were conferred,[22] and may not put themselves in a position where their personal interests conflict with those of the company.[23] The other main manifestation of the trusteeship strategy is the appointment of independent non-executive directors on boards. Since 2003 in the UK, listed company boards have been dominated by independent or outside directors.[24]

The reward strategy, by contrast, aims to exploit the selfishness of the agent for the benefit of the principal by structuring his or her incentives accordingly. Stock options, bonuses, LTIPs and other variable parts of executive remuneration are examples of the use of this strategy.

Finally, the affiliation strategy aims to facilitate the withdrawal of shareholders from the company at a fair price. In this way, the principal can terminate the agency relationship, if not satisfied with the agent's behaviour. In public companies, this is achieved by preventing the management from frustrating a hostile takeover bid,[25] so that shareholders are free to decide on the merits of an offer,

19 In private companies, the use of multiple voting rights can result to the entrenchment of directors who own the requisite number of shares. In particular, it is possible to issue shares that carry multiple votes only in the context of a vote to remove a director. See *Bushell v Faith* [1970] AC 1099. However, it is unlikely that the London Stock Exchange and the Financial Conduct Authority would allow the listing of a company whose articles provide for the above structure. See John Lowry and Arad Reisberg, *Pettet's Company Law: Company Law & Corporate Finance* (4th edn, Pearson Publishing, 2012), 191–192. In addition, dismissing a director (and minority shareholder) in the context of a small private company, where there is a close relationship of trust and confidence amongst members, may amount to unfair prejudice. See Companies Act 2006, ss 994–996; and *O' Neill v Philips* [1999] UKHL 24; 1 WLR 1126 (HL).

20 See Companies (Model Articles) Regulations 2008 (SI 2008/3229), reg 4, Schedule 3, arts 20 and 21.

21 See *Bristol & West Building Society v Mothew* [1998] 1 Ch 1; *Re Smith & Fawcett* [1942] Ch 304, esp 306; and Companies Act 2006, s 172.

22 Companies Act 2006, s 171 (b). See also *Hogg v Cramphorn Ltd* [1967] Ch 254.

23 Companies Act 2006, s 175. See also *Regal (Hastings) Ltd v Gulliver* [1942] 1 All ER 378.

24 Corporate Governance Code, Provision B.1.2 recommends that at least half the board, excluding the chairman, should consist of independent non-executive directors.

25 The Panel on Takeovers and Mergers, *The City Code on Takeovers and Mergers* (11th edn, RR Donnelley, 2013), General Principle 3.

thus enabling an active market for corporate control to operate.[26] Overall, agency theory supports the rationalisation of corporate law and corporate governance as a body of (generally) default rules that seek to protect the shareholders from managerial opportunism, mimicking the way the shareholders would have demanded to be protected, were they able to negotiate the terms of investing in public companies at zero cost.[27]

II. Limited liability as a necessary condition for shareholder risk neutrality

It is widely acknowledged that in order for businesses to make profits they need to take risks, as business activity necessarily entails making decisions with limited information. Similarly, investors require a risk premium (i.e. a higher expected return) to invest in more risky securities. For instance, generally, corporate bonds that carry the risk that the issuing company may go insolvent bear a higher interest rate than government bonds, which are presumed to be risk-free as the government is extremely unlikely to default on its debt.[28] Shares are even more risky investments as there is no specified return and share capital is the first to be lost if a company goes insolvent.

It would seem sensible, therefore, to expect shareholders to have a conservative view on risk-taking by companies as they are the first to lose if a risk goes badly. Nevertheless, it is widely accepted that shareholders are far from conservative in their attitude to risk. The attitude of shareholders towards risk-taking by companies is shaped by two phenomena, one dating back to the late 19th century and another that emerged in the 20th century. These are limited liability and portfolio diversification, which were mentioned in the previous chapter. Limited liability is a necessary condition for the emergence of portfolio diversification, as without it shareholders would be liable personally for companies' debts in the case of insolvency and would thus have a strong incentive to invest in a small number of companies and take an active part in their management. From a UK legal doctrine perspective, limited liability means that the liability of a member of any registered company limited by shares, to contribute to the company's assets in case the latter goes into insolvent liquidation, is limited to the amount unpaid[29] – if any – of the nominal value of the shares that the member has been allotted.[30] Practically the

26 Moreover, particularly important in this regard are 'sell-out' provisions, which are designed to prevent a minority shareholder being locked into a company against his will following a change in control. See Companies Act 2006, ss 983–985.

27 On this, see below Chapter 6, section I (a).

28 At least this is accurate for UK government bonds. However, the recent eurozone sovereign debt crisis demonstrates that eurozone government bonds are not necessarily of zero risk.

29 For private companies, there is no requirement that the nominal value of shares needs to be paid up at the time of allotment. See Companies Act 2006, ss 542–548. In the case of public companies, however, shares must be at least one-quarter paid up (Companies Act 2006, s 586).

30 Insolvency Act 1986, s 74 (2) (d). See also Companies Act 2006, s 3 (1) and (2); and *Salomon v Salomon & Co Ltd* [1896] UKHL 1, [1897] AC 22.

same rule applies to US corporations and to companies in other common law countries, as well as to certain company types with a minimum share capital in countries following the civilian legal tradition.[31]

The history of the introduction of limited liability in the UK is interesting in its own right,[32] but it is even more intriguing with regard to the adoption of limited liability by banking firms, which followed a slightly different path from other companies. This largely reflects the early recognition of the special features of the banking sector that make limited liability a potential threat to the public interest, as will be explained in Chapter 3. Indeed, limited liability became available for companies by virtue of the Limited Liability Act 1855, while the possibility of incorporating and acquiring separate legal personality by registration was introduced by the Joint Stock Companies Act 1844. Both Acts excluded banks from their scope, as did the Joint Stock Companies Act 1856, which codified and expanded company legislation.[33]

Indeed, in England until 1826, banks could only operate as common law partnerships with an upper limit of six partners having been introduced in the early 18th century.[34] Then the Banking Copartnerships Act 1826 allowed banks to become joint stock companies for the first time which had been common practice in other sectors for years.[35] Joint stock companies had no separate legal personality, and shares in them were really a share of the assets rather than an asset in its own right, and were not transferable without the approval of the directors. The Joint Stock Banks Act 1844 clarified that the Joint Stock Companies Act did not apply to banks, which could only obtain legal personality via a royal charter for a maximum duration of 20 years.[36] It was only when the Joint Stock Banking Companies Act 1857 was enacted that banks were allowed to incorporate as companies with legal personality without a charter and still with unlimited liability and a requirement of a minimum denomination of shares at £100. Limited liability first became available to banking companies in 1858 by virtue of the Joint Stock

31 See generally, Kaus J Hopt, 'Comparative Company Law' in Mathias Reimann and Reinhard Zimmermann (eds), *The Oxford Handbook of Comparative Law* (OUP, 2008). An historical discussion of limited liability from a US perspective can be found in William J Carney, 'Limited Liability Companies: Origins and Antecedents' (1995) 66 *University of Colorado Law Review* 855.

32 A comprehensive review of the relevant literature is not feasible within the scope of the present volume. See e.g. Robert A Bryer, 'The Mercantile Laws Commission of 1854 and the Political Economy of Limited Liability' (1997) 50 *Economic History Review* 37. From the perspective of banks, see e.g. Lucy A Newton, 'The Birth of Joint-stock Banking: England and New England Compared' (2010) 84 *Business History Review* 27. From a US perspective, see Stephen M Bainbridge and M Todd Henderson, *Limited Liability: A Legal and Economic Analysis* (Edward Elgar Publishing, 2016), 21–43.

33 John D Turner, *Banking in Crisis: The Rise and Fall of British Banking Stability, 1800 to the Present* (CUP, 2014), 39–41.

34 Ibid., 36.

35 Ibid., 38.

36 See Bishop C Hunt, *The Development of the Business Corporation in England, 1800–1867* (Harvard University Press, 1936), 96.

Banks Act 1858. The minimum denomination requirement was only abolished by the Companies Act 1862, thus completing the process of integrating the company law framework for banks within the framework for other companies, albeit with some minor modifications, a legacy which still stands today.[37]

However, banks were slow to adopt the legal form of a limited liability company, as depositors and other market players continued to rely heavily on bank shareholders' personal wealth as a reassurance that their deposits were safe. Indeed, by the mid-1870s only seven out of a significant number of existing English banks had incorporated as limited liability companies, although the Act was being adopted by most newly established banks.[38] This trend changed only after the infamous collapse of the City of Glasgow Bank in 1878, which led to catastrophic consequences for its shareholders, many of whom were middle-class families across the country.[39] By 1884, within a few years of that event, nearly all English banks had adopted limited liability. Still, most of them issued high amounts of uncalled share capital, thus maintaining the liability of certain shareholders to contribute up to that amount in case of insolvency and made avail of the possibility introduced by the Companies Act 1879 to issue reserve share capital,[40] which was similar to uncalled capital but could only be claimed in case of insolvency. Thus, in late 19th century Britain, a large percentage of deposits were covered by banks' called up capital, uncalled capital and reserve capital.[41] This faded gradually until the 1950s, when it reached the very low levels (of around 5%) at which it has more or less remained ever since.[42] The full adoption of limited liability by banks and other

37 On the application of the Act on insurance companies and companies formed 'for the purpose of carrying on the business of banking', see Companies Act 1862, ss 3–4. In the Act, banks were treated in the same way as other companies save for the following provisions: (a) banks had an additional obligation to publicise at their premises a statement of their share capital twice a year (s 44); (b) in banks the appointment of official inspectors to examine the affairs of the company required a petition by members representing one-third of the bank's share capital, while all other companies required one-fifth of the capita (s 56); and (c) any existing bank with unlimited liability which chose to register under the Act and adopt limited liability had to notify all its account holders 30 days in advance or else liability remained unlimited until notice was given (s 188). The full text of the Act can be found online at www.irishstatutebook.ie/eli/1862/act/89/enacted/en/print.html?printonload=true accessed 1 May 2017.

38 Turner (above n 33), 41 and 124.

39 An in-depth account of the events surrounding the bank's failure can be found in Leo Rosenblum, 'The Failure of the City of Glasgow Bank' (1933) 8 *The Accounting Review* 285, esp 289–291. See also Turner (above n 33), 120–123.

40 The difference between uncalled share capital and reserve share capital was that reserve capital was not callable at the directors' discretion but, rather, only if the bank went insolvent and had inadequate funds to repay depositors. On this generally, see Lewis T Evans and Neil C Quigley, 'Shareholder Liability Regimes, Principal-agent Relationships, and Banking Industry Performance' (1995) 38 *Journal of Law and Economics* 497.

41 Indeed, shareholder capital in a broad sense covered 70% of deposits in 1885, but only 40% in 1900. See Turner (above n 33), 128–129.

42 Ibid., 129–131.

financial institutions has meant that shareholders stand to benefit from any profits resulting from the taking of business risks, but only stand to lose the value of their shares if these risks turn out badly.

III. Aligning the risk appetite of senior managers and directors with that of the shareholders: the importance of positive incentives

Prima facie, corporate directors and senior managers have no direct reason to satisfy the risk appetite of the shareholders, as in widely held companies they enjoy in practice a very wide discretion to manage companies as they think fit, as they are freed from any shareholder interference other than in extraordinary circumstances.[43] Indeed, taking into account that managers are full-time employees of the company who have invested their personal capital in the company, it becomes clear that they are in general less prone to take risk compared to the shareholders. Human capital is not diversifiable and the potential failure of a company normally causes huge reputational damage to senior managers, which reduces their chance to obtain an equivalent position in the future. It follows that in a widely held company, senior managers can be expected to be less prone to take risks than shareholders, as only the latters' investment is fully diversified.

The above analysis assumes the relevant individuals to be risk-neutral, whereas in reality they tend to be risk-averse, as explained in Chapter 1. The standard economic explanation of the phenomenon of risk aversion is that it is due to the diminishing marginal utility of additional wealth for most individuals. Moreover, behavioural economic research suggests that individuals are even more risk-averse than this explanation suggests.[44] This, however, depends on whether individuals are faced with a gain or a loss, and whether they perceive the gain or loss to be of high probability or of low probability. Empirical evidence indicates that most individuals tend to be risk-averse in circumstances involving low-probability losses.[45] This means that in the context of decision-making that can impact a company's insolvency risk, which is likely to be perceived as a low-probability loss, senior managers paid only by a fixed salary in cash are likely to be strongly

43 The executive primacy of the board of directors is embedded in company law as the default position with regard to the governance of companies. Reflecting well-established case law, Model Article 3 for both public and private companies bestows the management of the business and affairs of a company on its board and Model Article 4 requires a special resolution to be passed by the shareholders in order to give directions to the board. See The Companies (Model Articles) Regulations SI 2008/3229, schedules 1, arts 3–4 and schedule 3, arts 3–4. See also *Automatic Self-Cleansing Filter Syndicate Co v Cunninghame* [1906] 2 Ch 34 (CA); *John Shaw & Sons Ltd v Shaw* [1935] 2 KB 113.

44 Matthew Rabin and Richard H Thaler, 'Anomalies: Risk Aversion' (2001) 15 *The Journal of Economic Perspectives* 219.

45 See Amos Tversky and Daniel Kahneman, 'Advances in Prospect Theory: Cumulative Representation of Uncertainty' (1992) 5 *Journal of Risk and Uncertainty* 297, 297–301.

risk-averse, and thus very far from the risk-neutral appetite of diversified equity investors.

The misalignment of risk appetite between managers and shareholders has been the target of academic criticism by contractarian scholars since the 1980s. Two major mechanisms have been used to re-align the risk appetite of the two groups: hostile takeovers and variable executive remuneration. A hostile takeover occurs when the majority of the shares – and hence the control – of a company are bought by another company without the approval of the target company's board. A hostile takeover leads to the target company becoming a subsidiary of the acquirer,[46] and the directors and senior managers of the target being replaced. It follows that the market for corporate control[47] ensures that companies' managers face a powerful incentive to do their best to maximise shareholder value, which includes adopting a neutral approach to risk-taking. This is the case because delivering shareholder value results in maintaining the company's share price at a high level and thus makes it unlikely that the company will be the target of a takeover. Indeed, for a hostile takeover offer to arise, the potential acquirer must be willing to pay the current shareholders of the target a premium above the market price of the shares, and still be able to cover the costs of the transaction and make a profit. This means that the share price must be lower than the underlying value of the company's assets from the bidder's perspective, which of course is very unlikely to be the case if the target is highly profitable and its share price reflects that.

Of course, it is well-established that in the financial services sector hostile takeovers are relatively uncommon both internationally[48] and in the UK.[49] This is – at least partly – due to regulatory obstacles.[50] However, major UK banks are sometimes engaged in hostile takeovers of foreign banks,[51] and do frequently resort to friendly mergers,[52] which are often facilitated by the implicit threat of a hostile

46 At least, this is the practice in the UK. In the US, it is common for the two companies to merge.

47 The American lawyer Henry Manne was the first author to introduce the concept of a market for corporate control. See Henry Manne, 'Mergers and the Market for Corporate Control' (1965) 73 *The Journal of Political Economy* 110.

48 See e.g. Ross Levine, 'The Corporate Governance of Banks: A Concise Discussion of Concepts and Evidence' (2004) World Bank Policy Research Working Paper 3404 http://elibrary.worldbank.org/doi/book/10.1596/1813-9450-3404 accessed 1 May 2017.

49 The only hostile takeover of a major UK bank in recent years was that of National Westminster Bank by the Royal Bank of Scotland in 2000, subsequent to a failed friendly merger of the former with Legal & General and a failed hostile takeover bid by the Bank of Scotland. The takeover was key to the rising of RBS to one of the Big Four clearing banks and made it one of the largest companies in the world.

50 Until the late 1980s, the Bank of England considered it necessary for a merger to be based on an amicable agreement of the parties in order to approve it.

51 An obvious recent example is the takeover of ABN AMRO by a consortium led by RBS.

52 Recent examples include the merger between Lloyds TSB and Halifax Bank of Scotland (HBOS) in 2009, the acquisition of Abbey National by Santander in 2004, the merger of Halifax and Bank of Scotland in 2001, and the acquisition of the Midland Bank by HSBC in 1992.

takeover. Therefore, although the pressures from the market for corporate control are somewhat limited in the banking sector, there is still an incentive for bank senior managers to maintain the share price of the bank so as to avoid takeover pressures.

The second mechanism used to achieve risk appetite alignment is variable executive remuneration.[53] Until the 1980s, executive remuneration in large US and UK companies was generally insensitive to performance, but rather akin to that in bureaucratic organisations. The influential work of Jensen and Murphy in 1990 demonstrated that the remuneration of US CEOs was not strongly linked to performance, and that the overall level of CEO pay in the 1980s was in real terms lower than in the 1930s.[54] They attributed this phenomenon to the political influence of trade unions, the media and certain shareholders, who opposed high levels of remuneration irrespective of performance sensitivity. Jensen and Murphy urged for an increase in variable remuneration, as better-aligned incentives would leave shareholders better-off despite the increase in executive remuneration. Indeed, the 1990s brought an explosive rise of variable remuneration (especially in the form of stock options) and of overall levels of pay both in the US[55] and the UK. The resulting remarkable increase in the overall levels of remuneration in recent years has captured the public imagination and is one of the core issues considered by a recent report published by the House of Commons Business, Energy and Industrial Strategy Committee.[56]

The traditional view of contractarian scholars on executive remuneration is the optimal contracting approach. This strand of scholarship[57] argues that executive

53 For an empirical study illustrating the significance of top management pay structure, see Mason A Carpenter and WM Gerard Sanders, 'Top Management Team Compensation: The Missing Link Between CEO Pay and Firm Performance?' (2002) 23 *Strategic Management Journal* 367.

54 Michael Jensen and Kevin Murphy, 'CEO Incentives – It's Not How Much You Pay, But How' (1990) *Harvard Business Review* 138. See also Bengt Holmstrom, 'Moral Hazard in Teams' (1982) 13 *Bell Journal of Economics* 324.

55 In the US the favourable tax treatment of variable remuneration since 1993 has further facilitated the shift towards performance-based pay. Section 162 (m) of the U.S. Internal Revenue Code 1993 eliminated the tax deductibility of executive compensation in excess of $1 million, unless it was performance-based.

56 Business, Energy and Industrial Strategy Committee, *Corporate Governance* (HC 2016–17, 702), paras 80–103. Indeed, the committee cautioned that shareholder engagement alone may not be able to restrain the growth of executive remuneration and recommended 'more transparency, better reporting, more employee involvement and tougher enforcement', and if these measures failed, 'more direct intervention' (para 103).

57 See for instance, Frank Easterbrook, 'Managers' Discretion and Investors' Welfare: Theories and Evidence' (1984) 9 *Delaware Journal of Corporate Law* 540; Daniel R Fischel, 'The Corporate Governance Movement' (1982) 35 *Vanderbilt Law Review* 1259; Sanford Grossman and Oliver Hart, 'An Analysis of the Principal-Agent Problem' (1983) 51 *Econometrica* 7; Bengt Holmstrom, 'Moral Hazard in Teams' (1982) 13 *Bell Journal of Economics* 324; and more recently Alex Edmans and Xavier Gabaix, 'Is CEO Pay Really Inefficient? A Survey of New Optimal Contracting Theories' (2009) 15 *European Financial Management* 486.

remuneration is not problematic, as it is restrained by market forces and aligns the interests (and risk appetite) of managers with those of the shareholders. The aims of executive employment contracts are to attract and retain talented individuals, to provide them with incentives to maximise shareholder value and to minimise overall transaction costs. This is achieved by paying the largest portion of executive remuneration in the form of bonuses, share options and performance shares that are payable only if certain performance thresholds are satisfied. An increase in overall levels of executive pay is an unavoidable consequence of making their pay more performance-sensitive, and therefore is not in itself evidence of rent extraction by managers.[58]

The introduction of independent remuneration committees that are expected to negotiate the remuneration of executive directors at arm's length,[59] and shareholder approval requirements in the UK since 2002 offer *prima facie* support to the view that there is no significant scope for managerial exploitation of shareholders in widely held companies. In particular, since 1 October 2013 UK quoted companies are expected to produce a remuneration policy statement and to submit it to shareholders' approval initially and then every three years, according to the Companies Act 2006, s 439. Companies are prohibited from making remuneration payments to directors, unless they are consistent with the approved remuneration policy, or *ad hoc* approved by the shareholders. Any obligation to make a payment in contradiction with this provision is void, and any monies paid are held by the recipient on constructive trust for the company (ss 226A–226E). In addition, since 2002 the Remuneration Report of quoted companies is put to a non-binding shareholder vote at each Annual General Meeting (AGM) (s 439). Failure of approval of the Remuneration Report now results in the company having to submit its remuneration policy for shareholder approval at the following AGM (s 439A).[60]

However, it is not clear whether variable remuneration achieves its intended goals or whether it is used as a device for managers to extract economic rents from shareholders. The influential work of Bebchuk *et al* asserts that managerial power shapes executive remuneration.[61] They argue that all the market forces that are

58 Also, senior managers may demand higher remuneration to compensate themselves for an increased risk of dismissal due to independent boards. On this, see Florian S Peters and Alexander F Wagner, 'The Executive Turnover Risk Premium' (2014) 69 *Journal of Finance* 1529; and Edward C Fee and Charles J Hadlock, 'Management Turnover Across the Corporate Hierarchy' (2004) 37 *Journal of Accounting and Economics* 3.

59 The UK Corporate Governance Code recommends that listed companies establish a board committee responsible for the remuneration of executive directors, consisting only of independent directors. Most UK companies abide by these recommendations. See CG Code, Provisions D.2.1 and D.2.2.

60 The recent reform was implemented by the Enterprise and Regulatory Reform Act 2013 ss 79–82. See also Department of Business, Innovations and Skills, 'Executive Pay: Shareholder Voting Rights Consultation' (BIS, 14 March 2012) www.bis.gov.uk/assets/biscore/business-law/docs/e/12-639-executive-pay-shareholder-voting-rights-consultation.pdf accessed 1 May 2017.

61 See Lucian Bebchuk, Jesse Fried and David Walker, 'Managerial Power and Rent Extraction in the Design of Executive Compensation' (2002) 69 *University of Chicago Law Review* 751, 789–794.

supposed to restrain managerial rent-seeking, according to the optimal contracting theory, are not strong enough to achieve this outcome. In parallel, formally independent remuneration committees are frequently loyal to CEOs and depend on them for relevant information and US shareholders have very limited direct powers to intervene in such issues. Hence, Bebchuk *et al* argue that managers have significant influence in deciding their own remuneration. If this is the case, then the design of variable remuneration may not actually reward managers for optimal performance, and may create perverse incentives for managers to take excessive risks that the shareholders would not approve. Indeed, various forms of performance-based remuneration have been criticised as depending on chance and rewarding executives for merely increasing the volatility of their company's share price rather than its profitability. Executive pay can therefore be a source of agency costs, rather than a tool to minimise them,[62] and can harm intrinsic motivation.[63]

Overall, the effect of the market for corporate control and variable remuneration reverses the problem of misalignment between the risk appetite of managers and shareholders. It is arguable that the current governance structure makes senior managers take even more risks than informed diversified shareholders would approve of, especially in the case of financial institutions whose assets are particularly opaque, as discussed in the previous chapter.[64]

IV. The development of directors' core duty of loyalty and the emergence of the profit maximisation norm

The Companies Act 2006 put directors' duties on a statutory footing for the first time,[65] with a view to increasing the accessibility and clarity of this area of the law, especially for the benefit of the directors of small and medium-size companies who lack expert legal advice. The codification was first proposed by the Law Commission in the late 1990s,[66] and was further supported by the Company Law Review Steering Group.[67] Nevertheless, the corresponding common law rules and

62 Jensen, Murphy and Wruck have criticised prevailing executive remuneration practices during the 1990s, and admitted in 2004 that executive pay was excessive and still not truly aligned with corporate performance. See Michael Jensen, Kevin Murphy and Eric Wruck, 'Remuneration: Where We've Been, How We Got to Here, What are the Problems, and How to Fix Them' (Harvard Business School NOM Research Paper No. 04–28, 12 July 2004), 98 http://ssrn.com/abstract=561305 accessed 1 May 2017.

63 On this, see Edward L Deci, 'Effects of Externally Mediated Rewards on Intrinsic Motivation' (1971) 18 *Journal of Personality and Social Psychology* 105.

64 This problem has given rise to a much greater emphasis on risk management at the board level in recent years. On this, see Marc T Moore, 'The Evolving Contours of the Board's Risk Management Function in UK Corporate Governance' (2010) 10 *Journal of Corporate Law Studies* 279.

65 See Part 10, ss 170–259 of the Act.

66 See Law Commission, *Company Directors: Regulating Conflicts of Interests and Formulating a Statement of Duties* (Law Com No 261, 1999), paras 4.1–4.24.

67 See Company Law Review Steering Group, 'Modern Company Law for a Competitive Economy: Final Report' (2001), para 1.56 http://webarchive.nationalarchives.gov.

equitable principles remain relevant as they continue to be used to guide the interpretation of the relevant statutory provisions.[68]

The duty of loyalty, similarly to all general directors' duties, is owed to the legal person of the company and not to the shareholders[69] and, therefore, it can be enforced only by the company itself,[70] with the exception of the limited possibility of shareholders bringing a derivative claim.[71] The duty is codified in section 172, which, although recognising that a well-managed company needs to take into account a series of broader considerations,[72] reasserts shareholder wealth maximisation as the corporate objective of UK companies. Indeed, company directors are required to act in the way they consider, in good faith, to be most likely 'to promote the success of the company for the benefit of its members as a whole', and in doing so they are required to have regard to six specified factors, namely: (a) the likely consequences of their decision in the long term; (b) the interests of the company's employees; (c) the need to foster business relationships; (d) the impact on the community and the environment; (e) the company's reputation; and (f) fairness between the shareholders.[73] This formulation reflects the so-called enlightened shareholder value (ESV) approach, which was adopted in the UK as a middle ground between pure shareholder wealth maximisation, and a pluralist approach to the corporate objective. ESV was intended to encourage directors to take a long-term view of the company's interests and to highlight the importance of balancing the interests of a range of stakeholders in order to ensure the success of companies for the benefit of the shareholders.

Nevertheless, the potential impact of section 172 and ESV is rather limited and most commentators agree that it falls short of challenging the norm of adopting short-term shareholder value maximisation as the corporate objective of UK companies.[74] First, the current formulation of the duty of loyalty results in giving

uk/20070603164510/http:/www.dti.gov.uk/cld/final_report/prelims.pdf accessed 1 May 2017.

68 See Companies Act 2006, s 170 (4).

69 Ibid., section 170(1). See also *Percival v Wright* [1902] 2 Ch 421; and *Greenhalgh v Arderne Cinemas Ltd* [1951] Ch 2.

70 See *Foss v Harbottle* (1843) 2 Hare 461.

71 Companies Act 2006, Part 11 introduced the statutory derivative claim. The restrictive judicial approach is evident in cases such as: *Mission Capital plc v Sinclair* [2008] EWHC 1339 (Ch); *Iesini v Westrip Holdings Ltd* [2009] EWHC 2526 (Ch); and *Franbar Holdings Ltd v Patel* [2008] EWHC 1534 (Ch).

72 See Company Law Review Steering Group, 'Modern Company Law for a Competitive Economy: Developing the Framework' (2000), paras 2.19–2.22 http://webarchive.nationalarchives.gov.uk/20121029131934/http://www.berr.gov.uk/files/file23245.pdf accessed 1 May 2017.

73 Companies Act 2006, s 172 (1).

74 It is debatable whether the codification merely reflects the pre-existing law or changes it. An in-depth analysis of the common law position with regard to directors' duty of loyalty can be found in John Parkinson, *Corporate Power and Responsibility: Issues in the Theory of Company Law* (OUP, 1993), 76–96. The Scottish Court of Session opined that the new wording of section 172 reflects pre-existing law. See *Re West Coast Capital (Lios) Ltd* [2008] CSOH 72 per Lord Glennie. However, Moore

the shareholders the privilege to define the meaning of 'the success of the company' which directors have to promote.[75] Although the law does not encourage short-term profit maximisation as the overriding consideration, there is nothing to prevent the shareholders from dictating a short-term approach to be followed by the board.[76] Second, the duty to have regard to a list of stakeholder interests does not effectively challenge the norm of profit maximisation, as those interests are only to be considered to the extent that doing so is consistent with the benefit of the members as a whole.[77] Therefore, stakeholder interests are not elevated to independent ends that can be balanced against the interests of the shareholders, but rather they are hierarchically subordinated to the overriding duty to promote the success of the company for the benefit of the shareholders.

The limited potential of the duty of loyalty to operate as a tool to foster a long-term view of companies' interests is further illustrated by the subjective nature of the duty and its deference to the good faith business judgment of directors. Indeed, the subjective nature of the duty is clearly expressed in section 172 and adopts the traditional common law position dating back to *Re Smith and Fawcett*.[78] It follows that to establish a breach of the duty of loyalty a claimant

argues that the codification of the duty led to the juridification of the relevant law by moving from reliance on directorial discretion towards a paternalistic approach, which determines in detail the process of board decision-making. See Marc T Moore, *Corporate Governance in the Shadow of the State* (Hart Publishing, 2013), 190–195.

75 According to Attorney-General Lord Goldsmith's speech in the Grand Committee of the House of Lords, '[t]he starting point is that it is essentially for the members of the company to define the objective they wish to achieve'. See HL Deb 6 February 2006, vol 678, col 255. Indeed, in *Greenhalgh v Arderne Cinemas Ltd* [1951] Ch 286 (CA), Evershed MR confirmed that: 'the phrase "the company as a whole" does not [...] mean the company as a commercial entity as distinct from the incorporators. However, in exceptional circumstances, as when a competitor attempts to acquire a company with the sole purpose of reducing it to "impotence and beggary", the interest of the company has been perceived as distinct from the collective interest of the shareholders.' See *Cayne v Global Natural Resources Plc* [1984] All ER 225. The same ratio was followed at first instance by Hart J in *Criterion Properties plc v Stratford UK Properties plc* [2002] EWHC 496.

76 In practice the fact that directors are elected by the shareholders and the ability of shareholders to remove directors by ordinary majority at any time (Companies Act 2006, s 168) makes it highly likely that directors will tend to comply with shareholder expectation with regard to corporate strategy.

77 See Andrew Keay, *The Enlightened Shareholder Value Principle and Corporate Governance* (Routledge, 2013), 128–129. Alcock suggests that the 2006 codification actually reinforced shareholder supremacy by explicitly subordinating stakeholder interests, while the pre-existing common law allowed for broader directorial discretion to follow corporate social responsibility policies. See Alistair Alcock, 'An Accidental Change to Director's Duties?' (2009) 30 *The Company Lawyer* 362.

78 See *Carlen v Drury* (1812) 1 Ves & B 154; *Regentcrest plc v Cohen* [2001] 2 BCLC 80; *Extrasure Travel Insurances Ltd v Scattergood* [2003] 1 BCLC 598. The dictum of Lord Greene MR in *Re Smith and Fawcett* sums up the point neatly: '[Directors] must exercise their discretion bona fide in what they consider – not what a court may consider – is in the interests of the company, and not for any collateral purpose.' See *Re Smith and Fawcett Ltd* [1942] Ch 304, 306.

must be able to show that directors did not honestly believe that their decisions would promote the success of the company.[79] Directors who act in good faith are immune from liability under the duty of loyalty, even if their decisions are unreasonable. In other words, the courts do not review the substantial merits of directors' business decisions and it is immaterial if a particular decision fails to benefit the company or even benefits the directors personally insofar as it is taken in good faith. That being said, directors cannot simply avoid liability by stating in court that they acted in good faith. The court will not give credence to their assertion in the absence of any rational link between the challenged decision and a potential benefit to the company.[80] Therefore, a decision that no rational director could have believed to be promoting the success of the company will lead to a finding of a breach of the duty of loyalty.

The subjective nature of the duty aside, the degree by which the duty of loyalty constrains directorial discretion is also limited due to the difficulties in enforcing a breach of the duty. From the perspective of a public company, unless the company has gone into liquidation,[81] the main enforcement option is for shareholders to bring a derivative claim.[82] Given the approach UK courts take, derivative claims are rarely successful generally, and even less successful in the case of public companies, as the statutory criteria in section 263 of the Companies Act are much

79 Still, it is worth noting that there is one situation where courts use an objective test to determine compliance with the duty of loyalty. Indeed, in *Charterbridge v Lloyds* it was held that when directors take a decision without actual consideration of the company's interests, the objective test of an intelligent and honest man is to be applied: 'The proper test I think, in the absence of actual separate consideration, must be whether an intelligent and honest man in the position of a director of the company concerned, could, in the whole of the existing circumstances, have reasonably believed that the transaction was for the benefit of the company.' See *Charterbridge Corp Ltd v Lloyds Bank Ltd* [1970] Ch 62, 74. See also *Extrasure Travel Insurance Ltd v Scattergood* [2003] 1 BCLC 598; and *Simtel Communications Ltd v Rebak* [2006] EWHC 572 (QB).

80 This is well established in the case law. For instance, Harman J emphasised that directors' actions cannot be justified by merely asserting that they acted in good faith. See *Re a Company (No 00370 of 1987) ex parte Glossop* [1988] BCLC 570. A similar approach was taken more recently by Arden LJ in *Item Software (UK) Ltd v Fassihi* [2004] EWCA Civ 1244. In particular, the unreasonableness of the alleged belief of the directors that their act promoted the success of the company may provide evidence that such belief was not honestly held. See *Extrasure Travel Insurance Ltd v Scattergood* [2003] 1 BCLC 598 [90]. Moreover, directors whose acts had a major detrimental effect on companies will find it more difficult to convince the court of their good faith, as suggested by Parker J in *Regentcrest plc v Cohen* [2001] 2 BCLC 80, 105.

81 In that case, the liquidator can bring a misfeasance action against directors on the grounds of breach of their duty of loyalty, based on section 212 of the Insolvency Act 1986.

82 An in-depth discussion of the legal nature of the derivative claim can be found in Brenda Hannigan, 'Drawing Boundaries Between Derivative Claims and Unfairly Prejudicial Petitions' (2009) *Journal of Business Law* 606.

more difficult to be satisfied in the case of companies where share ownership is effectively separated from managerial control.[83]

Given the subjective nature and enforcement difficulties associated with the duty, it becomes clear that corporate directors are not in practice compelled to follow any particular business strategy under the circumstances at hand. It is at their discretion to do any of the following: seek to maximise short-term shareholder value; pursue long-term shareholder value; balance the interests of various stakeholders equally;[84] or indeed safeguard the financial sustainability of the company, according to the corporate objective that will be proposed in this volume as the most appropriate for financial institutions. It follows that the current state of the law with regard to the duty of loyalty means that financial institution directors will not be held liable if they take excessive risks that initially maximise short-term shareholder value, but which ultimately lead to the failure of the institution in question.[85] The same analysis applies to banks that were partly nationalised after the 2007–2009 crisis, such as RBS, which remains 71.2% government owned, and, until recently, Lloyds,[86] as the UK government has resolved to manage its holdings (through UK Financial Investments Ltd) in a purely commercial way.[87]

The same conclusion is reached if we also take into account the legal position of corporate creditors within the framework of the duty of loyalty. The codification of 2006 did not bring any change to the position of creditors so that the relevant

83 A thorough examination of early cases decided after the coming into force of the statutory derivative claim under Part 11 of the Companies Act 2006 can be found in Arad Reisberg, 'Shadows of the Past and Back to the Future: Part 11 of the UK Companies Act 2006 (In)action' (2009) 2 *European Company and Financial Law Review* 219.

84 The subjective nature of the duty, the list of stakeholder interests to be taken into account, and the difficulties in bringing a derivative claim leave substantial discretion to directors insofar as they are honest. Courts have traditionally accepted that directors need not always focus on the narrow and immediate interests of shareholders. For instance, Berger J in *Teck Corporation v Millar* (1972) 33 DLR (3d) 288, 314, clarified that directors are entitled to consider the interests of the company's employees and the consequences of its actions on the community without breaching their duty of loyalty.

85 This accounts for the absence of any litigation alleging a breach of the duty of loyalty initiated by the Treasury after acquiring large interests in RBS and Lloyds in 2009.

86 The government sold off its last remaining shares in Lloyds in spring 2017. See Emma Dunkley, 'Lloyds Back in Private Ownership After Government Sells Out' *Financial Times* (London, 17 May 2017).

87 This was challenged unsuccessfully by People & Planet, an environmental protection non-governmental organisation (NGO). In *R (on the application of People & Planet) v HM Treasury* [2009] EWHC 3020 (Admin), [34], Sales J observed that if the government imposed its policy on climate change and human rights on the board of RBS it would be contrary to the duty of the directors to promote the success of RBS for the benefit of its shareholders, to the detriment of minority shareholders. See also Stephen Copp, 'S. 172 of the Companies Act 2006 Fails People and Planet' [2010] *The Company Lawyer* 406.

case law is still in force and remains unaltered.[88] The core principle is that although in solvent companies the interests of its shareholders qualify to be considered as the interests of the company, as soon as a company becomes insolvent it is the interests of the creditors which qualify to be regarded as the interests of the company.[89] The shift of focus of the duty of loyalty protects creditors from shareholder and managerial opportunism, when equity capital has already been depleted.[90] With regard to the exact meaning of the term 'creditors' in this context, it refers to the general creditors of a company as a whole rather than any particular creditor or group of creditors such as secured or preferential creditors.[91] In addition, recent authorities suggest that creditors' interests may have to be considered as a company approaches insolvency or when its solvency is dubious.[92] However, of course, this is essentially a duty of good faith which captures behaviours such as removing assets from an insolvent or near-insolvent company and therefore does not apply to excessively risky decisions taken in good faith.

88 See Companies Act 2006 section 172 (3).

89 Street CJ of the New South Wales Court of Appeal stated that: 'In a solvent company the proprietary interests of the shareholders entitle them as a general body to be regarded as the company when questions of the duty of directors arise. If, as a general body, they authorise or ratify a particular action of the directors, there can be no challenge to the validity of what the directors have done. But where a company is insolvent the interests of the creditors intrude. They become prospectively entitled, through the mechanism of liquidation, to displace the power of the shareholders and directors to deal with the company's assets. It is in a practical sense their assets and not the shareholders' assets that, through the medium of the company, are under the management of the directors pending either liquidation, return to solvency, or the imposition of some alternative administration.' See *Kinsela v Russell Kinsela Pty Ltd* (1986) 4 ACLC 215, 401. The dictum was adopted by the Court of Appeal in *West Mercia Safetywear Ltd v Dodd* [1988] 4 BCC 30, 33. See also Dan Prentice, 'Creditors' Interests and Director's Duties' [1990] *Oxford Journal of Legal Studies* 10, 265.

90 For an in-depth discussion of directors' duties to creditors under s 172 (3) and of the interplay between s 172 (3) and s 172 (1) of the Act, see Keay (above n 77), 218–230; Andrew Keay, 'Directors' Duties to Creditors: Contractarian Concerns Relating to Efficiency and Over-Protection of Creditors' (2003) 66 *Modern Law Review* 665; Andrew Keay, 'A Theoretical Analysis of the Director's Duty to Consider Creditor Interests: The Progressive School's Approach' (2004) 4 *Journal of Corporate Law Studies* 307.

91 See *Re Pantone 485 Ltd* [2002] 1 BCLC 266, esp 286–287 per Reid QC: 'In my view, where the company is insolvent, the human equivalent of the company for the purposes of the directors' fiduciary duties is the company's creditors as a whole, i.e. its general creditors. It follows that if the directors act consistently with the interests of the general creditors but inconsistently with the interests of a creditor or a section of creditors with special rights in a winding-up, they do not act in breach of duty to the company.'

92 In *Whalley v Doney* [2003] All ER (D) 509, Park J held that a director may breach his duty of loyalty if motivated only by the interests of shareholders and employees, provided that the company is in financial difficulties and creditors are at risk. See also *Brady v Brady* [1989] 3 BCC 535, 552.

V. Insulating directors from liability in case of failure: the lack of enforcement of the duty of care after the 2007–2009 financial crisis

Turning to negative incentives, this section seeks to demonstrate that the current legal position, with regard to directors' duty of care, facilitates excessive risk-taking by financial institution directors. This is primarily due to the judicial formulation of the standard of care for company directors which sets a relatively low threshold. It will be shown that the general standard of care for directors reflects the dominant conceptualisation of companies as private associations, and the policy to encourage entrepreneurship and risk-taking.

While the duty of loyalty refers to directors' state of mind, the duty of care determines the level of care and skill that they are expected to demonstrate in discharging their functions. The duty of care derives from the common law, whereas the other general duties of directors are fiduciary and thus equitable in nature. At present, the test to assess whether a director has breached the duty of care is a mixed one, comprising both a subjective and an objective component. Section 174 of the Companies Act 2006 codified the standard of care for corporate directors as being 'the care, skill and diligence that would be exercised by a reasonably diligent person with – (i) the general knowledge, skill and experience that may reasonably be expected of a person carrying out the functions carried out by the director; and (ii) the knowledge, skill and experience that the director has'. The statutory formulation of the duty of care reflects the evolution of the common law duty since the 1980s and is essentially identical to the wording of section 214 (4) of the Insolvency Act 1986 on wrongful trading.

To understand the duty of care in general and the problems arising in the context of banks in particular, it is expedient to provide a brief overview of its historical evolution. Traditionally, the standard of care for directors was very low.[93] The landmark case of *Re City Equitable Fire*,[94] following previous authorities,[95] confirmed that directors were not expected to possess any particular expertise or knowledge about the type of business the company engages in, and were only required to exercise their duty of care when attending board meetings. The standard of care was that of an ordinary man acting on his own behalf, but imbued with the

93 The first significant cases on the duty of care were: *Overend & Gurney Co v Gibb* (1872) LR 5 HL 480; and *Re Cardiff Savings Bank, Marquis of Bute's Case* [1892] 2 Ch 100. In the latter case the court refused an application of the liquidator of Cardiff Savings Bank to order the Marquis of Bute, the president of the bank, to contribute to its assets by way of compensation for his neglect or omission. The Marquis had been *de facto* president of the bank for four decades (since he was an infant) and had only attended a board meeting once. The court followed the decision in *Re Denham & Co* (1883) 25 Ch. D. 752, where a director who had not attended board meetings for four years was not found liable for damages caused by fraudulent behaviour of the other directors during that period.

94 *Re City Equitable Fire* [1925] Ch 407.

95 See *Re Brazilian Rubber Plantations and Estates* [1911] 1 Ch 425; *Lagunas Nitrate Company v Lagunas Syndicate* [1899] 2 Ch 39; *Re National Bank of Wales Ltd* [1899] 2 Ch 629; and *Dovey v Cory* [1901] AC 477.

actual knowledge and experience of the particular director whose behaviour is judged. In addition, the court confirmed that directors were entitled to delegate certain tasks to corporate officers and to rely on the honesty of the latter absent any grounds to suspect the contrary.[96]

Overall, the test for the duty of care was one of *crassa negligentia* (gross negligence),[97] and directors were not expected to take an active part in the running of their companies. It is worth noting that in the early 20th century there was no requirement for a director to be at least 16 years old, as is the current position.[98] In addition, English courts have traditionally been fully aware of the need to encourage risk-taking by businessmen and therefore avoided imposing an onerous duty of care that may force directors to behave in a risk-averse manner.[99] At any rate, the incompetence of a director was seen as a purely internal and private issue concerning the shareholders who selected the members of the board, and therefore negligence was clearly ratifiable by the majority of the shareholders in a General Meeting.[100]

96 'There are, in addition, one or two other general propositions that seem to be warranted by the reported cases: (1.) A director need not exhibit in the performance of his duties a greater degree of skill than may reasonably be expected from a person of his knowledge and experience. A director of a life insurance company, for instance, does not guarantee that he has the skill of an actuary or of a physician. [...] (2.) A director is not bound to give continuous attention to the affairs of his company. His duties are of an intermittent nature to be performed at periodical board meetings, and at meetings of any committee of the board upon which he happens to be placed. He is not, however, bound to attend all such meetings, though he ought to attend whenever, in the circumstances, he is reasonably able to do so. (3.) In respect of all duties that, having regard to the exigencies of business, and the articles of association, may properly be left to some other official, a director is, in the absence of grounds for suspicion, justified in trusting that official to perform such duties honestly.' *Re City Equitable Fire* (above n 94) 429, per Romer J.

97 On the contractarian rationalisation of the *crassa negligentia* standard, see Moore (above n 74), 150–157.

98 Companies Act 2006, s 157.

99 See *Overend & Gurney Co v Gibb* (above n 93) 494–495 (per Lord Hatherley LC): 'It would be extremely wrong to import into the consideration of the case of a person acting as a mercantile agent in the purchase of a business concern, those principles of extreme caution which might dictate the course of one who is not at all inclined to invest his property in any ventures of such a hazardous character. [...] [I]t would be a very fatal error in the verdict of any Court of justice to attempt to measure [...] the amount of prudence that ought to be exercised by the amount of prudence which the judge himself might think, under similar circumstances, he should have exercised.' This view was followed by Neville J in *Re Brazilian Rubber Plantations and Estates* (above n 95) 437–438. More recently, in the context of wrongful trading, Williamson QC emphasised that: 'it is easy to be wise with hindsight [and] I am also very conscious that the standard to be applied is that of the reasonably prudent businessman, a breed which is likely to be less temperamentally cautious than lawyers and accountants.' See *Re Brian D Pierson (Contractors) Ltd* [1999] BCC 26, 52.

100 See e.g. *Pavlides v Jensen* [1956] Ch 565; and *Macdougall v Gardiner* (1875) LR 1 Ch D 13 (CA). It followed that a derivative claim was not admissible for breach of the duty of

However, since the late 1980s the standard of care has developed into a more onerous one, which imposes some core and irreducible obligations on directors. The starting point was the wrongful trading provision introduced by section 214 of the Insolvency Act 1986, which holds the directors of insolvent companies liable unless they can show that they took every reasonable step to protect creditors' interests once they knew (or ought to have known) that there was no reasonable prospect for the company to avoid insolvent liquidation. The wrongful trading provision imposes a mixed objective-subjective test identical to the current wording of the duty of care. The importance of this test is that if a director has less skill than can reasonably be expected from a person carrying out his functions, he will still be held liable in negligence. The first cases that confirmed that the test included in the wrongful trading provision accurately describes the general standard of care for directors at common law were *Norman v Theodore Goddard*[101] and *Re D'Jan of London Ltd*,[102] both decided by Hoffmann LJ (as he then was).

In parallel, it has been made clear since the 1990s that there is a core irreducible nucleus of the duty of care, which cannot be avoided by delegating responsibilities to managers, or by refraining from taking any meaningful role in the company at all.[103] Independent directors are thus required to exhibit independence of judgement and to supervise executive management. While they are entitled to rely on

care. This was changed by the Companies Act 2006, s 260(3), but valid ratification, under s 239, is still a mandatory bar to a derivative claim, under s 263(2)(c) (ii) of the Act.

101 *Norman v Theodore Goddard* [1992] BCLC 1028.

102 *Re D'Jan of London Ltd* [1993] BCC 646. The following excerpt from the speech of Hoffmann LJ illustrates the change of judicial approach: 'Mr Russen [the counsel for the defendant] said that the standard of care which directors owe to their companies is not very exacting and signing forms without reading them is something that a busy director may reasonably do. I accept that in real life this often happens. But that does not mean that it is not negligent. People often take risks in circumstance in which it was not necessary or reasonable to do so. If the risk materialises, they may have to pay a penalty.'

103 The first case that acknowledges that doing nothing is no defence to an alleged breach of a director's duty of care was *Dorchester Finance v Stebbing* [1989] BCLC 497 decided in 1977. The leading case on the issue is *Equitable Life Assurance Society v Bowley* [2004] 1 BCLC 180. The facts of the case concerned the liability of the non-executive directors of an insurance company for breach of their duty of care because they approved a differential terminal bonus policy, which turned out to be illegal, relying on professional actuarial advice. Langley J held in paras 40–41 that: 'the extent to which a non-executive director may reasonably rely on the executive directors and other professionals to perform their duties is one in which the law can fairly be said to be developing and is plainly "fact sensitive". It is plainly arguable, I think, that a company may reasonably at least look to non-executive directors for independence of judgment and supervision of the executive management.' It was also clarified that *Re City Equitable Fire Insurance* does not represent the modern state of the law insofar as it allows unquestioning reliance by directors upon others. Similarly, it has been held that it is a breach of duty for directors to allow themselves to be dominated by one of their number, typically the CEO. See also *Re Brian D Pierson Ltd* (above n 99), 55, which confirms that 'one cannot be a sleeping director'.

executive directors for the provision of information and the implementation of the board's decisions, they must not allow themselves to be dominated by them.[104]

A landmark case in this context, which is of particular interest for bank corporate governance, is *Re Barings Plc (No 5)*.[105] This was part of the litigation caused by the failure of Barings, an investment bank with a long history in the City (of London), which was due to fraudulent dealings in securities by Mr Leeson, one of its employees in Singapore. The fraud was not detected by the board due to the absence of an adequate monitoring and internal control system. On the facts, three former directors of the bank were disqualified on grounds of unfitness. Parker J held that directors are under a continuous duty to acquire and maintain a sufficient knowledge of the company's business to enable them to discharge their functions properly. In addition, the court stressed that although delegation of responsibilities to management is permissible, directors cannot absolve themselves from the duty to supervise the discharge of the delegated functions. Cognisant of the various roles directors play on modern boards, the court clarified that the level of reward a director is entitled to and the particular position he or she has are relevant factors to determine the director's responsibilities.[106] It follows, for instance, that an executive director of a public company is expected to show much more attention to the company's affairs than a non-executive director of a small private company.

Still, despite the considerable reinforcement of the standard of care for company directors, the current state of the law is such that well-informed but risky business decisions are very unlikely to lead to finding a breach of the duty of care.[107]

104 See e.g. *Re Westmid Packing Services Ltd, Secretary of State for Trade and Industry v Griffiths* [1998] 2 BCLC 646, per Lord Woolf MR; and *Lexi Holdings plc (in admin) v Luqman* [2009] EWCA Civ 117 (CA). Furthermore, a recent Australian case indicates that in approving the financial statements of the company, directors are supposed to form a personal view with regard to their accuracy and to act as the final filter. Reliance on executive directors, accountants and audit committees does not absolve directors – be they executive or non-executive – from the duty to form their own opinion. See *Australian Securities and Investments Commission v Healey* [2011] FCA 717, discussed in John Lowry, 'The Irreducible Core of the Duty of Care, Skill and Diligence of Company Directors' (2012) 75 *Modern Law Review* 249. See also *Daniels v Anderson* (1995) 16 ACSR 607 (NSW CA).

105 *Re Barings plc (No 5), Secretary of State for Trade and Industry v Baker (No 5)* [1999] 1 BCLC 433.

106 Ibid., 435–436.

107 The point is summarised succinctly by Allen J, Chancellor of the Delaware Court of Chancery in *Gagliardi v Trifoods International Inc* 683 A 2d 1049 (Del 1996), 1052: 'Corporate directors of public companies typically have a very small proportionate ownership interest in their corporations and little or no incentive compensation. Thus, they enjoy (as residual owners) only a very small proportion of any "upside" gains earned by the corporation on risky investment projects. If, however, corporate directors were to be found liable for a corporate loss from a risky project on the ground that the investment was too risky (foolishly risky! stupidly risky! egregiously risky! – you supply the adverb), their liability would be joint and several for the whole loss (with I suppose a right of contribution). Given the scale of operation of modern public corporations, this stupefying disjunction between risk and reward for corporate

Insofar as directors inform themselves of the affairs of the company, follow reasonable decision-making procedures, and seek independent advice where necessary, their business decisions are unlikely to be successfully challenged in court. This view is confirmed by the recent experience of the failures of several major UK banks in 2008 and 2009. Although five British banks failed, none of their directors was sued for breach of his duty of care. Given the full or partial nationalisation of failed banks, it was perfectly feasible for the government to insist that the new boards pursue litigation on the ground of negligence against some of the previous directors. However, the boards of failed banks had followed reasonable processes to reach their decisions and had relied on expert advice and regulatory approval of their business models.[108] The limited judicial review of business decisions under the duty of care makes it clear that a potential action against the former directors of failed banks would – in all likelihood – have failed.

Moreover, the fact that troubled banks tend to be nationalised or – in the future – to enter into the special resolution regime (discussed in Chapter 4), rather than go into liquidation or administration, precludes the application of two provisions that complement the duty of care, namely the wrongful trading provision and the disqualification regime. The wrongful trading provision has already been briefly described in the preceding analysis of the duty of care. The disqualification of directors can be ordered by the court on various grounds specified by the Company Directors Disqualification Act 1986 (CDDA).[109] The broadest and most practically significant ground for disqualification is that a person who was a director of a company which has become insolvent is, in view of his or her conduct, unfit to be concerned with the management of limited liability companies.[110] Serious breaches of the duty of care owed by directors are a common example of conduct that leads to a finding of unfitness.[111]

directors threatens undesirable effects. […] Obviously, it is in the shareholders' economic interest to offer sufficient protection to directors from liability for negligence, etc., to allow directors to conclude that, as a practical matter, there is no risk that, if they act in good faith and meet minimal proceduralist standards of attention, they can face liability as a result of a business loss.'

108 For instance, Sir Ian Gibson, the senior independent director of Northern Rock, when giving evidence in Parliament, stressed that Northern Rock's business model was transparent to the shareholders and that the bank had sought advice from the FSA and legal advisers so that the board was 'fully satisfied that we did follow the best advice and follow[ed] it to the letter'. Treasury Committee, *The Run on the Rock* (HC 2007–2008 56–I), para 34.

109 A critical account of the Act can be found in Richard Williams, 'Disqualifying Directors: A Remedy Worse than the Disease?' (2007) 7 *Journal of Corporate Law Studies* 213. See also Maren Heidemann, 'Current Issues of Directors' Liability – The Scottish View' (2016) 27 *European Business Law Review* 243.

110 Company Directors Disqualification Act 1986, s 6 (1) and Schedule 1. An example of the use of disqualification in the banking context is provided by *Re Barings plc (No 5)* (above n 105). See also *Re Lo Line Electric Motors Ltd* [1988] Ch 477; and *Re Polly Peck International plc (No 2)* [1994] 1 BCLC 574.

111 See *Re Barings* (above n 105), 484.

Since 1 October 2015, a series of incremental changes to the directors' disqualification regime have been implemented,[112] partially as a response to the perceived weakness of director accountability exposed during the 2007–2009 financial crisis. Indeed, the relevant factors to be taken into account by courts in determining unfitness have been broadened,[113] and courts are now allowed to take into account overseas conduct.[114] The time limit to bring disqualification proceedings has been extended from two to three years.[115] Finally, there is now the possibility for the court to make a compensation order for company creditors who suffered losses due to the conduct of disqualified directors.[116]

The problem in the case of financial institution failures, however, is that public intervention usually pre-empts going into liquidation or administration.[117] As a result, the prerequisites for the application of the wrongful trading[118] and disqualification for unfitness[119] provisions are not satisfied.[120] The only remaining possibility to disqualify bank directors, under the current law, is subsequent to a Companies Act investigation.[121] Such investigations by the secretary of state are aimed at safeguarding the public interest.[122] However, they are a costly and cumbersome processes, especially in complex cases such as those of failed banks, and this probably explains the reasons for not using this process in the aftermath of the recent financial crisis. At any rate, even if the aforementioned process had been used, it does not seem particularly likely that a court would have found the

112 By virtue of the Small Business, Enterprise and Employment Act 2015, Part 9, which was brought into force by The Small Business, Enterprise and Employment Act 2015 (Commencement No. 2 and Transitional Provisions) Regulations 2015 (SI 2015/ 1689).

113 Company Directors Disqualification Act 1986, s 12C and Schedule 1, inserted by the Small Business, Enterprise and Employment Act 2015, s 106.

114 Company Directors Disqualification Act 1986, s 5A, inserted by the Small Business, Enterprise and Employment Act 2015, s 104.

115 Company Directors Disqualification Act 1986, s 7(2), as amended by the Small Business, Enterprise and Employment Act 2015, s 108.

116 Company Directors Disqualification Act 1986, s 15A, inserted by the Small Business, Enterprise and Employment Act 2015, s 110.

117 This was the case with RBS, HBOS, Lloyds and Northern Rock.

118 Insolvency Act 1986, s 214 (2) (a) requires the company to have gone into insolvent liquidation.

119 CDDA 1986, s 6 (2) defines insolvency as insolvent liquidation, administration, or administrative receivership.

120 For an in-depth analysis of the limits of the disqualification and wrongful trading provisions, especially in the case of banks, see Demetra Arsalidou, 'The Banking Crisis: Rethinking and Refining the Accountability of Bank Directors' (2010) *Journal of Business Law* 284. See also Edward Walker-Arnott, 'Company Law, Corporate Governance and the Banking Crisis' (2010) 7 *International Corporate Rescue* 3, 5–7.

121 See Companies Act 1985, s 437.

122 Arguably, there are strong arguments in favour of a Companies Act investigation, compared to a PRA investigation. First, the former can be made public while the latter cannot (due to FSMA 2000 s 348). Second, the Authority cannot be objective in such investigation as it may seek to conceal its own responsibilities for the failure. See Walker-Arnott (above n 120), 9–10.

directors of failed banks 'unfit' to engage with management of limited liability companies, given the legal position with regard to directors' duty of care.[123]

VI. Mitigating the problem of excessive risk-taking: independent boards and their limitations

The previous sections of this chapter manifest how corporate law and corporate governance rules facilitate risk-taking by corporate managers and ensure that their risk appetite is in line with the risk appetite of diversified equity investors. This section examines the principal available mechanism to constrain excessive (from the perspective of shareholders) risk-taking, namely independent boards of directors, which is the main mechanism used by the UK Corporate Governance Code to ensure effective governance. The criteria prescribed by the Code capture most types of relationships that can potentially undermine the independence of a director.[124] Of course, independent boards serve various functions including monitoring executive management and strategy formulation, but risk management has become a significant board function in recent years.[125]

There is rich literature – both theoretical and empirical – on the importance of board structure and, in particular, on the degree of board independence, which is generally assessed based on the percentage of independent non-executive directors sitting on a board.[126] An independent director is defined in the Corporate Governance Code as a person who does not have – and has not had for a sufficient period of time prior to his appointment – any substantial relationship with the company on whose board he serves, as a shareholder, employee, or business partner. The Code's criteria also capture family relations, interlocking directorships and other types of relationships.[127] Nearly all UK listed financial institutions follow the

123 Lowry and Edmunds argue that the Company Directors Disqualification Act had the potential to be used to disqualify at least some of the directors of RBS and HBOS, which is correct as a matter of statutory construction but does not defeat the point that the chances of a court doing so would have been limited. See John Lowry and Rod Edmunds, 'Directors Duties and Liabilities: Disqualifying "Unfit" Directors at Banks? Political Rhetoric and the Directors' Disqualification Regime' in Iris H-Y Chiu (ed), *The Law on Corporate Governance in Banks* (Edward Elgar Publishing, 2015), 93.

124 The independence criteria are set out in CG Code, Provision B.1.1. For a critique of the notion of directorial independence, see Suzanne Le Mire and George Gilligan, 'Independence and Independent Company Directors' (2013) 13 *Journal of Corporate Law Studies* 443.

125 On this see Moore (above n 64).

126 A review of general economic literature on the functioning of boards of directors can be found in Renee Adams, Benjamin Hermalin and Michael Weisbach, 'The Role of Boards of Directors in Corporate Governance: A Conceptual Framework and Survey' (2010) 48 *Journal of Economic Literature* 58; and Benjamin Hermalin and Michael Weisbach, 'Boards of Directors as an Endogenously Determined Institution: A Survey of the Economic Literature' (2003) 9 *Federal Reserve Bank of New York Economic Policy Review* 7. See also Ada Demb and Friedrich Neubaurer, *The Corporate Board* (OUP, 1992).

127 For a list of relationships and circumstances that are deemed to preclude independence, see UK Corporate Governance Code, para B.1.1.

Code's recommendations and have a high percentage of independent directors on their boards.[128] Formal independence is inevitably only a proxy for actual independence of mind, which also depends on the informal dynamics in the boardroom and the personalities of individual directors. Ensuring actual independence of mind is therefore far more difficult than merely safeguarding formal independence.

Using independent directors is generally viewed as a technique used by senior managers to signal to existing shareholders and potential investors that primary agency costs will be kept low. Therefore, within the standard contractarian account of corporate governance, independent boards are conceived as an institution responsible for monitoring executive directors and senior managers to the benefit of the shareholders.[129] Indeed, empirical evidence indicates that board independence is positively correlated with CEO turnover and thus independent boards lead to an increase in CEO accountability.[130]

Nevertheless, if the financial incentives faced by different types of directors are taken into account, it becomes clear why there is reason to assume that a strong independent component on boards will tend to lead to a lower level of risk-taking. Independent directors, in general, do not receive variable remuneration[131] to the

128 The percentage of independent directors in financial sector listed companies, as defined in the Corporate Governance Code, including independent chairmen, is as follows: 3i Group: 77.8%; Admiral Group: 70%; Aviva: 76.9%; Barclays: 84.6%; Direct Line Insurance Group: 70%; Experian: 60%; Hargreaves Lansdown: 66.7%; HSBC Holdings: 76.2%; Legal & General Group: 66.7%; Lloyds Banking Group: 76.9%; London Stock Exchange Group: 63.6%; Old Mutual: 69.2%; Provident Financial: 72.7%; Prudential: 56.3%; Royal Bank of Scotland Group: 76.9%; RSA Insurance Group: 81.8%; Schroders: 54.5%; St James's Place: 44.4%; Standard Chartered: 78.6%; Standard Life: 58.3%. Overall, all companies but one comply with the Code's guidance regarding the percentage of independent directors, the average percentage of independent directors in the sector being 69.1%. However, four institutions (out of 20) do not follow the Code's recommendation that the chairman of the board ought to be independent at the time of appointment, and in three more companies, board chairmen although independent on appointment, do not satisfy the criteria of independence at the time of writing due to having served on the board for more than nine years. The relevant data were taken from the institutions' corporate websites and were accurate as on 1 April 2017.

129 Alternatively, boards can be conceptualised as mediating hierarchies, balancing the interests of shareholders and other constituencies. See Lynn Stout, 'The Shareholder as Ulysses: Some Empirical Evidence on Why Investors in Public Corporations Tolerate Board Governance' (2003–2004) 152 *University Pennsylvania Law Review* 667.

130 See Steven N Kaplan and Bernadette A Minton, 'How Has CEO Turnover Changed?' (2012) 12 *International Review of Finance* 57; Volker Laux, 'Board Independence and CEO Turnover' (2008) 46 *Journal of Accounting Research* 137; and Michael S Weisbach, 'Outside Directors and CEO Turnover' (1988) 20 *Journal of Financial Economics* 431. On the psychological benefits of independent board chairmen, see Randall Morck, 'Behavioral Finance in Corporate Governance – Independent Directors, Non-Executive Chairs, and the Importance of the Devil's Advocate' (2004) 12 *Journal of Management and Governance* 179.

131 As recommended in CG Code, Provision D.1.3.

effect that they do not stand to benefit financially if a financial institution makes risky decisions and generates large profits,[132] while they stand to lose if it fails. Currently, their loss is confined to the reputational damage suffered and the ensuing difficulty in securing future non-executive appointments. In parallel, the presence of independent directors is likely to mitigate the problem of groupthink that tends to affect decision-making by boards and thus to prevent the unintended taking of excessive risks by over-optimistic senior executives.[133]

Still, several US empirical studies covering non-financial companies have failed to find any correlation between board independence and financial performance. Indeed, a number of studies show either a negative correlation between board independence and firm performance or at least the absence of a positive one.[134] Most notably, Bhagat and Black found that firms with only one or two executive directors on their board (a structure that they described as 'super-majority independent boards') performed significantly worse than other firms; and that in other firms there is no strong correlation between board independence and firm performance, measured by profitability and growth.[135] However, given that nearly all firms in their sample had at least 50% of independent directors, this evidence can be interpreted as demonstrating that the percentage of independent directors does

132 On the contrary, executive directors stand to benefit directly from increased profits due to variable remuneration. A discussion of the current regulatory framework for executive remuneration in banking can be found in Chapter 5, section II.

133 This is the so-called optimism bias. Empirical research suggests that people have a tendency to think that their level of skills and abilities is above average. In the bank governance context, bank directors – and especially executives who identify with the bank – may be prone to underestimate the risks the bank they serve faces as compared to other banks. See Neil Weinstein and William Klein, 'Unrealistic Optimism: Present and Future' (1996) 15 *Journal of Social and Clinical Psychology* 1.

134 See Anup Agrawal and Charles Knoeber, 'Firm Performance and Mechanisms to Control Agency Problems Between Managers and Shareholders' (1996) 31 *Journal of Financial and Quantitative Analysis* 377, 390; David Yermack, 'Higher Market Valuation of Companies with a Small Board of Directors' (1996) 40 *Journal of Financial Economics* 185, 195–202; Scott Barnhart and Stuart Rosenstein, 'Board Composition, Managerial Ownership, and Firm Performance: An Empirical Analysis' (1998) 33 *Financial Review* 1, 11–12; Benjamin Hermalin and Michael Weisbach, 'Boards of Directors as an Endogenously Determined Institution: A Survey of the Economic Literature' (2003) *FRBNY Economic Policy Review* 7; see Nikos Vafeas and Elena Theodorou, 'The Relationship between Board Structure and Firm Performance in the UK' (1998) 30 *British Accounting Review* 383, 395–399; Charlie Weir, David Laing and Philip McKnight, 'Internal and External Governance Mechanisms: Their Impact on the Performance of Large UK Public Companies' (2002) 29 *Journal of Business Finance and Accounting* 579, 594–603. A review of empirical studies on the relationship between corporate governance structures and firm performance can be found in Marc Goergen, *Corporate Governance and Complexity Theory* (Edward Elgar Publishing, 2010), 69–76.

135 See Sanjai Bhagat and Bernard Black, 'The Uncertain Relationship Between Board Composition and Firm Performance' (1999) 54 *Business Lawyer* 921; Sanjai Bhagat, 'The Non-Correlation between Board Independence and Long-Term Firm Performance' (2002) *Journal of Corporation Law* 231, 239.

not have a further positive effect once there is a critical mass of independent directors, and starts having a negative effect when only very few executives sit on the board.[136]

Indeed, boards where the CEO is the only executive director suffer from several shortcomings. First, there is only one source of inside information for non-executive directors, which makes it easier for the CEO to manipulate the board. Second, the absence of other executives on the board strengthens the position of the CEO in the executive pyramid. A major benefit of collective governance institutions, such as boards, is that they encourage hierarchically inferior members of an organisation to voice their opinion as equal members of a collective organ. Third, the presence of a larger number of executives may contribute to the avoidance of the biases of independent directors, in the same way that the presence of a majority of independent directors helps expose the biases of the executives.[137] A parallel potential disadvantage of super-majority independent boards is the trade-off between independence and collegiality which can undermine the effective flow of information from the CEO to independent directors.[138]

At any rate, these studies have limited value from the point of view of the present discussion. First, the scope of these studies covers public companies generally, and therefore their findings may not necessarily be valid for banks and other financial institutions. Second, these studies measure the effect of board structure on various metrics of profitability. Given the emphasis of this book on risk management and financial stability, it follows that profitability is not the relevant variable from our perspective.[139] Instead, it is crucial to enquire whether board independence makes banks and other financial institutions less prone to take excessive risks, and thus more resilient. It is therefore expedient to focus on financial institution-specific empirical studies that seek to assess the effect of board independence on risk-taking.

A particularly interesting study of 18 UK banks of various sizes from 2001 to 2006 concludes that there is a robust and statistically significant positive

136 In parallel, these studies do not capture the potential positive effect of independent boards on the market as a whole due to fostering accurate financial disclosure and enhanced market confidence. On this, see Jeffrey Gordon, 'The Rise of Independent Directors in the United States: Of Shareholder Value and Stock Market Prices' (2007) 59 *Stanford Law Review* 1465, 1505–1506.

137 See Donald Langevoort, 'The Human Nature of Corporate Boards: Law, Norms, and the Unintended Consequences of Independence and Accountability' (2001) 89 *Georgetown Law Journal* 797, 802–803.

138 Olson and Adams argue that there is a 'trade-off between proximity and objectivity'. See John Olson and Michael Adams, 'Composing a Balanced and Effective Board to Meet New Governance Mandates' (2004) 59 *Business Lawyer* 421, 429–430.

139 This is a point that has not been appreciated by legal literature on bank corporate governance. This explains why Hopt argues that recent empirical evidence undermined confidence in independent directors in the context of banks. See Klaus Hopt, 'Corporate Governance of Banks and Other Financial Institutions after the Financial Crisis' (2013) 13 *Journal of Corporate Law Studies* 219, 248–249.

correlation between the percentage of independent directors and three types of efficiency: technical, allocative, and cost-efficiency.[140] The same study did not find any statistically robust impact of board size on these types of efficiency. As the above types of efficiency demonstrate a financial institution's underlying performance but are not materially affected by risk-taking, the implication is that independent boards have a positive effect on financial institution resilience, as operationally efficient institutions are likely to be more stable financially in the long run.[141] Furthermore, other studies suggest that board independence is associated with *lower* levels of risk-taking in banks and other financial institutions. A study of a sample of relatively large US commercial and investment banks from 2003 to 2008 concludes that larger board size and independence are associated with lower levels of risk-taking.[142] In addition, an international study of 296 financial firms during the 2007–2008 crisis found that firms with more independent boards had worse returns on equity, but that this was due to the fact that they raised more equity capital as a response to the crisis.[143] This led to a net wealth transfer from shareholders to creditors, mainly bondholders.

This demonstrates that independent boards are associated with adopting more conservative/prudent capital structures which are not necessarily conducive to short-term shareholder value maximisation, but enhance the stability and reduce the insolvency risk of banks and other financial institutions.[144] However, the positive effect of independent boards on financial institution stability ought not to be exaggerated. Available evidence suggests that it is a relatively minor effect which, although welcome, does not in itself resolve the problem of excessive risk-taking. Board independence is a positive quality of boards, but cannot guarantee prudent risk management as indicated by the fact that all the banks that failed during the 2007–2009 crisis had independent boards.[145]

140 See Sailesh Tanna, Fotios Pasiouras and Matthias Nnadi, 'The Effect of Board Size and Composition on the Efficiency of UK Banks' (2011) 18 *International Journal of the Economics of Business* 441. A similar result was found recently by Cristina Stefanescu, 'Does a Strong Governance Mechanism Improve Efficiency in Banking System?' (2014) 20 *International Advances in Economic Research* 117.

141 On this issue, see Chapter 6, section III (a).

142 See Bernadette Minton, Jerome Taillard and Rohan Williamson, 'Do Independence and Financial Expertise of the Board Matter for Risk Taking and Performance?' (2011) Ohio State University, Fisher College of Business WP 2010-03-014 http://papers.ssrn.com/sol3/papers.cfm?abstract_id=1787126 accessed 1 May 2017.

143 David Erkens, Mingyi Hung and Pedro Matos, 'Corporate Governance in the 2007–2008 Financial Crisis: Evidence from Financial Institutions Worldwide' (2012) 18 *Journal of Corporate Finance* 389, esp 402.

144 Indeed, Walker-Arnott argues that solvency must be 'at the forefront of every director's mind'. Edward Walker-Arnott, 'Corporate Governance and Banks – The Role and Composition of the Board Corporate Governance' in Iris H-Y Chiu (ed), *The Law on Corporate Governance in Banks* (Edward Elgar Publishing, 2015), 71.

145 A detailed examination of the board composition of the UK banks that failed in 2007–2009 can be found in Walker-Arnott (above n 120), 19.

VII. Conclusions

Overall, this chapter has sought to illustrate how the private (corporate) law and soft-law framework facilitates risk-taking by corporate managers, both by creating positive incentives to take risks that are economically sensible for shareholders and by ensuring that honest directors following a reasonable decision-making process face no risk of legal liability should their companies fail. This is by no means intended as a criticism of the existing framework. Facilitating efficient risk-taking can support economic growth by ensuring that businesses innovate and take advantage of all available opportunities. However, in the special case of systemically important financial institutions whose potential failure has a significant negative impact on the economy as a whole, these legal doctrines facilitate taking risks that are not acceptable in the public interest, as explained in the previous chapter. The following three chapters document how public law, namely prudential regulation of banks and other financial institutions, has sought to tackle this problem before and after the 2007–2009 financial crisis.

3 The development of the prudential regulatory framework as a response to the problems posed by financial firms operating with limited liability

Having examined the role UK company law plays in facilitating risk-taking by company directors and managers, this chapter turns to the examination of the development of the regulatory framework that seeks to ensure financial stability, that is, micro- and macro-prudential regulation. It will be demonstrated that there is now a widely recognised public interest in maintaining the stability of the financial markets, and that the economic characteristics of banks and other financial institutions make it necessary that they are regulated and supervised to the effect of protecting financial stability. It will also be argued that the existence of a prudential regulation framework – be it formal or informal – is necessary as soon as banks and other major financial firms adopt limited liability in view of the incentives the latter creates. The structure of such regulatory arrangements will be shown to depend largely on political impetus generated by perceived regulatory failures usually relating to significant financial institution failures, and therefore to be susceptible to relatively frequent change. UK regulatory architecture will also be shown to have been influenced by developments in EU law, which poses the question of the likely impact of the UK's withdrawal from the EU on the country's prudential regulation framework. Finally, the discussion will seek to provide an overview of regulatory techniques and strategies, with a particular emphasis on reflexive regulation and meta-regulation, thus serving as necessary background to the examination of post-crisis regulatory reforms affecting risk-taking by financial institutions which will take place in the two following chapters.

To that effect, section I of the chapter examines the concept of financial stability and the relationship between risk-taking by individual financial institutions and systemic risk. Section II traces the historical development of prudential regulation in the UK with special emphasis on changes to regulatory architecture during the last two decades. Section III explores the – still under development – EU financial regulation architecture and discusses the likely impact of Brexit on UK prudential regulation. Section IV identifies the main types of prudential regulation strategies, as well as regulatory techniques and theories of regulation, and argues that the concepts of meta-regulation and enrolment of private actors help explain the emerging relationship between prudential regulation and corporate law. Section V concludes.

I. The rationale for prudential financial regulation: the public interest in financial stability

Broadly defined, financial regulation comprises the legislative, regulatory and soft-law rules and principles that apply to financial institutions and their senior employees.[1] In this sense, the regulatory framework includes both the applicable rules and principles *per se* and the process of supervision by the relevant authorities. It is conventional to distinguish between prudential regulation, on the one hand, and conduct of business regulation, on the other.[2] The former has two interconnected objectives, namely to protect the stability of the financial system as a whole (macro-prudential regulation) and to safeguard the safety and soundness of each financial institution (micro-prudential regulation).[3] Conduct of business regulation deals with customer protection and market integrity. The perspective of this study is that micro-prudential regulation ought to encompass the corporate law framework of financial institutions in order to increase its likelihood of success in achieving its objectives, thus also facilitating the fulfilment of the objectives of macro-prudential regulation. Therefore, the discussion herein will primarily focus on prudential regulation and the supervision on prudential grounds.

It is necessary to begin by reflecting on the economic rationale for prudential regulation.[4] While conduct of business regulation is justified on the basis of the information asymmetry and imbalance of bargaining power between financial institutions and (most of) their clients, prudential regulation has a different rationale. Indeed, due to systemic risk and the impact of financial crises on the real economy the protection of the stability of the financial system becomes a matter of public policy. The immediate response of governments to financial crises tends to be the provision of liquidity support (normally by the central bank)[5] and the setting up of deposit insurance schemes that practically guarantee bank deposits (up to a limit) to prevent creditors' runs on banks.[6] These tools of crisis management

1 For a general discussion of banking regulation and supervision globally, see James Barth, Gerard Caprio Jr and Ross Levine, *Rethinking Bank Regulation: Till Angels Govern* (CUP, 2006).

2 David Llewellyn, 'The Economic Rationale for Financial Regulation' (FSA Occasional Paper Series 1, April 1999), 10 www.fsa.gov.uk/pubs/occpapers/op01.pdf accessed 1 May 2017.

3 See Markus Brunnermeier and others, *The Fundamental Principles of Financial Regulation: Geneva Reports on the World Economy 11* (Center for Economic Policy Research, 2009), ch 3.

4 For a discussion of the economic rationales for financial regulation, see Llewellyn (above n 2). A brief discussion on why banks should be regulated can be found in Kenneth Spong, *Banking Regulation: Its Purposes, Implementation and Effects* (5th edn, Federal Reserve Bank of Kansas City Publications, 2000), 5–13.

5 For an in-depth analysis of the lender of last resort function of the Bank of England, its history and its recent evolution, see Andrew Campbell and Rosa Lastra, 'Revisiting the Lender of Last Resort – The Role of the Bank of England' in Iain MacNeil and Justin O'Brien (eds), *The Future of Financial Regulation* (Hart Publishing, 2010), esp 161–170.

6 On the limits of deposit protection, see above Chapter 1, n 80 and accompanying text. For a critical discussion of the relationship between deposit protection and moral

protect the financial system from immediate collapse, but come at the cost of exacerbating the problem in the long run, as explicit or implicit state support strengthens the incentives of financial institutions' managers and clients to take excessive risks.[7] This problem is known as moral hazard[8] and is due to the expectation of financial institution – especially bank – shareholders and senior managers that government intervention will rescue ailing institutions or at least prevent the collapse of the financial system thus mitigating the negative externalities generated by risk-taking. Of course, as was explained in the previous chapter, even without any expectation of government support, the doctrine of limited liability itself creates a degree of moral hazard in a sector where the failure of one firm is likely to generate considerable negative externalities. It is therefore of little surprise that safeguarding the stability of the UK financial system[9] is currently one of the core regulatory objectives of the UK financial regulation authorities enshrined in primary legislation.

It is worth noting that the legislative emphasis on financial stability is very recent and has clearly been a response to the 2007–2009 financial crisis. Indeed, the Banking Act 2009 added to the list of the statutory objectives of the Bank of England a financial stability objective.[10] Similarly, the Financial Services Act 2010 added financial stability to the objectives of the Financial Services Authority.[11] Furthermore, the Financial Services Act 2012 amended the formulation of the financial stability objective by asserting that the Bank ought to 'protect and enhance the stability of the financial system of the UK' rather than merely to contribute 'to the protection and enhancement' of financial stability, as the

hazard, see Jenny Hamilton, 'Depositor Protection and Co-insurance after Northern Rock: Less a Case of Moral Hazard and More a Case of Consumer Responsibility?' in Johanna Gray and Orkun Akseli (eds), *Financial Regulation in Crisis? The Role of Law and the Failure of Northern Rock* (Edward Elgar Publishing, 2011), 19–24.

7 For instance, Picciotto argues that the existing regulatory and institutional framework (including limited liability, the lender of last resort function, and tax avoidance through off-shore vehicles) resulted in ineffective hyper-regulation, regulatory arbitrage, perverse incentives and market distortions. See Sol Picciotto, *Regulating Global Corporate Capitalism* (CUP, 2011), 288–290.

8 The concept of moral hazard originated from insurance contracts. Arrow's seminal work on the medical care market explored the effects of moral hazard in that context. See Kenneth Arrow, 'Uncertainty and the Welfare Economics of Medical Care' (1963) 53 *The American Economic Review* 941, esp 961–962. See also Mark Pauly, 'The Economics of Moral Hazard: Comment' (1968) 58 *The American Economic Review* 531.

9 Financial stability, although intuitively appealing, is an elusive concept and one that is hard to give a precise definition to or measure. For instance, Davies and Green argue that it is very difficult to say *ex ante* if a given financial system is stable or not, but with the benefit of hindsight one can define instability as loss of normalcy and resilience. See Howard Davies and David Green, *Banking on the Future: The Rise and Fall of Central Banking* (Princeton University Press, 2010), ch 3.

10 Banking Act 2009, s 238(1) inserting s 2A to the Bank of England Act 1998.

11 Financial Services Act 2010, s 1(3) inserting s 3A into the Financial Services and Markets Act 2000. The Act will be henceforth abbreviated as 'FSMA 2000'.

previous statutory formulation was.[12] In addition, the 2012 Act set up the Financial Policy Committee of the Bank of England which is charged with contributing to the achievement of the Bank's financial stability objective.[13] Finally, the recent restructuring of the financial regulatory landscape, which will be explored in the next section, can be said to prioritise macro-prudential issues, and separates prudential regulation from conduct of business regulation, thus potentially allowing for greater emphasis on financial stability than under the previous regime. Safeguarding financial stability entails *inter alia* maintaining the safety and soundness of individual systemic banks and other financial institutions in order to reduce their insolvency risk. The other main objectives of financial regulation – namely, maintaining market confidence, protecting consumers and reducing financial crime[14] – refer to conduct of business regulation and hence are not directly relevant from the perspective of this study. The following paragraphs identify the specific economic characteristics of the financial sector, and of banks in particular, that explain why financial stability is a public good in the strict sense of the term.[15]

First, it is necessary to explain the vital importance of the financial sector and of banks in particular for any modern economy. As financial intermediaries, banks efficiently transfer liquidity from depositors and bondholders to individual, corporate and sovereign borrowers, allowing for economic growth and expansion. In fact, they generate liquidity, as they fund illiquid assets (loans) using the money deposited in them.[16] Indeed, by accepting deposits and relending the greatest part of them and then reaccepting the funds back and relending them, and so on, circulating money is multiplied several times. This is the so-called money multiplying effect, which explains the need for authorities charged with monetary policy to supervise the overall level of lending in the economy.[17] Other financial institutions also act as risk intermediaries, for instance, insurance firms.

12 Financial Services Act 2012, s 2(2).

13 See Bank of England Act 1998, s 9C (inserted by the Financial Services Act 2012, s 4).

14 See FSMA 2000, ss 2–6.

15 A genuine public good is a good or service that is both non-excludable (i.e. no person can be excluded from its use) and non-rivalrous (i.e. use by one individual does not diminish its value for others). Public goods are an example of market failure, as markets tend to under-produce them. See Paul Samuelson, 'The Pure Theory of Public Expenditure' (1954) 36 *Review of Economics and Statistics* 387. For a discussion of financial stability as a 'framework-type' public good, see Mads Andenas and Iris H-Y Chiu, *The Foundations and Future of Financial Regulation: Governance for Responsibility* (Routledge, 2014), 8–10, and 18–20. See also David S Bieri, 'Regulation and Financial Stability in the Age of Turbulence' in Robert W Kolb (ed), *Lessons from the Global Financial Crisis* (John Wiley & Sons, 2010), 327.

16 Of course, financial intermediation has not been the only activity of banks in recent years. It has been illustrated that the financial intermediation role of banks is nowadays less important than in the past, as their main sources of income are fees and trading activities rather than the margin between interest rates paid by borrowers and interest rates paid to depositors. See e.g. Franklin Allen and Anthony Santomero, 'What Do Financial Intermediaries Do?' (2001) 25 *Journal of Banking & Finance* 271.

17 In the UK, monetary policy is independently administered by the Bank of England (and the Bank's Monetary Policy Committee) within the inflation target set by the

Moreover, banks operate a complex payment services system which facilitates the transactions of their private and corporate clients (*inter alia*) via cheques, credit cards, debit cards, cash cards, electronic purses, money transfers, and standing orders. In this way, banks can be said to resemble public utility firms providing an intangible network of essential importance for society as a whole. Banks and other financial institutions are also large employers, especially in countries like the UK where the financial sector accounts for nearly 10% of GDP. In parallel, financial institutions exert a significant influence on the corporate governance of other large companies. Institutional investors such as insurance companies, pension funds, unit trusts, investment trusts, hedge funds and – to some extent – banks and other financial institutions hold the majority of the shares of listed companies in the UK.[18] Banks influence the governance of companies they lend funds to through debenture covenants, informal monitoring of financed companies, and by screening companies before loans are advanced.

As a result, financial crises have detrimental effects on the real economy. In a typical crisis scenario, bank lending is curtailed as ailing banks seek to reduce their loan portfolios. The resulting credit crunch undermines the ability of firms to raise debt and expand, and can thus cause the economy as a whole to enter into a recession[19] and unemployment to rise.[20] To make matters worse, government spending to prevent the failure of large banks (and thus the collapse of the financial system) and to respond to the overall economic recession, leads to the inescapable consequence of increasing the public debt with serious long-term consequences for the economy.[21] It seems that whatever policy is followed to manage a crisis, serious negative externalities are generated when a large financial institution fails, and the losses are borne not only by other financial institutions but also by the real economy and/or the taxpayers. The consequences of financial crises are so severe that it is highly unlikely that any benefits accruing from profitable risk-taking during the period leading up to a crisis outweigh the cost of a crisis, although formal economic evidence on this is difficult to obtain.[22]

Treasury. See Bank of England Act 1998 s 10 which abolishes the power of the Treasury to give directions to the Bank with regard to monetary policy; and s 11 which lexically prioritises the Bank's objective to maintain price stability vis-à-vis its duty to support the economic policy of the government.

18 On this, see Chapter 1, n 14 and accompanying text.

19 For instance, in 2009, UK GDP declined by 4% as a result of the 2008 financial crisis.

20 The unemployment rate rose from around 5.3% in 2007 to 8% in 2011. See European Economic Forecast Autumn 2009 (Commission, August 2009) 156 http://ec.europa.eu/economy_finance/publications/publication_summary16053_en.htm accessed 1 May 2017; and European Economic Forecast Autumn 2013 (Commission, August 2013) 101 http://ec.europa.eu/economy_finance/eu/forecasts/2013_autumn_forecast_en.htm accessed 1 May 2017.

21 The UK national debt to GDP ratio increased from 43.30% at the end of the 2007–2008 fiscal year to 88.10% at the end of 2012–2013. Ibid.

22 The UK government's support to the banking sector peaked at £1,162 billion in 2009 and in 2013 stood at £141 billion. The exact final cost to UK taxpayers is difficult to calculate as it will ultimately depend on the price at which the Treasury's shares in rescued banks are sold. Taking into account the share prices of RBS and Lloyds on 31

So far it has been demonstrated that financial institutions play a vital economic role and that financial instability following a crisis harms the real economy. However, one might ask in which ways the failure of individual financial institutions affects the system as whole. No doubt, the key feature of the financial sector which makes financial stability a public good is systemic risk.[23] Indeed, if the failure of one institution left its competitors strengthened and the system intact, as is the case in most other industries, there would be no threat to financial stability. However, the failure of any financial institution of significant size and complexity has spill-over effects on the entire system. Other major institutions are likely to suffer and a series of failures may be triggered. Problems in a few institutions can thus infect the whole system and lead to a serious crisis, as happened in the UK in 2007–2009. Institutions whose failure can cause negative effects on the financial system are described in regulatory terms as systemically important financial institutions,[24] and include not only banks but also large insurance companies and investment companies, even if only acting on the wholesale market.[25]

Economic literature identifies the main cause of systemic risk as the very high interconnectedness and interdependence of financial institutions which conduct a major part of their business *inter se*.[26] UK regulators have identified two types of systemic risk, namely, cyclical risk and structural risk.[27] Banks, for instance, rely on the inter-bank lending market to ensure that they have adequate liquidity to meet their liabilities, especially in times of low depositor confidence as will be explained below. Activities on the derivatives and foreign exchange markets are other examples of the interconnected nature of banking, as banks are the major players in these markets. Counterparty risk is hence conducive to systemic risk.

Another component of systemic risk is the reputational one. The failure of an important bank or other financial institution may cause a crisis of confidence in the

March 2013, the loss to the Treasury stood at £28 billion. Another £3 billion was the cost of resolving Northern Rock and Bradford & Bingley. The additional interest paid by the Treasury to fund its investments in the banking sector amounts to £20 billion in four years. Overall, the cost of the 2007–2009 crisis to the Treasury can be estimated at £51 billion. See HM Treasury, *Annual Report and Accounts 2012–13* (2013–2014, HC 34).

23 For a detailed examination of the various components of systemic risk, see Steven L Schwarcz, 'Systemic Risk' (2008) 97 *Georgetown Law Journal* 193; and also Steven L Schwarcz and Lucy Chang, 'The Custom to Failure Cycle' (2012) 62 *Duke Law Journal* 767.

24 The Basel Committee has identified five features of systemically important financial institutions, namely their size, linkages, global footprint, complexity and substitutability of services. On this see below Chapter 4, n 14.

25 As evinced by the state rescue of American wholesale insurer AIG in 2008. On this, see Andenas and Chiu (above n 15), 93 and 305.

26 See Peter O Mulbert, 'Corporate Governance of Banks after the Financial Crisis – Theory, Evidence, Reforms' (2010) ECGI Working Paper No 130/2009, 11–12 http://papers.ssrn.com/sol3/papers.cfm?abstract_id=1448118 accessed 1 May 2017.

27 See Bank of England and Financial Services Authority, 'Instruments of Macroprudential Policy' (December 2011) www.bankofengland.co.uk/publications/Documents/other/financialstability/discussionpaper111220.pdf accessed 1 May 2017.

system as a whole and depositors' runs may affect other banks, or at least an increase in withdrawals may occur. Due to the maturity mismatch between, on the one hand, deposits, which are typically payable on demand, and on the other, loans, which are to be repaid after a fixed period, it follows that no bank can meet a significant fraction of its liabilities at any given time. Banks cannot even do so relatively quickly, as their assets are illiquid and cannot therefore be sold *en masse* at short notice, other than at very low prices. If a large number of depositors are persuaded that their bank is in a precarious position and rush to draw their funds, they will cause the collapse of the bank, no matter how healthy it is. In other words, the inability of rational depositors to co-ordinate their actions can lead to a creditors' run, which is a typical collective action problem. Therefore, any deposit-taking institution is constantly dependent on the confidence of its depositors and can at any time be diminished to cash flow insolvency merely as a result of a crisis of public confidence.

Finally, the opacity of the sector *per se* is a cause of systemic risk.[28] The inability of other financial institutions to value the assets of an ailing institution precipitates the collapse of the latter.[29] In parallel, the inability of financial markets to distinguish between sound and unsound banks in times of crisis can paralyse the inter-bank lending market and make it more difficult for banks to raise equity capital. Similarly, the general inability of depositors to distinguish between banks precipitates a crisis of confidence once one major bank collapses.[30] The same opacity problem applies to insurance companies and other financial institutions as their assets mostly consist of debt and equity financial instruments which are difficult to value accurately.

To appreciate the magnitude of the threat that systemic risk poses to financial stability it is necessary to refer to a few particular characteristics of banks, namely, their heavy reliance on debt financing. In financial institutions, as in all limited liability companies, insolvency risk increases the higher the company's leverage is. Indeed, if a company's activities are mostly funded by equity, then there is a large buffer to absorb losses and hence insolvency is unlikely. Conversely, if a company relies primarily on debt capital, it runs a higher risk of insolvency.[31] This can

28 A recent empirical study on banks found evidence that opacity causes contagion by exacerbating the cycles of bubbles and crashes. In other words, more opaque banks benefit in times of euphoria and then suffer in times of crisis. See Jeffrey Jones, Wayne Lee and Timothy Yeager, 'Opaque Banks, Price Discovery, and Financial Instability' (2012) 21 *Journal of Financial Intermediation* 383.

29 On the opacity of banks' assets, see Chapter 1, section III.

30 Indeed, immigrants to the US who have experienced a bank crisis in their country of origin are less likely to open a bank account. See Una Okonkwo Osili and Anna Paulson, 'Bank Crises and Investor Confidence: An Empirical Investigation' (2009) Federal Reserve Bank of Chicago Policy Discussion Paper PDP2009-9 www.chicagofed.org/webpages/publications/policy_discussion_papers/2009/pdp_9.cfm accessed 1 May 2017.

31 If markets were perfect and there were no taxes, agency costs and administrative costs associated with insolvency, the capital structure of a company would not matter with regard to its profitability, as posited by the Modigliani-Miller Theorem which proves that in perfect market conditions, the additional cost of borrowing would fully

happen if for any reason the company becomes unable to pay its debts as they fall due (e.g. due to a reduction in the income of the company or a failure to roll over short-term debt), or if the value of the company's assets decreases to the extent that it becomes lower than the company's liabilities.[32] Unlike most other large companies, banks rely heavily on debt capital. A typical bank is approximately 95% debt financed[33] and only 5% equity financed. This gives a gearing ratio of 19:1 which is remarkably higher than the gearing ratios of most other companies, which are conventionally considered to be highly geared as soon as the ratio exceeds the level of 1:1.

The reason why banks are far more highly leveraged than other companies is that their profitability rises as their equity-to-assets ratio falls.[34] Unlike generic companies, banks do not incur debt in order to do business, but rather their core business activity is to incur debt by accepting deposits and lending the funds out to borrowers. Hence, if we apply the balance sheet test of insolvency on banks, they will always be near-insolvent, as their liabilities are nearly equal to their assets. Therefore, even when banks are perfectly healthy, their capital structure resembles that of a near-insolvent non-financial company, while bank directors are – arguably – subject to no special duties to creditors, as explained in Chapter 2. The outcome of this is that bank shareholders have stronger ongoing incentives to support a high level of risk-taking than the shareholders of generic companies. As banks are very highly leveraged, shareholders have the incentive to push managers to adopt very risky strategies as – due to limited liability – they risk only their relatively small investment while reaping the benefits from betting the whole amount of banks' assets.

Finally, investment banking activities such as trading in securities, on behalf of clients or on the banks' own behalf, exposes banks to the volatility of the financial markets. It follows that investment banks, which in the UK are often integral parts of major bank groups, are susceptible to sharp changes in their risk profile due to their sensitivity to the conditions of financial markets. It is often argued that the combination of retail and investment banking activities further increases the risks faced by banks, and that this accounts for the series of smaller and larger banking crises that have happened globally since the integration of the financial sector during the 1980s and 1990s both in the UK and internationally.[35]

outweigh any benefits accruing to the shareholders from increasing leverage. See Franco Modigliani and Merton Miller, 'The Cost of Capital, Corporation Finance and the Theory of Investment' (1959) 48 *American Economic Review* 261.

32 The two main tests of insolvency, namely the cash flow test and the balance sheet test, are set out in the Insolvency Act 1986, s 122.

33 See Jonathan Macey and Maureen O'Hara, 'The Corporate Governance of Banks' (2003) 9 *Federal Reserve Bank of New York Economic Policy Review* 91, 91–92.

34 An economic explanation of the reason why banks are so highly leveraged can be found in Harry DeAngelo and Rene M Stulz, 'Liquid-Claim Production, Risk Management, and Bank Capital Structure: Why High Leverage is Optimal for Banks' (2013) Fisher College of Business Working Paper 2013-03-08 http://papers.ssrn.com/sol3/papers.cfm?abstract_id=2254998 accessed 1 May 2017.

35 The regulatory initiatives that have been taken to tackle this problem such as ring-fencing will be discussed in the following chapter.

II. The evolution of UK regulatory architecture in response to perceived regulatory failures

Most accounts of the history of banking regulation and supervision in the UK place its inception in the late 1970s[36] and emphasise the fact that a formal licensing requirement and supervisory regime for all banking institutions was only introduced by the Banking Act 1987.[37] However, if a broader notion of regulatory function is adopted, it is evident that the Bank of England had been exercising a proto-regulatory function since much earlier. Indeed, since the onset of World War I, the Bank of England stopped competing against other banks and assumed the effective leadership of the banking system.[38] This happened despite the absence of any formal licensing, regulatory or supervisory powers of the Bank. Instead, the persuasive authority of the Bank of England was based on the fact that commercial banks relied on the Bank of England to restrict entry to the market, thus insulating them from competition,[39] and was facilitated by close social links between the Bank and major UK banks. Ultimately an omnipresent implicit threat of nationalisation, existing during the whole period from the 1930s until the 1970s, ensured compliance with the instructions and guidance provided by the Bank of England.[40] By the 1930s the Bank's informal control over major banks encompassed crucial corporate decisions such as the payment of dividends and amalgamations.[41] Thus the development of effective regulatory arrangements closely followed the full adoption of limited liability and the abandoning of the practices of using reserve capital and uncalled capital in the early 20th century, as was explained in Chapter 2.

The introduction of formal supervisory arrangements since 1979 has been associated with frequent overhauls of the regulatory architecture. The original structure put in place a two-tier system whereby banks of high reputation and standing were not subject to licensing and supervisory requirements, whereas smaller deposit-takers were.[42] A formal deposit protection scheme was also introduced.[43] This structure came under heavy criticism after the collapse of Johnson

36 As a result of the Banking Act 1979 which was a response to the secondary banking crisis of 1973–1975. For a concise discussion of the crisis, see Margaret Reid, *The Secondary Banking Crisis, 1973–75: Its Causes and Course* (Macmillan Publishers, 1982).

37 See e.g. Andenas and Chiu (above n 15) 5–6; and Christopher Ryan, 'Transfer of Banking Supervision to the Financial Services Authority' in Michael Blair and others (eds), *Blackstone's Guide to the Bank of England Act 1998* (Blackstone Press, 1998), 39–40.

38 On this, see Charles AE Goodhart, *The Evolution of Central Banks* (MIT Press, 1988), 44–55.

39 See Fred Hirsch, 'The Bagehot Problem' (1977) 45 *The Manchester School* 241, 248.

40 See John D Turner, *Banking in Crisis: The Rise and Fall of British Banking Stability, 1800 to the Present* (CUP, 2014), 175.

41 Ibid., 176–177.

42 See Andenas and Chiu (above n 15), 5.

43 Banking Act 1979, s 29 (as originally enacted) provided for a protection limit of £10,000 of which 75% could be claimed.

Matthey, an established bank, in 1984. As a result, the Banking Act 1987 introduced a comprehensive regime of authorisation and supervision for all deposit-takers[44] as well as the requirement that entities and senior persons are fit and proper to engage in banking.[45] At the same time, insurance companies were regulated by the Department of Trade and Industry and other financial sector firms were regulated by five self-regulating organisations,[46] which were overseen by the Securities and Investment Board (SIB), a statutory body under the Financial Services Act 1986, which in due course evolved into the Financial Services Authority, and eventually into the present-day Financial Conduct Authority.

This heavily fragmented and partially self-regulatory structure of financial supervision was seen as highly problematic by the mid-1990s, especially in view of the collapse of Bank of Credit and Commerce International in 1991 and of Barings Bank in 1995.[47] It is of little surprise that the Labour administration which came into power in 1997 set out to rectify this problem by creating a single financial regulator, especially given the trend of integration in the financial services sector.[48] Indeed, the SIB was renamed in October 1997 as the Financial Services Authority (FSA),[49] and assumed the *de facto* role of regulating investment firms and insurance companies. In June 1998 the responsibility for regulating banks was transferred from the Bank of England to the FSA by virtue of the Bank of England Act 1998.[50] At the same time, the Act made the Bank of England independent from the Treasury in matters of monetary policy.[51] Eventually, in December 2001 the FSA was given full regulatory and supervisory authority over the whole

44 Banking Act 1987, ss 8–14 (as originally enacted).

45 A detailed examination of the Act can be found in Graham Penn, *Banking Supervision: Regulation of the UK Banking Sector under the Banking Act 1987* (Butterworths, 1989).

46 The five self-regulating organisations, known as SROs, were the following: the Association of Futures Brokers and Dealers (AFBD), the Financial Intermediaries, Managers and Brokers Regulatory Association (FIMBRA), the Investment Management Regulatory Organisation (IMRO), the Life Assurance and Unit Trust Regulatory Organisation (LAUTRO), and The Securities Association (TSA). In 1991 the AFBD and TSA were replaced by the Securities and Futures Authority (SFA), and in 1994 the FIMBRA and LAUTRO were replaced by the Personal Investment Authority (PIA), thus reducing the number of SROs to three. On this, see Eilís Ferran, 'Examining the UK's Experience in Adopting the Single Financial Regulator Model' (2003) 28 *Brooklyn Journal of International Law* 257, 266–267.

47 For a discussion of the events surrounding the failure of these banks and especially Barings, see Christos Hadjiemmanuil, 'The Bank of England and the Lessons from Barings: UK Banking Regulation under Parliamentary Scrutiny' (1996) 1 *Yearbook of International Financial and Economic Law* 333.

48 For a discussion of the policy rationales behind the creation of the FSA, see Ferran (above n 46), 270–271.

49 See E Peter Ellinger, Eva Lomnicka and Christopher VM Hare, *Ellinger's Modern Banking Law* (5th edn, OUP, 2011), 28.

50 Section 21.

51 Sections 10–19. An in-depth discussion of the concept of independent regulatory agencies can be found in Kirti Datla and Richard Revesz, 'Deconstruing Independent Agencies (and Executive Agencies)' (2013) 98 *Cornell Law Review* 769.

financial industry sector – including banking, insurance and investment business – by virtue of the Financial Services and Markets Act 2000.[52] This was a period characterised by a profound belief in the ability of market discipline – in most circumstances – to ensure customer protection and financial stability,[53] and hence by a dominant conception of the appropriate role of regulation as one exclusively concerned with tackling market failures.[54]

Unsurprisingly, the failures of several UK banks during the 2007–2009 global financial crisis undermined confidence in the efficacy of the single regulator model whereby the FSA regulated and supervised all financial firms for all purposes.[55] The reform initiative was taken by Chancellor of the Exchequer George Osborne, in his 2010 Mansion House speech, which manifested the government's intention to restore the prudential regulatory functions of the Bank of England.[56] Subsequently, the Treasury published two consultation papers[57] and the Financial Services Act was passed in December 2012. The Bank of England had been preparing for the transition since 2011 and has published several policy documents delineating its regulatory approach.[58] In brief, the Financial Services Act 2012 abolished the FSA as a single financial regulator and transformed it into the Financial Conduct Authority (FCA), while entrusting micro-prudential regulation of systemically important financial institutions with the Bank of England through a new subsidiary, the Prudential Regulation Authority (PRA).[59]

52 Section 19 of the Act contains a general prohibition for any person to carry on a regulated activity unless it is authorised by the FSA, and Schedule 2 provides a list of regulated activities covering *inter alia* deposit taking, insurance and dealing in financial instruments as principal or agent.

53 On the limitations of market discipline to act as a prudential regulatory tool, see Chapter 1, sections III and IV.

54 On this, see Harry McVea, 'Financial Services Regulation under the Financial Services Authority: A Reassertion of the Market Failure Thesis?' (2005) 64 *Cambridge Law Journal* 413.

55 On the impact of the failure of several major UK banks in 2007–2009 on regulatory architecture, see Joanna Gray, 'Financial Regulation Before and After Northern Rock' in Joanna Gray and Orkun Akseli (eds), *Financial Regulation in Crisis? The Role of Law and the Failure of Northern Rock* (Edward Elgar Publishing, 2011).

56 For a discussion of the initial stages of the reform process, see Phillip Rawlings, 'Bank Reform in the UK: Part II – Return to the Dark Ages?' (2011) 8 *International Corporate Rescue* 55. See also Eilís Ferran, 'The Break-up of the Financial Services Authority' (2011) 31 *Oxford Journal of Legal Studies* 455.

57 See HM Treasury Consultation Papers: 'A New Approach to Financial Regulation: Judgement, Focus and Stability' (2010); and 'A New Approach to Financial Regulation: Building a Stronger System' (2011).

58 See PRA, 'The PRA's Approach to Banking Supervision' (2012); and 'The PRA's Approach to Insurance Supervision' (2012) www.fsa.gov.uk/about/what/reg_reform/pra accessed 1 May 2017.

59 This approach, however, is inconsistent with empirical evidence suggesting that strict separation of macro-prudential regulation from micro-prudential regulation alleviates the problem of regulatory capture. See Pierre Boyer and Jorge Ponce, 'Regulatory Capture and Banking Supervision Reform' (2012) *8 Journal of Financial Stability* 206, esp 207–208.

In parallel, a new Financial Policy Committee of the Bank of England (FPC) is now responsible for macro-prudential regulation.[60] The FPC operates as a sub-committee of the Bank's Court of Directors with two main objectives: to contribute to the achievement of the financial stability objective of the bank and to support the economic policy of the government, as specified by the Treasury.[61] The main functions of the FPC are: (a) to monitor the stability of the financial system with a view to identifying systemic risks; (b) to prepare financial stability reports; and (c) to give binding directions to the FCA and PRA in order to ensure the implementation of its macro-prudential policies.[62]

The PRA is the new micro-prudential regulator for all systemic financial institutions. This category includes all deposit-takers (banks, building societies and credit unions), large insurance firms, and major investment firms.[63] The common characteristic of these firms is that their potential failure poses a threat to the stability of the financial system and could disrupt the continuity of the provision of financial services. The particular activities that fall within the scope of the PRA's prudential regulation were specified by the Treasury according to the Act.[64] Firms that seek to engage in such activities will have to be licensed by the PRA, while all other financial firms will be licensed by the FCA.[65] A second objective of the PRA focuses on insurance firms regulated by it. The PRA is thus required to ensure an appropriate degree of protection for present and potential policy-holders.

60 A detailed analysis of the reform can be found in Andreas Kokkinis, 'The Financial Services Act 2012: The Recent Overhaul of the United Kingdom's Financial Regulatory Structure' (2013) *International Corporate and Commercial Law Review* 325.

61 Bank of England Act 1998, ss 9C and 9D (inserted by Financial Services Act 2012, s 4).

62 FSMA 2000 s 9G (inserted by Financial Services Act 2012, s 4).

63 Overall, the PRA is currently responsible for the prudential regulation and supervision of 1,700 financial institutions. See www.bankofengland.co.uk/pra/Pages/default.aspx accessed 1 May 2017.

64 FSMA 2000 s 22A (inserted by Financial Services Act 2012, s 9). The Financial Services and Markets Act 2000 (PRA-regulated Activities) Order 2013 (SI 2013/556) came into force on 1 April 2013. Accepting deposits, effecting or carrying out a contract of insurance, and acting as a managing agent at Lloyd's fall automatically within the regulatory scope of the PRA (art 2). Dealing in investments as principal is a PRA-regulated activity only if the relevant firm is designated by the PRA after consulting with the FCA (art 3). Art 8 of the Order requires the PRA to issue a statement of policy with respect to its exercise of the power to designate investment firms. In its statement, the PRA identified the following factors that will be considered to decide whether or not to designate an eligible investment firm: (a) the firm's balance sheet exceeding an average of £15 billion in gross assets over four quarters; (b) the balance sheet of all firms in the same group exceeding the above threshold; (c) if the firm is part of the group of a PRA-regulated firm, whether its revenues, balance sheet and risk-taking is significant relative to those of the group as a whole. See PRA, 'Designation of Investment Firms for Prudential Supervision by the Prudential Regulation Authority' (Statement of Policy, March 2013) paras 8–12 www.bankofengland.co.uk/publications/Documents/other/pra/designationofinvestmentfirms.pdf accessed 1 May 2017.

65 FSMA 2000 s 55A (inserted by Financial Services Act 2012, s 11).

The FCA is now the authority regulating and supervising the market conduct of all financial institutions whether they are licenced by it or by the PRA. It is responsible for securing an appropriate degree of consumer protection, enhancing the integrity of the financial system and promoting effective competition in the interests of consumers. The FCA has discretion to determine the level of consumer protection but must have regard to a list of matters specified in the Act, including the general principle that consumers should take responsibility for their decisions.[66] The integrity of the financial system includes its resilience, the avoidance of financial crime and market abuse, its orderly operation and transparency in price formation.[67] Furthermore, the FCA has assumed the role of the UK Listing Authority.

It is worth noting that the PRA is given a veto power over the exercise of the FCA's regulatory powers with respect to firms authorised by the former. The PRA may exercise its veto power where the FCA is proposing to exercise its regulatory powers in a way that the PRA considers to be threatening the stability of the UK financial system or likely to result in the failure of a systemic institution.[68] Finally, the Treasury is given the power to give binding directions to the Bank of England in circumstances where the Treasury provides financial assistance to a financial institution, incurs expenditure in connection with the Banking Act 2009,[69] or provides financial assistance or a loan to the Financial Services Compensation Scheme manager. As a result, in any case where public funds are committed to the rescue of a financial institution, or where the failure of an institution results in public funds being used to compensate its depositors, the Treasury can give directions to the Bank of England, with a view to protecting the public interest. This, in a way, creates a hierarchy of decision-making with the Treasury at the top followed by the Bank of England, which includes the PRA, and with the FCA at the bottom.

III. The development of the EU financial regulation and supervision framework and the potential consequences of Brexit

In recent years, the architecture of European financial regulation has undergone dramatic changes. Across the EU, there is harmonisation of the substantive rules regarding capital adequacy, liquidity, deposit protection and banking resolution, and there is a platform to facilitate co-operation between financial regulatory authorities, namely the European System of Financial Supervision (ESFS). The ESFS comprises the European Supervisory Authorities (ESAs) and the European Systemic Risk Board (ESRB).[70] There are three ESAs, namely, the European

66 FSMA 2000 s 1C (2) (d) (inserted by Financial Services Act 2012, s 6).
67 FSMA 2000 s 1D (inserted by Financial Services Act 2012, s 6).
68 FSMA 2000 s 3I (inserted by Financial Services Act 2012, s 6).
69 The stabilisation options introduced by the Act will be analysed in Chapter 4, section III.
70 Regulation (EU) No 1092/2010 of the European Parliament and of the Council of 24 November 2010 on European Union macro-prudential oversight of the financial

Banking Authority (EBA),[71] the European Securities and Markets Authority (ESMA),[72] and the European Insurance and Occupational Pensions Authority (EIOPA).[73] The EBA, in particular, plays a crucial role in promulgating the new Banking Single Rulebook, i.e. the harmonisation of banking prudential regulation rules across the EU. Indeed, the EBA is authorised by relevant primary legislation to issue binding technical standards[74] on the implementation of the relevant rules as well as guidelines and recommendations addressed to national competent authorities.[75]

In parallel, the experience of the global financial crisis and the eurozone sovereign debt crisis highlighted the problems resulting from the absence of a unified European approach to banking regulation, supervision and crisis management, especially given the adoption of the euro as the common currency of 19 member states. As corollary to the currency union, the banking union was established consisting of two pillars, the Single Supervisory Mechanism (SSM) and the Single Resolution Mechanism (SRM). As part of the SSM, the European Central Bank (ECB) has assumed since late 2014 the direct responsibility for supervising all systemically important banks in the eurozone.[76] Under the new regime the ECB is currently supervising 125 large banks,[77] representing approximately 85% of banking assets in the eurozone.[78] The banking union is also open to member states

system and establishing a European Systemic Risk Board [2010] OJ L331/1. A discussion of the ESRB's role can be found in Andenas and Chiu (above n 15) 49–52.

71 Regulation (EU) No 1093/2010 of the European Parliament and of the Council of 24 November 2010 establishing a European Supervisory Authority (European Banking Authority), amending Decision No 716/2009/EC and repealing Commission Decision 2009/78/EC [2010] OJ L331/12 (EBA Regulation), art 1.

72 Regulation (EU) No 1095/2010 of the European Parliament and of the Council of 24 November 2010 establishing a European Supervisory Authority (European Securities and Markets Authority), amending Decision No 716/2009/EC and repealing Commission Decision 2009/77/EC [2010] OJ L331/84, art 1.

73 Regulation (EU) No 1094/2010 of the European Parliament and of the Council of 24 November 2010 establishing a European Supervisory Authority (European Insurance and Occupational Pensions Authority), amending Decision No 716/2009/EC and repealing Commission Decision 2009/79/EC [2010] OJ L331/48, art 1.

74 EBA Regulation, art 8 (1) (a).

75 EBA Regulation, art 8 (1) (a) and (e).

76 Council Regulation (EU) No 1024/2013 of 15 October 2013 conferring specific tasks on the European Central Bank concerning policies relating to the prudential supervision of credit institutions [2013] OJ L287/63 (Banking Union Regulation) introduced the single supervisory mechanism, which came into force on 4 November 2014. See also Regulation (EU) No 1022/2013 of the European Parliament and of the Council of 22 October 2013 amending Regulation (EU) No 1093/2010 establishing a European Supervisory Authority (European Banking Authority) regarding the conferral of specific tasks on the European Central Bank pursuant to Council Regulation (EU) No 1024/2013 [2013] OJ L287/5.

77 This is accurate as of 1 January 2017. See European Central Bank, 'List of Supervised Entities' (2017) www.bankingsupervision.europa.eu/banking/list/who/html/index.en.html accessed 1 May 2017.

78 For a detailed discussion of the new regime, see Eilís Ferran and Valia Babis, 'The European Single Supervisory Mechanism' (2013) 13 *Journal of Corporate Law Studies* 255.

that have not adopted the euro to opt in,[79] but no non-eurozone countries have joined at the time of writing. In addition, as part of the SRM, a Single Resolution Board was established on 1 January 2015 with the task of fast-track crisis management and with the responsibility to administer the Single Resolution Fund to be built up gradually from 2016 to 2023 from levies on eurozone banks.[80]

Even before the Brexit referendum, there was little doubt that the UK was not interested in opting into the Banking Union. Still, since the UK is currently home to four global systemically important banks (G-SIBs),[81] the PRA as the UK's national authority has to maintain a memorandum of understanding with the ECB so as to facilitate the co-operation of the two authorities.[82] It follows that despite the fact that the UK is not part of the Banking Union, so long as it remains a member of the EU, it is still affected by the harmonisation of banking regulation standards and of their implementation, and the PRA and Bank of England will now have to work closely with the EBA, the ECB and other relevant EU authorities. Of course, the outcome of the EU membership referendum held on 23 June 2016 and the subsequent notification of withdrawal served by the UK on 29 March 2017 mean that the UK will be exiting the EU and all associated treaties on 29 March 2019 – unless an extension of negotiations is agreed between the UK and the remaining 27 member states unanimously, or a withdrawal agreement comes into force before that time.[83] This has caused widespread concern amongst financial institutions as to the applicable regime post-Brexit.

It is essential to note that the extent of the legal impact of the referendum will depend heavily on the form that the UK's withdrawal from the EU will take. This will of course depend on the outcome of the negotiations that commenced after the UK invoked article 50 of the Treaty on European Union and cannot be predicted with any degree of accuracy at this stage. In the following paragraphs, it will

79 Banking Union Regulation, art 7.

80 Regulation (EU) No 806/2014 of the European Parliament and of the Council of 15 July 2014 establishing uniform rules and a uniform procedure for the resolution of credit institutions and certain investment firms in the framework of a Single Resolution Mechanism and a Single Resolution Fund and amending Regulation (EU) No 1093/2010 [2014] OJ L 225/1.

81 These are HSBC, Barclays, RBS and Standard Chartered. Lloyds was removed from the list of G-SIBs in November 2012. See Financial Stability Board, '2015 Update of Group of Global Systemically Important Banks (G-SIBs)' (2015) www.fsb.org/2015/11/2015-update-of-list-of-global-systemically-important-banks-g-sibs/ accessed 1 April 2017.

82 Banking Union Regulation, art 3 (6).

83 Consolidated version of the Treaty on European Union [2012] OJ C326/1 (TEU), art 50 (3). Article 50 was introduced by the Treaty of Lisbon of 13 December 2007 and came into effect on 1 December 2009. According to art 50 (2), a withdrawal agreement requires a qualified majority of the Council of the EU and the consent of the European Parliament. Art 50(4) clarifies that the representative of the departing member state is disqualified from voting at the Council of the EU and that the term qualified majority has the meaning given in art 238 (3) (b) of the Treaty on the Functioning of the European Union [2012] OJ C326/1 (TFEU), that is, 55% of the member states representing at least 65% of the EU population.

be demonstrated that the legal consequences of the UK's withdrawal from the EU in financial regulation will depend first and foremost on whether the UK will eventually continue to be part of the Single Market.[84] Certain areas of EU law that derive from the fundamental rules on the free movement of goods, persons,[85] services and capital enshrined in the Treaty for the Functioning of the European Union[86] (TFEU) are equally applicable to countries that are not EU member states but are members of the Single Market. Therefore, the Single Market extends to all countries that are members of the European Economic Area[87] (EEA) – that is, all 28 EU member states as well as three of the European Free Trade Association (EFTA) member states, Norway, Lichtenstein and Iceland,[88] and – to a limited extent – to Switzerland through bilateral treaties.[89] Essentially

84 An in-depth analysis of the potential consequences of an exit from the Single Market on corporate and financial transactions can be found in Andreas Kokkinis, 'The Impact of Brexit on the Legal Framework for Cross-border Corporate Activity' (2016) 27 *European Business Law Review* 959.

85 Crucially, Articles 43 and 48 TEU protect freedom of establishment within the EU. As a result, a member state cannot generally refuse to recognise a company incorporated in another member state on the grounds that the company does not abide by the host state's real seat requirement. See *R v HM Treasury and Commissioners of Inland Revenue, ex parte Daily Mail and General Trust* (Case 81/87) [1988] ECR 5483; *Centros Ltd v Erhverrs* (C-212/97); *Ueberseering BV v Nordic GmbH* (C-208/00); and *SEVIC Systems AG* (C-411/03). Nevertheless, a member state may still demand that companies incorporated under its own law maintain their actual centre of administration (real seat) within the borders of that state and refuse to recognise the personality of a company that contravenes this requirement. See *Cartesio Octato es Szolgaltato bt* (C-210/06) [2009] ECR I-9641.

86 TFEU art 26 (2). Specific provisions on the free movement of goods, customs union and competition law harmonisation are set out in arts 28–44. Detailed provisions on the free movement of individuals, services and capital, including the right of establishment for natural and legal persons and the prohibition of discrimination on grounds of nationality, are set out in arts 45–66.

87 The European Economic Area was created by the Agreement on the European Economic Area which was signed in Porto on 2 May 1992 [1994] OJ L1/3 and became effective on 1 January 1994. It is an international treaty originally between the 12 European Economic Community (EEC) member states and the European Free Trade Association states, which were at the time the following: Norway, Lichtenstein and Iceland (which are still members of EFTA and the EEA), Austria, Sweden and Finland (which joined the EU in 1995), and Switzerland, which never ratified the Agreement due to its rejection by a referendum in December 1992.

88 The European Free Trade Association is an intergovernmental organisation established by a Convention on 4 January 1960. Its original signatories were the United Kingdom, which played a primary role in the creation of the organisation as a countervailing force to the EEC founded in 1958, Austria, Denmark, Norway, Portugal, Sweden and Switzerland. Iceland joined in 1970, Finland in 1986 and Lichtenstein in 1991. However, as many of the members joined the EEC (and later EU), the importance of EFTA gradually declined. Indeed, the UK and Denmark left in 1973, Portugal in 1986 and Austria, Finland and Sweden in 1995. As a result, EFTA has currently only four members: Iceland, Lichtenstein, Norway and Switzerland.

89 Switzerland remains an EFTA member but is not a member of the EEA. Still, it is part of the European Single Market by virtue of a series of bilateral treaties with the EEA.

the whole of EU legislation that is relevant to financial services regulation falls within the scope of the Single Market *acquis*, although this does not apply fully to Switzerland, as will be explained below.

Non-EU EEA countries are obliged to implement all EU law rules that fall within the scope of the EEA Agreement subject to their formal approval by special joint committees that include representatives from both sides. As the EEA Agreement does not entail the delegation of any legislative or other powers by EEA states to EU institutions, all new EU legislation has to be incorporated into the EEA Agreement by consensus of all EEA states in order to become binding. In theory, EEA countries have the right to refuse the application of new EU legislation, but this right has never been used as it would give the EU the right to terminate the whole EEA Agreement. A number of EEA/EFTA bodies mirror EU institutions and administer those EU law rules that are applicable to EEA states. The most important of these bodies are the EFTA Standing Committee which comprises the ambassadors of the three EEA states to the EU, the EFTA Surveillance Authority which oversees the implementation of and monitors compliance with the relevant rules, and the EFTA Court which hears cases of alleged infringement of the relevant rules brought by the Surveillance Authority.[90]

The incorporation of new rules into the EEA Agreement is led politically by the EEA Council (of foreign ministers). The actual decision to incorporate applicable EU legislation into the Agreement is taken by consensus by the EEA Joint Committee which consists of the EFTA Standing Committee and the European External Action Service.[91] The procedure entails notification of the Joint Committee as soon as an EEA-relevant piece of legislation is proposed, and further notification when it is adopted. Then the act is scrutinised by the Joint Committee to ensure it falls within the scope of the EEA Agreement and if approved, a draft decision is sent to the Commission for review to ensure the coherence of the law relating to the Single Market. Although in principle incorporation ought to occur as soon as possible so that new rules are implemented at approximately the same time throughout the EEA, in practice the process is often protracted and can last several years.

However, the position of the UK government is currently against remaining in the Single Market as doing so would, in the government's view, fail to deliver the mandate of the referendum as the UK would continue to be subject to EU law and especially to the freedom of movement principle. Therefore, the Swiss model becomes highly relevant to the UK as it would be the option allowing the closest possible relationship with the EU without full membership of the Single Market.

By way of background, the EEC Switzerland Free Trade Agreement [1972] OJ L300/189 which was signed in Brussels on 22 July 1972 and came into force on 1 January 1973, covered trade in goods other than agricultural products.

90 An analysis of the jurisprudence of the EFTA Court during the first 20 years of its existence can be found in EFTA Court, *The EEA and the EFTA Court* (Hart Publishing, 2015).

91 This is an agency established for this purpose in 2010. Until then it was the role of the Commission to represent the EU on the EEA Joint Committee.

It is important to note that although all EU law that relates to the free movement of goods, services, people and capital applies to EEA countries, the same is not the case with Switzerland. EU law that is based on the free movement of persons (natural and legal) applies to Switzerland, but EU rules on financial regulation, prospectuses and their passporting and the passporting rights of financial firms do not apply. A special bilateral agreement allows Swiss general insurance firms to set up agencies and branches in EEA states and vice versa.[92] Another crucial difference is that the bilateral treaties between the EU and Switzerland[93] do not provide for the incorporation of new pieces of EU legislation. Any expansion of Switzerland's participation to the Single Market is achieved by concluding additional bilateral treaties which over the years has led to a proliferation of treaties which now exceed 120. The EU Council has stated that no further bilateral treaties will be concluded and has demanded that an appropriate institutional framework be set up to ensure the coherence of the Single Market, incorporation of new rules and dispute resolution.[94]

Furthermore, it is worth noting that Switzerland, in the last three years, faced a political crisis that bears similarities to the UK's position on migration. A referendum was held in February 2014 where the majority of Swiss people approved a motion to introduce quotas on migration including EU migration.[95] This created fears that, once implementing the referendum, Switzerland would fail to comply with freedom of movement and would thus lose access to the Single Market. However, in December 2016 Switzerland and the EU agreed on a compromise whereby Swiss law now requires employers to prioritise Swiss candidates but no quotas are imposed on EEA migration.[96] This demonstrates that even limited access to the Single Market is inextricably linked to freedom of movement and at any rate it remains to be seen if a model of bilateral treaties between the UK and EU could cover financial regulation.

92 Agreement between the European Economic Community and the Swiss Confederation of 26 July 1989 on direct insurance other than life insurance [1991] OJ L205/3, which became effective on 1 January 1992.

93 The ten bilateral treaties granting Switzerland partial membership of the Single Market were signed in two phases: the first seven in 1999 and the last three in 2004. They cover areas such as the free movement of persons, technical trade barriers, public procurement, agriculture, air and land transport, and Switzerland's participation in the Schengen and Dublin agreements. For an in-depth discussion of the position of Switzerland vis-à-vis the Single Market, see Stephan Breitenmoser, 'Sectoral Agreements between the EC and Switzerland: Contents and Context' (2003) 40 *Common Market Law Review* 1137.

94 See Aydan Bahadir and Fernando Garcés de los Fayos, 'The European Economic Area (EEA), Switzerland and the North' (European Parliament, November 2016) www.europarl.europa.eu/atyourservice/en/displayFtu.html?ftuId=FTU_6.5.3.html accessed 1 May 2017.

95 The referendum resulted in an amendment to the Swiss Constitution. See Federal Constitution of the Swiss Confederation of 18 April 1999, art 121a (inserted by the Federal Council Decree of 13 May 2014).

96 See Eric Maurice, 'EU and Switzerland Agree on Free Movement' *Eurobserver* (22 December 2016) https://euobserver.com/justice/136398 accessed 1 May 2017.

In any case, whatever form the UK's withdrawal from the EU takes, it is in the interests of both the UK and other EU member states that close co-operation in the area of banking regulation and supervision is maintained.[97] From the perspective of the UK, adopting a policy of light regulation to attract financial institutions from the rest of the EU that seek to engage in regulatory arbitrage[98] could seriously undermine financial stability and would mean that UK regulatory requirements would not be treated as equivalent by EU authorities. At the same time, Brexit could also serve as an opportunity to dispense with some EU financial regulation rules that are of questionable value – an issue to which we will return in the last chapter of this volume.

IV. The rise of reflexive regulation techniques until the 2007–2009 crisis and its continuing significance post-crisis

This section seeks to explain the concept of reflexive regulation and to provide some examples of reflexive regulatory techniques. My discussion of reflexive law is necessarily brief and cannot do justice to the richness of the relevant literature.[99] Generally, reflexive regulation in the financial context focuses on principles and procedures rather than prescriptive rules, requires regulated persons to take a proactive rather than a reactive position with regard to compliance, and devolves several crucial regulatory tasks to private entities.

As such, reflexive techniques mark a departure from command and control regulation,[100] which is based on the direct imposition of prescriptive mandatory rules that seek to regulate all the relevant aspects of the conduct of the regulated persons.[101] For instance, reflexive regulatory techniques are common in labour law. The

97 Brener demonstrates the vital need for post-Brexit co-operation given the complexity and cross-border nature of financial institutions. See Alan Brener, 'No-Man is an Island: UK and EU Banking Regulatory Engagement after "Brexit"' (2016) 27 *European Business Law Review* 1029.

98 Of course, regulatory competition in the area of company law has already been happening and the UK has been one of the preferred member states to incorporate companies and get listed. On this, see Lars Hornuf, *Regulatory Competition in European Corporate and Capital Market Law: An Empirical Analysis* (Intersentia, 2012). See also John C Coffee Jr, 'Racing Towards the Top?: The Impact of Cross-Listings and Stock Market Competition on International Corporate Governance' (2002) 102 *Columbia Law Review* 1757.

99 The concept of reflexivity originates in the work of Teubner. See Gunther Teubner, *Law as an Autopoietic System*, Anne Bankowska and Ruth Adler trs, Zenon Bankowski ed (Blackwell, 1993).

100 A general academic discussion of 'new governance' regulatory techniques and their interplay with conventional forms of regulation can be found in David Trubek and Louise Trubek, 'New Governance & Legal Regulation: Complementarity, Rivalry, and Transformation' (2006–2007) 13 *Columbia Journal of European Law* 539, 542–547.

101 For a general discussion of the regulatory trend towards modern regulatory techniques in developed economies, see Rauf Gonenc, Maria Maher and Giuseppe Nicoletti, 'The Implementation and the Effects of Regulatory Reform: Past Experience and Current Issues' (2000) OECD Working Paper 251 (ECO/WKP(2000)24) http://papers.ssrn.com/sol3/papers.cfm?abstract_id=238213 accessed 1 May 2017.

key mechanism to regulate industrial relations – i.e. collective bargaining between employers and trade unions – can be analysed as an instance of reflexive regulation which prescribes a procedure rather than an outcome.[102] The same applies to the requirement for employers to give employees an opportunity to defend themselves in a disciplinary meeting before being dismissed on grounds of misbehaviour or incompetence.[103] In addition, international labour law is a good example of reflexive law as it is mainly based on non-binding guidelines promulgated by the International Labour Organization (ILO),[104] the OECD[105] and the United Nations.[106]

The reasons why command and control regulation is unlikely to work effectively in the financial context lie in the extreme complexity and highly dynamic nature of the sector, which make it highly likely that command and control regulation will lead to unintended consequences.[107] Indeed, financial innovation is an omnipresent characteristic of developed financial markets, so that new business models or products pose a permanent threat to financial stability, irrespective of the framework of duties and prohibitions that regulators may impose. At any rate, regulators lack the resources, expertise and motivation to micro-manage banks effectively.[108] A further argument against inflexible command and control regulation is that – generally – when inflexible and onerous regulation is introduced in a regulated sector of the economy, that sector shrinks as firms move to the unregulated sector. Broadly speaking, the shadow banking system consists of largely unregulated financial entities that do not accept deposits, such as investment banks, hedge funds, monolines, conduits and structured investment vehicles (SIVs).[109] Recent economic research indicates that shadow banking poses a significant threat to the stability of the financial system.[110] It can thus be argued that command and control regulation inevitably leads to a degree of inefficiency and increased costs.[111]

102 See Ralf Rogowski, *Reflexive Labour Law in the World Society* (Edward Elgar Publishing, 2013), ch 3.

103 See Advisory, Conciliation and Arbitration Service, *Code of Practice 1: Disciplinary and Grievance Procedures* (The Stationery Office, 2009), esp paras 9–16.

104 See e.g. ILO, 'ILO Declaration on Fundamental Principles and Rights at Work' (18 June 1999) www.ilo.org/declaration/thedeclaration/textdeclaration/lang–en/index.htm accessed 1 May 2017.

105 OECD, *OECD Guidelines for Multinational Enterprises* (OECD Publishing, 2011).

106 The UN Global Compact Principles on labour (principles 3–6) can be found online at www.unglobalcompact.org/AboutTheGC/TheTenPrinciples/labour.html accessed 1 May 2017.

107 An excellent account of the failures of command and control regulation can be found in Julia Black, 'Paradoxes and Failures: "New Governance" Techniques and the Financial Crisis' (2012) 75 *Modern Law Review* 1037, 1038–1041.

108 A fundamental problem faced by financial regulators is how to recruit appropriately skilled and talented individuals, as such persons are likely to choose to work for banks and other financial institutions.

109 The PRA is responsible for monitoring the shadow banking sector.

110 See Roland Meeks, Benjamin Nelson and Piergiorgio Alessandri, 'Shadow Banks and Macroeconomic Instability' (2014) Bank of England Working Paper No 487 www.bankofengland.co.uk/research/Pages/workingpapers/2014/wp487.aspx accessed 1 May 2017.

111 See Brunnermeier and others (above n 3), 67–73.

Given the relative practical advantages of modern reflexive regulatory techniques, it is of no surprise that many such flexible techniques were heavily relied on by regulators in the UK and internationally in the years leading up to the recent financial crisis, and indeed continue to be relied on despite the contrary regulatory rhetoric. In her seminal work, Julia Black identifies four such techniques, namely: principles-based regulation; risk-based regulation; the enrolment of gatekeepers; and meta-regulation.[112] The FSA adopted principles-based regulation[113] as its landmark approach in areas such as the fair treatment of customers. The essence of the approach is the use of broad principles that regulated persons are expected to follow instead of rigid rules. Risk-based regulation marked the FSA's approach to the supervision of individual banks; regulatory resources were focused on those firms that were perceived to pose the higher risks to regulatory objectives.[114] In parallel, the enrolment of private gatekeepers, such as auditors and credit rating agencies, was a crucial component of the capital adequacy regime and continues to be important, despite the CRD IV reforms.

Perhaps the best example of reflexive regulation in the area of financial regulation is meta-regulation. Meta-regulation is essentially a regulatory approach that does not prescribe the mode of compliance, but rather invites regulated persons to adopt their own policy for the achievement of regulatory objectives, and to actively monitor their own compliance with it, under the oversight of the relevant authority. Meta-regulation is a common regulatory technique in various areas of public law including health and safety and environmental regulation, and to an extent labour law. In the area of health and safety regulation,[115] each employer is required to adopt its own health and safety policy which attributes key responsibilities (e.g. prevention of accidents, provision of training, consultation with employees, implementation of emergency procedures) to particular individuals, and identifies the specific health and safety risks, and actions to be taken to mitigate them.[116] In parallel, there are a series of activity-specific codes of practice which are drafted by industry bodies and approved by the Health and Safety Executive.[117] Similarly, environmental regulation has in recent years partially moved from command and control to reflexive (or new governance) techniques

112 See Black (above n 107), 1042–1056.

113 For a discussion of the merits and challenges of principles-based regulation see Julia Black, Martyn Hopper and Christa Band, 'Making a Success of Principles-based Regulation' (2007) 1 *Law and Financial Markets Review* 191.

114 An overview of the adoption of risk-based regulation by the FSA can be found in Andenas and Chiu (above n 15), 78–83. An analysis of the significance of risk management as a regulatory technique and of its inherent limitations can be found in Julia Black, 'The Emergence of Risk-based Regulation and the New Public Risk Management in the United Kingdom' (2005) *Public Law* 512.

115 For an in-depth examination of the use of reflexive regulatory techniques in this area, see Neil Gunningham and Richard Johnstone, *Regulating Workplace Safety: System and Sanctions* (OUP, 1999), 143–172.

116 See Health and Safety Executive, 'Write a Health and Safety Policy for your Business' www.hse.gov.uk/simple-health-safety/write.htm accessed 1 May 2017.

117 See Health and Safety at Work etc. Act 1974, s 16.

subsequent to rising concerns about the efficiency and effectiveness of the command and control approach.[118] Indeed, private environmental governance[119] includes self-regulation through voluntary codes of practice, the disclosure of relevant information, environmental certification mechanisms by private not-for-profit bodies,[120] and the elaboration of environmental policies by companies.[121]

In the case of financial regulation, the complexity of financial institutions and the nature of financial transactions as inherently risky and inevitably based on limited information makes it impossible to assess *ex ante* which behaviours or business strategies are excessively risky. If that were feasible, the management of financial institutions could be entrusted to regulators, and no discretion would need to be left to bank directors and senior managers.[122] It is evident that capital adequacy regulation, and the Internal Ratings Based (IRB) Approach to the calculation of credit risk in particular, are examples of meta-regulation. As will be explained in the following chapter, the CRD IV framework actively encourages banks to adopt internal models to calculate credit risk instead of relying on credit rating agencies, and thus further expands the use of meta-regulation. In parallel, regulatory tools such as remuneration policies and recovery and resolution plans, which are prepared by the regulated firms in accordance with broad guidance and approved by the regulators, are further instances of the use of meta-regulation in this context.

V. Conclusions

It is evident from the discussion in this chapter that profitable risk-taking by individual financial institutions often harms the stability of the financial system, and

118 A discussion of the limitations of command and control environmental regulation from a US perspective can be found in Richard Steward, 'A New Generation of Environmental Regulation?' (2001) 29 *Capital University Law Review* 21.

119 A thorough examination of the phenomenon of private environmental governance and of the likely impact of the global financial crisis in this area can be found in Marc Allen Eisner, 'Private Environmental Governance in Hard Times: Markets for Virtue and the Dynamics of Regulatory Change' (2011) 12 *Theoretical Inquiries in Law* 489.

120 One such example is the Soil Association, which is a registered charity founded in 1973. The Soil Association certifies organic products in a range of industries including food, beverages, textiles and personal care products.

121 On the operation of sustainability indexes and the legitimacy implications of environmental self-regulation, see Oren Perez, 'Private Environmental Governance as Ensemble Regulation: A Critical Exploration of Sustainability Indexes and the New Ensemble Politics' (2011) 12 *Theoretical Inquiries in Law* 543.

122 The PRA emphasises the vital role of bank boards and management with regard to safeguarding the financial sustainability of banks: 'It is the responsibility of each firm's board of directors and senior management to manage their firm prudently, with a view to maintaining its safety and soundness, thereby contributing to the continued stability of the financial system. This will be in firms' collective interest as well as in the public interest. It is vital that boards and senior management understand and uphold this objective, and establish within their firms a culture that supports it.' See Bank of England, Prudential Regulation Authority, 'The PRA's approach to banking supervision' (2012), 4 www.bankofengland.co.uk/pra/Pages/publications/bankingappr1210.aspx accessed 1 May 2017.

hence the overall economy, and that there is, therefore, a strong public interest in safeguarding the public good of financial stability. Prudential regulation, mostly of banks, but recently also of other major financial institutions, has been the public law response to this problem, while the corporate law regime applying to financial institutions had been – until a decade ago – excluded from the scope of prudential regulation in tandem with the regime applicable to any other large public company. In the two chapters that follow, we will see that post-crisis regulatory reforms have had a significant impact on the corporate law framework for financial institutions, although the two areas of law have maintained their formal autonomy.

4 Post-crisis reforms and their limitations

Regulating financial institutions' capital and corporate structure

The first two chapters of the book demonstrated that in the case of large financial institutions the current corporate law regime leads to potentially very high negative externalities in the form of undermining the stability of the financial system. This, however, does not necessarily imply that regulation ought to prescribe corporate governance principles, structures and procedures for financial institutions. As Chapter 3 illustrated, there is in place an elaborate framework of regulatory rules and principles that aim to safeguard financial stability. Indeed, the conventional position until the 2007–2009 crisis was that any externalities arising out of running banks as profit-maximising entities could be – and actually were – effectively dealt with by regulating bank capital. We will see in this chapter that this framework focuses post-crisis on regulating directly the capital structure and the corporate structure of banks and to some extent of other major financial institutions. Similarly, those who assume that the reinforced (post-crisis) regulatory framework is adequate to respond to externalities and market failures, would reject any reform proposal with regard to the internal corporate governance of banks as being superfluous and hence value-decreasing.[1]

This chapter explores one set of post-crisis regulatory reforms, namely rules affecting the capital and corporate structure of financial institutions, while Chapter 5 will focus on reforms relating to the internal governance, risk management and senior manager liability regimes in financial institutions. If the rules analysed here were sufficient to respond fully to the market failures identified in Chapter 1 it would follow (within the dominant contractarian understanding of corporate law)[2] that financial regulation should not encroach upon the corporate governance of

1 Economists such as John Kay, Sir David Walker and Sir John Vickers tend to view the existing corporate governance framework and duty of loyalty as consistent with financial stability. Similarly, the UK government recently rejected the idea of introducing a duty of bank directors to maintain financial stability which would override their duty to shareholders. See Department of Business, Innovations and Skills, 'Transparency & Trust: Enhancing the Transparency of UK Company Ownership and Increasing Trust in UK Business: Government Response' (April 2014), paras 249–258 www.gov.uk/government/consultations/company-ownership-transparency-and-trust-discussion-paper accessed 1 May 2017.

2 An examination of the contractarian theory of corporate law can be found below in Chapter 6, section I (a).

financial institutions, but rather should set the limits within which institutions – and their shareholders – are free to pursue the objectives they choose in the manner they think fit, that is, in practice, the maximisation of profits. Advocating the stringent regulation of banks' conduct, while preserving the facilitative nature of their internal corporate governance would thus be consistent with the orthodox contractarian account of corporate law, which accepts mandatory regulation of companies in the public interest insofar as it does not undermine the purely facilitative character of corporate law.[3]

The aim of this chapter is therefore to demonstrate that it is still necessary to regulate the internal corporate governance structures of financial institutions, instead of exclusively relying on the regulation of their capital and corporate structure. Indeed, it will be shown that the current shareholder-centric corporate law framework can seriously undermine the effectiveness of the aforementioned types of prudential regulation, and that – at any rate – such regulatory measures have their own inherent limitations. To this effect, section I explores rules regarding capital adequacy and liquidity, section II focuses on the ring-fencing of retail banking activities that is being introduced in the UK and on other alternative forms of structural regulation, and section III explores the newly minted EU recovery and resolution framework for banks.

I. The Basel III and CRD IV capital adequacy framework and its limitations

a. An overview of the regulatory framework

As explained in Chapter 3, micro-prudential regulation seeks to reduce the likelihood that a systemic institution fails and, in the event of failure, to mitigate its consequences. The principal tool used to reduce the likelihood of bank failures is the adoption of minimum capital requirements which demand that banks have a minimum level of equity capital available to absorb potential losses in tandem with their risk exposures. In this regard, there is a substantial degree of international harmonisation due to the broad acceptance of the standards promulgated by the Basel Committee since the 1980s.[4] Post-crisis capital adequacy rules have been strengthened and new liquidity and leverage standards have been introduced to reduce the likelihood of bank failures by ensuring that there is adequate shareholder equity to absorb potential losses and by reducing shareholder incentives to encourage institutions' managers to take excessive risks. The Basel Committee's

3 This is the position taken by most contractarian scholars. See e.g. Brian R Cheffins, 'Did Corporate Governance "Fail" During the 2008 Stock Market Meltdown? The Case of the S&P 500' (2009) ECGI Working Paper No 124/2009 http://papers.ssrn.com/sol3/papers.cfm?abstract_id=1396126 accessed 1 May 2017.

4 The Basel Committee on Banking Supervision is an institution created in 1974 by the governors of the central banks of major Western economies, which has enormously influenced banking regulation in the last three decades and has contributed to the international harmonisation of prudential regulation.

current recommendations, known as Basel III,[5] have been fully adopted by the EU and therefore are an integral part of the UK's regulatory framework[6] and will probably continue to be so post-Brexit, given the need to ensure that UK financial institutions have the broadest possible access to EU markets.

To appreciate the significance of the reforms introduced post-crisis it is expedient to explain briefly the previous regulatory position. Under Pillar 1 of Basel II, banks had to maintain minimum capital equivalent to 8% of their risk-weighted assets, half of which ought to be Tier 1 capital,[7] i.e. shareholders' equity and disclosed reserves, while Tier 2 capital comprised certain forms of long-term debt.[8] In this context, the term risk-weighted assets refers to a measure of a bank's exposure to credit risk (i.e. the risk that borrowers may default), market risk, and operational risk which is calculated as a percentage of the actual value of a bank's assets. In parallel, Pillar 2 required banks to assess their own capital adequacy regarding any residual risks not covered by Pillar 1, and gave regulators the discretion to demand that banks hold additional capital. Pillar 3 required banks to disclose relevant information to enable market participants to assess banks' capital adequacy, thus reinforcing market discipline.

Since the coming into force of CRD IV which implemented Basel III with effect from the beginning of 2015, Tier 1 capital must be no less than 6% of risk-weighted assets, while the core of it, Common Equity Tier 1 (CET1), must be at least 4.5% thereof.[9] CET1 consists exclusively of ordinary share capital,[10] retained earnings and disclosed reserves. It follows that preference shares do not qualify as CET1. The PRA has also confirmed that, for the purposes of Pillar 2, capital should be of the same quality as the capital held to meet the Pillar 1 requirement, i.e. at least 56% of CET1, and no more than 25% Tier 2 capital.[11] In addition,

5 See Basel Committee on Banking Supervision, *Basel III: A Global Regulatory Framework for more Resilient Banks and Banking Systems* (rev edn, Bank for International Settlements Publications, 2011). From now on it will be abbreviated as Basel III.

6 See Directive 2013/36/EU of the European Parliament and of the Council of 26 June 2013 on access to the activity of credit institutions and the prudential supervision of credit institutions and investment firms, amending Directive 2002/87/EC and repealing Directives 2006/48/EC and 2006/49/EC [2013] OJ L176/338, from now on to be abbreviated as CRD IV; and Regulation (EU) No 575/2013 of the European Parliament and of the Council of 26 June 2013 on prudential requirements for credit institutions and investment firms and amending Regulation (EU) No 648/2012 [2013] OJ L176/1, from now on to be abbreviated as CRR. CRD IV and CRR are implemented in the UK via the regulatory rules of the PRA.

7 See Bank for International Settlements, *International Convergence of Capital Measurement and Capital Standards: A Revised Framework-Comprehensive Version* (Bank for International Settlements Publications, 2006) para 40. From now on to be abbreviated as 'Basel II'.

8 Ibid., para 49 (i).

9 See CRR, art 92.

10 Basel III, para 53. There is a list of criteria for the classification of an instrument as a common share.

11 See PRA, 'Strengthening Capital Standards: Implementing CRD IV, Feedback and Final Rules' (Policy Statement PS 7/13, 13 June 2013), para 3.6 www.bankofengland.co.uk/pra/Pages/publications/implemcrdiv.aspx accessed 1 May 2017.

under the new framework, banks are now expected to hold the following types of additional capital, all of them being of the highest-quality CET1 capital:[12] (a) a capital conservation buffer; (b) a systemic risk buffer depending on the size of each bank; and (c) a countercyclical buffer, in times of economic growth. The capital conservation buffer is a permanent buffer of 2.5% of risk-weighted assets, applying fully from the beginning of 2019.[13]

Furthermore, there is an additional capital buffer which aims to cover the risks that an individual institution poses to the financial system. If an institution is classified as a global systemically important institution (G-SII),[14] it has to hold a special G-SII buffer the size of which depends on the systemic importance of the institution for the global financial system.[15] Indeed, the Financial Stability Board issues annually a list of global systemically important banks classified into five groups of descending systemic importance.[16] If an institution is not a G-SII but is still systemically important for the EU or a member state, it qualifies as an 'other systemically important institution' (O-SII),[17] and has to maintain a buffer of up to 2% of its risk-weighted assets. CRD IV also enables competent authorities to impose a systemic risk buffer of 1% to 3% on appropriate institutions, which applies instead of the G-SII buffer (or the O-SII buffer) if it is higher.[18] Finally, Basel III recommends that banks hold additional capital during periods of financial growth,[19] and CRD IV provides that member states must require individual banks to maintain a countercyclical buffer of up to 2.5%,[20] in line with Basel III recommendations.[21] The combined effect of these requirements is that – depending on

12 See CRD IV, arts 129 (1), 130 (5), 131 (4)–(5), and 133 (3).

13 CRD IV, arts 129 (1) and 160 (1) to (5). For 2017 the capital conservation buffer is set by the PRA at 1.25% and for 2018 at 1.875%. See PRA Rulebook, CRR Firms, Capital Buffers, 2.2.

14 The criteria to identify a G-SII include its size, interconnectedness, substitutability of the services provided, complexity and cross-border activity. Ibid., art 131 (2).

15 The buffer can be 1%, 1.5%, 2%, 2.5% or 3.5% depending on the subcategory to which each institution belongs. CRD IV, art 131(9).

16 The Financial Stability Board (FSB) was founded in 2009 as a successor of the Financial Stability Forum, with a mandate to assess risks to the global financial system and promote the co-ordination of national authorities. It brings together the regulatory authorities of 23 countries and several international organisations such as the World Bank and the International Monetary Fund (IMF). Its secretariat is located in Basel and hosted by the Bank for International Settlements (BIS).

17 See CRD IV art 131 (3).

18 CRD IV, art 133.

19 Basel III, paras 122–135.

20 See CRD IV, art 130, and 136–140. Each designated authority is expected to set for every quarter a buffer rate which should reflect any deviation of the ratio of credit to GDP from its long-term trend within the relevant national economy (art 136 (2)). With regard to non-EU countries, the ESRB may recommend an appropriate buffer rate if the one set by the relevant country's authority is not sufficient to protect EU credit institutions (art 138). The countercyclical buffer for each institution will be the weighted average of the buffer rates applicable to the jurisdictions where the institution's credit exposures are located (art 140 (1)).

21 Basel III, paras 139–148.

their size and the phase of the economic cycle – banks will have to maintain CET1 capital of between 7%[22] and 13% of their risk-weighted assets (and hence total capital of 10.5% to 16.5%), plus any additional capital required by the national regulators under Pillar 2.[23]

Furthermore, Basel III and CRD IV introduced a total leverage ratio to prevent the risk of excessive leverage. According to the new rules, Tier 1 capital must be no less than 3% of the overall exposures of a bank.[24] For these purposes, Tier 1 capital is defined in the same way as for the purposes of the capital ratio, so it must consist of at least 75% CET1 capital. Exposures include a bank's consolidated group assets as well as certain off-balance sheet items and commitments so that the regulatory leverage ratio of a bank tends to be lower than its equity-to-assets ratio.[25] Regulators can also impose additional leverage ratio buffers on systemically important banks and a countercyclical buffer at times of rapid economic growth.[26] The leverage ratio was introduced in the UK on 1 January 2016,[27] and applies to banks and building societies with total retail deposits of at least £50 billion either individually or on a group consolidated basis.[28]

In parallel, as a response to the liquidity shortages faced by major institutions during the 2007–2009 financial crisis,[29] CRD IV and Basel III include explicit rules on bank liquidity. Indeed, from 2018 banks will be required to hold liquid assets adequate to cover the difference between their liquidity outflows and inflows under gravely stressed conditions for a period of 30 days (Liquidity Coverage Ratio).[30] In addition, banks have to ensure that their long-term obligations are funded by a variety of stable funding instruments even under stressed

22 Indeed, the seven major UK deposit-taking institutions, namely, Barclays, HSBC, Lloyds Banking Group, Nationwide, Royal Bank of Scotland, Santander UK and Standard Chartered, have been expected by the PRA to maintain a CET1 capital ratio of 7% from 1 January 2016 unless a special capital plan has been agreed. See PRA, 'Capital Requirements for Major UK Banks and Building Societies' (Supervisory Statement SS3/13, November 2013) www.bankofengland.co.uk/pra/Pages/publications/ss/2015/ss313update.aspx accessed 1 May 2017.

23 The new buffers generally apply from 1 January 2016 with the exception of the G-SII buffer which is coming into force gradually from 2016 and will be fully implemented by 2019. See CRD IV, art 162 (2) and (5).

24 See Basel III, paras 153–164. CRR envisages the introduction of a binding leverage ratio by the end of 2018 (CRR, Preamble para 94).

25 On the precise calculation of the leverage ratio see CRR arts 429–430.

26 From a UK perspective, see PRA Rulebook: CRR Firms: Leverage Ratio Instrument 2015 (PRA 2015/89), s 4.

27 Ibid., para E.

28 Ibid., s 1.1

29 For a policy discussion of the role of liquidity and liquidity ratios, see Markus Brunnermeier and others, *The Fundamental Principles of Financial Regulation: Geneva Reports on the World Economy 11* (Center for Economic Policy Research, 2009), 39–48.

30 See Basel III paras 40–42 and CRR art 412. The requirement will be introduced gradually from 2015 and will apply fully from 1 January 2018. The Commission is empowered to specify the details of the requirement (CRR art 460). See also Basel Committee on Banking Supervision, *Basel III: The Liquidity Coverage Ratio and Liquidity Risk Monitoring Tools* (Bank for International Settlements, 2013).

conditions.[31] To further strengthen liquidity in the banking system, the Basel Committee is currently developing a net stable funding ratio (NSFR) which is intended to be introduced in the EU from 2018.[32] The aim of the NSFR will be to minimise the risk that disruptions of funding erode the liquidity position and thus threaten the viability of a bank.[33]

Finally, it is worth noting that although capital adequacy ratios are unique to deposit-taking institutions, there is a legal requirement for large insurance companies to maintain sufficient equity capital to ensure their solvency in view of calculable risks, by virtue of the Directive known as Solvency II.[34] Broadly speaking, an insurance undertaking that falls within the scope of the Directive[35] must review its capital on an annual basis[36] to ensure that it complies with the solvency capital requirement.[37] The latter includes the Basic Solvency Capital Requirement,[38] the capital requirement for operational risk and the adjustment for the loss-absorbing capacity of technical provisions and deferred taxes.[39]

b. The crucial interplay between senior managers' incentives and capital adequacy rules

There is little doubt that the aforementioned reforms enhanced the capital adequacy framework by responding to a series of deficiencies that were exposed

31 CRR, art 413.
32 See CRR, Preamble para 112.
33 The relevant consultation outlines the regime as follows. Banks' available amount of stable funding will have to eventually reach 100% of the required amount of stable funding. The latter is calculated by attributing a factor to each type of asset which seeks to measure the liquidity risk associated with the asset. For instance, all assets that are encumbered (i.e. are the subject matter of a security interest) for more than one year carry a factor of 100%, while cash and deposits in central banks carry a factor of 0%. See Basel Committee on Banking Supervision, *Basel III: The Net Stable Funding Ration: Consultative Document* (Bank for International Settlements Publications, 2014).
34 Directive 2009/138/EC of the European Parliament and of the Council of 25 November 2009 on the taking-up and pursuit of the business of Insurance and Reinsurance (Solvency II) (recast) [2009] OJ L335/1 to be abbreviated from now on as 'Solvency II'.
35 Solvency II, art 2 (1) defines its *prima facie* scope very broadly as applying to all life and non-life insurance undertakings established within the EU. However, articles 3–12 of the Directive exclude from its scope of application a range of insurance firms, *inter alia*: social security institutions, small undertakings, many mutual undertakings and the providers of funeral coverage.
36 Solvency II, art 102 (1).
37 Solvency II, art 100.
38 This includes at least the following five individual risk modules: non-life underwriting risk; life underwriting risk; health underwriting risk; market risk; counterparty default risk. Solvency II, art 104 (1). Each risk module must be 'calibrated using a Value-at-Risk measure, with a 99,5 % confidence level, over a one-year period'. Solvency II, art 104 (4).
39 Solvency II, art 103.

during the 2007–2009 financial crisis. Nevertheless, the successful operation of the new rules largely depends on banks' senior management being co-operative and honestly doing their best to ensure that banks are well capitalised, in view of their risk exposures and the unique features of each institution. The main argument here is that the incentives faced by the senior management of banks, which is partly a corporate law and corporate governance issue, are relevant to the successful implementation of capital adequacy standards. It follows that the effectiveness of the capital adequacy regime depends to a considerable extent on the incentives faced by key decision-makers within banks and the efficacy of banks' internal governance procedures.[40] Similarly, the incentives structure for middle-layer bank managers can support or jeopardise the successful implementation of capital standards.[41] The following paragraphs will explore the main areas of the capital adequacy framework where banks have significant discretion and hence incentives matter.

The calculation of credit risk – which largely determines the size of risk-weighted assets and hence the amount of capital banks are required to maintain – is the main area where misaligned incentives can seriously undermine the effectiveness of the capital adequacy regime. There are two different methodologies to assess credit risk, namely the Standardised Approach and the IRB Approach, the use of the latter requiring the approval of the competent authority.[42] Under the Standardised Approach, assets are risk-weighted based on their falling within broad categories prescribed by CRR,[43] i.e. claims against central governments, banks, commercial companies, mortgages, etc.[44] Each asset is weighted by a multiplier (of 0%, 20%, 50%, 100% or 150%) depending on the type of borrower and the borrower's credit rating.[45] For instance, loans to central governments, insofar as they have a top credit rating, are weighted at 0% so that such loans trigger no capital requirement.

Nevertheless, recent evidence suggests that credit rating agencies are likely to consistently underestimate the risks associated with certain debts, due to conflicts of interest and the inherent limits of human rationality.[46] It follows that it may

40 Evidence suggests that differences in banking regulation regimes across countries were not correlated with bank performance during the recent crisis. See Andrea Beltratti and René Stulz, 'The Credit Crisis Around the Globe: Why Did Some Banks Perform Better?' (2012) 105 *Journal of Financial Economics* 1.

41 On this issue, see Future of Banking Commission, 'Final Report' (2010) 10 (recommendation 25) http://i.telegraph.co.uk/telegraph/multimedia/archive/01656/Bankpdf_1656684a.pdf accessed 1 May 2017.

42 See Basel II, paras 50–51; and CRR, art 143.

43 This area has remained largely the same as it was under Basel II despite the implementation of Basel III, CRD IV and CRR. The Standardised Approach is now set out in CRR arts 111–134.

44 CRR, art 112 identifies 17 different classes of exposure (assets).

45 In order for ratings to be eligible, that agency must qualify as an External Credit Assessment Institution (ECAI) under CRR, arts 135(1) and 138.

46 An in-depth analysis of the role and incentives of Credit Rating Agencies can be found in John Hunt, 'Credit Rating Agencies and the "Worldwide Credit Crisis": The Limits

well be the case that borrowers who are rated as risk-free (or of low risk), such as OECD governments and large banks, may turn out not to be creditworthy. Apart from failed financial institutions, the most notable example is the Greek government, the private creditors of which lost a substantial portion of their claims.[47] Banks have been responding to the said regulatory incentives by forwarding large amounts of credit to such creditors, which caused them to incur large losses in recent years. The serious failure of credit rating agencies to detect the forthcoming failures of large financial institutions and the eurozone sovereign debt crisis in a timely manner has undermined regulatory reliance on their ratings. Indeed, CRD IV (in line with Basel III)[48] requires competent authorities to encourage large institutions to develop internal capacity to assess credit risk, and to ensure that their methodologies do not rely solely or mechanistically on external credit ratings, but rather take into account other relevant information.[49]

Once the IRB Approach[50] is adopted, the importance of senior managers' incentives becomes even more evident. There are two versions of the IRB Approach: the foundation and the advanced.[51] Banks using the IRB Approach are expected to follow their own models to rate the creditworthiness of debtors and generally the risk associated with each type of asset they hold, within broad guidelines set by the relevant legislation and regulatory authorities. Indeed, CRR includes a series of technical requirements for institutions with permission to use the IRB Approach, which cover the classification of exposures into categories, the calculation of the probability of default and expected loss for various types of loans, and maturity adjustments.[52] Banks are thus given substantial discretion to calculate their own capital requirements with regard to credit risk.[53] Large UK banks follow the advanced IRB Approach for the majority of their assets, while they follow the foundation IRB Approach or the Standardised Approach for the rest of their assets.[54]

Given the emphasis of CRD IV on banks using their own methodologies to calculate credit risk, it can be safely assumed that the IRB Approach will continue to

of Reputation, the Insufficiency of Reform, and a Proposal for Improvement' (2009) *Columbia Business Law Review* 109.

47 Private bondholders suffered a haircut of 53.5%. See Eurogroup, 'Statement of 21 February 2012' (2012) www.consilium.europa.eu/uedocs/cms_data/docs/pressdata/en/ecofin/128075.pdf accessed 1 May 2017.

48 Basel III, para 119 requires banks not to rely totally on credit rating agencies and to consider whether the risk weights attached to their exposures, according to external ratings, are adequate.

49 CRD IV, arts 77–79.

50 See CRR, arts 142 and following.

51 Basel II, para 245.

52 See CRR, arts 151–184.

53 Similarly, banks can use their own methodologies to calculate operational risk. Broadly speaking, there is a choice between the Basic Indicator Approach, the Standardised Approach, and the Advanced Measurement Approach (CRR, art 312).

54 This can be seen in the annual reports and accounts of Barclays, HSBC, Lloyds Banking Group, Royal Bank of Scotland and Standard Chartered for 2016.

be the dominant method of calculating credit risk used by large UK banks. This regulatory technique is an example of reflexive regulation which aims to make the regulated entities take a proactive approach in ensuring that they are well capitalised. However, at the same time this structure creates a potential risk that banks will deliberately underestimate their credit risk exposures so as to escape stringent capital standards and thus increase their profits.[55] Granted, regulatory approval of the use of the internal approach and continuous supervision aim to prevent banks from underestimating their capital needs. Still, such regulatory measures cannot be relied on totally, because banks know more than regulators about the creditworthiness of their clients, and regulators lack the necessary resources to embark on an in-depth analysis of the exposures of all regulated banks. The opacity of banks' assets, explored in Chapter 1, is not only a limitation on market discipline but also a severe obstacle to the effective supervision of banks' asset quality by the relevant authorities.

Therefore, strengthening regulatory capital ratios does not necessarily imply that banks have adequate capital, as the experience of the last two decades suggests. Table 4.1 shows the evolution of the regulatory Tier 1 capital ratio[56] for major UK banks,[57] while Table 4.2 shows the evolution of their equity-to-assets ratio which is a measure of their overall leverage.[58] Equity includes called-up share capital, preference shares, the share premium account, the profit and loss account, other reserves, and minority interests (in subsidiaries of the group that are not wholly owned), so it is defined in the same way as Tier 1 capital.

Table 4.1 Tier 1 regulatory capital of major UK banks 2000–2016

Bank	*31/12/2000*	*31/12/2006*	*31/12/2012*	*31/12/2016*
Barclays	7.2%	7.7%	13.3%	14.2%
HSBC	9.0%	9.4%	13.4%	16.1%
HBOS	7.9%	8.1%	–	–
Lloyds	8.5%	8.2%	13.8%	17.0%
RBS	6.9%	7.5%	12.4%	15.2%
SCB	7.0%	7.5%	13.4%	15.7%

55 This claim is consistent with economic theory on capital requirements. An overview of relevant economic literature can be found in João Santos, 'Bank Capital Regulation in Contemporary Banking Theory: A Review of the Literature' (2001) 10 *Financial Markets, Institutions & Instruments* 41.

56 The CET1 ratio at the end of 2016 was: Barclays 12.4%, HSBC 13.6%, Lloyds 13.6%, RBS 13.4%, Standard Chartered Bank (SCB) 15.7%.

57 The group of major UK banks studied here includes all banks considered as major by the PRA (see above n 22), except for Nationwide which is a building society and hence has no equity capital, and Santander UK because it is a wholly owned Subsidiary of Grupo Santander SA.

58 All data are taken from the annual reports and accounts of the relevant banks, which can be found online.

Table 4.2 Equity-to-asset ratio of major UK banks 2000–2016

Bank	*31/12/2000*	*31/12/2006*	*31/12/2012*	*31/12/2016*
Barclays	4.17%	2.83%	4.22%	5.88%
HSBC	6.49%	5.97%	6.20%	7.69%
HBOS	4.10%	3.58%	–	–
Lloyds	4.57%	3.35%	4.83%	5.97%
RBS	7.22%	4.60%	5.19%	6.19%
SCB	5.74%	5.22%	7.24%	7.52%

The argument that, under the present corporate law framework, bank senior managers face a continuous incentive to seek to evade the effects of capital adequacy requirements is supported by the fact that the increased demands to hold regulatory capital in recent years (which is calculated as a percentage of risk-weighted assets) has not been consistently matched by a commensurate reduction in total leverage. Indeed, Table 4.1 demonstrates that all major UK banks *increased* their leverage during the 2000–2006 period, while at the same time they kept their regulatory capital stable or actually strengthened it. In this way, compliance with Basel II has arguably been used by banks to falsely demonstrate to the markets that they were strengthening their capital, while in reality they were taking more risks and increasing their leverage to unsustainable levels. This phenomenon is due to the opacity of banks' assets, and at the same time further exacerbates banks' opacity by using formal compliance with regulatory standards to signal substantial financial strength to the relevant markets. Of course, since 2007 there has been a considerable reduction in leverage but, still, one that does not match the impressive improvement in regulatory capital ratios.

At any rate, it is unclear whether modest decreases in leverage actually reduce the rational financial incentives of bank shareholders to support risk-taking.[59] In addition, to the extent that bank shareholders have a limited understanding of the amount of risk taken by banks, the risk appetite reduction effect of decreased leverage is weakened, as bank managers may take risks of which the shareholders are not fully aware, in order to achieve positive financial results. For instance, capital adequacy rules can lead to unintended consequences which undermine the stability of the financial system, if they are manipulated by profit-seeking bank managers. As explained above, capital adequacy rules create a powerful incentive for banks to move assets from their balance sheet to special purpose vehicles by securitising loans, as the experience of the 2007–2009 crisis suggests. Indeed, extensive use of securitisation during the years leading up to the recent crisis

59 *Prima facie*, reducing leverage should make rational bank shareholders more risk-averse, as they stand to lose more in case a bank fails. However, they 'may choose to compensate the loss in utility from the reduction in leverage with the choice of a riskier portfolio'. See Santos (above n 55), 53.

seriously undermined financial stability and contributed to the severity of the crisis by exacerbating the opacity of banks.[60]

II. Banks' corporate structure: ring-fencing as a partial revival of the separation between investment and retail banking

a. An overview of the UK ring-fencing regime and its limitations

One of the explanations for the 2007–2009 global financial crisis pointed to the combination of retail and investment banking activities in large financial conglomerates in the years leading up to the crisis.[61] The argument goes as follows. Retail banks are fundamentally simple to manage and are low-risk businesses that – under appropriate regulation and a deposit insurance scheme – would be very unlikely to fail and cause a systemic crisis. Conversely, investment banks are, by their very nature, high-risk entities which engage in speculative investments and are hence prone to insolvency. Therefore, some degree of separation of retail and investment banking activities, which might also have the positive side effect of reducing the overall size of very large financial institutions, has been proposed as a key reform to enhance financial stability and address the so-called too-big-to-fail problem.

Historically, a strict separation of retail and investment banking was followed in the US from the 1930s until the 1990s,[62] and in the UK until the mid-1980s.[63] Conversely, Germany and other European countries have traditionally supported financial conglomeration and universal banking under the assumption that it leads to greater stability. The 2007–2009 crisis has led to a limited reintroduction of structural separation of banking activities in the US, where the so-called Volcker rule prohibits banks from engaging in proprietary trading of securities and from investing in hedge funds and private equity funds.[64] In parallel, a milder form of

60 On the ways in which the securitisation of mortgages contributed to the 2007 crisis in the US, see Viral Acharya and Matthew Richardson, 'Causes of the Financial Crisis' (2009) 21 *Critical Review Journal of Politics and Society* 195. See also Orkun Akseli, 'Was Securitisation the Culprit? Explanation of Legal Processes Behind Creation of Mortgage-backed Sub-prime Securities' in Joanna Gray and Orkun Akseli (eds), *Financial Regulation in Crisis? The Role of Law and the Failure of Northern Rock* (Edward Elgar Publishing, 2011).

61 Mervyn King, the former governor of the Bank of England, and Vince Cable, the former UK business, innovation and skills secretary, have publicly supported the separation of retail and investment banks.

62 In the US, the Banking Act of 1933, commonly referred to as the Glass-Steagall Act, introduced the compulsory separation of retail and investment banking. The separation was abolished by the Financial Services Modernization Act of 1999 (known as the Gramm, Leach, Bliley Act), which allowed banks, brokerages and insurance companies to merge.

63 In the UK, until the mid-1980s, there was a uniform practice of separating retail and investment banking.

64 See Wall Street Reform and Consumer Protection Act of 2010 (Dodd-Frank Act), s 619.

separation, broadly known as ring-fencing, has been adopted in the UK.[65] Furthermore, the European Commission recently proposed the introduction of a rule similar to the Volcker rule for large EU banks,[66] which had a successful first reading at the Council in June 2015, but the relevant Regulation has not been passed yet.[67]

In the UK, the Financial Services (Banking Reform) Act 2013 introduced the ring-fencing of retail banking activities,[68] along the lines proposed in the influential report by the committee chaired by Sir John Vickers.[69] In brief, each banking group is expected to incorporate its domestic retail banking activities as a separate legal entity, the ring-fenced body, which will have to meet separate capital requirements. Certain activities, most notably deposit-taking,[70] money withdrawal facilities and overdraft facilities offered in the UK,[71] must be undertaken by the ring-fenced entity, while several other activities can be undertaken by it, with the exception of excluded activities such as proprietary trading.[72] The statutory aims of ring-fencing are to ensure the continuity of the provision of core financial services in the UK[73] and to protect depositors.[74] As envisaged by Vickers, ring-fencing is intended to facilitate the resolution of troubled banking groups and, in particular, to make it possible to allow the non-ring-fenced part of the group to fail, while securing the survival of the ring-fenced part and hence the undisrupted provision of key financial services.[75] The ring-fencing rules are expected to come

65 The Financial Services (Banking Reform) Act 2013 ss 1–12 introduced the ring-fencing of domestic retail banking activities within financial conglomerates as was proposed by the Vickers Report (below n 69) in 2011.

66 See Commission, 'Proposal for a Regulation of the European Parliament and of the Council on Structural Measures Improving the Resilience of EU Credit Institutions' *COM* (2014) 43 final, esp art 6. The proposal is based on the recommendations of the Liikanen Report. See Erki Liikanen, 'High-level Expert Group on Reforming the Structure of the EU Banking Sector: Final Report' (2012) http://ec.europa.eu/internal_market/bank/docs/high-level_expert_group/report_en.pdf accessed 1 May 2017.

67 See European Council, 'Structural Reform of EU Banking Sector: Improving the Resilience of Credit Institutions' (7 April 2016) www.consilium.europa.eu/en/policies/banking-structural-reform/ accessed 1 May 2017.

68 For a discussion of the benefits and limits of ring-fencing initiatives internationally, see Leonardo Gambacorta and Adrian van Rixtel, *Structural Bank Regulation Initiatives: Approaches and Implications* (BIS Working Paper 412, Bank for International Settlements Publications, 2013).

69 The Vickers Report recommended a mild form of separation of retail banking from investment banking known as ring-fencing of domestic retail activities, which are to be undertaken by a separate subsidiary with stronger capital and supervision. See Independent Commission on Banking, *Final Report: Recommendations* (Domarn Group 2011), esp para 9.2.

70 FSMA 2000 s 142B (2) to be inserted by Banking Reform Act s 4.

71 FSMA 2000 s 142C (2) to be inserted by Banking Reform Act s 4.

72 FSMA 2000 s 142D (2) to be inserted by Banking Reform Act s 4.

73 FSMA 2000 s 2B (3) (c) to be inserted by Banking Reform Act s 1.

74 FSMA 2000 s 142B (4) (a) to be inserted by Banking Reform Act s 4.

75 See Vickers Report (above n 69) paras 3.23 and 3.95–3.99.

into force on 1 January 2019 but, of course, most major UK banks have been preparing for their introduction since 2012.[76]

However, ring-fencing is only a mild form of separation of retail and investment banking activities within banking groups and hence its potential contribution to financial stability should not be overestimated.[77] In particular, ring-fencing is unlikely to enable the government to allow the non-ring-fenced part of banks to fail.[78] Indeed, it would be highly unlikely that ring-fenced entities would be able to survive the failure of the rest of the relevant banking group even if they were separately capitalised. It must be borne in mind that retail banks depend on the confidence of their depositors for their survival and that a serious crisis of confidence can diminish any retail bank to insolvency.[79] Allowing the biggest part of a banking group to fail would in all probability cause a creditors' run on the ring-fenced entity, which would then have to be supported by the government to prevent its collapse. Taking into account that the collapse of Lehman Brothers and other investment banks led to systemic contagion in various banks across the world, it is highly likely that the collapse of the investment banking part of a banking group would lead to devastating consequences for the ring-fenced entity. Moreover, the collapse of the non-ring-fenced part of a large banking group would be likely to trigger a systemic crisis *per se*, as the non-ring-fenced parts of groups are expected to include at least two-thirds and up to four-fifths of large banks' assets.[80]

The argument here does not seek to downplay the importance of ring-fencing. Ring-fencing is likely to serve as a useful crisis management tool[81] by ensuring that

76 There have been, at the time of writing, 11 Commencement Orders relating to the Banking Act 2013, two of which are relevant to ring-fencing. Indeed, the Financial Services (Banking Reform) Act 2013 (Commencement No. 1) Order 2014 (SI 2014/377) brought into force section 6 and Schedule 1 of the Act on ring-fencing transfer schemes on 1 March 2014; and the Financial Services (Banking Reform) Act 2013 (Commencement No. 10) Order 2016 (SI 2016/512) brought into force section 4 of the Act on ring-fencing of certain activities for the purposes of inserting section 142H into the FSMA 2000 (enabling the PRA to issue ring-fencing rules) on 21 April 2016. The relevant PRA instrument will come into force on 1 January 2019. See PRA Rulebook: CRR Firms and Non-Authorised Persons: Ring-fencing Instrument 2017, para E.

77 For a critical analysis of ring-fencing, see Policy Exchange, *Ringfencing UK Banks: More of a Problem than a Solution*, James Barty ed (Heron, Dawson and Sawyer, 2013).

78 On this, see Mads Andenas and Iris H-Y Chiu, *The Foundations and Future of Financial Regulation: Governance for Responsibility* (Routledge, 2014), 304.

79 On this see Chapter 3, section I.

80 The services that must be provided by ring-fenced entities amount to 18% of UK banks' assets, while those that may be provided by them amount to another 18%. Vickers Report (above n 69), para 3.40. It can be reasonably expected that banks will keep ring-fenced entities as small as possible to avoid any additional regulatory burden.

81 At the same time, the international implementation of varying degrees of ring-fencing may encourage globally active banks to adopt complex business structures that are ultimately more difficult to supervise and resolve. See Gambacorta and van Rixtel (above n 68), 16–17.

vital utility-type services are not disrupted in times of crisis. Still, ring-fencing cannot *per se* solve the fundamental problem emanating from the fact that the failure of a large (retail or investment) bank leads to negative consequences for the financial system as a whole. It follows that the introduction of ring-fencing does not undermine the importance of aligning corporate law as it applies to financial institutions with the objectives of prudential regulation, as advocated in the present study. Indeed, the Vickers Report envisages that the board of the ring-fenced entity will be focused on preserving the safety and soundness of the ring-fenced entity.[82]

This is, of course, contingent on the corporate law and corporate governance rules that will apply to ring-fenced entities. More broadly, given the fact that the ultimate parent or holding company will continue to exercise effective control over the boards of ring-fenced bodies, by virtue of its power to appoint and remove their members, it follows that for ring-fencing to be effective the corporate governance regime for the entire banking group – including the ultimate parent company – needs to be aligned to the regulatory objectives. Therefore, the pending introduction of ring-fenced retail banking subsidiaries within banking groups does not build a case for implementing a special corporate governance regime only for the ring-fenced entities, but rather for entire banking groups. At any rate, the same reasons that support the introduction of a special governance regime for ring-fenced entities also apply to other parts of banking groups. Indeed, systemic risk, asset opacity, and peculiar capital structure are characteristics of all main types of banking activities.[83] Furthermore, any such differentiation would create a powerful incentive for banks to move activities outside ring-fenced bodies so as to avoid any additional regulatory governance requirements imposed exclusively on ring-fenced bodies.

b. The limitations of an alternative policy of strict separation

A strict separation of retail and investment banking would entail the complete break-up of financial conglomerates, as investment and retail banking activities would have to be undertaken by completely separate corporate entities with no material share ownership links.[84] It follows that retail banking activities ought to be completely separate from investment banking activities so that the failure of an

82 To that effect, the Vickers Report recommends that the majority of the directors of the ring-fenced entity be independent and different from the directors of the parent. See Vickers Report (above n 69) para 9.2 (5) (g).

83 On asset opacity see Chapter 1, section III; and on systemic risk see Chapter 3, section I.

84 A similar proposal forwarded by Avgouleas advocates a three-tier separation as follows: banks that are only allowed to engage in retail banking; retail banks that can also engage in a limited set of capital market transactions; and investment banks that cannot accept deposits. See Emilios Avgouleas, 'The Reform of the "Too-Big-To-Fail" Bank: A New Regulatory Model for the Institutional Separation of "Casino" from "Utility" Banking' (2010) https://papers.ssrn.com/sol3/papers.cfm?abstract_id=1552970&rec=1&srcabs=1525670&alg=1&pos=6 accessed 1 May 2017.

investment bank would have no immediate consequence on retail banks. It is envisaged that under a regime of strict separation, the relevant national government would be able to allow investment banks to fail, and thus market discipline would be restored. It is also argued that a strict separation would reduce contagion and systemic risk in the financial sector, and that the economic benefits of combining retail and investment banking activities are overstated. An argument in favour of this approach is that structural separation has the potential to restore public confidence in banking and to mitigate existing concerns about a perceived lack of legitimacy with respect to the enormous economic influence of financial conglomerates.[85] According to this school of thought, a special corporate law regime is not necessary either for retail or for investment banks: the former are presumed to be inherently safe and sound utility-type institutions under strict regulation, and the latter would be allowed to take risks and potentially fail in the same way as any other non-financial company.[86]

It is not within the scope of the present monograph to assess the substantive merits of a strict separation of retail and investment banking, as such evaluation would require balancing the expected costs and benefits that such a reform would bring, which is ultimately a matter for empirical econometric research. It is sufficient to say that a reintroduction of a strict separation of banking activities would be very costly (due to the loss of economies of scale and scope[87] and the costs of transition), and would place UK banks at a competitive disadvantage compared to other banks, while it is not automatically clear that it would prevent the occurrence of financial crises or resolve the too-big-to-fail conundrum. Indeed, longer-term empirical evidence also undermines the presumption that the stability of a financial system is related to its structure.[88]

The experience of the recent crisis demonstrates that bank failures were primarily triggered by losses incurred by the retail banking activities of banks and that most losses ultimately originated from such activities (primarily from mortgage lending).[89] Indeed, Northern Rock and HBOS were mostly focused on retail

85 In this vein, Zingales has argued that structural separation would promote competition and limit the lobbying power of large banks. See Luigi Zingales, *Capitalism for the People: Recapturing the Lost Genius of American Capitalism* (Basic Books, 2012).

86 For instance, Kay has advocated the creation of narrow banks to fulfil retail banking functions that are completely separate from entities providing other financial services, with the latter being allowed to fail and thus being fully subject to market forces. See John Kay, 'Narrow Banking: The Reform of Banking Regulation' (2009) www.johnkay.com/2009/09/15/narrow-banking/ accessed 1 May 2017.

87 There is strong evidence on economies of scale and scope in continental European banking systems. See Yener Altunbas and Phil Molyneux, 'Economies of Scale and Scope in European Banking' (1996) 6 *Applied Financial Economics* 367.

88 On this, see John D Turner, *Banking in Crisis: The Rise and Fall of British Banking Stability, 1800 to the Present* (CUP, 2014), 65.

89 Indeed, Wallison argues that structural reform cannot prevent bad business decisions that can make any type of financial institution fail, even a narrow bank. See Peter Wallison, 'Did the "Repeal" of the Glass-Steagall Have any Role in the Financial Crisis? Not Even Close' (2009) 106 *Public Lawyer* 102.

banking, while RBS's losses came primarily from the retail banking part of the group.[90] In addition, the far-reaching consequences of allowing Lehman Brothers to fail in 2007 and the subsequent state rescue of AIG undermines the argument that investment banks can be allowed to fail without any consequences to financial stability, on the basis that they do not accept deposits.[91] Even more importantly, a strict separation could increase the concentration of risk to the non-retail sector thus increasing systemic risk.[92]

Furthermore, a mandatory strict separation of retail and investment banking would create a strong incentive for UK banks to move to other jurisdictions, and would place the UK banking industry in an unfavourable position in relation to foreign competitors. A globally harmonised approach to this issue would address these concerns, but such harmonisation is very unlikely to happen in the foreseeable future. A separation would also reduce the capacity of retail banks to advance credit, as part of bank lending is funded by activities other than deposit-taking. A restriction of available funding[93] would significantly delay economic growth and thus lead to a lower level of economic development in the long run. Finally, under a strict separation regime the profitability of retail banks would significantly decrease, as the investment banking activities of universal banks generally contribute a disproportionately high percentage of banks' total profits. This would make it more difficult for retail banks to raise enough equity capital to comply with the strengthened capital adequacy requirements.[94] At the same time, shadow banking, that is unregulated entities engaging in financial transactions, would – in all likelihood – develop exponentially with all the possible risks that this would engender for financial stability and consumer protection.[95]

At any rate, it is highly unlikely that a strict separation of retail and investment banking will be implemented in the UK. Given that reforming bank corporate governance is much easier to implement than introducing a strict separation of banking activities, the approach proposed herein can be viewed as a realistic alternative to a radical structural reform of the banking sector, even if one takes the

90 See Policy Exchange (above n 77), ch 3.

91 A succinct account of the reasons that led Lehman to fail can be found in Joel Spina, 'The Failure of Lehman Brothers' (10 July 2013) http://papers.ssrn.com/sol3/papers.cfm?abstract_id=2337124 accessed 1 May 2017.

92 Julian TS Chow and Jay Surti, 'Making Banks Safer: Can Volcker and Vickers Do it?' (IMF Working Paper WP/11/236, October 2011) https://papers.ssrn.com/sol3/papers.cfm?abstract_id=1945623&rec=1&srcabs=1945621 accessed 1 May 2017.

93 'British banks adopted this new model enthusiastically, and by 2008 were lending out around £800bn more than they had on deposit.' See Parliamentary Commission on Banking Standards, *Changing Banking for Good* (2013–14, HL 27-II, HC 175-II) 14.

94 This would be caused by the reluctance of investors to buy bank shares due to the lower profitability of the latter.

95 For a detailed discussion of the notion of shadow banking, see Melanie L Fein, 'The Shadow Banking Charade' (2013), 3–11 https://papers.ssrn.com/sol3/papers.cfm?abstract_id=2218812 accessed 1 May 2017.

view that such structural reform would undermine the importance of corporate governance reforms.

III. The EU banking recovery and resolution framework and its implementation in the UK

The final area of regulation that relates to bank capital and corporate structure to be discussed is the rules regarding bank recovery and resolution. Amongst other weaknesses, the 2007–2009 crisis exposed the inadequacy of the previously available regulatory tools to respond to bank distress and failure. To resolve this problem, the Banking Act 2009 introduced a special insolvency framework for banks which focuses on rescuing their business, described as the special resolution regime.[96] The regime originally consisted of three stabilisation options, namely: private sector purchase, creation of a bridge bank as a subsidiary of the Bank of England, and temporary public ownership.[97] A fourth option, bail-in stabilisation, was added as a result of the Financial Services (Banking Reform) Act 2013.[98] In cases where rescuing a troubled bank is not considered to be necessary by reference to the relevant statutory objectives, a special bank administration and bank liquidation procedure apply.[99] The threshold for the exercise of the relevant powers of the Bank of England is satisfied when a bank fails or is likely to fail to meet the general authorisation criteria set out by the FSMA 2000.[100]

In parallel, the Financial Services Act 2010 introduced a requirement for regulated institutions to draft recovery and resolution plans, also known as living wills.[101] Recovery plans aim to facilitate the rescue of the business of a troubled financial company as a going concern so as to avoid systemic contagion which may be triggered by a failure. Resolution plans aim to ensure an orderly winding-up in the event of failure in order to minimise systemic disruption.[102] Recovery and resolution plans are to be evaluated by the relevant authority, currently the PRA, and if found inadequate, the institution in question must take all appropriate steps

96 For a conceptual framework of the functions and objectives of special resolution regimes see Gustaf Sjoberg, 'Banking Special Resolution Regimes as a Governance Tool' in Wolf-Georg Ringe and Peter Huber (eds), *Legal Challenges in the Global Financial Crisis* (Hart Publishing, 2014). See also Andrew Campbell, 'Northern Rock, the financial crisis and the Special Resolution Regime' in Joanna Gray and Orkun Akseli (eds), *Financial Regulation in Crisis? The Role of Law and the Failure of Northern Rock* (Edward Elgar Publishing, 2011).

97 Banking Act 2009, ss 1 (3), 11, 12, 13.

98 Banking Act 2009 new ss 12A-12B (to be inserted by Banking Reform Act 2013 Schedule 2, s 2).

99 Banking Act 2009, s 4 (4)–(10).

100 Banking Act 2009, s 7.

101 Financial Services Act 2010, s 7 introduced ss 139B – 139F into FSMA 2000.

102 A discussion of the complex issues arising out of the resolution of systemic banks can be found in Stijn Claessens, Richard Herring and Dirk Schoenmaker, *A Safer World Financial System: Improving the Resolution of Systemic Institutions* (Centre for Economic Policy Research, 2010).

to amend them. Of course, there is now a harmonised recovery and resolution framework across the EU subsequent to the full coming into force of the Bank Recovery and Resolution Directive (BRRD) at the beginning of 2016.[103]

The principal aim of BRRD is to harmonise the process for resolving ailing financial institutions with a view to achieving an orderly resolution, particularly in the case of cross-border institutions, while ensuring the continuity of failed institutions' critical financial and economic functions.[104] This is envisaged to be achieved by placing the cost of failure first on shareholders and then on unprotected creditors while the Directive seeks to minimise any cost to taxpayers.[105] To this effect, BRRD requires credit institutions and investment firms to draw up recovery plans and resolution plans which are then to be approved by the competent national resolution authority[106] – in the case of the UK, the PRA, which has issued a policy statement setting out the regulatory rules that implement the Directive.[107] Interestingly, resolution plans cannot assume any extraordinary public financial support nor any emergency liquidity assistance provided by a central bank.[108] Of crucial importance from our perspective are the BRRD provisions on bail-in which seek to ensure that some of the obligations of financial institutions are converted into equity or written down in case of failure. Indeed, BRRD emphasises the use of debt capital as a means to absorb bank losses in advance of using public funds,[109] thus implementing relevant international standards.[110] State aid can only be provided once at least 8% of an ailing bank's liabilities have been written off.[111]

Nevertheless, the Directive excludes from the scope of the bail-in tool several categories of liabilities, most notably: protected deposits; liabilities arising out of holding clients' assets; liabilities by virtue of fiduciary relationships; liabilities to

103 Directive 2014/59/EU of the European Parliament and of the Council of 15 May 2014 establishing a framework for the recovery and resolution of credit institutions and investment firms and amending Council Directive 82/891/EEC, and Directives 2001/24/EC, 2002/47/EC, 2004/25/EC, 2005/56/EC, 2007/36/EC, 2011/35/EU, 2012/30/EU and 2013/36/EU, and Regulations (EU) No 1093/2010 and (EU) No 648/2012, of the European Parliament and of the Council [2014] OJ L173/190, art 130 (1).

104 Ibid., Preamble paras 3–4.

105 Ibid., Preamble para 5. On this, see Christos Hadjiemmanuil, 'The Bank Recovery and Resolution Directive in Context' in Jens-Hinrich Binder and Dalvinder Singh (eds), *Bank Resolution: The European Regime* (OUP, 2016).

106 BRRD, arts 5–12. Discussed in Dalvinder Singh, 'Recovery and Resolution Planning: Reconfiguring Financial Regulation and Supervision' in Jens-Hinrich Binder and Dalvinder Singh (eds), *Bank Resolution: The European Regime* (OUP, 2016).

107 PRA, 'Implementing the Bank Recovery and Resolution Directive' (Policy Statement PS1/15, January 2015) www.bankofengland.co.uk/pra/Pages/publications/ps/2015/recoveryresolutionupdate.aspx accessed 1 May 2017.

108 BRRD, art 10 (3).

109 Ibid., arts 34, 40–44 and 63.

110 International resolution standards were drafted by the FSB and endorsed by G-20 leaders in 2011. See Financial Stability Board, 'Key Attributes of Effective Resolution Regimes for Financial Institutions' (2011) www.fsb.org/wp-content/uploads/r_111104cc.pdf accessed 1 May 2017.

111 BRRD, art 37 (10) (a).

employees in relation to accrued salaries, debts to commercial or trade creditors for the supply of goods or services that are critical for the daily operations of the institution; and debts to tax and social security authorities.[112] These exemptions are consistent with the Directive's policy to protect depositor and customer confidence in financial institutions and also to safeguard public funds and vulnerable creditors such as employees.

Of course, it remains to be seen whether the use of bail-in powers will actually enhance financial stability or not. Hadjiemmanuil, for instance, highlights the inherent inconsistency between: on the one hand, the policy objective of reducing moral hazard by ensuring that shareholders and debt-holders suffer losses; and, on the other, the objective of reducing contagion when a crisis occurs, which militates against imposing losses to debt-holders as doing so undermines investor confidence in other banks within the same financial system.[113] Overall, although these reforms have undermined the perception of an implied government guarantee on bonds issued by banks, it remains to be seen to what extent they will be used in practice when a systemic crisis occurs.[114] The possibility of regulatory authorities or governments negotiating with ailing bank boards and offering them indirect state aid remains open, although of dubious legality under EU law, as suggested by the example of the crisis faced by the Italian Banca Monte dei Paschi di Siena S.p.A.[115] In the UK, in view of Brexit, there may be, in the foreseeable future, even broader legal flexibility to provide ailing financial institutions with state aid. In any case, even if bail-in is uniformly implemented in the future, it does not remove the fundamental problem of bank asset opacity.

112 BRRD, art 44 (2). For a detailed discussion of the new bail-in powers of the PRA, see Stephen J Connelly, 'The Implementation of the EU Bank Recovery and Resolution Directive's Derivative Bail-in Powers in the UK' in Jens-Hinrich Binder and Dalvinder Singh (eds), *Bank Resolution: The European Regime* (OUP, 2016). See also the speech given by the director of the Bank of England Special Resolution Unit, Andrew Gracie, 'A Practical Process for Implementing a Bail-in Resolution Power' (British Bankers' Association, London, September 2012) www.bankofengland.co.uk/archive/Documents/historicpubs/speeches/2012/speech600.pdf accessed 1 May 2017.

113 A critical discussion of special resolution regimes can be found in Christos Hadjiemmanuil, 'Special Resolution Regimes for Banking Institutions: Objectives and Limitations' in Wolf-Georg Ringe and Peter Huber (eds), *Legal Challenges in the Global Financial Crisis* (Hart Publishing, 2014), 232–234.

114 Avgouleas and Goodhart argue that the bail-in regime will fail to eradicate the need to inject public funds where several banks have simultaneously entered into difficulties, and therefore that its use will be limited to idiosyncratic bank failures. See Emilios Avgouleas and Charles Goodhart, 'Critical Reflections on Bank Bail-ins' (2015) 1 *Journal of Financial Regulation* 3.

115 The Italian government attempted in December 2016 to recapitalise the ailing bank, claiming it is solvent so as to avoid the application of the bail-in provisions. The implementation of the recapitalisation was, at the time of writing, still pending as ECB and Commission approval had not yet been granted. See Alex Barker, Claire Jones and Rachel Sanderson, 'Brussels and ECB Split on Monte dei Paschi's Capital Proposals' *Financial Times* (London, 23 February 2017).

Furthermore, an additional tool for the recovery and resolution of financial institutions advocated by the Basel Committee is the use of bonds known as contingent convertible bonds.[116] When an institution's recovery plan is triggered, any contingent convertible bonds are converted into common equity thus increasing the institution's core capital ratio and facilitating its recovery. Such bonds have been issued successfully by Lloyds in the UK and by several European banks.[117] Crucially from our perspective, contingent convertible bonds can in theory play a corporate governance function as it is clearly in the best interests of their holders for financial institutions to follow prudent strategies that guarantee their solvency in the long term.[118] In this sense, the holders of contingent convertible bonds have very different interests from shareholders who, as explained in Chapter 1, are keen for institutions to take any risks that maximise their total expected value. However, the opacity of bank assets makes it difficult for such benefits to materialise,[119] especially since bank directors owe no fiduciary duties to bondholders, and bondholders have no voting rights or other form of corporate representation. At any rate, any such governance benefits can only materialise if contingent convertible bonds become a major source of capital for institutions.[120]

IV. Conclusions

The discussion in this chapter highlighted the range of ambitious reforms in the areas of capital adequacy, bank structure and bank resolution that have been implemented since the 2007–2009 financial crisis, and the limitations of such reforms. By analysing these limitations, it was by no means intended to undermine the positive contribution of the reforms in question to financial stability. Rather, the aim of the chapter was to demonstrate that a supporting corporate law and corporate governance regime – that is, one aligning directorial and managerial incentives with regulatory objectives – could work as a vital complement to capital adequacy, ring-fencing and resolution rules. Conversely, the current corporate law regime, which – in practice if not in theory – is prone to align managers' interests with the short-term interests of existing shareholders, is likely to operate

116 See Basel Committee on Banking Supervision, *Resolution Policies and Frameworks – Progress So Far* (Bank for International Settlements Publications, 2011), para 83. See also Charles W Calomiris and Charles M Kahn, 'The Role of Demandable Debt in Structuring Optimal Banking Arrangements' (1991) 81 *American Economic Review* 497.

117 See Jennifer Hughes, 'Cocos and Bail-in Share Common Goal' *Financial Times* (London, 20 February 2011).

118 There is also empirical evidence confirming that bondholders influence issuing companies to manage their risks more prudently. See Tao-Hsien Dolly King and Min-Ming Wen, 'Shareholder Governance, Bondholder Governance and Managerial Risk-taking' (2011) 35 *Journal of Banking and Finance* 512.

119 See Chapter 1, section IV.

120 On this, see Charles W Calomiris and Richard J Herring, 'Why and How to Design a Contingent Convertible Debt Requirement' (2011) https://ssrn.com/abstract=1815406 accessed 1 May 2017.

antagonistically to the capital adequacy regime and thus to undermine the effectiveness of the new rules.

It follows that a complete prudential regulatory framework ought to incorporate the corporate law and governance framework for systemically important financial institutions. This, of course, would necessitate a radical reconceptualisation of financial institution corporate governance, moving from the current facilitative and shareholder-centric approach to a regulatory approach. The next chapter illustrates that this has already been partially accepted by policy-makers and that there is currently an extensive nexus of regulatory rules affecting board structure, selection of directors and senior managers, executive remuneration, risk management, and director and senior manager liability in banks and – to some extent – other financial institutions. However, it will also be argued that this framework remains incomplete and that further reform is necessary to align the corporate law framework for financial institutions with regulatory objectives.

5 Post-crisis reforms and their limitations

Regulating the qualities and incentives of financial institution directors and senior managers

This chapter explores the regulatory rules affecting financial institutions' internal governance that have been introduced in the aftermath of the 2007–2009 crisis. Some of these rules regulate areas that were never regulated before such as institutions' board structure, risk management function and executive remuneration, while others strengthen long-standing areas of prudential regulation such as the requirement that senior managers are fit and proper, and the power of the authority to impose regulatory sanctions on senior managers. It will be shown that the combined effect of all these rules is the creation of a unique corporate governance framework for banks and other financial institutions, which shares some elements with the broader corporate law framework applicable to all public companies but is clearly distinct from it, as it contains many regulatory rules that are mandatory in nature and aim to safeguard systemic stability rather than maximise shareholder value.[1] However, it will also be demonstrated that the resulting framework remains heavily influenced by the traditional corporate law emphasis on shareholder empowerment and shareholder value maximisation, and therefore that the incipient transformation of the corporate law framework for financial institutions remains unfinished.

To that effect, the chapter is structured as follows. Section I sets out the soft-law and regulatory rules regarding financial institutions' board structure and the organisation of their risk management function. Section II explores the detailed regulatory framework in place on senior executive remuneration in banks with special emphasis on the CRD IV rules that limit the amount of variable remuneration paid as a percentage of fixed remuneration. Section III will trace the evolution of the 'fit and proper' requirement for bank senior managers and will focus on the recently introduced Senior Persons Regime applicable to banks, investment firms and insurance companies. Then, section IV will examine the regulatory rules that enable regulators to pursue individual enforcement against

1 Of course, the gradual 'juridification' of corporate governance is by no means exclusive to bank corporate governance, albeit it is more evident in this context. Indeed, in recent years the regulatory aspects of general corporate governance law have increased exponentially both in the UK and the US. On this see Marc T Moore, *Corporate Governance in the Shadow of the State* (Hart Publishing, 2013), 177–226.

financial institutions' senior managers and will explore the way the PRA has used these powers in recent enforcement cases arising out of the Co-operative Bank crisis in 2013. Section V concludes.

I. Regulating financial institutions' board structure and internal risk management function

Part of the international regulatory response to the 2007–2009 financial crisis was a series of reforms in financial institution corporate governance beginning with the publication of the Basel Principles for Enhancing Corporate Governance in late 2010.[2] The Principles focus on effective boards, sound risk management, executive remuneration, the simplification of group structures, and transparency. They are modelled on the OECD Principles of Corporate Governance,[3] which are not bank-specific. Indeed, apart from their emphasis on risk management evinced in the requirements for a board risk committee, a chief risk officer (CRO) and the scrutiny of new products and mergers, the Basel Principles do not differentiate financial institution corporate governance from the governance of non-financial companies.

Although significant in achieving a degree of international convergence in the area, the Basel Principles did not add much to the UK corporate governance regime for financial institutions, as their recommendations were already in place, subsequent to the regulatory implementation of the Walker Review, discussed below, and the 2010 revision of the UK Corporate Governance Code which emphasised the importance of risk management.[4] From the point of view of the discussion herein, the most notable contribution of the Basel Principles is that they illustrate the attitude of major regulators worldwide about corporate governance in financial institutions. First, it is acknowledged that corporate governance is 'of great relevance'[5] both at the micro-level of individual institutions and at the macro-level of the stability of financial systems, since it can provide proper incentives to senior managers, facilitate supervision and foster market confidence. Second, the recent crisis is seen as partly due to governance failures,[6] since poor

2 See Working Group on Corporate Governance of the Basel Committee, *Principles for Enhancing Corporate Governance*, Nouy Daniele and others (Bank for International Settlements Publications, 2010).

3 The Principles were last revised in April 2004 and are at the time of writing under review. See Organisation for Economic Co-operation and Development, 'G20/ OECD Principles of Corporate Governance' (2004) www.oecd.org/corporate/oecdprinciplesofcorporategovernance.htm accessed 1 May 2017.

4 On this, see Marc T Moore, 'The Evolving Contours of the Board's Risk Management Function in UK Corporate Governance' (2010) 10 *Journal of Corporate Law Studies* 279, 297–300.

5 See *Principles for Enhancing Corporate Governance* (above n 2), 1–2.

6 This is also widely accepted in the literature. See e.g. Jaap Winter, 'The Financial Crisis: Does Good Corporate Governance Matter and How to Achieve it?' in Eddy Wymeersch, Klaus Hopt and Guido Ferranini (eds), *Financial Regulation and Supervision: A Post-crisis Analysis* (OUP, 2012).

governance is liable to lead both to individual failures and to wider problems, due to loss of confidence in the financial markets.[7] Third, great emphasis is placed on the role of supervisors[8] who are expected to evaluate the corporate governance structures of individual financial institutions – including the expertise and integrity of prospective directors and senior managers – and to have formal powers to take remedial action should the governance of a bank be judged to be defective. For instance, the experience of the recent crisis illustrates that the failure of boards to be involved meaningfully in strategy-setting, and the consequent complete delegation of strategy development to executive management was central to the governance failures of both RBS[9] and HBOS.[10] Therefore, the effective safeguarding of financial stability requires prudential regulators to assess the adequacy of the governance practices followed by financial institutions.

From a regulatory perspective, firms are required to have in place an effective governance system to ensure that their governing body – that is the board of directors in the case of companies – has overall responsibility to ensure compliance with the relevant regulatory rules and principles. This entails having a clear and transparent organisational structure, sound administration and accounting procedures, and effective risk management processes.[11] The requirement to have in place appropriate systems and controls applies in a way that is proportionate to firm size, complexity, diversity of operations, volume of transactions and level of risk.[12]

In the UK, the influential review by Sir David Walker[13] introduced, for the first time, a set of corporate governance rules and principles applicable exclusively to banks and other major financial institutions.[14] Similarly to the UK Corporate Governance Code, the Review intended its recommendations to be enforced on a comply-or-explain basis.[15] The Review does not challenge the shareholder-centric orientation of bank corporate governance but rather limits itself to incremental improvements without proposing a new conceptual framework which would serve as the basis for a more fundamental re-evaluation of the

7 See *Principles for Enhancing Corporate Governance* (above n 2), 5.
8 Ibid., 30–32.
9 See FSA, 'The Failure of the Royal Bank of Scotland: Financial Services Authority Board Report' (2011), paras 591–593 www.fsa.gov.uk/pubs/other/rbs.pdf accessed 1 May 2017.
10 See Parliamentary Commission on Banking Standards, *'An Accident Waiting to Happen': The Failure of HBOS* (2012–13, HL 144, HC 705), paras 91–92.
11 See CRD IV, art 76 (1) and (2) applying to deposit-taking institutions; and Solvency II, arts 40–41 applying to insurance undertakings.
12 PRA Rulebook, CRR Firms, Risk Control 2.5.
13 David Walker, 'A Review of Corporate Governance in UK Banks and Other Financial Industry Entities: Final Recommendations' (2009) www.icaew.com/en/library/subject-gateways/corporate-governance/codes-and-reports/walker-report accessed 1 May 2017. To be abbreviated from now on as the 'Walker Review'.
14 Ibid., para 1.22.
15 Ibid., paras 2.16–2.19. It is notable that despite the original intention of Sir David Walker there is no formal obligation for banks to disclose whether they comply with the recommendations or not, as is the case with respect to the UK Corporate Governance Code.

corporate governance of banks.[16] Its recommendations remain within the traditional agency costs paradigm, dominant since the time of the Cadbury Committee. Consequently, the Review preserves the corporate objective of profit maximisation at the heart of banks' corporate governance model. Admittedly, it would not be feasible for the Review to introduce a change in this regard, as the shareholder-centric orientation of UK corporate governance is embedded in statutory provisions,[17] but the Review actively endorsed shareholder value maximisation as the key duty of bank and other financial institution directors rather than proposing an alternative perspective on the purposes of corporate governance in financial institutions.

Instead, the Review focused on three areas of financial institution corporate governance, perceived to be weak, namely: the competence of independent directors; risk management; and the remuneration of executive directors and senior managers, which will be discussed in the next section. Regarding independent director competence, the Review recommends that a majority of non-executive directors (NEDs) possess relevant financial experience, and that NEDs are offered individually tailored induction and training, and thematic business awareness sessions.[18] Notably, the Review recommends that more time must be committed by financial institution NEDs than was previously the case, and that normally this should mean 30–36 days annually, compared to a pre-existing practice of approximately 25 days annually,[19] and that board chairmen devote around two-thirds of their working time to their role.[20]

In addition, CRD IV introduced several mandatory rules regulating the structure of bank boards. The Directive's approach to the composition of bank boards is based on the acceptance of five uncontroversial general principles, namely sufficient collective knowledge, time commitment, adequate resources, diversity, and honesty.[21] Crucially, CRD IV precludes banks from combining the positions of CEO and chairman of the board without the consent of the regulator,[22] and requires nomination committees to consist exclusively of non-executive directors.[23] Although these requirements coincide with the existing recommendations of the Corporate Governance Code[24] and – to a large extent – with the actual practice of

16 Ibid., Annex 3, 137 states that: 'To dilute the primacy of the duty of the BOFI director to shareholders to accommodate a new accountability to other stakeholders would risk changing fundamentally *the contractual and legal basis on which the UK market economy operates.* It would introduce potentially substantial new uncertainty for shareholders as to the value of their holdings and would be likely to lead to shareholder exodus from the sector and a rise in the cost of capital for BOFIs' (emphasis added).
17 See Companies Act 2006, ss 168, 171, 172, 304, 305, 314, 561 and 983.
18 Walker Review (above n 13), paras 3.13 and 3.16.
19 Ibid., para 3.23.
20 Ibid., para 4.18.
21 See CRD IV art 91 (1), (2) and (7)–(9).
22 CRD IV art 88 (1) (e).
23 CRD IV art 88 (2).
24 See CG Code, paras A.2.1 and B.2.1, respectively.

UK banks,[25] the 'juridification' of the relevant rules from 'comply-or-explain' soft law (enforceable by market pressure) to compulsory regulatory standards is noticeable. Furthermore, CRD IV imposes a cap on parallel board appointments to the effect that the same person cannot hold more than: either one executive and two non-executive appointments; or four non-executive appointments.[26] Appointments at not-for-profit organisations and charities are excluded from the cap,[27] and competent regulators are given the discretion to allow bank directors to hold one additional non-executive position.[28]

With regard to risk management,[29] the Walker Review emphasises that the risk mitigation function of bank boards should be no longer confined to peripheral risks but, rather, cover risks that are intrinsic to banks' business. All of the main recommendations of the Review are now included in the PRA Rulebook as mandatory requirements, and many are also part of the new CRD IV framework. Bank boards are thus expected to shape the risk appetite and tolerance of banks in a forward-looking way.[30] Boards are expected to be served by risk committees consisting of non-executive directors,[31] which should focus on major prudential risks[32] and encourage due diligence and in-depth risk scrutiny by the board of major strategic transactions, such as acquisitions and disposals.[33] Moreover, large financial institutions should be served by a CRO[34] to oversee risk on an enterprise-wide basis. CROs are to have a substantial degree of independence from CEOs, in the sense that they can only be removed by the board and they have direct access to the board.[35] Beyond this, the rules require that a firm's risk management function be independent from its operational functions and able to report directly to the board.[36]

25 All major UK banks operate fully independent nominations committees, and have a separate board chairman and CEO, although board chairmen are not always independent, the most notable example being the case of HSBC. On this, see Chapter 2, n 128 and accompanying text.
26 The cap will be effective on 1 July 2014. See CRD IV art 91 (3).
27 CRD IV art 91 (5).
28 CRD IV art 91 (6).
29 A general discussion of the nature of risk and of risk management in complex organisations can be found in Power's work. Michael Power, *Organized Uncertainty: Designing a World of Risk Management* (OUP, 2007). For a post-crisis critique, see Gabriele Sabato, 'Financial Crisis: Where Did Risk Management Fail?' (2010) 2 *International Review of Applied Financial Issues and Economics* 315.
30 Walker Review (above n 13), para 6.22.
31 CRD IV, art 76 (3) requires member states to ensure that large banks establish a risk committee. See also PRA Rulebook, CRR Firms, Risk Control 3.1 (1).
32 Walker Review (above n 13), para 6.21. The functions of risk committees are set out in detail in PRA Rulebook, CRR Firms, Risk Control 3.1 (2) and (3).
33 Walker Review (above n 13), para 6.31.
34 For an early discussion of the role of chief risk officers, see Andre Liebenberg and Robert Hoyt, 'The Determinants of Enterprise Risk Management: Evidence from the Appointment of Chief Risk Officers' (2003) 6 *Risk Management & Insurance Review* 37.
35 PRA Rulebook, CRR Firms, Risk Control 3.5. See also Walker Review (above n 13), para 6.12.
36 PRA Rulebook, CRR Firms, Risk Control 3.4.

At the European level, the EBA has recently issued a consultation paper as part of the process to amend its guidelines on firms' internal governance in order to further emphasise the risk oversight duty of boards and board committees.[37]

Overall, the discussion above shows that the prevalent regulatory approach to banks' internal risk management is to require banks to have ultimate responsibility for the design and implementation of their processes, which is an example of meta-regulation.[38] The problem with meta-regulation in this context is of course the tension between the business objectives of financial institutions and the regulatory objectives.

II. Post-crisis regulation of executive remuneration in financial institutions

Executive remuneration attracted major policy attention after the 2007–2009 crisis. For instance, the stated purpose of the CRD IV approach to remuneration is to prevent the creation of financial incentives for excessive risk-taking which is perceived as one of the main causes of bank failures and financial instability generally. Indeed, the preamble of the Directive states that: 'Weaknesses in corporate governance in a number of institutions have contributed to excessive and imprudent risk-taking in the banking sector which has led to the failure of individual institutions and systemic problems in Member States and globally.'[39] The Directive introduced a detailed set of rules on executive remuneration which, however, has not generally had much practical impact on the UK regulatory framework, as the latter already had most of those rules in place before the coming into force of the Directive.[40] Of course, this does not apply to the Directive's assertion that high relative levels of variable remuneration are a major governance weakness[41] and to the ensuing introduction of a controversial upper limit with regard to the ratio between fixed and variable remuneration, commonly described as a bonus cap.[42]

37 The Consultation closed on 28 January 2017 and the revised guidelines are expected to be published in mid-2017. See EBA, 'Consultation on Guidelines on Internal Governance (Revised)' (EBA/CP/2016/16, 2016) www.eba.europa.eu/regulation-and-policy/internal-governance/guidelines-on-internal-governance-revised-/-/regulatory-activity/consultation-paper accessed 1 May 2017.

38 On this, see Iris H-Y Chiu, 'Corporate Governance and Risk Management in Banks and Financial Institutions' in Iris H-Y Chiu (ed), *The Law on Corporate Governance in Banks* (Edward Elgar Publishing, 2015) 191–192.

39 CRD IV, Preamble para 53.

40 For a detailed doctrinal discussion of the legal framework for executive remuneration in banks, see Marc T Moore, 'Design and Control of Remuneration in UK Banks' in Iris H-Y Chiu (ed), *The Law on Corporate Governance in Banks* (Edward Elgar Publishing, 2015).

41 For an academic critique of the mismatch between bank executive remuneration and long-term performance, see Lucian Bebchuk, Alma Cohen and Holger Spamann, 'The Wages of Failure: Executive Compensation at Bear Stearns and Lehman 2000–2008' (2010) 27 *Yale Journal on Regulation* 257.

42 See CRD IV, Preamble para 65.

However, before examining the latter, it is expedient to examine the broader regulatory framework on executive remuneration in banks.

Reform impetus in the area of remuneration began with the publication of the Walker Review which recommended that the scope of remuneration committees' oversight be extended to cover setting remuneration policy at the group level[43] and approving the remuneration of all high-end employees.[44] It also recommended that half of an officer's performance-based remuneration be in the form of a long-term scheme, whereby half is vested in no less than three years and half in five years. Bonus awards, meanwhile, should be paid over a three-year period.[45] Moreover, it was recommended that high-end employees and executive directors retain a shareholding in the company in proportion to their overall remuneration.[46] Indeed, the Financial Services Act 2010[47] vested the PRA with new responsibilities on executive remuneration, including the duty to require regulated firms to adopt a remuneration policy consistent with the effective management of risk[48] and, most importantly, the power to prohibit relevant persons from being remunerated in a way that contravenes the above standards. Indeed, the PRA Rulebook requires significant CRD IV-regulated firms to have a remuneration committee.[49]

The provision of guaranteed variable remuneration is prohibited other than to new staff and for the first year of their employment.[50] The fixed component of remuneration must be high enough to enable firms not to pay any variable remuneration at all when performance is poor.[51] Furthermore, the rules require that at least 50% of variable remuneration be paid in shares, share-linked instruments or capital instruments rather than cash.[52] The rules also require UK banks to defer at least 60% of variable remuneration for at least seven years, for persons performing a senior management function, which includes executive directors.[53]

43 Walker Review (above n 13), para 7.7.
44 Ibid., para 7.10.
45 Ibid., para 7.34.
46 Ibid., para 7.35.
47 Section 6, which inserted section 139A into FSMA 2000.
48 According to FSMA 2000, s 139A (3) (b), the policy must also be consistent with the 2009 Implementation Standards for Principles for Sound Compensation Practices issued by the Financial Stability Board.
49 PRA Rulebook, CRR Firms, Remuneration 7.4.
50 PRA Rulebook, CRR Firms, Remuneration 15.7.
51 PRA Rulebook, CRR Firms, Remuneration 15.9 (2).
52 PRA Rulebook, CRR Firms, Remuneration 15.15.
53 PRA Rulebook, CRR Firms, Remuneration 15.17 and 15.18. All CRD IV-regulated firms are expected to defer 40% of variable remuneration of all material risk-takers. However, in the case of payments in excess of €500,000 and payments to directors of significant firms, 60% of remuneration must be deferred. The monetary limit was introduced by CRD IV, article 94 (1) (m). A discussion of the policy behind the seven-year deferral period can be found in PRA, 'Strengthening the Alignment of Risk and Reward: New Remuneration Rules' (PRA PS12/15, 2015) 7–8 www.bankofengland.co.uk/pra/Pages/publications/ps/2015/ps1215.aspx accessed 1 May 2017.

The deferred element must be vested no faster than on a *pro rata* basis, i.e. equally on each anniversary of the grant, with none taking place until three years after the award. Moreover, banks are required to reduce any unvested deferred variable remuneration and take reasonable steps to recover any vested variable remuneration in case an individual is found guilty of misconduct or there is a significant failure of risk management.[54]

Another important aspect of the PRA rules concerns the metrics used to measure performance. Consistent with its overall emphasis on sound risk management, the PRA demands that firms risk-adjust profit-related metrics used to assess financial performance.[55] It is also worth noting that the old Combined PRA and FCA Handbook warned banks of the danger that executives seek to boost earnings per share and total shareholder return in the short term, mainly by increasing leverage, to the detriment of the long-term financial health of the firm.[56] As a result, all major UK banks currently use a variety of non-profit-related metrics alongside profit-related ones to determine the vesting of bonuses and performance share awards.[57] Non-profit-related criteria include the following: capital strength, liquidity, minimisation of bad loans, customer satisfaction, compliance, risk management, corporate reputation, and strategy development. In parallel, profitability is no longer exclusively assessed by relative total shareholder return and earnings per share (EPS), but rather some major banks use return on risk-weighted assets. The latter metric is less prone to create an incentive to increase a bank's leverage.

With regard to rules on the structure of senior executive remuneration packages, CRD IV contains a range of principles that were already part of the UK framework. The scope of these rules is broad and covers all material risk-takers including 'senior management, risk-takers, staff engaged in control functions and any employee receiving total remuneration that takes them into the same remuneration bracket as senior management'. However, in addition to the aforementioned provisions, CRD IV introduced a cap on all forms of variable remuneration paid to the senior management of credit institutions (banks) and certain investment firms as a percentage of their fixed remuneration. Broadly speaking, variable pay cannot exceed 100% of fixed remuneration,[58] unless the shareholders of a bank approve a higher rate, which cannot exceed 200% of fixed remuneration.[59] The Directive prescribes the procedure to be followed in detail. All shareholders must be given a reasonable notice period in advance of the relevant meeting and must be provided with a detailed statement by the institution on the impact of the proposed increase of variable pay on the bank's ability to maintain a sound capital base. In addition, the resolution approving the increase must be passed by at least 66% of the share

54 PRA Rulebook, CRR Firms, Remuneration 15.22 and 15.23, respectively.
55 PRA Rulebook, CRR Firms, Remuneration 11.2–11.6.
56 PRA and FCA Handbook, SYSC 19A.3.24 (as it was before 1 July 2015).
57 Data on the remuneration practices of major UK banks are taken from their 2013 remuneration reports which are included in their annual reports and accounts. This is now required by CRD IV article 94 (1) (a).
58 See CRD IV, article 94 (1) (g) (i).
59 See CRD IV, article 94 (1) (g) (ii).

capital, provided that at least 50% of the shares are represented at the meeting, or by 75% of the share capital. Any shareholders who are affected by the decision (e.g. directors or managers of the bank) are disqualified from voting. Therefore, given that all major UK banks except for RBS have obtained shareholder approval to extend variable pay to 200% of fixed pay and take full advantage of the discounted rate, the bonus cap rules allow variable remuneration to be up to 66.7% of the total remuneration package, which marks a significant departure from previous practice for major UK banks.[60]

In parallel, CRD IV enables member states to allow banks to apply a discounted rate of up to 25% of variable remuneration[61] if it is paid in instruments that are deferred for at least five years in accordance with guidelines prepared by the European Banking Authority. The guidelines take into account four factors to calculate the discount rate, namely the national inflation rate, the average interest rate paid on EU sovereign bonds, the length of the deferral period, and any additional retention period requirement.[62] According to the complex formula used, assuming that 25% of variable remuneration is paid in appropriate instruments and is deferred for five years, variable remuneration can reach up to 114.19% of fixed remuneration (or 228.38% with shareholder approval).[63] Most major UK banks have not yet made use of this possibility.

Unsurprisingly, given that CRD IV imposes no restriction regarding the overall level of remuneration, all major UK banks have responded to the new rules by introducing new forms of fixed remuneration to counterbalance the effect of the bonus cap.[64] These payments, typically described as 'fixed-pay allowances', are reviewed annually and are of questionable compliance with CRD IV's notion of fixed remuneration. According to recent EBA guidance, all components of fixed remuneration have to be pre-determined for the whole period of an employee's employment, irrespective of past or future performance, and therefore any elements that are subject to unilateral alteration at the employer's discretion must be classified as variable remuneration.[65] This, of course, does not prevent UK banks from

60 At the end of 2012, the maximum potential variable remuneration for executive directors as a percentage of fixed salary was as follows: 900% in HSBC, 750% in Barclays, 600% in RBS and Standard Chartered, and 425% in Lloyds (500% for Lloyds' CEO). The data are taken from the banks' respective annual reports and accounts for 2012.

61 CRD IV, article 94 (1) (g) (iii).

62 See EBA, 'Guidelines on the Applicable Notional Discount Rate for Variable Remuneration' (EBA/GL/2014/01, 27 March 2014) www.eba.europa.eu/regulation-and-policy/remuneration/guidelines-on-discount-rate-for-variable-remuneration accessed 1 May 2017.

63 Ibid., 22.

64 This can be seen in the 2014, 2015 and 2016 annual reports and accounts issued by Barclays, HSBC, Lloyds Banking Group, the Royal Bank of Scotland and Standard Chartered.

65 See European Banking Authority, 'Guidelines on Sound Remuneration Policies under Articles 74(3) and 75(2) of Directive 2013/36/EU and Disclosures under Article 450 of Regulation (EU) No 575/2013' (EBA/GL/2015/22, 2015) 120–123 www.eba.

using employment contracts of annual duration for their senior executives, so that the amount of the fixed-pay allowance is renegotiated annually in compliance with the letter but not with the spirit of the EBA's rules.

The bonus cap has been met with scepticism by the PRA, which noted that the unintended outcome of the bonus cap – that is, the rise in fixed remuneration – is likely to weaken banks in times of crisis due to its less flexible nature.[66] In a similar vein, the Treasury launched in September 2013 an unsuccessful legal challenge against the bonus cap before the European Court of Justice on the grounds of lack of competence by the EU to legislate in the area.[67] There is also considerable academic opposition to the bonus cap rule, pointing out that variable remuneration is a sound risk management tool,[68] and that the rule brings unintended consequences.[69] Most academic contributions in favour of the cap are written from a perspective of distributive justice and reducing the overall level of senior manager remuneration rather than regarding its potential contribution to financial stability.[70]

Of course, whether the bonus cap rule will continue to be part of the UK regulatory framework post-Brexit remains to be seen and will depend on the ultimate agreement between the UK and the rest of the EU on the terms of the UK's withdrawal. What is reasonably clear, however, is that if not required to apply this

europa.eu/documents/10180/1314839/EBA-GL-2015-22+Guidelines+on+Sound +Remuneration+Policies_EN.pdf accessed 1 May 2017.

66 Mark Kleinman, 'Bank Watchdog Steps Up Bonus Cap Opposition' Sky News (London, 23 September 2013) http://news.sky.com/story/1145453/bank-watchdog-steps-up-bonus-cap-opposition accessed 1 May 2017. See Bank of England: Prudential Regulation Authority, 'Strengthening Capital Standards: Implementing CRD IV, Feedback and Final Rules' (PRA Policy Statement PS7/13, 2013) para 4.7 www.bankofengland.co.uk/pra/Pages/publications/implemcrdiv.aspx accessed 1 May 2017.

67 Case C-507/13 *United Kingdom v Parliament and Council* [2013] was lodged on 20 September 2013 and was removed from the register on 4 May 2015. One of the grounds for the legal action was the alleged illegality of the delegation of the power to determine the staff on which the new rules will apply to the European Banking Authority in article 94 (2).

68 See e.g. John Thanassoulis, 'The Case for Intervening in Bankers' Pay' (2012) 67 *The Journal of Finance* 849.

69 Kevin J Murphy, 'Regulating Banking Bonuses in the European Union: A Case Study in Unintended Consequences' (2013) 19 *European Financial Management* 631.

70 For instance, Moore views the introduction of the bonus cap positively as an example of regulation that seeks to enhance pay equity by reducing the disparity in remuneration between senior managers and ordinary employees. Marc T Moore, 'Corporate Governance, Pay Equity, and the Limitations of Agency Theory' (2015) 68 *Current Legal Problems* 431, 438–441. See also Alan Dignam, 'Remuneration and Riots: Rethinking Corporate Governance in the Age of Entitlement' (2013) 66 *Current Legal Problems* 401. On the other hand, a positive appraisal of the bonus as a tool to reduce excessive risk-taking can also be found in Andrew Johnston, 'Preventing the Next Financial Crisis? Regulating Bankers' Pay in Europe' (2014) 41 *Journal of Law and Society* 6, 23–26.

rule as part of such an agreement, the UK is unlikely to retain it.[71] At any rate, it is doubtful whether the bonus cap rule has any effect in reducing banks' insolvency risk or indeed in reducing incentives to take excessive risk, as the latter depend on a whole range of factors including the prospect of increases in fixed remuneration and the type of instruments in which remuneration is paid (such as shares, options, etc.).

Despite the reforms introduced by the aforementioned provisions, financial institution remuneration committees retain significant discretion to determine the components of executive remuneration packages. Although diminished, variable remuneration continues to represent the largest component of executive pay, and profitability remains the most important criterion to assess executive performance. Given the subjectivity of non-profit-related criteria, it can be surmised that remuneration committees are likely to consider them achieved in most cases.[72] On the contrary, profit-related performance benchmarks are objectively defined with reference to specific financial outcomes, such as the relative performance of an institution compared to a group of similar institutions globally. It follows that the actual dependence of executives' actual remuneration on profitability may be greater than it seems, as subjective non-financial criteria are likely to operate in practice as quasi-fixed remuneration.

III. The fit and proper requirement and the new Senior Managers Regime

The Banking Reform Act 2013 introduced a new Senior Managers Regime (and Senior Insurance Managers Regime), which replaced the pre-existing Approved Persons Regime (APER), with effect from 6 April 2016.[73] The new regime sits within the established legislative framework requiring senior employees in regulated entities to be fit and proper. Before exploring the new regime, it is expedient to investigate the evolution of the role of regulators in approving senior appointments in financial institutions. We will see that a relatively light-touch approach was followed up until the 2007–2009 financial crisis and that, since then, prudential regulators have adopted a more inquisitive and proactive stance emphasising the competence of proposed bank directors as much as their honesty.[74]

71 On this, see Longjie Lu, 'The End of Bankers' Bonus Cap: How Will the UK Regulate Bankers' (2016) 27 *European Business Law Review* 1091.

72 Insofar as the remuneration committee has discretion to decide the achievement of an open-ended non-financial goal such as adherence to values, the rigour of the scrutiny of executive performance depends on the substantial independence of the members of the remuneration committee. If most of them are psychologically beholden and loyal to the CEO, the scrutiny is likely to be unexacting.

73 Part 4 of the Act amended Parts II and III of FSMA 2000. The relevant provisions were brought into force on 7 March 2016 by the Financial Services (Banking Reform) Act 2013 (Commencement No. 9) Order 2015 (SI 2015/490). However, the new regulatory rules were put in place on 6 April 2016.

74 A detailed discussion of the evolution of the fit and proper test until early 2012 can be found in Andreas Kokkinis, 'The Reformed "Fit and Proper" Test: A Call for a Broader Rethink of Bank Corporate Governance?' (2012) 9 *International Corporate Rescue* 5.

Under the Banking Act 1987, it was a condition for the authorisation of a bank that its directors, managers and controllers were fit and proper persons.[75] The Bank of England had no direct power to oppose the nomination or demand the replacement of bank directors and shadow directors, but could refuse, revoke or restrict the authorisation of a bank that failed to comply with instructions in this regard. On the other hand, the Bank of England had direct power to oppose the acquisition of substantial blocks of shares by prospective investors and there was in place a system of notification of the Bank once a person crossed certain thresholds of share ownership.[76] The criteria to determine whether a person was 'fit and proper' included probity, competence and soundness of judgement, with special regard to their past record. Any serious doubt about a person's fitness or any material danger to depositors' interests was adequate for the person to be deemed improper. The Bank of England was therefore entrusted with a broad discretion to assess the reputation, character, competence and professionalism of proposed individuals,[77] in stark contrast with the situation in non-financial companies whose directors are not submitted to any regulatory approval process.

The Financial Services and Markets Act 2000 empowered the FSA (now the PRA for systemically important firms, and the FCA for other financial firms)[78] to scrutinise and approve any person who performs a controlled function in an authorised entity such as a bank.[79] FSMA 2000 identifies two groups of such individuals: on the one hand, members of the governing bodies of financial firms, i.e. members of the board of directors; and on the other, senior managers to whom significant functions have been delegated. In deciding whether to approve a person, the Authority has to assess his or her fitness and propriety.[80] Given that the role of the PRA in this area only goes back to 2013, it is worth examining how the FSA discharged these functions until its abolition. It will be seen that the FSA's approach underwent significant change after 2008.

Under the FSA Handbook, which survives now as the FCA Handbook,[81] when assessing whether a person is fit and proper, the Authority had to have regard to the proposed person's honesty, competence and financial soundness.[82] The

75 Banking Act 1987, Schedule 3.

76 See Section 105 (4) of the Banking Act 1987 as replaced by the Banking Coordination (Second Council Directive) Regulations (SI 1992/3218), reg 43(2).

77 For a detailed discussion of some instances of regulatory vetoing of directorial appointments, see Christos Hadjiemmanuil, *Banking Regulation and the Bank of England* (LLP Publishing, 1996), 241–249.

78 A discussion of the recent abolition of the FSA, and an examination of the division of supervisory competence between the PRA and FCA can be found in Chapter 3, section II.

79 FSMA 2000, s 59 (1).

80 FSMA 2000, s 61 (1).

81 Therefore, references will be made to the current FCA Handbook, which of course does not apply to systemically important financial institutions, as it is identical to the rules of the FSA Handbook that applied at the time to all financial institutions.

82 FCA Handbook, FIT 2.

Handbook[83] contained detailed criteria for assessing honesty, such as prior convictions, disciplinary proceedings, regulatory breaches, dismissals from fiduciary positions, and the insolvency of a company or partnership in which the candidate was concerned. Conversely, scarce guidance was offered on competence; the relevant criteria included the person's training, experience and available time to devote to their post.[84] As regards the financial soundness of proposed persons, it tended to be assumed, unless the relevant person had been declared bankrupt or entered similar proceedings.[85] It is not surprising, therefore, that up until the recent financial crisis, the FSA was mainly focusing on the honesty rather than the competence of proposed persons and largely deferred to banks' commercial judgement with regard to the fitness of senior persons, consistent with its general light-handed approach to financial regulation.[86] It should also be noted that until the crisis the Approved Persons Regime operated in the same manner for all financial firms without distinguishing between large systemically important institutions such as banks, and small financial firms.

Prior to the 2007–2009 crisis the FSA mostly concentrated on the honesty and financial soundness of proposed bank directors and accepted any high-level general business experience as sufficient evidence of competence.[87] At board level, running a bank was generally thought to be no different from running any other large company. Post-crisis, however, competence has become a major regulatory concern and relevant financial experience is normally sought.[88] The lack of financial expertise on bank boards was broadly identified as one of the governance failures that contributed to the recent crisis,[89] and led to the Walker Review placing a substantial focus on directors' expertise.[90] Indeed, in 2010 the FSA publicised its intended change of regulatory approach from principles-based and reactive regulation towards outcomes-based and proactive regulation. This entails judging the

83 FCA Handbook, FIT 2.1.3.
84 FCA Handbook, FIT 2.2.1.
85 FCA Handbook, FIT 2.3.
86 For a critical discussion of the light-touch approach to financial regulation, see Roman Tomasic, 'Beyond "Light Touch" Regulation of British Banks after the Financial Crisis' in Iain MacNeil and Justin O'Brien (eds), *The Future of Financial Regulation* (Hart Publishing, 2010), esp 104–112.
87 For instance, Sir Frederick Goodwin, the CEO of RBS from 2001 to 2009, who is considered partly responsible for the unsustainable expansion of RBS and especially the merger with ABN AMRO, which precipitated its collapse, was a chartered accountant prior to moving to banking in 1995.
88 'We made clear that we are now seeking to ensure that firms are adequately assessing the individual's competence, particularly in terms of technical skills.' See FSA, 'Effective Corporate Governance (Significant Influence Controlled Functions and the Walker Review)' (FSA Consultation Paper 10/3, 2010) para 1.9 www.fsa.gov.uk/pubs/cp/cp10_03.pdf accessed 1 May 2017.
89 For instance, the lack of a banking background of the CEOs of RBS and HBOS has been identified as a possible cause of their collapse. See Parliamentary Commission on Banking Standards, *Changing Banking for Good* (2013–14, HL 27-II, HC 175-II), para 128.
90 See Walker Review (above n 13), para 3.6.

business models and product features of regulated firms on their substantive merits.[91] In the context of Approved Persons, the FSA clarified that it was prepared to scrutinise meticulously the competence of proposed individuals rather than merely to rubber stamp banks' decisions.[92]

The procedure that was followed by the FSA from 2008 until its abolition included four stages, namely application by a bank, assessment of the candidate by the Authority, interview of the candidate, and ongoing review of the candidate's suitability. Interviews took place at the discretion of the regulators on the basis of the following criteria: the size of the firm, the importance of the position the candidate was proposed to assume, and the candidate's record and qualifications. It was therefore reasonable to assume that proposed bank directors would normally be called for an interview.[93] The interview stage was evidently the most inquisitive one and marked the departure from the previous approach as it enabled regulators to form their own opinion about the candidate's competence and expertise.

Evidence from the annual reports prepared by the FSA, in the years after the crisis and until its abolition, confirm the radical change of approach with regard to the Approved Persons Regime. Interviews were first implemented in 2008 and in the first six months of implementing the new approach 51 interviews were held and a number of candidates were withdrawn by regulated firms subsequent to the interviews.[94] During the 2009–2010 financial year, the FSA completed 377 interviews of candidates who would exercise a significant influence function, which resulted in the withdrawal of 27 candidates.[95] Similarly during the 2010–2011 financial year, the FSA held 409 interviews and firms withdrew 25 candidates, of whom 21 were withdrawn for competence reasons.[96] Evidence is not available for

91 For instance, Mr Ashley-Fenn from the FSA argued in 2010 that: 'We now have a much greater willingness to make judgements, for example, about individuals performing key roles and the sustainability of business models of firms. […] We cannot simply rely on monitoring systems and controls or assuming that firms' senior management are necessarily always best placed to make these judgements alone.' See Graeme Ashley-Fenn, 'Corporate Governance – An FSA Perspective' (Building Societies Association Corporate Governance Seminar, London, 2010) www.fsa.gov.uk/pages/Library/Communication/Speeches/2010/0303_gaf.shtml accessed 1 May 2017.

92 'Let me be clear – gone are the days when we receive a phone call to say that a firm wishes to appoint X to be the new chairman or CEO and expecting us to nod them through as approved within two days because that is when the firm wishes to publicly make the announcement.' Ibid.

93 The Walker Review (above n 13) recommends (in paras 3.24–3.25) that the FSA hold interviews when proposed non-executive directors of banks do not bring relevant recent financial industry experience. In such cases, the interviewing panel should include at least one person with board-level (or just below board-level) financial industry experience.

94 FSA, 'Annual Report 2008/09' (2009), 19 www.fsa.gov.uk/static/pubs/annual/ar08_09/ar08_09.pdf accessed 1 May 2017.

95 FSA, 'Annual Report 2009/10' (2010), 22 www.fsa.gov.uk/pubs/annual/ar09_10/ar09_10.pdf accessed 1 May 2017.

96 FSA, 'Annual Report 2010/11' (2011), 28–29 www.fsa.gov.uk/pubs/annual/ar10_11/ar10_11.pdf accessed 1 May 2017.

the period after 2011, but the final report of the FSA in 2013 emphasises the efforts made by the Authority in 2012 to economise on its resources by reducing the number of interviews.[97]

Despite the change of regulatory approach, Parliament was not satisfied that the defects of the Approved Persons Regime had been adequately remedied. The Commission on Banking Standards in its 2013 report criticised heavily the operation of the Approved Persons Regime, and proposed the introduction of a new, more rigorous approval regime for systemically important institutions, distinct from that applied to other financial firms.[98] The government responded to the report promptly and most of its recommendations became part of the Banking Reform Act 2013.

The scope of the new Senior Managers Regime is crucial, as individuals who are deemed to perform a senior management function are subject to the provision that requires firms to submit a statement of responsibilities for each senior manager,[99] and also to a reversed burden of proof in case there is a regulatory breach within the area of responsibility of a senior manager.[100] A senior management function is defined as a function that satisfies two criteria. First, that the relevant person will be managing one or more aspects of the affairs of a relevant authorised person (financial firm). This includes non-executive directors and directors of a parent company.[101] Second, that the activities of the relevant person involve a risk of serious consequences for the authorised financial institution or for business interests in the UK.[102] The Act also ensures that, for all PRA-regulated firms, only persons exercising a senior management function will be designated as exercising controlled functions so that the two categories will practically be merged.[103] The regime thus covers the senior managers of all firms within the scope of CRD IV, including all UK incorporated banks, building societies and credit unions, and some investment firms, which will be referred to as financial institutions, the term on this occasion excluding insurance firms for which there is a special senior managers regime.[104]

A CRD IV firm must not make an approval application unless it is satisfied that the relevant person is fit and proper to perform the senior management function,[105] and in doing so it has to consider the person's good repute, integrity,

97 FSA, 'Annual Report 2012/13', 33 www.fca.org.uk/news/firms/fsa-annual-report-2012-13 accessed 1 May 2017.
98 See Parliamentary Commission on Banking Standards (above n 89), ch 6.
99 FSMA 2000, ss 60 2A–2C, inserted by Banking Reform Act 2013, s 20.
100 FSMA 2000, ss 66A–66B, inserted by Banking Reform Act 2013, s 32. This will be discussed in the next section of the present chapter.
101 See Banking Reform Act 2013, Explanatory Notes, para 174.
102 FSMA 2000, s 59 ZA, inserted by Banking Reform Act 2013, s 19.
103 FSMA 2000, s 59 (6), inserted by Banking Reform Act 2013, s 18 (3).
104 The meaning of the term 'relevant authorised person' is defined in Banking Reform Act 2013, s 33, which will insert s 71A into the FSMA 2000, as an institution with permission to accept deposits other than an insurer, or an investment firm with permission to deal in investments as principal insofar as it is regulated by the PRA with regard to that activity.
105 PRA Rulebook, CRR firms, Fitness and Propriety, 2.1.

knowledge, experience, qualifications and training.[106] Crucially, financial institutions have to accompany approval applications with a statement of responsibilities detailing the particular aspects of their affairs that the candidate is intended to undertake.[107] If the functions of a senior manager change significantly, institutions have to submit to the regulator a revised statement of responsibilities. These provisions aim to facilitate the apportionment of individual responsibility to senior bank managers in case of regulatory failures and thus enhance their accountability, as will be explained in the next section.

To that effect, the PRA has prescribed a list of senior management functions for which specific regulatory approval is required, including six executive functions (chief executive officer, chief finance officer (CFO), chief risk officer, head of internal audit, head of key business area, and group entity senior manager), and five non-executive functions (board chairman, chairmen of the audit, remuneration and risk committees, and senior independent director).[108] It is worth noting that the role of the chairman of the nominations committee is not a senior management function probably because it is very common practice for companies to combine the roles of chairman of the board and chairman of the nominations committee. The range of senior management functions is currently much more detailed than it was before the crisis but still the role of non-executive directors who are not chairing a board committee is not recognised as a senior management function, contrary to FCA-authorised firms.[109] Still, when CRD IV firms appoint non-executive directors who do not perform a senior management function, they have to provide the PRA with information that allows it to assess whether they are fit and proper.[110]

In addition, the Banking Reform Act introduced a number of provisions enabling the PRA (and the FCA) to approve a candidate for a senior management function subject to conditions or for a limited period of time, and impose or vary such conditions at any time after approval is given. Each regulator must issue a statement of policy with regard to these issues.[111] Another innovation introduced by the Act is the duty imposed on banks and other relevant firms to ensure that all senior managerial candidates who apply for approval are fit and proper to perform the relevant function.[112] In particular, banks are required to have regard to the candidates' qualifications, past or current training, competence and personal characteristics.[113] To strengthen the effect of this provision institutions are also

106 PRA Rulebook, CRR firms, Fitness and Propriety, 2.6.
107 FSMA 2000, s 62A, inserted by Banking Reform Act 2013, s 24.
108 PRA Rulebook, CRR firms, Senior Management Functions, 3.2–3.7, 4.2–4.6 and 5.2. These functions do not apply to credit unions, for which there is only the credit union senior management function (6.1–6.3).
109 FCA Handbook, SUP 10A.6.12. Indeed, there is a different range of controlled functions for FCA-authorised firms. These rules are not within the scope of this study as they do not apply to PRA-regulated entities.
110 PRA Rulebook, CRR firms, Fitness and Propriety, 4.2.
111 FSMA 2000, ss 63ZD and 63ZE, inserted by Banking Reform Act 2013, s 27.
112 FSMA 2000, s 60A, inserted by Banking Reform Act 2013, s 21.
113 FSMA 2000, s 60A (2) (a)–(d).

required to review annually the fitness of senior managers and to notify the regulator if they believe that there are any grounds on which the latter could withdraw approval.[114]

With regard to bank employees who do not perform senior management functions, but rather only perform a significant-harm function, the Act sets out a simplified regime whereby banks will be required to assess whether these employees are fit and proper persons to discharge significant-harm functions, and issue a certificate.[115] A 'significant-harm function' is one that involves performing such duties that may cause significant harm to the bank or its customers.[116] Certificates have to specify the aspects of the affairs of the bank with which the employee will be involved, and are valid for 12 months.[117]

Moreover, there are special rules applying to insurance firms that are regulated by the PRA, deriving from the Solvency II Directive. Indeed, Solvency II requires insurance and reinsurance firms to ensure that persons who effectively run their business are fit and proper, and to notify their supervisory authorities if there is any change in the identity of the persons who perform control functions.[118] Senior Insurance Management Functions mirror the senior management functions for CRD IV banks and other financial institutions, with one exception, namely that there is no head of key business area executive function.[119] The same applies to large insurance firms that are not within the scope of the Solvency II Directive.[120] UK insurance firms within the scope of Solvency II must apply for PRA approval of the persons who will be performing senior management functions before they commence performing the relevant activities.[121]

In parallel, there is a framework to ensure that regulatory authorities have control over the share ownership of financial institutions. Sections 178–192 of FSMA 2000 require investors to notify the PRA or the FCA, as appropriate, prior to acquiring control of 10% of the shares of a regulated firm so that the PRA can assess the prospective acquirer and its directors and managers.[122] Further notification duties – and regulatory approval – are triggered once a shareholder crosses the 20%, 30% and 50% thresholds.[123] The assessment criteria include the

114 FSMA 2000, s 63 (2A), inserted by Banking Reform Act 2013, s 25.
115 FSMA 2000, ss 63E and 63F, inserted by Banking Reform Act 2013, s 29.
116 FSMA 2000, s 63E (5).
117 FSMA 2000, s 63F (5).
118 Solvency II, art 42.
119 PRA Rulebook, Solvency II firms, Insurance – Senior Insurance Management Functions, 3.1–3.4, 4.1–4.5 and 5.1.
120 PRA Rulebook, Non-SII Firms, Large Non-Solvency II Firms – Senior Insurance Management Functions, 3.1–3.4, 4.1–4.5 and 5.1. For these purposes, 'large' means having assets (relating to regulated activities) that exceed £25 million during the two previous financial years.
121 PRA Rulebook, Solvency II firms, Senior Insurance Managers Regime – Applications and Notifications, 2.1.
122 In non-financial companies, there is only a significant share ownership disclosure regime which mainly serves transparency purposes. See FCA Handbook, DTR 5.
123 FSMA 2000, s 182.

reputation of the prospective controller, the reputation and competence of the persons who will direct the firm subsequent to the acquisition, and financial soundness of the acquiring firm.[124] The formal powers of prudential regulators in this context have not been changed in response to the crisis, despite the deleterious effect that the takeover of ABN AMRO had on RBS,[125] but the approach to be followed by UK regulators in the future in similar cases is likely to be more interventionist, in line with the broader change of regulatory approach. It is worth noting that this is an area of extensive EU harmonisation as the Qualifying Holdings Directive, which amended several pre-existing directives, requires potential acquirers to notify the relevant national supervisory authority and prescribes a detailed procedure for the prudential assessment of proposed acquisitions.[126] The share ownership threshold that triggers the duty to notify is set at 10% but member states are allowed to require notification at a lower threshold. Other than that, the Directive is a maximum harmonisation directive.

The examination of the framework relating to regulatory oversight of the qualifications and honesty of persons performing senior management functions in financial institutions highlights the heavy reliance on meta-regulatory techniques after the crisis. Indeed, emphasis is now on financial institutions to assess the fitness and propriety of individuals who are entrusted with controlled functions, and to communicate all relevant information to the authorities. This is reasonable in view of the costs and unintended consequences associated with interventionist regulatory approaches to senior appointments but raises the perennial issue of financial institutions' incentive to co-operate with regulators and support regulatory objectives.

IV. Holding financial institutions' senior managers accountable: post-crisis regulatory enforcement, and new administrative and criminal sanctions

a. Post-crisis regulatory enforcement cases

In the financial sector, company law directors' duties are not the only available accountability device. The PRA and the FCA are empowered by FSMA 2000 to prescribe codes of conduct of relevant approved persons[127] and to impose sanctions in case of breach.[128] The scope of these codes of conduct is broader than

124 FSMA 2000, s 186.
125 On this, see Chapter 6, n 94 and accompanying text.
126 Directive 2007/44/EC of the European Parliament and of the Council of 5 September 2007 amending Council Directive 92/49/EEC and Directives 2002/83/EC, 2004/39/EC, 2005/68/EC and 2006/48/EC as regards procedural rules and evaluation criteria for the prudential assessment of acquisitions and increase of holdings in the financial sector [2007] OJ L247/1. Discussed in Georgina Tsagas, 'The Market for Corporate Control in the Banking Industry' in Iris H-Y Chiu (ed), *The Law on Corporate Governance in Banks* (Edward Elgar Publishing, 2015) 300–302.
127 FSMA 2000, ss 64–65.
128 FSMA 2000, ss 66–67.

directors' duties as they cover all approved persons including senior managers.[129] FSMA 2000 specifies the general process to impose regulatory sanctions.[130] If sanctions are imposed, the relevant person is allowed to appeal to the Upper Tribunal which can review the substance of the decision of the PRA or FCA.[131] Then a further appeal is allowed to the Court of Appeal on questions of law only.[132] Indeed, the PRA Rulebook sets out seven general principles of conduct for PRA-authorised persons. Firms must contractually require PRA-approved persons and non-executive directors to act with integrity and due skill, care and diligence (thus effectively replicating the company law duties of loyalty and care), and to co-operate with and disclose information to the regulators.[133] In addition to this, firms must contractually require PRA-approved persons to 'take reasonable steps to ensure that the business of the firm for which they are responsible' is effectively controlled and complies with regulatory rules, and that 'any delegation of their responsibilities is to an appropriate person and that they oversee the discharge of the delegated responsibility effectively'.[134]

Given the similarity between the company law duty of care and the relevant regulatory rule, the discussion in Chapter 2 on the limitations of the duty of care in the context of bank failures also explains why the FSA was reluctant to pursue enforcement cases against the directors of failed UK banks after the recent crisis. For instance, the FSA concluded that there was no prospect of success in seeking to impose regulatory sanctions on the former directors and senior managers of RBS as:

> Errors of commercial judgement are not in themselves sanctionable unless either the processes and controls which governed how these judgements were reached were clearly deficient, or the judgements were clearly outside the bounds of what might be considered reasonable. The reasonableness of judgements, moreover, has to be assessed within the context of the information available at the time, and not with the benefit of hindsight.[135]

129 A detailed analysis of the relevant rules can be found in section III of this chapter.
130 FSMA 2000, s 67.
131 FSMA 2000, s 67 (7). The Financial Services and Markets Tribunal was established by FSMA 2000 s 132. Its powers were later transferred to the Upper Tribunal. See The Transfer of Tribunal Functions Order 2010 (S.I. 2010/22), s 2 (2). The proceedings before the Tribunal are regulated by FSMA 2000, ss 133–133B. It is worth noting that, given the availability of the special dispute resolution process provided for by FSMA 2000, judicial review of a PRA decision is not available save in the most exceptional circumstances. See *R (on the application of Davies) v Financial Services Authority* [2003] EWCA Civ 1128; and *R (on the application of Christopher Willford) v Financial Services Authority* [2013] All ER (D) 114.
132 Tribunals, Courts and Enforcement Act 2007, s 13.
133 PRA Rulebook, CRR firms, Fitness and Propriety, 3.1.
134 PRA Rulebook, CRR firms, Fitness and Propriety, 3.2. It is worth noting that their duty to oversee the discharge of delegated responsibilities does not apply to non-executive directors who do not perform a senior management function contrary to the duty to supervise delegated function under the company law duty of care.
135 See FSA (above n 9), 9. For a detailed discussion of the reasons for not imposing any sanctions, see ibid. 354–356 and 399–406.

However, there have been a few instances of enforcement arising out of the bank failures that occurred in 2007–2009. For example, Christopher Willford, the former group finance director of Bradford & Bingley plc, was fined £30,000 in 2013 after a long enforcement procedure, for breaching APER Principle 6 (duty to act with due skill, care and diligence) in May 2008 by failing to disclose relevant financial information about the bank to the board.[136] It is evident that the level of the fine is too low to deter excessive risk-taking in view of the remuneration paid to bank executives. Another example of regulatory enforcement is the investigation of the behaviour of Johnny Cameron, a former executive at RBS (chairman of global markets). Mr Cameron undertook not to perform any significant influence function in relation to any regulated activity and not to work full-time in the financial services sector.[137] Also, Peter Cummings, CFO at HBOS, was fined £500,000 and banned from undertaking significant influence functions for breach of APER Principle 6, as it then stood.[138]

Moreover, there has been a noteworthy instance of regulatory enforcement against directors of the Co-operative Bank, which faced financial distress and was recapitalised in December 2013. The Co-operative Bank was until then a wholly owned subsidiary of the Co-operative Group which had merged in 2009 with a larger institution, the Britannia Building Society, and – partly as a result thereof – disclosed significant loan impairments in summer 2013, mostly affecting its corporate loan book. The recapitalisation was achieved partly by bailing-in the bank's bondholders and partly by issuing new shares so that, at the end of the process, the stake of the Co-operative Group was reduced to approximately 20% of the bank's equity capital and voting rights.[139] The PRA has pursued two enforcement cases and imposed both a financial penalty (based on FSMA 2000 s 66) and a prohibition on the bank's CEO and on one of its executive directors serving at the relevant time, to perform any significant influence function in PRA-regulated firms (based on FSMA 2000 s 66).

Indeed, Mr Tootell, who was the bank's CFO from January 2009 and then its CEO from September 2012 until December 2013, was imposed a penalty of £248,289 which represents 35% of his relevant income during the tax year preceding the end of the period of the regulatory breach, eventually reduced by 30%

136 FCA, 'Final Notice for Mr Willford' (Reference Number: CXW01232, 11 December 2013) www.fca.org.uk/static/documents/final-notices/christopher-willford.pdf accessed 1 May 2017.

137 See FSA, 'FSA Statement on Johnny Cameron' (FSA/PN/081/2010, 2010) www.fsa.gov.uk/pages/Library/Communication/PR/2010/081.shtml accessed 1 May 2017.

138 For a discussion of the enforcement case against Peter Cummings, see Iris H-Y Chiu, 'Comparing Directors' Duties in the Financial Services Sector with Regulatory Duties under the Senior Persons Regime – Some Critical Observations' (2016) 27 *European Business Law Review* 261, 275–276.

139 For a vivid discussion of the near-failure of the Co-operative Bank, see Christine Mallin, 'The Co-Operative Bank – What Went Wrong?' in Christine Mallin (ed), *Handbook on Corporate Governance in Financial Institutions* (Edward Elgar Publishing, 2016).

to £173,802 as Mr Tootell settled.[140] The relevant findings of fact regarding Mr Tootell's behaviour highlight his role in fostering 'a culture which encouraged prioritising the short-term financial position of the Firm at the cost of taking prudent and sustainable actions to secure the longer-term capital position of the Firm',[141] and his failure to bring to the attention of the board, in a timely manner, various key issues including the acquisition of Britannia Building Society, and a change of the accounting treatment of the bank's corporate loan book. More broadly, the PRA criticised the bank's risk management process as faulty and inadequate in ensuring that the bank's business decisions were in line with its stated risk appetite.[142] The measure of the financial penalty imposed was influenced by the fact that Mr Tootell was not found to have breached any regulatory principles deliberately or recklessly.[143]

As far as the second enforcement case is concerned, Mr Alderson, who was an executive director responsible for the bank's Corporate and Business Banking Division from 2010 until 2014, was imposed a final financial penalty of £88,890, calculated in the same way as in Mr Tootell's case, and again was found not to have breached any regulatory principles deliberately or recklessly.[144] In particular, Mr Alderson was found to have failed to: (a) apply due diligence in connection to the acquisition of Britannia; (b) ensure that the bank's policies where implemented when making lending decisions; and (c) provide the board with adequate information.[145] More crucially, with regard to impairments affecting the bank's corporate loan book, Mr Alderson actively 'challenged figures that were proposed to him for impairment provisions',[146] thus encouraging the taking of an over-optimistic approach.

It follows that the pre-existing legal framework was inadequate to achieve the level of bank director accountability sufficient to protect the stability of the financial system. Taking risky decisions, which may be beneficial for risk-neutral shareholders but eventually lead to the failure of a bank, is clearly not sanctionable insofar as the decisions are made following a reasonable process, and are not totally unreasonable in the circumstances. In view of the inherently risky nature of financial services, this test amounts to little more than a gross negligence test, which is unlikely to be satisfied in the majority of cases.[147]

140 See PRA, 'Final Notice for Mr Tootell' (Reference Number: BXT01184, 14 January 2016), 1–2 www.bankofengland.co.uk/publications/Pages/news/2016/022.aspx accessed on 1 May 2017.

141 Ibid., 39.

142 Ibid., 40.

143 Ibid., 41–44.

144 See PRA, 'Final Notice for Mr Alderson' (Reference Number: KBA01005, 14 January 2016), 1–2 www.bankofengland.co.uk/publications/Pages/news/2016/022.aspx accessed on 1 May 2017.

145 Ibid., 42–46.

146 Ibid., 40.

147 An analysis of the regulatory enforcement powers and a critique of the FSA's approach to enforcement, see Dalvinder Singh, *Banking Regulation of the UK and US Financial Markets* (Ashgate, 2007), 121–135.

b. The new regulatory (administrative) and criminal sanctions

Still, it is necessary to examine the effect of the recent amendments to FSMA 2000 introduced by the Banking Reform Act 2013. Essentially, findings of misconduct by bank senior managers will be facilitated due to the reversed burden of proof applicable when a regulated firm contravenes one of the relevant rules of conduct.[148] Indeed, senior managers who are responsible for the management of the activities 'in relation to which the contravention occurred'[149] will be guilty of misconduct unless they satisfy the PRA (or the FCA) that they took all steps that a person in their position could reasonably be expected to take to prevent the contravention.

This reform will undoubtedly facilitate taking enforcement action against bank senior managers in the context of regulatory breaches by banks such as the LIBOR scandal. However, as it relies on successful enforcement action being brought against a bank for breach of a particular rule of conduct,[150] and on a senior manager being personally responsible for the relevant activities, its effect seems to be limited in practice to cases of breaching conduct of business regulation. This interpretation is supported by the fact that the Banking Reform Act expressly addresses the issue of bank failures in section 36 which is discussed below. It follows that, despite the welcome strengthening of regulatory enforcement powers brought by the forthcoming reform, regulatory sanctions will continue to be inadequate to ensure that bank directors and senior managers face strong incentives to prevent bank failures, as they continue to rely on the finding of fault in directors' and senior managers' individual conduct. The mere taking of excessive business risks, and making errors of commercial judgement, will remain unimpeachable even after the full implementation of the Banking Reform Act 2013.

The final existing accountability mechanism for bank directors to be examined is the new criminal offence widely known as reckless banking.[151] Section 36 of the Banking Reform Act 2013, which came into force on 7 March 2016,[152] introduced a criminal offence relating to decisions causing a financial institution to fail. It will be argued that the new offence, although clearly evincing the determination of the government to hold the directors and senior managers of failed banks accountable, is unlikely to deter excessive risk-taking to a significant degree due to its formulation and the inevitable limitations of using criminal law to regulate corporate conduct.

148 Section 32 of the Banking Reform Act 2013 will insert ss 66A and 66B into the FSMA 2000.
149 See forthcoming FSMA 2000 ss 66A (5) (c) and 66B (5) (c).
150 This can be any rule included in the PRA or the FCA Handbook.
151 The introduction of the criminal offence goes against the recent tendency of decriminalising regulatory offences. On the phenomenon of decriminalisation, see Singh (above n 147), 118–121. An economic analysis of the use of criminal sanctions can be found in Steven Shavell, 'Criminal Law and the Optimal Use of Non-Monetary Sanctions as Deterrents' (1985) *Columbia Law Review* 1232.
152 See Financial Services (Banking Reform) Act 2013 (Commencement No. 9) Order 2015 (SI 2015/490).

The new offence applies to senior managers[153] of financial institutions, i.e. institutions accepting deposits and investment firms regulated by the PRA.[154] To establish that a person committed the offence, the following elements must be proved: (a) the institution has failed;[155] (b) the failure was caused by the implementation of a particular decision; (c) the defendant was a senior manager at the time the decision was taken; (d) the defendant agreed to take the decision or failed to take all possible steps to prevent the decision; (e) at the time the decision was taken, the defendant was aware of a risk that its implementation might cause the failure of the institution; and (f) the defendant's conduct with regard to the decision falls far below what could reasonably be expected of a person in his or her position.[156] On conviction on indictment, the offence is punishable by imprisonment for up to seven years and/or an unlimited fine.[157]

All the elements of the offence, apart from the failure of the institution and the position of the defendant as a senior manager, are very difficult to establish, especially under the criminal standard of proof.[158] In particular, establishing causation between a specific decision and the failure of an institution is a very difficult task. Recent experience demonstrates that it is usually a combination of strategic decisions that contributes to the failure of a bank.[159] It follows that the 'but for' test of causation[160] will be particularly difficult to satisfy as it is often unclear whether a bank would have failed anyway if a particular decision had not been taken. Furthermore, proving that the defendant was aware of the risk posed by the relevant decision to the viability of the financial institution – in other words proving recklessness – will be a formidable task. In this context, given the complexity of financial institutions and the sophisticated risk management models in use,[161] it will be very unlikely that a senior manager can be proven to have taken a decision being aware of such a risk, especially as the term 'risk' is normally

153 On the interpretation of the term senior manager, see Banking Reform Act 2013, s 37 (7)–(8).

154 Banking Reform Act 2013, s 37 (2)–(6).

155 According to s 37 (9)–(10), an institution is regarded as having failed if it enters into any insolvency procedure or if the stabilisation powers of the Bank of England or the role of the Financial Services Compensation Scheme are invoked.

156 Banking Reform Act, s 36 (1) (c).

157 Banking Reform Act, s 36 (4).

158 In *Woolmington v Director of Public Prosecutions* [1935] UKHL 1, 7 Viscount Sankey LC emphasised that: 'Juries are always told that if conviction there is to be the prosecution must prove the case beyond reasonable doubt. [...] No matter what the charge or where the trial, the principle that the prosecution must prove the guilt of the prisoner is part of the common law of England and no attempt to whittle it down can be entertained.'

159 See e.g. FSA (above n 9), 21–27, where a series of different factors are identified as having contributed to the failure of RBS.

160 See *R v White* [1910] 2 KB 124.

161 An overview of risk models used by banks and a critical evaluation of the capacity of the models to quantify extreme downward risks can be found in Christophe Bucher, 'Risk Models-at-risk' (2014) 44 *Journal of Banking & Finance* 72.

construed by the courts as excluding very low-probability events.[162] Similarly, establishing that the defendant did not do all that he or she could have done to prevent the decision being taken will be complicated in the case of large banks where a number of management organs and committees share different responsibilities.[163]

Most crucially, the offence imposes liability only if the defendant's conduct was grossly negligent. Given the difficulty in establishing even ordinary negligence, as explained above, it becomes clear that establishing beyond reasonable doubt that the defendant's conduct fell far below the reasonably expected standard will only be achieved in the most extreme cases of mismanagement. It is submitted that even a situation similar to the facts in *Re Barings*[164] would not necessarily lead to the successful enforcement of the criminal offence, as the requirements that the defendant was aware of the risk posed by a decision and that his conduct fell far below what is reasonably expected would be difficult to satisfy.

Overall, the review of accountability mechanisms establishes that financial institution directors and senior managers who follow profit maximisation strategies entailing excessive risk-taking, but are in good faith, are still unlikely to face personal liability despite the reinforced power of regulators to impose sanctions on individuals and the introduction of criminal liability for taking a risky decision that causes the failure of a financial institution.

V. Conclusions

This chapter demonstrated that the reaction to the 2007–2009 financial crisis has led to a substantial expansion of regulatory intervention in the internal governance of financial institutions, especially in the areas of executive remuneration and the selection of directors and senior managers. However, despite these reforms, financial institutions' senior managers continue to face strong incentives to seek to maximise shareholder value, and board members still owe the same duties to shareholders as the directors of any other company. It follows that the profit maximisation norm, which is inextricably linked to a high level of risk-taking, continues to dominate financial institution corporate governance despite the constraints recently imposed by prudential regulation. At the same time, the new

162 According to Lord Diplock in *R v Lawrence* [1982] AC 510, 526, 'Recklessness on the part of the doer of an act presupposes that there is something in the circumstances that would have drawn the attention of an ordinary prudent individual to the possibility that his act was capable of causing the kind of serious harmful consequences that the section that created the offence was intended to prevent, and that *the risk of those harmful consequences occurring was not so slight* that an ordinary prudent individual would feel justified in treating them as negligible' (emphasis added).

163 On this, see John Lowry and Rod Edmunds, 'Directors Duties and Liabilities: Disqualifying "Unfit" Directors at Banks? Political Rhetoric and the Directors' Disqualification Regime' in Iris H-Y Chiu (ed), *The Law on Corporate Governance in Banks* (Edward Elgar Publishing, 2015), 96.

164 [1999] 1 BCLC 433.

regulatory rules rely heavily on regulated entities making their own efforts to comply with regulatory objectives, for instance by designing appropriate risk management procedures and remuneration policies and by scrutinising senior appointments. The next chapter argues that it is therefore necessary to engage in a broader rethink of the corporate law and governance regime in the financial sector with a view to bringing it in line with regulatory objectives.

6 The need to reform the corporate law framework as it applies to financial institutions

Towards financial sustainability

The previous chapters argued that despite the broad range of post-crisis reforms, the shareholder-centric character of financial institution corporate governance persists through the significant remaining components of variable remuneration, the pressures from the market for corporate control and institutional shareholders, and the application of directors' duties on financial institutions in the same manner as in generic companies. In the same vein, most scholars[1] still perceive financial institution corporate governance as an exercise of aligning the interests of senior managers with those of dispersed shareholders,[2] thus obfuscating the potential complementarity between the corporate regime and prudential regulation.

The argument advanced here is that revisiting the theoretical understanding of corporate law, as applying to the financial sector, under the prism of a regulatory approach is a prerequisite to the successful implementation of existing reforms. Indeed, reconsidering financial institutions' corporate law framework through the perspective of prudential regulation objectives would serve as a clear theoretical basis for a radical reform of financial institutions' corporate objective and directors' duties (to be discussed in the next chapter) to reflect the change of focus from profit maximisation to entity preservation. However, doing so raises a series of possible counter-arguments stemming from the contractarian account of corporate law,[3] which asserts that corporate law ought to act as a standard-form contract and

1 At the same time, some authors suggest that a distinct approach should be taken to the corporate governance of banks which detracts from the generally accepted facilitative approach. See e.g. Blanaid Clarke, '"Corporate Governance" an Oxymoron? The Role of Corporate Governance in the Current Banking Crisis' in Iain MacNeil and Justin O'Brien (eds), *The Future of Financial Regulation* (Hart Publishing, 2010).

2 For instance, White reviews the interplay between corporate governance and financial regulation, and assumes that corporate governance necessarily aims to protect the interests of the shareholders. He thus concludes the achievement of regulatory objectives requires a worsening of bank corporate governance. See Lawrence White, 'Corporate Governance and Prudential Regulation of Banks: Is There Any Connection?' in James Barth, Chen Lin and Clas Wihlborg (eds), *Research Handbook on International Banking and Governance* (Edward Elgar Publishing, 2012).

3 Corporate contractarianism is based on the law and economics methodology which explores the rationale for legal rules and evaluates their social desirability using neoclassical economic theory (mostly micro-economics). See e.g. Richard A Posner and

as market infrastructure rather than as an area of regulatory law with top-bottom imposition of values and objectives.

To that effect, section I of this chapter engages closely with the dominant economic theory of the corporation and identifies that the social utility of a market-facilitative approach to corporate law rests on several factual assumptions which may very well be convincing for non-financial companies but are not so in the case of financial institutions. Section II explains that the relationship between corporate law and prudential regulation, which is currently antagonistic, could be instead symbiotic; and identifies the potential positive contribution of a supportive internal governance framework to the objectives of prudential regulation. Then section III explores the main features of a regulatory-driven corporate law framework for financial institutions focusing primarily on the appropriate corporate objective for financial institutions. Finally, section IV concludes.

I. Why a regulatory approach to financial institutions' corporate law framework is consistent with economic analysis of corporate law

a. An overview of corporate contractarianism

It is trite to say that the prevailing view of the firm, and hence the dominant theory of company law since the late 1970s, is the so-called nexus of contracts theory[4] and the closely related agency costs theory. They both stem from the law and economics tradition and are based on an economic explanation of the existence of companies and of the exclusive privileges attributed to shareholders by business practice and company law. Until then – with one notable exception – economics viewed the firm as a 'black box' and could not account for the emergence of companies, while company law theory was dominated by managerialist thoughts. The latter viewed large widely held companies as quasi-public institutions which are free to act – and ought to act – in the best interests of the community, after the demise of shareholder control, which was first documented in the ground-breaking work of Berle and Means in 1932.[5] Berle and Means provided empirical evidence

Kenneth E Scott, *Economics of Corporation Law and Securities Regulation* (Little, Brown, 1980); and Richard Posner, *Economic Analysis of Law* (8th edn, Wolters Kluwer, 2011). For an in-depth discussion of corporate contractarian theory, see Marc T Moore, 'Private Ordering and Public Policy: The Paradoxical Foundations of Corporate Contractarianism' (2014) 34 *Oxford Journal of Legal Studies* 693; and Andrew Johnston, *EC Regulation of Corporate Governance* (CUP, 2009), 21–58.

4 Still, the entity conception of the corporation as a public institution remains relevant. For a comparison of the two, see William T Allen, 'Our Schizophrenic Conception of the Business Corporation' (1992) 14 *Cardozo Law Review* 261.

5 See Adolf Berle and Gardiner Means, *The Modern Corporation and Private Property* (rev edn, Harcourt, Brace & World, 1967). Thorstein Veblen was the intellectual predecessor of Berle and Means's work, mainly in *Absentee Ownership and Business in Recent Times* (Viking Adult, 1923). However, Berle himself did not initially view the separation of ownership and control as a positive evolution; it was Dodd who first argued that the modern corporation is public in nature and that corporate managers,

that most large US companies were practically controlled by their managers due to the high dispersal of their share ownership, a phenomenon they famously labelled as the separation of ownership and control.[6]

The exception alluded to in the previous paragraph is the path-breaking article of Ronald Coase who proposed in 1937 that the firm is an alternative to market transactions, whereby resource allocation is accomplished by managerial authority, rather than by entering into contracts.[7] In other words, the choice of whether an activity is to be pursued through the market using the process of bargaining or internally in the firm using the command power of the manager over employees and corporate assets, depends on transaction costs. It must be noted that this analysis purports to explain the emergence of all types of firms including sole traders, partnerships and companies.

Following on this tradition, in the early 1970s Alchian and Demsetz explained the firm as a team productive process whereby managers monitor the activity of other members to prevent shirking and reward hard work.[8] They argued that firms develop when team effort increases production and it is impossible to measure the marginal contribution of each input provider. Therefore, the classical capitalistic firm was analysed as a contractual structure with the following core features: (a) production based on joint input; (b) multiple input owners (e.g. employees, creditors, etc.); (c) one party who is common to all contracts, negotiates each contract independently, holds the residual claim to the output and has the right to sell his or her status. This latter party is the employer/owner of the firm.

Jensen and Meckling were the first to affirm that the company is a mere legal fiction, nothing more than an administrative convenience that consists of a nexus of contracting individuals,[9] namely its managers, directors, shareholders,

freed now from shareholder control, should exercise their power for the public good. See Merrick Dodd, 'For Whom are Corporate Managers Trustees?' (1932) 45 *Harvard Law Review* 1145, esp 1162. Berle later adopted this position and ascertained that the modern corporation should be viewed '*not as a business device but as a social institution in the context of a revolutionary century*'. See Adolf Berle, *The 20th Century Capitalist Revolution* (Harcourt, Brace & Co, 1954), 24.

6 A similar observation in Germany gave rise to the entity theory. 'The property rights are fragmented and flexible to such an extent that the enterprise obtains a proper life [...] an objective existence, like it was embodied by state and church in earlier times.' See Walther Rathenau, *Von kommenden Dingen* (Berlin, S Fischer, 1917), 142. The translation is taken from Martin Lupold and Gerhard Schnyder, 'Horse, Cow, Sheep, or "Thing-in-itself"? The Cognitive Origins of Corporate Governance in Switzerland, Germany, and the US, 1910s-1930s' (2008) http://ssrn.com/abstract=1018413 accessed 1 May 2017.

7 See Ronald Coase, 'The Nature of the Firm' (1937) in Peter Buckley and Jonathan Michie (eds), *Firms, Organizations and Contracts (A Reader in Industrial Organisation)* (OUP, 1996).

8 Armen Alchian and Harold Demsetz, 'Production, Information Costs, and Economic Organisation' (1972) 62 *American Economic Review* 777, 777–780.

9 See Michael Jensen and William Meckling, 'Theory of the Firm: Managerial Behavior, Agency Costs and Ownership Structure' (1976) 3 *Journal of Financial Economics* 305. Jensen and Meckling speak about firms in general and not about companies as such.

employees, suppliers, creditors and customers.[10] It is obvious to company lawyers that this analysis of the company is incorrect from a technical legal perspective,[11] as the doctrine of separate legal personality means that in law it is the company that enters into contracts with input providers.[12] However, the economic view of the company purports to capture its economic substance rather than legal technicalities. According to the nexus of contracts view, shareholders are not in any sense the owners of the company, as the company does not exist and hence there is nothing to be owned,[13] but they provide one of the inputs, i.e. equity capital.

The next logical step in the contractarian project is to explain company law itself in contractual terms. The ground-breaking work of Easterbrook and Fischel analyses company law as a standard form contract which offers default terms that can be overridden by express agreement of the parties.[14] Easterbrook and Fischel make two claims that must be clearly distinguished: a positive claim that US corporate law is (in most cases) facilitative/enabling rather than directive/regulatory;[15] and the normative claim that corporate law should contain rules that mimic the terms that the relevant parties would have agreed to if they were able to negotiate in the absence of transaction costs. Corporate law should not generally impose mandatory rules, but rather should seek to predict the set of rules that would be chosen by rational parties, if they were negotiating on an arm's length basis.[16] Which

However, from the point of view of corporate governance, we are concerned only with companies and for this reason I substitute 'company' for 'firm' in the present discussion. See also Melvin Eisenberg, 'The Conception that the Corporation is a Nexus of Contracts and the Dual Nature of the Firm' (1999) 24 *Journal of Corporation Law* 819.

10 See Jensen and Meckling (above n 9), 313. From a doctrinal legal perspective, the corporate constitution binds the company and its members contractually. See Companies Acts 2006, s 33 and *Borland's Trustee v Steel Bros & Co Ltd* [1901] 1 Ch 279.

11 Bainbridge, for instance, observes that corporate constituents do not contract with each other but with the corporation, and that the board is the nexus of contracts. See Stephen M Bainbridge, 'Director Primacy: The Means and Ends of Corporate Governance' (2002–2003) 97 *Northwestern University Law Review* 547, 554–556.

12 For instance, employees are employed by the company, assets are purchased and held by the company and loans are taken by the company.

13 For a criticism of the contractarian attempt to deny the existence of companies as separate entities, see Paddy Ireland, 'The Myth of Shareholder Ownership' (1999) 62 *Modern Law Review* 32, 52–57.

14 See Frank H Easterbrook and Daniel R Fischel, *The Economic Structure of Corporate Law* (Harvard University Press, 1991).

15 In the UK context, a similar analysis is offered by Cheffins, who concludes that entities akin to limited liability companies existed before special company legislation was enacted and thus that companies are creatures of business practice (private contracting) and not of the law, as the old concession theory claimed. See Brian R Cheffins, *Company Law: Theory, Structure and Operation* (OUP, 1997), 31–41.

16 It is worth citing the thesis of Easterbrook and Fischel in their own words: 'We treat corporate law as a standard form contract, supplying terms most venturers would have chosen but yielding to explicit terms in all but a few instances. The normative thesis of the book is that corporate law should contain the terms people would have negotiated, were the costs of negotiating at arm's length for every contingency sufficiently low. The positive thesis is that corporate law almost always conforms to this model. It

particular default rules are chosen matters, as high transaction costs may prevent corporate constituencies from negotiating and agreeing on different rules, and hence inefficient default rules can be hard to opt out of.[17] Broadly speaking, most American contractarian scholars are convinced that the existing doctrinal position of US corporate law is efficient due to regulatory competition. Indeed, company law falls within the domain of individual states and therefore company promoters can select the state of incorporation and hence the applicable company law regime they prefer, irrespective of the state where the company will be having its real centre of administration. It has thus been argued that regulatory competition is a race to the top where each state seeks to formulate the most efficient company law rules to attract incorporations.[18]

Most contractarians agree that the default position of corporate law with regard to the internal organisation of companies should be that directors are empowered to run the business of the company insulated from shareholder interference but that, at the same time, directors owe a duty to promote the collective interests of the shareholders, and are elected by the shareholders who are the only corporate constituency having voting rights. Shareholders are also unique in their right to appropriate the residual profits of the company, after all fixed contractual claims are satisfied, via the payment of dividends or the distribution of corporate assets in the case where a company is wound up. This way of structuring the internal governance of companies, which is characteristic of the UK and US systems,[19] is described by some authors as shareholder primacy.[20]

is enabling rather than directive. The standby terms grant great discretion to managers and facilitate actual contracts.' Easterbrook and Fischel (above n 14), 15.

17 For a more nuanced view which identifies a property-law function of company law, i.e. asset partitioning, see Henry Hansmann and Reinier Kraakman, 'The Essential Role of Organizational Law' (Harvard Law and Economics Discussion Paper 284, April 2000) http://ssrn.com/abstract=229956 accessed 1 May 2017.

18 See e.g. Ralph Winter, 'State Law, Shareholder Protection and the Theory of the Corporation' (1977) 6 *Journal of Legal Studies* 251; and Frank Easterbrook, 'Managers' Discretion and Investors' Welfare: Theories and Evidence' (1984) 9 *Delaware Journal of Corporate Law* 540. The state that attracts most incorporations is Delaware. For a general discussion of the Delaware corporate law system, see Lawrence A Hamermesh, 'The Policy Foundations of Delaware Corporate Law' (2006) 106 *Columbia Law Review* 1749. For a critical analysis of state competition to attract incorporations in the US, see Lucian Bebchuk, 'Federalism and the Corporation: The Desirable Limits on State Competition in Corporate Law' (1992) 105 *Harvard Law Review* 1435.

19 The emphasis placed by UK corporate managers on shareholders' financial interests has been empirically confirmed. Indeed, a mid-1990s study found that 71% of UK managers gave first priority to shareholder interests. See Masaru Yoshimori, 'Whose Company Is It? The Concept of Corporations in Japan and the West' (1995) 28 *Long Range Planning* 33, 34.

20 For a discussion of the modern emphasis of Delaware corporate law on shareholder value, see Edward B Rock, 'Adapting to the New Shareholder-Centric Reality' (2013) 161 *University of Pennsylvania Law Review* 1907.

The reason why all corporate constituencies are likely to agree to the above structure and why it therefore should be the default legal position is the following. Granting all the company powers to the board and thus insulating the board from direct intervention by shareholders (or by any other group of constituents such as employees) is the only workable way to run a complicated and large organisation. Direct involvement by the shareholders, who are – at least in public companies – numerous, relatively uninformed about the business, and lacking a uniform view on what is good for the company, would lead to inefficient and confused decision-making.[21] The same would apply to other groups. Conversely, granting all powers to the board of directors – similarly to a representative democracy where all power is delegated to a sovereign parliament – provides a workable governance structure.

The second key characteristic of Anglo-American company law, which contractarian theory defends, is more difficult to establish. One first needs to understand why all corporate constituents would accept shareholder exclusivity with regard to the corporate objective and voting rights. It seems *prima facie* strange that out of all constituents it is only the shareholders' interests that directors are required to promote,[22] and it is only them who appropriate all residual profit and who enjoy voting rights.[23] Indeed, shareholders appear to be similar to creditors, as both groups provide capital to the company, and seem to have a less intricate involvement with the company than say employees, whose livelihood largely depends on the company's fate, while shareholders only stand to lose the financial value of their investment.

The reason why mainstream contractarian scholars support shareholder exclusivity is the unique vulnerability of the shareholders due to the special nature of the terms of their 'contract' with the company. Contrary to all other corporate constituencies who are entitled to a predetermined financial return on their investment in the company,[24] shareholders are not entitled in law to any return other than in the case where the company is wound up. In the latter case, any net

21 See Stephen M Bainbridge, 'Director Primacy and Shareholder Disempowerment' (2006) 119 *Harvard Law Review* 1735, 1749–1751; Bainbridge (above n 11), 557–563.

22 In the UK, Companies Act 2006 s 172 states that directors must act in the way they consider (in good faith) to be most likely to promote the success of the company to the benefit of the shareholders as a whole. A detailed examination of directors' duties in UK company law can be found in Chapter 2, sections IV and V. In the US, the landmark decision of the Supreme Court of Michigan in *Dodge v Ford Motor Co* 204 Mich 459, 507; 170 NW 668 (Mich 1919) confirmed that '[a] business corporation is organized and carried on primarily for the profit of the stockholders'.

23 In the UK, Model Articles 20 and 21 for public companies (Companies (Model Articles) Regulations SI 2008/ 3229, Schedule 3) provide that directors are appointed by an ordinary resolution of the members or by a decision of the board, and that any director appointed by the board, or one who has not been reappointed in the last two AGMs, is to retire and may offer himself for re-election at the next AGM.

24 For instance, a bank that has lent money to a company expects the capital to be repaid with the agreed interest; bondholders expect a fixed rate of return and, at some point, a redemption of the capital; employees expect to be paid the agreed salary; and suppliers of goods and services expect to be paid the agreed price.

value remaining after all creditors have been paid and the expenses of the liquidation have been covered, is distributed to the shareholders.[25] Outside liquidation, holders of ordinary shares have no contractual right to a fixed income stream from the company. It is entirely at the discretion of companies to declare a dividend, provided that doing so is allowed by the relevant legal rules.[26]

From a contractarian perspective, it follows that if corporate constituents were able to negotiate *ex ante* in a zero transaction costs world, they would assign primacy to shareholders' interests, as they are the group the most vulnerable to managerial opportunism, their contracts being incomplete and them bearing the residual risk.[27] This argument justifies shareholder value maximisation as the sole legitimate corporate objective by following the hypothetical bargain methodology.[28] The fact that shareholders are the last to be paid in liquidation, and may only receive a dividend if the company has profits (i.e. there is surplus after all contractual liabilities are met) renders the shareholders the residual risk-bearers in a company as their investment is the first one to be lost if things go wrong; and in that sense it is more risky than the investment of company creditors in the broader sense of the term.[29] So, naturally shareholders would demand to reap the rewards of corporate success given that they are the first to bear the consequences of corporate failure.[30]

25 See Insolvency Act 1986, s 107.

26 There is an elaborate body of law which restricts the ability of companies to pay dividends and ensures that the capital of the company is not returned to the shareholders. These rules aim to protect companies' creditors and can be found in Companies Act 2006 ss 829–853. See also *Trevor v Whitworth* (1887) App Cas 409 (HL).

27 See Easterbrook and Fischel (above n 14), 11; and Bainbridge (above n 11), 584–591.

28 Generally, the two main dimensions of the hypothetical bargain are the generality and idealisation of the parties. For a detailed discussion of the various alternative constructions of the hypothetical bargain, see David Charny, 'Hypothetical Bargains: The Normative Structure of Contract Interpretation' (1991) 89 *Michigan Law Review* 1815, 1820–1823.

29 In a broad sense, any party that has a contractual claim against the company (e.g. employees with regard to unpaid wages, suppliers with regard to unpaid goods/services they supplied, and tort victims with regard to the damages they are owed) is a creditor.

30 It must be emphasised, however, that this proposition is hotly contested in corporate theory as numerous scholars support the view that employees, rather than shareholders, are the main residual risk bearers in a company. See Lawrence Mitchell, *Progressive Corporate Law* (Westview Press, 1995); and Lorraine Talbot, *Progressive Corporate Governance for the 21st Century* (Routledge, 2013), 132–134. In addition, other scholars argue that there are many residual risk bearers in companies and hence shareholders are not unique. See Lynn Stout, 'Bad and Not-so-Bad Arguments for Shareholder Primacy' (2001–2002) 75 *Southern California Law Review* 1189, 1194–1195; Margaret Blair, *Ownership and Control: Rethinking Corporate Governance for the 21st Century* (Brookings Institute, 1995); Gavin Kelly and John Parkinson, 'The Conceptual Foundations of the Company: A Pluralist Approach' in John Parkinson, Gavin Kelly and Andrew Gamble (eds), *The Political Economy of the Company* (Hart Publishing, 2000), esp 113–121; and Oliver Williamson, *The Mechanisms of Governance* (OUP, 1996), ch 7.

Once it is accepted that shareholders are entitled to residual profits, it follows that they are the best constituency to be given governance rights.[31] Given that other constituencies are protected by explicit contracts against the risk that managers may misuse corporate assets and under-perform, it is purportedly sensible to grant voting powers to the shareholders and to make them the beneficiaries of directors' fiduciary duties. Apart from being necessary for the protection of shareholder interests, this structure also benefits other constituencies indirectly, as shareholders are the group that is most likely to use its voting power in a way which is beneficial for the company as whole.[32] This is because shareholders appropriate most of the marginal gains and suffer most of the marginal losses.[33] Conversely, constituents who have contractual rights *against* the company should not be given voting rights as they would be able to use them opportunistically to renegotiate the terms of their explicit contracts to the detriment of the company.

In the context of the selection of corporate governance norms by shareholders and managers, contractarian theory has to explain how private ordering actually works in practice, given the absence of explicit bargaining between managers and shareholders with regard to the corporate objective and the corporate governance structures of each company. The response given by contractarian theory is that shareholders agree to the terms of governance offered by a company by purchasing its shares.[34] A share is essentially a bundle of rights including a right to dividends, and typically the right to vote for the board, approve some decisions and have the company run in the shareholders' interests. These rights cannot be negotiated individually but resemble the standard terms and conditions in consumer contracts.[35] Evidently, if investors are not satisfied with the governance terms offered by a particular company, they will not buy its shares. It is thus accurate to describe shareholder exclusivity as the outcome of a notional agreement between shareholders and senior managers, insofar as it is not dictated by the law but naturally prevails in corporate practice by the operation of the forces of the capital market.[36] This of course assumes that the prices at which the shares

31 The existence of voting *per se* is explained as performing a gap-filling function. This is necessary as it is impossible for companies' constitutions and corporate law to provide for every possible contingency. The same explanation is given with regard to fiduciary duties of directors. See Frank Easterbrook and Daniel Fischel, 'Voting in Corporate Law' (1983) 26 *Journal of Law and Economics* 395, 401–403.

32 For instance, Blair and Stout, although they reject shareholder exclusivity with regard to the corporate objective, accept (limited) shareholder voting rights as being beneficial for all corporate constituencies. See Margaret Blair and Lynn Stout, 'A Team Production Theory of Corporate Law' (1999) 24 *Journal of Corporation Law* 751, 796.

33 See Easterbrook and Fischel (above n 14), 403–406.

34 See Easterbrook and Fischel (above n 14), 287 and 293–295.

35 Investors' choice is still free to the extent that many companies are offering shares and other investment opportunities. Given the large number of listed companies in which an investor can invest, it is realistic to say that companies compete to attract equity capital.

36 Companies with governance practices that do not meet shareholders' expectations will suffer from lower share prices, as potential investors will discount governance failures

trade reflect their internal governance structures, as – presumably – potential investors monitor companies' corporate governance and respond to perceived improvements or deteriorations of governance structures accordingly.

The principal normative implication of corporate contractarianism is that the appropriate role of corporate law is to facilitate free contracting amongst the relevant interested parties by providing default rules that mimic the likely outcome of the parties' bargain. Contractarian theory thus rejects the use of mandatory rules. Indeed, insofar as the consent of all parties to an agreement or activity is substantively free,[37] and no third parties suffer any harm, it must be true that allowing them to act as they freely choose leads to the maximisation of aggregate social wealth.[38] In particular, it is argued that when a company operates with the objective of maximising its profits, it necessarily maximises social wealth as the economic profits of firms are equal to the value of their output minus the value of their input. It follows that any profit made increases social wealth by at least the amount of that profit and hence maximising profits maximises social wealth,[39] which eventually benefits all members of society.[40]

when deciding whether to buy shares in a company. In addition, current shareholders who are dissatisfied with the corporate governance of their company are likely to sell their shares. Ultimately, the hypothesis is that companies which do not adopt the governance structures favoured by shareholders will face a higher cost of capital, as their share prices will be lower than they would otherwise be. Managers are thus incentivised to offer investors the governance regime that they prefer. Easterbrook and Fischel assert that the 'mechanism by which stocks are valued ensures that the price reflects the terms of governance and operation'. See Frank Easterbrook and Daniel Fischel, 'The Corporate Contract' (1989) 89 *Columbia Law Review* 1416, 1430.

37 In order for the consent of the parties to qualify as substantively free of coercion there must be alternative suppliers of the relevant good or service. See Milton Friedman, *Capitalism and Freedom* (40th anniversary edn, The University of Chicago Press, 2002), 28. In other words, if a market is monopolistic, free contracting will not maximise social wealth, as the output under monopoly is smaller than under competition because some consumers switch to (more costly) alternative products. In addition, monopolist producers are in a position to transfer wealth from the consumers to themselves. For an explanation of the economic consequences of monopoly, see Posner (above n 3), 351–368. The problems caused by monopolies and market power are dealt with by competition law which falls outside the scope of this monograph.

38 This assumes that aggregate social wealth is defined as the sum of the wealth of all members of a given society and that all involved individuals are rational and well informed.

39 On this see Michael C Jensen, 'Value Maximization, Stakeholder Theory, and the Corporate Objective Function' (2001) 14 *Journal of Applied Corporate Finance* 8, 11–13. The same idea was introduced in a less precise manner by Friedman. See Milton Friedman, 'The Social Responsibility of Business is to Increase its Profits' *New York Times Magazine* (New York, 13 September 1970), 32.

40 This claim overlooks the crucial issue of the distribution of benefits amongst individuals. As soon as concerns of distributional justice are admitted, the maximisation of total social wealth does not necessarily coincide with the public interest. On this, see John Parkinson, *Corporate Power and Responsibility: Issues in the Theory of Company Law* (Clarendon Press, 1993), 48–50. See also Ian B Lee, 'Efficiency and Ethics in the Debate about Shareholder Primacy' (2006) 31 *Delaware Journal of Corporate Law* 533.

b. The assumptions underlying the claim that a market-facilitative corporate law framework leads to maximum social utility

The present study does not question the normative assumption that the maximisation of social wealth is the appropriate objective of corporate law, and hence the relevant criterion against which to assess the current legal framework. However, it aims to establish that in the financial sector it is necessary to regulate corporate governance outcomes by mandatory rules with a view to protecting the public good of financial stability. To this effect, this section analyses the normative contractarian thesis and exposes the factual assumptions that underpin the alleged link between shareholder exclusivity and the maximisation of aggregate social wealth.

Contractarian theory does not fail to acknowledge the problem of negative externalities and other market failures which require the introduction of mandatory regulation.[41] To the extent that efficiency is socially valued, individual behaviour and interpersonal agreements fall outside the scope of the regulatory state so far as there is no market failure such as irrationality, information asymmetry, public goods,[42] monopoly or externalities. If one of the above types of market failure applies then the regulatory state needs to interfere with the behaviour or agreement in question so as to ensure the maximisation of aggregate social wealth.[43]

However, corporate contractarianism asserts that corporate law should not undermine its exclusive focus on the maximisation of shareholder wealth,[44] but rather that any necessary intervention to tackle market failures and achieve the democratically agreed level of social justice should be implemented in other areas of law such as tort law, employment law and taxation.[45] In this way, the

41 The pioneering work of Coase explains the need to impose a tortious duty to compensate for the harm caused to third parties (negative externalities), in situations where transaction costs are high enough to prevent the relevant parties from negotiating and agreeing to a solution. See Ronald Coase, 'The Problem of Social Cost' (1960) 3 *Journal of Law and Economics* 1.

42 The nature of corporate information as a public good which, absent mandatory disclosure obligations, is prone to be under-produced justifies the mandatory nature of securities law. See e.g. Frank Easterbrook and Daniel Fischel, 'Mandatory Disclosure and the Protection of Investors' (1984) 70 *Virginia Law Review* 669, 681–682.

43 However, contractarian theory contends that such intervention should, if possible, be implemented by public law means, so as to preserve the enabling nature of company law, which is essentially private in nature.

44 The argument is simply that there is no need to regulate companies any differently from other persons with regard to externalities. According to this view, companies should only be obliged to comply with the general law of the land as any other legal or natural person. See Bainbridge (above n 11), 591.

45 Friedman was the first to explicitly argue that the redistribution of income should take place through reverse income tax alone and not by interfering with various markets or paying a series of specific benefits. See Friedman (above n 37), 161–195. Kaplow and Shavell demonstrate that using a legal rule to redistribute income is less efficient than effecting the same redistribution by taxation, as redistribution through legal rules is a blunt tool compared to taxation, and is likely to fail as prices adjust to reflect the expected cost of (inefficient) legal rules. See Louis Kaplow and Steven Shavell, 'Why

fundamentally positive effect of companies behaving as self-interested rational wealth maximisers remains. The benefit to society from profit-seeking by companies can thus be enjoyed, while externalities are remedied by making companies compensate tort victims, pay taxes, or by directly regulating aspects of their external behaviour.[46] It is argued that if corporate law required companies to seek to achieve an objective different from shareholder value maximisation, much of the benefits accruing from the private sector ownership of companies would be lost[47] as corporate managers would be left free to exploit shareholders and pursue policy objectives of their own choice to the detriment of society as a whole.[48] Therefore, contractarians accept the general regulation of corporate conduct by the ordinary law of the land, but reject any special regulation of corporate governance outcomes as being economically inefficient and value-decreasing.

Therefore, if it is accepted that corporate law's ultimate goal should be the maximisation of social wealth, then the claim that corporate law's operational objective must be shareholder value maximisation rests on two factual assumptions. The first assumption is that: (a) either there are no negative externalities resulting from profit maximisation per se, or (b) negative externalities arising out of corporate profit-seeking activity can be fully dealt with outside the realm of corporate governance law. Evidently, if regulating the external conduct of companies while preserving the facilitative nature of company law and the shareholder wealth maximisation norm is not sufficient to internalise externalities, the whole claim that the current regime maximises aggregate social wealth fails. The second factual assumption is that the private ordering process of shaping the internal corporate governance of companies is superior to interventionist state regulation

the Legal System is Less Efficient than the Income Tax in Redistributing Income' (1994) 23 *Journal of Legal Studies* 667, esp 669–675.

46 Bruner argues that the corporate governance systems of the UK, Canada and Australia have been able to focus predominantly on shareholder wealth maximisation without causing social instability due to the implementation of robust social welfare policies. On the other hand, the failure of the US to introduce a comparable social welfare system led to increasing demands on corporate governance to accommodate the interests of stakeholders. See Christopher Bruner, *Corporate Governance in the Common-Law World: The Political Foundations of Shareholder Power* (CUP, 2013), esp 214–220.

47 The shareholder value maximisation norm restores the private entrepreneurial nature of companies. If managers were allowed to seek private benefits, companies would not behave as rational wealth maximisers and hence Adam Smith's invisible hand argument would fail. On this, see Marc T Moore, *Corporate Governance in the Shadow of the State* (Hart Publishing, 2013), 75–76.

48 This argument is based on the idea that if directors are made accountable to more than one group of corporate constituents (as the stakeholder theory suggests) they will be in fact accountable to no one and thus they will be free to pursue their own self-interest. See e.g. Bainbridge (above n 11), 581–582. However, Blair and Stout challenge this assumption and explain the role of boards as that of a mediating hierarchy that balances the claims of different corporate constituents. See Blair and Stout (above n 32), esp 767–778.

by mandatory rules. The following paragraphs establish that neither of the two assumptions holds true in the case of financial institutions.

Let us begin from the externalities point. In the first place, it needs to be clarified that the existence of negative externalities that are not internalised by regulation does not necessarily mean that the current regime is not conducive to the maximisation of aggregate social wealth. If the benefits accruing to the shareholders are outweighed by the costs borne by third parties, total social wealth is still maximised. If this is the case, the social desirability of shareholder wealth maximisation has to be empirically ascertained based on the best available evidence, and cannot be simply derived by economic theory.[49] To that effect, Chapter 1 demonstrated the causal link between profit maximisation and excessive risk-taking in financial institutions and explained that the long-term interests of rational shareholders do not necessarily support sustainable business strategies. Rational diversified shareholders tend to be risk-neutral, while limited liability and the very high leverage of banks ensure that the negative consequences of risk-taking are not fully internalised by financial institution shareholders. It follows that the profit maximisation norm, which is embedded in the UK corporate law framework as explained in Chapter 2, is *prima facie* inconsistent with protecting financial stability. Then, Chapters 3, 4 and 5 established that other regulatory techniques cannot on their own fully tackle this problem as they rely on meta-regulatory techniques which require a supportive incentives framework within the regulated entity. Therefore, it follows that the focus of corporate law on profit maximisation does not – in the special case of financial institutions – contribute to the maximisation of social wealth as it damages the public good of financial stability to an extent that is probably higher than any benefits accruing from profit maximisation.

Turning to the point of efficient governance norm selection by the capital market, it is worth noting that this claim assumes two further propositions. The first one is that capital markets are efficient. According to the semi-strong version of the efficient capital markets hypothesis (ECMH),[50] the prices at which shares trade fully reflect all publicly available information about the issuing companies, so that share (and bond) prices reflect *inter alia* the appropriateness of the corporate governance structures chosen by companies.[51] The efficiency of capital markets is supported by some empirical evidence,[52] but is by no means settled in economic literature. The second proposition is that there is adequate available information to

49 See Moore (above n 47), 247–256.

50 An excellent overview of the ECMH can be found in Eugene F Fama, 'Efficient Capital Markets: A Review of Theory and Empirical Work' (1970) 25 *The Journal of Finance* 383. For a critical analysis of the ECMH, see Lynn Stout, 'The Mechanisms of Market Inefficiency' (2003) 28 *Journal of Corporation Law* 635.

51 The strong form of the Efficient Markets Hypothesis states that prices reflect all relevant information. The semi-strong form, which is more plausible, asserts that prices reflect publicly available information. The weak form states that the current price of a security reflects its past prices.

52 The seminal work of Fama reviews early empirical evidence that supports the hypothesis. See Fama (above n 50).

enable investors to assess the corporate governance of companies and monitor the behaviour of senior managers. However, if information is not available or cannot be properly understood by the investors, the prices of shares will not reflect the fundamental value of a company's assets, prospects, governance and strategy, but merely the erroneous perceptions of misinformed investors.

It follows that even if one accepts the validity of the semi-strong version of the efficient markets hypothesis, it is still possible that the absence of relevant information – or the inability of investors to understand it – prevents the prices of shares from reflecting the fundamental value of a company and of its corporate governance. Thus, if shares are mispriced by the market for a long period of time, there is no assurance that prevailing corporate governance norms are optimal and it becomes logically possible that the law can prescribe superior structures to the ones actually prevailing. This demonstrates that state regulation may potentially lead to better governance structures (for equity investors and creditors) than the ones favoured by the markets. To establish this claim, Chapter 1 showed that financial institutions are opaque in the sense that markets cannot value their assets, risk and governance structures accurately, and hence market discipline through monitoring by equity and debt investors fails.

The two arguments are interrelated as the presence of both (a) negative externalities that cannot be dealt with by regulating external conduct, and (b) opacity that prevents effective private monitoring, demonstrates that the present regime is sub-optimal both for society as a whole and for financial institutions' equity and debt investors, thus establishing a strong *economic* case for legal reform. However, the externalities argument offers a more powerful justification for regulation as it calls for regulation to protect the public interest, while the opacity argument calls for regulation to protect private investors.

II. How an alternative corporate law framework could complement reflexive regulatory techniques: the potential symbiotic relationship between corporate law and prudential regulation

Before proceeding to illustrate the potential positive contribution of regulating financial institution corporate governance to the overall prudential regulation regime, a caveat is necessary. When alluding to a regulatory approach, it is not necessarily meant that the emphasis will be on regulatory discretion and hence on rule-making and supervision by administrative authorities,[53] but rather the term '*regulatory*' is used in its broader sense to include legislative measures.[54] Essentially, a regulatory approach, as opposed to the current facilitative approach, would be implemented by appropriate legislative reform which would be supplemented

53 A discussion of the most influential theories on regulation can be found in Bronwen Morgan and Karen Yeung, *An Introduction to Law and Regulation: Text and Materials* (CUP, 2007).

54 The discussion alludes to using 'regulatory law', i.e. legal rules that seek to promote and protect the public interest.

by new regulatory rules and supervision by the relevant authorities. It follows that a regulatory approach does not necessarily equate to requiring prudential regulators to micro-manage financial institutions, but rather to setting the right incentives and procedures to ensure that institutions will be managed in a way consistent with the public interest in financial stability.

The main prospective benefit of extending the micro-prudential regulatory framework to include the corporate law framework for financial institutions, is the alignment of the incentives of directors and senior managers with the objectives of prudential regulation, which is crucial for reflexive regulatory techniques to work in practice.[55] Indeed, the main weakness of meta-regulation, and reflexive regulation in general, stems from its main strength, i.e. the reliance on regulated entities to implement their own internal policies and comply with them. If the incentives faced by the relevant persons inside an institution – i.e. the board and senior management – are not aligned with regulatory objectives, it is highly likely that institutions will try to manipulate regulatory standards or will comply only in letter but not in spirit. Internal risk management, audit and control functions can be marginalised from core decision-makers and reduced to a mere compliance exercise which is seen as unnecessary and is not seriously taken into account.[56] This observation highlights the significance of the corporate governance regime, and at the same time indicates that corporate governance reform ought to create appropriate incentives as much as procedures. It follows that a regulatory approach to financial institution corporate governance would be primarily focused on aligning the incentives of directors and senior managers with regulatory objectives.

On the contrary, to the extent that there remains a significant divergence between the incentives faced by managers and directors, and regulatory objectives, the following two risks threaten financial stability. First, regulation may prove to be ineffective in practice, as regulators can easily be captured by financial institution managers, who benefit from the availability of enormous resources to substantiate their own views and present them as well-grounded. In addition, given that senior regulators are appointed by the government, they may succumb to political pressures demanding them to take a light-touch approach, as it is extremely unpopular to restrain financial institution activities in periods of economic growth.[57] Second, in the case that regulators do manage to materially restrict the discretion of managers to pursue personal interests, the latter are likely to attempt to bypass regulatory obstacles by engineering transactions and business models accordingly. Conversely, constraints imposed by the appropriate design of financial institution directors' and

55 On the notion of reflexive law and regulation, see Chapter 3, section IV.

56 See Julia Black, 'Paradoxes and Failures: "New Governance" Techniques and the Financial Crisis' (2012) 75 *Modern Law Review* 1037, 1046–1047.

57 'Regulation, in effect, provided little or no check, nor barrier, to the decisions taken by banks [...] in the pursuit of (short-term) profit maximisation. It was not adapted to changes in the underlying vulnerabilities of the system as a whole [...] and allowed financial engineering to avoid its impact.' Markus K Brunnermeier and others, *The Fundamental Principles of Financial Regulation: Geneva Reports on the World Economy* 11 (Center for Economic Policy Research, 2009), 1.

senior managers' incentives and governance structures can effectively complement external regulation. Ensuring that corporate law is successful in aligning directors' and senior managers' behaviours with regulatory objectives, would thus contribute both to the effectiveness of prudential regulation and the mitigation of the costs related to financial institutions' attempts to evade it.

In addition, robust internal governance procedures severely curtail the risk that serious fraud undermines the stability of an institution.[58] Although the UK bank failures that marked the recent crisis were not directly associated with such practices,[59] the recent LIBOR scandal indicates that fraudulent and criminal practices can persist in large and well-established financial institutions with seemingly exemplary governance mechanisms.[60] Such behaviours – apart from harming customers and other parties – are a potential threat to the stability of the financial system, due to the ensuing financial loss, regulatory sanctions and reputational damage of the institution concerned. Of course, such practices are already outlawed, and are clearly inconsistent with the present corporate governance system. However, the strong incentives faced by senior managers to maximise short-term profitability, and the limited ability of shareholders to monitor the adequacy of internal controls,[61] demonstrate the potential for a regulatory model to reduce fraud, regulatory breaches and other forms of misconduct.

Another usual cause of failures, and hence a potential source of systemic risk, is the frequent lack of understanding by boards of institutions' business models, risk profiles and products. The whole corporate governance debate revolves around these issues and most corporate governance rules aim to facilitate the successful discharge by the board of its responsibilities, by making provision for (*inter alia*) board structure, selection process, information flows, and incentives. Indeed, the high expectations that regulators have of financial institution boards require directors to play a meaningful role in the management of financial institutions' businesses. Boards and senior executives are the regulators' first point of contact and the main subjects of regulatory incentives; if they do not properly understand and control the business strategy and risk exposures of the institution they serve,

58 The Bank of Credit and Commerce International (BCCI) ceased trading in July 1991, after it became apparent that it had engaged in money-laundering activities. Barings, a very old merchant bank that had not faced troubles since its 1890 reorganisation, collapsed in 1995 due to vast losses incurred on the Singapore Stock Exchange, by Mr Nick Leeson, a local manager. For a vivid description of the Barings failure, see David Kynaston, *The City of London – Volume IV: A Club No More, 1945–2000* (Pimlico, 2002), 762–768.

59 For instance, no evidence of malpractice or any type of intentional misconduct was identified in the case of RBS, despite the in-depth investigation carried out by the FSA. See FSA, 'The Failure of the Royal Bank of Scotland: Financial Services Authority Board Report' (2011) Part III www.fsa.gov.uk/pubs/other/rbs.pdf accessed 1 May 2017.

60 On the LIBOR scandal, see HM Treasury, *The Wheatley Review of LIBOR: Final Report* (Government Publications, 2012) www.gov.uk/government/publications/the-wheatley-review accessed 1 May 2017.

61 On this, see Chapter 1, section III.

the whole concept of a constructive dialogue between regulators and regulated persons falls apart.

Fundamentally, the failures of RBS,[62] HBOS[63] and Northern Rock[64] were due to their business models, which were approved by their directors.[65] Indeed, directors and senior managers are entrusted with a critical function to decide the strategy and supervise the operations of financial institutions.[66] Given the fact that senior managers possess superior information and expertise with regard to the affairs of the institution they run, it cannot be the role of regulators to take operating and business decisions;[67] boards must be responsible for deciding institutions' risk profile and strategy.[68] Thus, regulators now attach additional importance to boards, and see it as their duty to ensure that financial institutions' governance mechanisms are effective.[69] It is therefore unsurprising that the Basel Principles for Corporate Governance[70] urge bank boards to ensure that internal control functions are well-resourced, independent and effective. From this perspective, financial institutions are more vulnerable than most other companies due to their size, product and market diversification, and complexity, therefore more rigorous internal control procedures ought to be put in place.

Furthermore, a regulatory-driven corporate law regime would undoubtedly ensure that financial institutions manage their risks effectively, and that their boards are kept informed of material risks, and also monitor whether the institution's strategy is consistent with its risk profile as decided by the board. Sound corporate governance structures can lead to more efficient management of risks and hence mitigate the danger of financial collapse at the micro-level, with positive effects on the stability of the financial system at the macro-level. It was explained earlier in this chapter how the internal models for calculating credit, market and operational

62 See FSA (above n 59), paras 572–573.

63 See Parliamentary Commission on Banking Standards, *'An Accident Waiting to Happen': The Failure of HBOS* (2012–13, HL 144, HC 705), paras 122–126.

64 See Treasury Committee, *The Run on the Rock* (HC 2007–08 56–I), paras 37–42.

65 For an in-depth case study of the failure of Northern Rock, see Roman Tomasic, 'The Failure of Corporate Governance and the Limits of Law: British Banks and the Global Financial Crisis' in William Sun, Jim Stewart and David Pollard (eds), *Corporate Governance and the Global Financial Crisis: International Perspectives* (CUP, 2011).

66 See CG Code, para A4.

67 Restrictions of bank activities and government ownership of banks have been found to be negatively correlated with bank performance and stability, and the latter positively correlated with corruption. See James Barth, Gerard Caprio and Ross Levine, 'Bank Regulation and Supervision: What Works Best?' (2004) 13 *Journal of Financial Intermediation* 205, 229–231.

68 See Kenneth Spong, *Banking Regulation: Its Purposes, Implementation and Effects* (5th edn, Federal Reserve Bank of Kansas City Publication, 2000), 12.

69 '[O]ur regulatory approach before the crisis underestimated the importance of governance. We are, however, determined to put this right …' See Graeme Ashley-Fenn, 'Corporate Governance – An FSA Perspective' (Building Societies Association Corporate Governance Seminar, London, 2010) www.fsa.gov.uk/pages/Library/Communication/Speeches/2010/0303_gaf.shtml accessed 1 May 2017.

70 Paras 32–33.

risk highlight the crucial importance of regulating financial institution corporate governance. In the same vein, appropriate corporate governance reforms could tackle the problem of short-termist pressures by institutional investors, and could ensure that executive remuneration in financial institutions does not create inappropriate incentives from the perspective of financial stability, a policy which is already pursued by the CRD IV framework.

Moreover, corporate governance structures have a vital role to play in ensuring that CEOs do not dominate the board of directors, but instead that the board – and its independent directors in particular – engage in robust scrutiny of the CEO's strategy. Indeed, a major cause of failure for any type of company[71] is a dominant, self-assertive CEO, who stifles the opinions of his or her colleagues, is over-optimistic about his or her plans, fails to delegate functions properly, and may also be extravagant and arbitrary. For instance, the domination of RBS's board by its charismatic CEO has been identified as one of the major causes of the bank's downfall.[72] This indicates that existing corporate governance structures did not succeed in maintaining an appropriate balance of power in banks, and thus supports the need for regulatory intervention in the area.

Finally, corporate law has the potential to influence the corporate culture of large companies, including banks and other financial firms.[73] This can be achieved both directly by emphasising several principles – such as accountability, transparency, probity and sustainability[74] – and indirectly by setting up procedures that require the board to decide on the values of the company and monitor whether day-to-day management is consistent with those values. More crucially certain corporate governance law rules can play an important educational role, especially the provision on directors' core duty of loyalty. Indeed, the inclusion of the interests of several stakeholders and the environment as matters to have regard to under the duty of loyalty in section 172 of the Companies Act 2006 has arguably influenced corporate boards towards a more inclusive approach to corporate governance, under the auspices of the 'enlightened' shareholder value approach.[75] Likewise, the Stewardship Code[76] attempts to change the behaviour of institutional shareholders towards a model of responsible ownership. In the case of

71 Vanessa Finch, *Corporate Insolvency Law: Perspectives and Principles* (2nd edn, CUP 2009), 159.

72 See FSA (above n 59), paras 607–613.

73 On the potential role of culture in financial regulation, see Dan Awrey, William Blair and David Kershaw, 'Between Law and Markets: Is There a Role for Culture and Ethics in Financial Regulation?' (2013) 38 *Delaware Journal of Corporate Law* 191.

74 See CG Code, Governance and the Code.

75 An in-depth examination of the evolution and operation of the Enlightened Shareholder Value approach can be found in Andrew Keay, *The Enlightened Shareholder Value Principle and Corporate Governance* (Routledge, 2013).

76 See Financial Reporting Council, 'The UK Stewardship Code' (2012), 5 www.icaew.com/en/library/subject-gateways/corporate-governance/codes-and-reports/uk-stewardship-code accessed 1 May 2017. For a critical analysis of the potential impact of the Code, see Brian Cheffins, 'The Stewardship's Code Achilles' Heel' (2010) 73 *Modern Law Review* 985. On the uncertain notion of stewardship, see Arad Reisberg,

financial institutions, the creation of a distinct set of corporate governance rules could be used as a tool to emphasise the urgent need for sustainable development and prudent business strategy, and to cultivate a norm of meaningful compliance with prudential regulatory rules and principles.[77]

III. Towards a new corporate objective for financial institutions: maintaining the financial sustainability of the entity in the long term

a. Introducing the new corporate objective

The key distinctive feature of a regulatory approach to corporate law for financial institutions is the change of focus from the private interests of shareholders to the public interest. The public interest in maintaining financial stability as a vital public good has already been explored in Chapter 3. Since the unqualified pursuit of profit maximisation is incompatible with safeguarding financial stability, it follows that a regulatory approach to financial institution corporate governance would undoubtedly prioritise the preservation of financial stability over the maximisation of profits for the benefit of financial institutions' shareholders.

The preceding analysis suggests that the appropriate corporate objective for financial institutions is to maintain, safeguard and enhance the financial sustainability of the entity[78] in the long term. The term 'corporate objective' refers to the ultimate beneficiary of the actions of a company; it is the answer to the question of in whose interests companies are run.[79] The link between financial stability as a

'The Notion of Stewardship from a Company Law Perspective' (2011) 18 *Journal of Financial Crime* 126.

77 UK regulators already acknowledge the importance of appropriate corporate culture in financial institutions. See Ashley-Fenn (above n 69).

78 Acceptance of the corporate objective proposed herein does not presuppose the acceptance of the entity theory of the company, which asserts that companies are real entities rather than mere aggregations of contracts, as previously discussed. This study adopts the broad contractarian theoretical framework, and builds an economic case to run financial institutions in a sustainable manner, as the only possible way to prevent negative externalities in the form of financial instability. Nevertheless, the corporate objective proposed here would also be likely to be accepted by scholars following the real entity theory. Some of the most notable works in the area include: Gunther Teubner, 'Enterprise Corporatism: New Industrial Policy and the "Essence" of the Legal Person' (1988) 36 *American Journal of Comparative Law* 130; Katsuhito Iwai, 'Persons, Things, and Corporations: The Corporate Personality Controversy and Comparative Corporate Governance' (1999) 47 *American Journal of Comparative Law* 583; David Gindis, 'From Fictions and Aggregates to Real Entities in the Theory of the Firm' (2009) 5 *Journal of Institutional Economics* 25; and Martin Lupold and Gerhard Schnyder (above n 6). For an in-depth discussion of the old natural entity theory in the US context, see David Millon, 'Theories of the Corporation' (1990) 39 *Duke Law Journal* 201, 211–220.

79 The corporate objective must be distinguished from the object of a company which may be prescribed in its objects clause and specifies a particular activity for the company to pursue or limit the industry sectors in which it may get involved. It is worth noting that companies are no longer required to include an object clause in their

public good and the safety and soundness of individual financial institutions is due to systemic risk and contagion as was explained in Chapter 3. This is not to say that protecting the safety and soundness of individual institutions is a sufficient condition to prevent financial crises. There are many other factors and parameters that are dealt with by macro-prudential regulation. Still, minimising the likelihood of failure or distress of individual financial institutions is a necessary condition to achieve a stable financial system.

It is therefore a necessary complement to micro-prudential regulation to acknowledge that the appropriate corporate objective for financial institutions is to safeguard and enhance their financial sustainability in the long term. By ***financial sustainability*** it is meant the continuous ability of a financial institution to meet its obligations and generate sufficient profit to maintain a strong capital base. Indeed, the term sustainability is widely used in corporate social responsibility literature which distinguishes between environmental, social and economic sustainability.[80] In the latter sense, sustainability refers to the preservation of natural, social and economic capital in the long term.[81] Here, financial sustainability essentially refers to the survival of the institution as a going concern, which includes the prevention of insolvency and also the preservation of a sound capital base in compliance with regulatory requirements and expectations.

Of course, the long term is an inherently vague concept which is difficult to define in a precise manner.[82] Long-term planning can be defined as formulating a plan which seeks to meet future needs, based on current needs and their projected trajectory.[83] An example of medium-term planning can be found in the provisions

constitution (Companies Act 2006, s 31(1)) and that ultra vires acts are now perfectly valid (Companies Act 2006, s 39). For a critical analysis of the corporate governance implications of the abolition of the ultra vires doctrine, see Lorraine Talbot, 'Critical Corporate Governance and the Demise of the Ultra Vires Doctrine' (2009) 38 *Common Law World Review* 170.

80 See e.g. Thomas Dyllick and Kai Hockerts, 'Beyond the Business Case for Corporate Sustainability' (2002) 11 *Business Strategy and the Environment* 130, esp 132. See also Teun Hardjono and Peter de Klein, 'Introduction on the European Sustainability Framework (ECSF)' (2004) 55 *Journal of Business Ethics* 99, 99–100.

81 See Robert Goodland, 'The Concept of Environmental Sustainability' (1995) 26 *Annual Review of Ecology and Systematics* 1. Goodland defines environmental sustainability as 'holding the scale of the human economic subsystem to within the biophysical limits of the overall ecosystem on which it depends'. This entails keeping waste emissions within assimilative capacity; harvesting renewable sources within regeneration rates; and depleting non-renewable sources at the same rate as renewable substitutes are created. Ibid., 3.

82 The concept of the long term in the corporate context has been criticised as being very hard to assess. See Einer Elhauge, 'Sacrificing Corporate Profits in the Public Interest' (2005) 80 *New York University Law Review* 733, 756. In addition, Chancellor Allen, formerly of the Delaware Court of Chancery, dismissed the concept as a 'murky distinction between long-term profit maximization and short-term profit maximization'. See William Allen, 'Our Schizophrenic Conception of the Business Corporation' (1992) 14 *Cardozo Law Review* 261, 273.

83 See e.g. BusinessDictionary.com, www.businessdictionary.com/definition/long-term-planning.html accessed 1 May 2017.

setting out the streamlined capital reduction procedure available to private companies. Each director is expected to confirm that 'the company will be able to pay its debts as they fall due during the year immediately following' the solvency statement.[84] This provision requires directors to plan the financial needs of the company for one year and to ensure that it will have adequate resources to meet its obligations within this timeframe. Of course, it is impossible to prescribe the exact length of a long-term timeframe, but it would definitely be long enough to transcend economic cycles in the financial sector. This would suggest managing a financial institution with a view to ensuring its sustainable development during good economic times, so as to be able to sustain any losses occurring in bad times.

Maintaining financial sustainability appears to be a limited and conservative objective which does not set a positive goal, such as the maximisation of share price, profits, revenue or market share, but rather sets an absolute minimum of performance. It is submitted, however, that the only effective way to enhance the financial sustainability of a financial institution – and any other company that does business in a competitive market – is to seek profitability in a sustainable manner by increasing the cost efficiency[85] and operational efficiency[86] of the business and constantly improving the quality and design of the products or services provided.[87] This appears to be contradicting the argument advanced in the previous chapters that seeking to maximise profits leads to a higher rate of failure, but in reality it is not. There are five main determinants of short-term firm profitability at any given time, namely: (a) productive efficiency; (b) the level of risk associated with a firm's assets and activities; (c) capital structure; (d) the level of competition in the relevant markets;[88] and (e) macroeconomic factors.[89]

84 Companies Act 2006, s 643 (1) (b) (ii).

85 A cost-efficiency (or business-efficiency) ratio is typically defined as the ratio between the expenses and revenues of a business (i.e. expenses/revenue).

86 Operational efficiency (or productivity) is typically defined as the ratio between the inputs that are used to maintain a business operation and the outputs that the operation generates.

87 It is widely accepted that a reasonable level of profits is necessary to ensure the survival of a firm, and that a firm which does not grow is likely to fail in the long run. See Myron Gordon, *Finance, Investment and Macroeconomics: The Neoclassical and a Post-Keynesian Solution* (Edward Elgar Publishing, 1994), 94–95; Lawrence Mitchell, *Corporate Irresponsibility* (Yale University Press, 2001), 11; and David Schrader, 'The Corporation and Profits' (1987) 6 *Journal of Business Ethics* 589, 590.

88 It seems that increased market concentration fosters higher profits and hence supports financial stability, despite its general wealth-reducing effect to consumers. On the interplay between financial stability and competition in the financial sector, see Barbara Casu, Claudia Girardone and Philip Molyneux, 'Is There a Conflict Between Competition and Financial Stability?' in James Barth, Chen Lin and Clas Wihlborg (eds), *Research Handbook on International Banking and Governance* (Edward Elgar Publishing, 2012).

89 A recent empirical study by Dietrich and Wanzenried on the profitability of 10,165 commercial banks from 118 countries during the 1998–2012 period, confirms that cost efficiency and market concentration are two major determinants of bank profitability. Another relevant factor is whether the bank is privately owned or owned by the state, state-owned banks being significantly less profitable. See Andreas Dietrich and

Increasing financial institution profitability in the short term by taking excessive risks or by increasing leverage is inconsistent with financial stability as it increases the likelihood of failure. However, improving the productive efficiency of a financial institution by minimising the costs it incurs to offer its services (including financing cost, capital cost, operational cost and labour cost), materially strengthens the present profitability of an institution, without increasing its insolvency risk in the long term. As a matter of fact, cost efficiency-driven profitability can substantially decrease insolvency risk if profits are used to strengthen the capital ratio of the relevant institutions.[90] This, of course, does not mean that the sustainability objective would necessarily require financial institutions to minimise labour and other costs to the detriment of their long-term profitability, but rather that pursuing stakeholder-friendly policies should not come at the expense of increasing insolvency risk. This differentiates the regime proposed herein from the currently followed Enlightened Shareholder Value approach.[91] Under the latter, companies are encouraged to have regard to the interests of non-shareholder constituencies to the extent that doing so is believed to benefit the company and its members in the long run. On the other hand, under the sustainability objective, financial institutions would be allowed to take into account stakeholder interests only to the extent that doing so enhances their financial sustainability both in the short and long term.[92]

Overall, the objective of long-term entity preservation encapsulates the pursuit of sustainable profitability, especially to the extent that the latter is driven by cost

Gabrielle Wanzenried, 'The Determinants of Commercial Banking Profitability in Low-, Middle-, and High-income Countries' (2014) 54 *The Quarterly Review of Economics and Finance* 337. See also: Ugo Albertazzi and Leonardo Gambacorta, 'Bank Profitability and the Business Cycle' (2009) 5 *Journal of Financial Stability* 393; Panayiotis Athanasoglou, Sophocles Brissimis and Matthaios Delis, 'Bank-specific, Industry-specific and Macroeconomic Determinants of Bank Profitability' (2008) 18 *Journal of International Financial Markets, Institutions and Money* 121; Giuliano Iannotta, Giacomo Nocera and Andrea Sironi, 'Ownership Structure, Risk and Performance in the European Banking Industry' (2007) 31 *Journal of Banking and Finance* 2127; Fotios Pasiouras and Kyriaki Kosmidou, 'Factors Influencing the Profitability of Domestic and Foreign Commercial Banks in the European Union' (2007) 21 *Research in International Business and Finance* 222.

90 See Dietrich and Wanzenried (above n 89).

91 A doctrinal discussion of directors' duty of loyalty can be found in Chapter 2, section IV.

92 Broadly speaking, balancing the interests of all corporate constituencies can enhance the long-term value of a company by fostering sound relationships with employees, communities and business partners, and by encouraging firm-specific investment. However, protecting labour can discourage innovation. For instance, Vitols argues that UK companies, which operate within a shareholder-oriented governance framework, are more likely to develop radically innovative products and services than German companies, which operate within a framework that balances profitability with employment protection. The author notes that UK banks were quick to use information technology to reduce labour costs in the 1990s unlike their German counterparts. See Sigurt Vitols, 'Varieties of Corporate Governance: Comparing Germany and the UK' in Peter Hall and David Soskice (eds), *Varieties of Capitalism: The Institutional Foundations of Comparative Advantage* (OUP, 2001), 350–355.

efficiency, which is a necessary condition to achieve a well-capitalised financial system. Of course, it must be emphasised that financial sustainability would be the overriding corporate objective for financial institutions, and profit-seeking would be pursued only to the extent that it is consistent with financial sustainability.[93] Under the new corporate objective, financial institutions would no longer be run with a view to maximising shareholder wealth within the limits set by prudential regulation and other areas of law. Therefore, directors would be required to abstain from any strategy or policy that threatens the viability of the institution, even if it was the best available option to maximise its present share price.

To explain the practical implications of the new corporate objective the discussion will now provide some examples of strategies that tend to engender a high insolvency risk, and hence ought to be avoided. Most of these examples are based on the circumstances surrounding the failure of several UK banks, most notably the Royal Bank of Scotland, Halifax Bank of Scotland and Northern Rock. To begin with, acquiring a controlling stake in another bank or financial institution without appropriate due diligence can seriously undermine the financial position of an institution, especially when the acquisition is financed primarily by debt.[94] Generally, the success of a takeover from the perspective of the acquiring company and its shareholders depends on the materialisation of expected synergies and economies of scale and scope.[95] In the case of banks, asset opacity renders takeovers a particularly risky endeavour as the difficulty in assessing the asset quality of the target bank means that the acquirer may overpay for the shares of the target and hence its capital base may be compromised.

Relying on short-term lending from the wholesale markets to finance long-term exposures is another strategy that exposes a financial institution to danger if liquidity in the relevant markets decreases sharply, as was the case in 2007.[96] In the same vein, a large discrepancy between the deposits held by a bank and the loans advanced by it (to the effect that deposits are significantly less than loans) tends to indicate a risky funding strategy that raises concerns about the bank's liquidity. More significantly, pursuing asset expansion to the detriment of asset quality is the archetypical risky strategy that contributes to increased short-term profits, but can cause large losses due to loan impairments in the long run.

93 Other scholars have proposed reforms of bank corporate governance that detract from the dominant shareholder-centric paradigm. See e.g. Lucian Bebchuck and Holger Spamann, 'Regulating Bankers' Pay' (2010) 98 *Georgetown Law Journal* 247.

94 See FSA (above n 59), 46 and 54–56.

95 Empirical evidence suggests that takeovers do not have any significant effect on the fundamental value of companies despite the fact that they do increase overall profitability. See Paul Guest, Magnus Bild and Mikael Runsten, 'The Effect of Takeovers on the Fundamental Value of Acquirers' (2010) 40 *Accounting and Business Research* 333. See also Robert Conn and others, 'The Impact on UK Acquirers of Domestic, Cross-Border, Public and Private Acquisitions' (2005) 32 *Journal of Business Finance & Accounting* 815; Eugene F Fama, 'Market Efficiency, Long-Run Returns, and Behavioral Finance' (1998) 49 *Journal of Financial Economics* 283.

96 See FSA (above n 59), 43–47. The same business practice characterised Northern Rock. See Treasury Committee (above n 64), paras 15–17.

Aggressive expansion tends to entail: the advancement of loans without the necessary checks on the financial position of prospective borrowers; large individual credit exposures; and failing to obtain appropriate collateral for loans, especially in the context of mortgages.[97] Such practices boost a financial institution's short-term performance as they improve its market share and revenues, but can deplete capital if large losses occur.[98] Aggressive expansion is facilitated by offering loans that are intended to be syndicated as this exposes the original lending bank to the risk that other banks may decide to stop participating in such syndications.[99]

In parallel, investing in high-risk debt and equity securities is another example of a risky strategy that is liable to erode the asset quality of a financial institution.[100] The same is true of investing in debt that is highly rated but not fundamentally creditworthy, as happened with senior tranches of credit derivatives where the underlying assets consisted of sub-prime loans,[101] and with sovereign debt issued by governments that were already heavily indebted, and had a limited ability to raise revenue. Similarly, engaging in proprietary trading of complex financial instruments, the inherent risks of which are not fully understood by the board and senior management, can alter the risk profile of a financial institution and expose it to serious losses.[102] Failing to respond to market signals, which indicate that market conditions are deteriorating in an effort to maintain high profits in the short term is another example of a risky and myopic strategy.[103]

Moreover, increasing the leverage ratio of a financial institution is a strategy that tends to favour current shareholders in the short term at the expense of stability. Generally, if total equity is too meagre to absorb potential losses, insolvency risk raises significantly. A related practice is the use of securitisation to remove assets from the balance sheets of banks and thus to evade capital requirements, despite the fact that the relevant banks remain committed to back the entity to which the loans are transferred (i.e. the special purpose vehicle) due to reputational

97 FSA (above n 59), 126–131. Probably the most striking example of a bank suffering huge loan impairments after a period of rapid asset expansion is that of HBOS. See Parliamentary Commission on Banking Standards (above n 63), paras 30–32.

98 For instance, it is estimated that between 2008 and 2011 HBOS's loan impairments amounted to £25 billion, that is, 20% of the total value of the bank's loan book in 2008. Ibid., para 28.

99 This problem particularly affected HBOS. Ibid., para 28.

100 Again, HBOS provides a good example. Ibid., para 24.

101 On this issue, see e.g. John Hull, 'Credit Ratings and the Securitization of Subprime Mortgages' (Up from the Ashes: The Financial System after the Crisis, Atlanta, Georgia, May 2010) http://citeseerx.ist.psu.edu/viewdoc/download?doi=10.1.1.169.5692&rep=rep1&type=pdf accessed 1 May 2017.

102 It is widely argued that financial innovation led to the creation of financial instruments that are too complex to be understood even by expert bank personnel. See James Crotty, 'Structural Causes of the Global Financial Crisis: A Critical Assessment of the New Financial Architecture' (2009) 33 *Cambridge Journal of Economics* 563, 566–567.

103 Such decisions were taken by the boards of RBS and HBOS in the 2006–2008 period. See FSA (above n 59), 52–54; and Parliamentary Commission on Banking Standards (above n 63), para 26.

reasons.[104] Similarly, underestimating the risks associated with the assets of a financial institution and hence its capital needs, can lead to excessive leverage.[105]

Finally, risky strategies that jeopardise the safety and soundness of financial institutions include any instance of unlawful behaviour which is likely to lead to legal liability in the form of fines or compensation to relevant parties, and serious reputational damage. Again, these strategies may maximise *ex ante* shareholder wealth calculated on the basis of the probability of a sanction being imposed compared to the benefit accruing from the unlawful behaviour, but they are clearly inconsistent with the goal of safeguarding the sustainability of the entity, as if the breach is detected, the ensuing regulatory sanctions are likely to weaken the capital base of the errant financial institution (financial sanction) and harm its reputation.

b. Distinguishing and defending the new corporate objective

The corporate objective proposed herein is based on (but not identical to) the objective proposed by Andrew Keay as part of the Entity Maximisation and Sustainability (EMS) model of corporate governance.[106] In his influential work, Keay critically analyses the shareholder value and stakeholder value maximisation views of the company, and finds that they both suffer from several deficiencies.[107] Under Keay's proposed approach, the aim of the company is to maximise the wealth of the entity, and to secure its long-term survival,[108] which inevitably advances the common interest of all investors (e.g. shareholders, creditors, employees, customers and communities), without preferring the interests of one group or resorting to a balancing exercise.[109] Sustainability refers to the survival of the company and focuses on its ability to remain solvent.[110] No long-term maximisation strategy ought to be adopted if it threatens the viability of the company in the short run. Conversely, no strategy that brings short-term gains should be adopted if it threatens viability in the long run. The model is based on conceptualising the company as a real entity, which is legally and substantively separate from those

104 On the risk transfer effect of the use of special purpose vehicles and its limitations, see Basel Committee on Banking Supervision, *The Joint Forum Report on Special Purpose Entities* (Bank for International Settlements Publications, 2009), 26–30.

105 This problem was analysed in Chapter 4, section I (b).

106 See Andrew Keay, *The Corporate Objective* (Edward Elgar Publishing, 2011), 173–275; 'Ascertaining the Corporate Objective: An Entity Maximisation and Sustainability Model' (2008) 71 *Modern Law Review* 663; and 'The Ultimate Objective of the Public Company and the Enforcement of the Entity Maximisation and Sustainability Model' (2010) 10 *Journal of Corporate Law Studies* 35.

107 Both shareholder primacy and stakeholder theories are criticised as being vague and laden with uncertainties. In addition, Keay affirms that shareholder primacy neglects the fact that other stakeholders bear part of the residual risk of the company, while stakeholder theories are prone to be abused by self-serving corporate managers. See Keay, *The Corporate Objective* (above n 106), 96–109 and 144–160.

108 Ibid., 174–175.

109 Ibid., 198–201.

110 Ibid., 218–219.

who invest in it.[111] As such, the interest of the company itself is enshrined as the final determinant of corporate strategy and as a guide to assist managers in taking difficult decisions, say with regard to the pricing of the company's products, potential relocation of production, and mass redundancies.[112]

The financial sustainability corporate objective is distinguishable from the EMS model in the following respects. First, while EMS accepts the sustainability and wealth maximisation of the entity as two concurrent and mutually reinforcing goals, here it is suggested that financial institutions should clearly prioritise sustainability, and only pursue profitability to the extent that it is conducive to – or at least consistent with – sustainability. Second, in the EMS model the maximisation of the wealth of the entity does not equate to long-term profitability for the benefit of the shareholders, and hence is closer to continental European entity theory.[113] The approach proposed here does not rely on ascertaining the distinct interests of financial institutions as autonomous corporate entities, but rather focuses on protecting the public interest by preserving their long-term financial sustainability. In other words, the corporate objective proposed herein would require directors to take all possible steps to ensure the long-term financial health of the financial institution. This inevitably entails being prudent and conservative when making strategic decisions and setting the risk appetite of the institution, and seeking to maximise the institution's operational efficiency within the limits set by conduct of business regulation and other areas of law.[114] The pursuit of operational efficiency, which incidentally benefits shareholders, is not an independent objective, but rather one of the policies which are likely to enhance long-term financial sustainability.

Third, the statutory implementation of the EMS model is envisaged to entail a mild reform of section 172 of the Companies Act, which would remove any references to specific investor interests from the section.[115] On the contrary, the proposed implementation of the new corporate objective advocated here entails the introduction of a new statutory provision, which would envisage departing from current managerial practice by exposing directors and senior managers to a significant risk of civil liability should a financial institution fail, as will be seen in Chapter 7.

111 Ibid., 178–183.
112 Ibid., 211–217.
113 'This means that the common interest of all who have invested is to be fostered … But, rather than the focus being on the investors and their interests, as stakeholder theory requires, the focus is on the entity and what will enhance its position.' Keay, 'Ascertaining the Corporate Objective' (above n 106), 685.
114 Conversely, Keay favours an entity concept of the interests of the corporation which would detract from shareholder value maximisation whenever a strategy that furthers shareholder value does not maximise the value of the entity which includes its reputation and adherence to corporate social responsibility norms. 'Reputation can be viewed as including a company operating within its social license, namely being constrained to fulfil the expectations of society in carrying out its business activities …' Keay, 'Ascertaining the Corporate Objective' (above n 106), 686.
115 Keay, *The Corporate Objective* (above n 106), 226.

Furthermore, the regulatory approach to financial institutions' corporate objective outlined here would escape the 'multiple servants' criticism that has been voiced against stakeholder theories.[116] Unlike stakeholder theories,[117] the proposed corporate objective does not require directors to balance the conflicting interests of an ill-defined range of stakeholder groups,[118] so that there is no danger that directors will ultimately serve their own interests, under the pretext of balancing the interests of all stakeholders.[119] The requirement to adopt prudent strategies that safeguard the long-term financial sustainability of financial institutions provides much clearer guidance to directors and does not allow them to behave opportunistically. Under the present model, there is no need for boards to balance different objectives or interests; instead, there is lexical prioritisation of long-term financial sustainability as the single ultimate corporate objective to the effect that any other objective can only be pursued to the extent that it is consistent with sustainability. At any rate, during the years leading up to the recent financial crisis, directors have arguably been taking more risks than rational fully

116 Bainbridge elegantly summarises this point: 'directors who are responsible to everyone are accountable to no one.' See Bainbridge (above n 11), 581–582.

117 It is not possible within the scope of the present book to do justice to the rich and diverse stakeholder literature. The first academic proponent of the stakeholder view of the corporation was Merrick Dodd, whose lively academic conversation with Adolf Berle defined the contours of the modern corporate governance debate. See Dodd (above n 5); Adolf Berle, 'For Whom Corporate Managers are Trustees: A Note' (1932) 45 *Harvard Law Review* 1365. A good account of the stakeholder theory can be found in Edward Freeman, *Strategic Management: A Stakeholder Approach* (Pitman/Ballinger, 1984); Thomas Donaldson and Lee Preston, 'The Stakeholder Theory of the Corporation: Concepts, Evidence, Implications' (1995) 20 *Academy Management Review* 65; Thomas Clarke, 'The Stakeholder Corporation: A Business Philosophy for the Information Age' (1998) 31 *Long Range Planning* 182. An historical analysis of the issue can be found in Harwell Wells, 'The Cycles of Corporate Social Responsibility: An Historical Retrospective for the Twenty-first Century' (2002–2003) 51 *Kansas Law Review* 77. In parallel, the influential work of Parkinson asserts that company law ought to be designed in a way consistent with the public interest. See John Parkinson, *Corporate Power and Responsibility: Issues in the Theory of Company Law* (Oxford Clarendon Press, 1993), esp chs 1–3; John Parkinson, 'Disclosure and Corporate Social and Environmental Performance: Competitiveness and Enterprise in a Broader Social Frame' (2003) 3 *Journal of Corporate Law Studies* 3. For a critical evaluation of stakeholder theories, see Andrew Keay, 'Stakeholder Theory in Corporate Law: Has it Got What it Takes?' (2010) 9 *Richmond Journal of Global Law & Business* 240.

118 The absence of a clear objective outcome of the balancing process is criticised as prone to lead to confusion. See Michael Jensen, 'Value Maximisation, Stakeholder Theory and the Corporate Objective' (2001) 7 *European Financial Management* 297, 301–302. The lack of clarity is exacerbated by the absence of a generally accepted notion of stakeholder groups. Indeed, there are more than 100 stakeholder groups identified in the relevant literature. See Yves Fassin, 'The Stakeholder Model Refined' (2009) 84 *Journal of Business Ethics* 113, 120.

119 On the negative accountability effect of the stakeholder approach, see Lucian Bebchuk, 'The Case for Increasing Shareholder Power' (2004–2005) 118 *Harvard Law Review* 833, 910–911.

informed shareholders would have accepted.[120] It follows that, rather than weakening directorial accountability, introducing the new corporate objective would actually curtail the scope for opportunistic behaviour by directors against shareholders, while at the same time insulating directors against pressures by short-termist shareholders to maximise current profitability in an unsustainable manner at the expense of financial stability.

In that respect, it is submitted that the regulatory approach to financial institution corporate governance is conducive to greater clarity than the EMS model, since the latter would require directors to ascertain the interests of the company in order to identify the strategies that are likely to maximise the wealth of the entity.[121] Such enquiry would inevitably entail a subjective element and leave wide discretion to corporate directors to identify and operationalise the interest of the entity. On the contrary, the corporate objective of financial sustainability provides a clear functional objective rather than a general standard. This of course is not intended as a criticism to the EMS model's broader application to public companies as the discussion here is limited to the examination of the corporate governance in the financial services sector where the public interest in safeguarding financial stability overrides broader concerns which are totally legitimate outside this context. Nevertheless, the effect of the regulatory approach would, in practice, be that of maximising the collective wealth of all involved parties by virtue of minimising the probability of the occurrence of financial crises. This is evident with regard to depositors, bondholders, and other financial institution creditors who would directly benefit from the reduction in insolvency risk brought by the implementation of the new corporate objective. Indeed, maintaining the long-term viability of a financial institution directly benefits its creditors, whose claims become more secure, especially given the fact that – in the financial sector – higher risk is not fully compensated by increased interest rates paid to the creditors of financial institutions.

The same can largely be said about the other stakeholders of financial institutions such as business partners and local communities, since they all stand to suffer from financial crises with no corresponding benefits. In particular, the interests of employees (except for senior managers) are hugely affected when a financial institution faces financial difficulties, as they are likely to be dismissed.[122] This causes them to lose the value of their firm-specific expertise and to incur the financial and

120 On this, see Chapter 1, section III.

121 Keay rejects the assertion that a company is merely a vehicle to satisfy the interests of groups of natural persons, citing Lord Cullen in *Dawson International plc v Coats Paton plc* (No 1) [1989] BCLC 233. Instead he explains: 'My argument is that for the purposes of the corporate objective directors are to work to enhance the benefit of the entity, but I must add that in doing so natural people will ultimately and necessarily benefit, that is, the investors' interests will be fostered.' See Keay, *The Corporate Objective* (above n 106), 195.

122 For instance, the number of RBS employees (excluding temporary staff) fell from 226,400 on 31 December 2007 to 118,079 on 31 December 2013, and further to 77,000 on 31 December 2016, according to the bank's annual reports and accounts for the relevant years, which is a reduction by almost two-thirds in nine years.

non-financial costs of finding alternative employment. Similarly, it is in the interests of the customers of financial institutions in their capacity as borrowers to maintain safety and soundness, since financial institution failures tend to lead to crises during which the advancement of credit is seriously curtailed.[123]

Granted, the proposed change of paradigm would appear to be value-decreasing for financial institution shareholders as their private interests would cease to be the overriding criterion of good corporate governance. However, given the tendency of directors, under the existing shareholder-centric regime, to take risks that are excessive even from the perspective of shareholders, it follows that the loss of alignment of directors' interests and risk appetite with those of shareholders would be – at least partially – compensated by the avoidance of excessive risk-taking.[124] At any rate, moving towards a financial services sector characterised by lower profits in periods of economic growth but also by safer institutions and less frequent crises, would appeal to a substantial number of potential equity investors.[125] Long-term-oriented investors such as pension funds, insurance companies, sovereign wealth funds, and individuals[126] would have no reason to refrain from investing in the shares of financial institutions which would be less profitable but also less risky. This view is supported by the fact that although recent prudential-regulatory reforms have already substantially decreased the profitability of banks,[127] UK banks are still able to raise equity capital comfortably.[128] The

123 The availability of credit to UK households and businesses reduced dramatically in late 2008 and remains at very low levels compared to the pre-crisis period, despite the efforts of the Bank of England. See Daniel Monteiro, *The Flow of Credit in the UK Economy and the Availability of Financing to the Corporate Sector* (Economic Papers 509, EU, 2013) http://ec.europa.eu/economy_finance/publications/economic_paper/2013/pdf/ecp509_en.pdf accessed 1 May 2017.

124 See Chapter 1, conclusions.

125 The scope for regulatory arbitrage may be smaller than is usually assumed given the enormous practical difficulties an institution would face if it chose to incorporate elsewhere and the strong comparative advantages of London vis-à-vis other financial centres. See Parliamentary Commission on Banking Standards, *Changing Banking for Good* (2013–14, HL 27-I, HC 175-I), paras 240–242.

126 Institutional investors such as pension funds and insurance companies seek to obtain a stable income that allows them to meet their long-term obligations to pensioners and policy holders. Sovereign wealth funds are similarly seen as long-term investors which aim to contribute to the development of the economy of the relevant state in the long run. See also Matthias Burghardt, *Retail Investor Sentiment and Behavior* (Gabler Verlag, 2011).

127 A KPMG analysis of major UK banks' average return on equity (ROE) between 2005 and 2013 reveals a reduction of more than 50%, from close to 20% in 2005 to less than 10% in 2013. See KPMG, 'Road to Recovery? What the Future Holds for UK Banks: Half Year Results 2013' (2013), 9 www.criticaleye.com/insights-servfile.cfm?id=3740 accessed 1 May 2017.

128 An example of this is Lloyds' floating of 35% of the shares of TSB in late June 2014, which rose to 50% by the end of 2014. The original target was to float 25% of TSB's shares, but demand was unexpectedly high. Data are taken from Lloyds annual report and accounts 2014.

proposed reform would only dissuade short-termist arbitrageurs from investing, a development which would be welcome as it would further foster financial stability.

The feasibility of moving towards financial sustainability as the overriding objective of financial institutions is further illustrated by the continuous existence of building societies and other forms of co-operative banks in the UK and abroad, despite the undeniable trend for such institutions to demutualise since the 1980s.[129] Indeed, building societies[130] provided most of mortgage lending in the UK until the late 1980s,[131] and continue to play a significant role in this market. Similarly, in many continental European countries, various forms of co-operative banks maintain a high market share.[132] Building societies have no shareholders and equity capital,[133] but are owned by qualifying depositors and mortgage holders. To be a qualifying borrowing member, one's indebtedness must be no lower than £100,[134] and each member has one vote, irrespective of their investment or borrowing. Apart from these differences, most building societies follow the UK Corporate Governance Code. If having no shareholders at all is workable, being a public company, but departing from the profit maximisation norm must be workable as well.

It is therefore submitted that departing from profit maximisation in favour of financial sustainability is a clear, feasible and necessary reform. Indeed, the preceding discussion suggests that the concerns expressed in the Walker Review with regard to a potential reform of financial institutions' corporate objective are not compelling reasons to preclude such reform.[135] The Review cautioned against diluting the single focus of financial institution directors on shareholder wealth as it argues that such a change would mark the abandonment of the contractarian basis of UK company law, lead to great uncertainty, create the danger that shareholders might become reluctant to invest in financial institutions, and dilute board focus on risk management. Admittedly, all these objections would be valid against a proposed move towards a stakeholder model of corporate governance. Such

129 For a critical analysis of the impact on UK building societies of the profit maximisation norm prevalent in the corporate sector, see Lorraine E Talbot, 'Keeping Bad Company: Building Societies A Case Study' (2009) 60 *Northern Ireland Legal Quarterly* 443.

130 A building society is a mutual financial institution mainly engaging in mortgage lending. In the UK, all building societies are members of the Building Societies Commission.

131 See Tomas Valnek, 'The Comparative Performance of Mutual Building Societies and Stock Retail Banks' (1999) 23 *Journal of Banking & Finance* 925. In 2010 UK building societies had 2,000 branches, 15 million savers (21% market share) and 3 million borrowers (31% market share). See Stephen Valdez and Philip Molyneux, *An Introduction to Global Financial Markets* (6th edn, Palgrave Macmillan, 2010), 25.

132 The deposits share of co-operative banks was, in 2006, particularly high in the following European countries: France (43.6%), the Netherlands (39.0%), Austria (34.9%), Finland (32.7%), Italy (30.3%) and Germany (15.8%). Ibid., 24.

133 Building Societies Act 1986, s 7, allows them to issue shares, but most of them do not.

134 Ibid., Schedule 2, s 29 (2) and 36 (1).

135 See David Walker, 'A Review of Corporate Governance in UK Banks and Other Financial Industry Entities: Final Recommendations' (2009), Annex 3 www.icaew.com/en/library/subject-gateways/corporate-governance/codes-and-reports/walker-report accessed 1 May 2017.

concerns, however, are not justified in relation to the corporate objective proposed in this book. The regulatory approach proposed herein is compatible with the broader contractarian paradigm insofar as it is accepted that a pure private ordering model of financial institution corporate governance is inconsistent with the public interest in financial stability. Moreover, it has been established that the proposed change of paradigm would be unlikely to lead to an exodus of shareholders from the financial services sector. This line of argumentation seems to be much more acceptable now than a few years ago, as manifested by the view of the Banking Commission that the safety and soundness of banks ought to be placed above the duties owed by bank directors to shareholders.[136]

Inevitably, the regulatory approach proposed in this book would be likely to weaken the incentives of shareholders to monitor financial institution performance. This, however, is not necessarily problematic from the perspective of the corporate objective of financial sustainability, as shareholder activism tends to pressurise boards to take excessive risk.[137] The beneficial effects of shareholder monitoring are generally uncertain[138] and the potential of shareholders to act as effective monitoring agents in the financial sector is limited. Nevertheless, the new corporate objective would attract investors with a lower-risk appetite and a longer-term investment horizon, as it would act as a signal that investing in a financial institution is a relatively safe investment. This potential change in the profile of investors would thus hopefully encourage closer engagement and dialogue between institutional shareholders and financial institutions, to the benefit of both private investors and financial stability.

IV. Conclusions

This chapter sought to establish that: (a) reforming the corporate law framework as it applies to systemically important financial institutions with a view to enhance financial stability would be consistent with the law and economics jurisprudence; and (b) that the core objective of such reform ought to be to change the corporate objective of financial institutions. Of course, achieving a change to the corporate objective of financial institutions entails legal and regulatory reforms and it will be the purpose of the next chapter, the last substantive chapter of the book, to outline a series of concrete reforms to that effect.

136 Parliamentary Commission on Banking Standards (above n 125), para 124, emphasises that: 'The obligations of directors to shareholders in accordance with the provisions of the Companies Act 2006 create a particular tension between duties to shareholders and financial safety and soundness in the case of banks.'

137 On this see Chapter 1, section II.

138 Empirical evidence suggests that institutional shareholders do not perform any monitoring. See Marc Goergen, Luc Renneboog and Chendi Zhang, 'Do UK Institutional Shareholders Monitor their Investee Firms?' (2008) 8 *Journal of Corporate Law Studies* 39, 55–56.

7 Reforming the civil liability regime for financial institution directors and senior managers to foster financial sustainability

The aim of this chapter is to articulate concrete and workable law reform proposals applying to systemically important financial institutions giving effect to the corporate objective of financial sustainability which was discussed in the previous chapter. A new legal provision is thus proposed which would effectively implement the new corporate objective and ensure that financial institution directors and senior managers face powerful financial incentives to refrain from taking decisions that increase the insolvency risk of their institution. The new provision would be in line with the spirit of the recommendations of the Parliamentary Commission on Banking Standards, and would respond to the inadequacy of the present regulatory regime highlighted by the reluctance of the FSA to pursue the cases against the directors and senior managers of several banks that failed during the 2007–2009 crisis.

Unlike the recently introduced criminal offence of reckless banking, which will inevitably be very difficult to enforce, the proposed provision would impose civil liability to contribute to the assets of a financial institution that has entered the Special Resolution Regime or otherwise failed. Subsequent to a petition from the PRA, from the institution's shareholders or its non-insured creditors, liability would be imposed by the court, which would have the discretion to reduce or exclude liability provided that defendants are able to prove that the financial institution had been managed in accordance with the corporate objective of financial sustainability. Liability would not depend on bad faith or negligence, but would be capped and made proportional to director and senior manager remuneration, so as to avoid excessive deterrence.

To this effect, the chapter is structured as follows. Section I explains why company law, rather than prudential regulatory reform, is necessary, and sets out the main parameters of the proposed new provision focusing on its scope, liability standard and enforcement mechanisms. Section II explores a range of collateral legal reforms that would support the effectiveness of the new provision in the areas of directors' duties and corporate governance. Section III explains why the implementation of the new corporate objective does not necessitate an overhaul of shareholder voting rights nor the attribution of voting rights to financial institution creditors. Section IV brings the various strands of discussion together and concludes.

I. Introducing statutory civil liability triggered by bank and other financial institution failures

a. Why company law reform is necessary

The discussion in the previous chapters highlighted that the proposed corporate objective of financial sustainability to be applied to financial institutions cannot be accommodated within the existing legal framework of the company law and regulatory duties owed by financial institution directors and senior managers. Indeed, there is a clear misalignment between the company law duties that effectively prioritise the interests of the shareholders and the objective of safeguarding the sustainability of a financial institution in the long term. Cognisant of this problem, the Parliamentary Commission on Banking Standards called on the government to initiate a consultation on the duties of bank directors in the Companies Act 2006 in order to ensure that the safety and soundness of banks is placed above the duties owed to bank shareholders.[1] As an interim solution, the Commission proposed an amendment to the UK Corporate Governance Code which would acknowledge the tension between, on the one hand, maintaining the safety and soundness of banks, and on the other, pursuing shareholder wealth maximisation.

However, the government recently rejected the idea of introducing 'a new primary duty on bank directors to promote the financial stability of their companies over the interests of shareholders'.[2] Part of the relevant academic literature also rejects the idea of reforms to the company law regime to the extent that it applies to financial institutions. For instance, Chiu argues that the company law framework for directors' duties and the prudential regulatory framework on senior managers have distinct purposes and ought to remain distinct.[3] However, the analysis herein suggests that the regulatory framework and regulatory enforcement are *per se* insufficient to ensure the removal of incentives to undermine financial stability, and therefore additional legal reform in the area of company law is necessary, as will be explained further when discussing the enforcement of the proposed new civil liability provision.[4] Although it is correct to say that under the current legal

1 See Parliamentary Commission on Banking Standards, *Changing Banking for Good* (2013–14, HL 27-I, HC 175-I), paras 702–708.

2 See Department of Business, Innovations and Skills, 'Transparency & Trust: Enhancing the Transparency of UK Company Ownership and Increasing Trust in UK Business: Government Response' (April 2014), para 249 www.gov.uk/government/consultations/company-ownership-transparency-and-trust-discussion-paper accessed 1 May 2017.

3 Iris H-Y Chiu, 'Comparing Directors' Duties in the Financial Services Sector with Regulatory Duties under the Senior Persons Regime – Some Critical Observations' (2016) 27 *European Business Law Review* 261. See also Mads Andenas and Iris H-Y Chiu, *The Foundations and Future of Financial Regulation: Governance for Responsibility* (Routledge, 2014), 392.

4 Reforms in this area have indeed been proposed in the past. Macey and O'Hara, for instance, advocate the imposition of a higher standard of care for bank directors than for other companies, and suggest that bank directors' duty of loyalty ought to encompass fixed claimants as well as shareholders. See Jonathan Macey and Maureen O'Hara, 'The Corporate Governance of Banks' (2003) 9 *Federal Reserve Bank of New*

framework financial institution directors would not face any substantial risk of liability if they chose to adopt financial sustainability as their core objective,[5] this is by no means the same as positively requiring financial institution directors to do so, which is necessary to implement the regulatory approach to financial institution corporate governance. Given the strong financial and broader incentives for financial institution directors and senior managers to take risks that are excessive from the point of view of financial stability,[6] implementing sustainability as financial institutions' corporate objective would require imposing personal liability on directors and senior managers if they fail to prioritise and do their best to safeguard sustainability.

Clearly, the only effective way to impose civil liability in this context is legislative reform. Relying on soft-law recommendations such as the UK Corporate Governance Code would be inadequate due to the lack of enforcement mechanisms other than market discipline.[7] The latter would not be effective in this context as excessively risky behaviour may actually be perceived as beneficial for financial institution shareholders and therefore be rewarded rather than penalised by the markets, especially given the limited ability of market players to assess the risks taken by financial institutions.[8] This was recognised by the Parliamentary Commission, which only proposed a reform to the Code as an interim solution.[9]

York Economic Policy Review 91, 102. It has also been proposed by the Independent Commission on Banking that the boards of ring-fenced entities and their parent companies should be under a duty to preserve the integrity of the ring-fenced entity. See Independent Commission on Banking, *Final Report: Recommendations* (Domarn Group, 2011), para 9.2 (5) (i).

5 On the generally restrictive approach that English courts follow with regard to derivative claims, even after the introduction of the statutory derivative claim in the Companies Act 2006, see Arad Reisberg, 'Shadows of the Past and Back to the Future: Part 11 of the UK Companies Act 2006 (In)Action' (2009) *6 European Company and Financial Law Review* 219; Arad Reisberg, *Derivative Actions and Corporate Governance* (OUP, 2007), ch 4.

6 On this, see Chapter 1, sections I and II.

7 Listed companies are required to disclose in their annual financial report how they apply the main principles of the Code and whether they have complied with the provisions of the Code. Companies are further required to specify any provisions they have not complied with, the period of non-compliance, and give reasons for their choice to do so. See FCA Handbook, LR 9.8.6 (5)–(6). Empirical evidence confirms the limited effect of the comply-or-explain approach. See Sridhar Arcot and Valentina Bruno, 'In Letter but not in Spirit: An Analysis of Corporate Governance in the UK' (2006) http://papers.ssrn.com/sol3/papers.cfm?abstract_id=819784 accessed 1 May 2017.

8 The inadequacy of Code reforms to tackle the problem has been observed by Hannigan. See Brenda Hannigan, 'Board Failures in the Financial Crisis – Tinkering with Codes and the Need for Wider Corporate Governance Reforms: Part 1' (2011) 32 (12) *The Company Lawyer* 363; ibid., 'Part 2' (2012) 33(2) *The Company Lawyer* 35.

9 'The Commission recommends that the UK Corporate Governance Code be amended to require directors of banks to attach the utmost importance to the safety and soundness of the firm and for the duties they owe to customers, taxpayers and others in interpreting their duties as directors.' Parliamentary Commission on Banking Standards (above n 1), para 124.

Furthermore, legislative reform would strongly signal the change of corporate governance paradigm with regard to financial institutions. This would be likely to contribute to the development of a new corporate culture in financial institutions, which would enshrine the viability of the entity as the foremost priority of directors and senior managers.[10] Finally, it is submitted that the relevant statutory provision imposing civil liability in the case of financial institution failures ought to be drafted in a precise and specific manner that achieves the maximum possible degree of legal certainty, as this is necessary in order to ensure the effectiveness of the provision.[11]

Drafting an effective statutory provision to perform the functions identified in the preceding analysis is a complicated task. The behaviour that the new rule is intended to discourage is taking or approving highly risky business decisions, which increase financial institutions' insolvency risk, and may actually result in a financial institution requiring public support. It follows that, as the riskiness of particular business decisions can only be evaluated *ex post facto*, after a financial institution has failed, the relevant duty ought to be triggered accordingly, after the failure of a financial institution.[12] In that respect, the proposed provision would be similar to wrongful trading, which is triggered once a company enters insolvent liquidation. Given the nature of the proposed rule, it is submitted that it should be inserted into the Insolvency Act 1886 to reflect the change intended to the corporate law framework applicable to financial institutions. The main parameters of any provision imposing civil liability are the following: the scope of the provision; the behaviour or event that triggers liability; whether liability is strict, or based on negligence; and enforcement mechanisms. The following discussion addresses these key aspects of the proposed new provision, with a view to implement the corporate objective of financial sustainability.

b. The scope of the new provision

The scope of the civil liability provision ought to be tailored in a manner that effectively safeguards the stability of the UK financial system. With regard to the

10 It is widely accepted that the introduction of the Enlightened Shareholder Value principle, in the formulation of the duty of loyalty in section 172 of the Companies Act 2006, has played an educational role for company directors, drawing their attention to the importance of considering the interests of stakeholders. See e.g. Andrew Keay, *The Enlightened Shareholder Value Principle and Corporate Governance* (Routledge, 2013), 260–262.

11 Of course, this does not necessarily mean that the new provision ought to consist exclusively of rules rather than standards. Given the complex nature of managing banks, a mixture of rules and standards will be proposed to structure the new provision. On the fundamental distinction between rules and standards, see Julia Black, *Rules and Regulators* (Clarendon Press, 1997), 20–30.

12 In parallel, inappropriate behaviour by a director or senior manager at any time, can lead to the revocation of their authorisation to perform their function. For a detailed discussion of the new regulatory powers in approving senior personnel, see Chapter 5, section III.

financial institutions covered by the new provision, it is submitted that – consistent with the rationale of protecting systemic stability – it must apply to all financial institutions that are deemed systemically important and are thus regulated by the PRA,[13] insofar as they are limited liability companies. The reason why it is argued that only institutions that have the form of a body corporate should be covered, is that in such institutions the misalignment between the private interests of the shareholders and the public interest necessitates a change of corporate governance paradigm.[14] It follows that the scope of the new provision would be broader than the scope of the criminal offence of causing a financial institution to fail. Indeed, section 37 of the Banking Reform Act 2013 interprets the term 'financial institution' as including any institution permitted to accept deposits,[15] and any investment firm that deals in investments as a principal and is regulated by the PRA[16] (apart from an insurance firm or credit union). However, for the purposes of the civil liability regime, insurance firms and any other institutions regulated by the PRA ought to be included. Including all (corporate) financial institutions within the ambit of statutory liability would ensure that both UK-incorporated banks and subsidiaries of overseas banks are covered. This is crucial in view of the large market share and potential systemic importance of foreign banks such as Santander UK Group Holdings plc, which is a wholly owned subsidiary of the Spanish group Banco Santander SA.[17]

With regard to the individuals exposed to civil liability, it is submitted that the approach taken by the criminal offence of causing a bank to fail ought to be followed, amended, of course, to reflect the wider scope of financial institutions covered. This would mean that both directors and other senior managers of financial institutions would be subject to the provision.[18] It could be argued that holding members of the board accountable is sufficient as they can structure the incentives and monitor the conduct of senior managers accordingly.[19] However, the importance of not restricting the scope only to directors is two-fold. First, evidence suggests that financial institution boards are prone to fail to maintain a full understanding of the business decisions taken by senior managers.[20]

13 The range of firms regulated by the PRA was explained in Chapter 3, section II.
14 Whether the civil liability regime proposed herein ought to be extended to building societies and other mutual deposit-takers is an interesting topic for future research, but falls outside the scope of this study.
15 Banking Reform Act 2013, s 37 (3).
16 Banking Reform Act 2013, s 37 (4).
17 At the end of March 2017, Santander UK reported £173.8 billion of total UK customer deposits and £200.2 billion of customer loans. See Santander UK Group Holdings plc, 'Quarterly Management Statement for the Three Months Ended 31 March 2017' (2017) www.santander.co.uk/uk/about-santander-uk/investor-relations/santander-uk-group-holdings-plc accessed 1 May 2017.
18 See Banking Reform Act 2013, s 37 (7)–(8).
19 This would be in line with the approach taken by the Companies Act 2006.
20 For instance, the report on the failure of HBOS concludes that: 'The effects of the culture were all the more corrosive when coupled with a lack of corporate self-knowledge at the top of the organisation, enabling the bank's leaders to persist in the

Therefore, senior managers ought to have a direct personal incentive to ensure they do not contribute to the failure of the financial institution, as board oversight may not be effective in practice. Second, it must be kept in mind that it is currently the practice of major UK financial institutions to structure their boards so that they consist nearly exclusively of non-executive directors, which means that, apart from the CEO, a very limited number of senior managers, if any, sit on boards.[21] It is hence expedient to ensure that liability for failure extends to the persons who actually take crucial decisions rather than merely to a few executive directors and the independent directors who oversee them.

The notion of failure under the new provision should be broad in order to include any relevant insolvency procedures and situations where a distressed financial institution is rescued by public intervention. Therefore, the approach taken by section 37 (9)–(10) of the Banking Reform Act 2013 ought to be followed for the purposes of civil liability as well. This would mean that failure would include: the exercise by the Bank of England of any of the stabilisation options of the Banking Act 2009;[22] inability or likely inability to satisfy claims for the purposes of the Financial Services Compensation Scheme;[23] liquidation; administration, bank insolvency; bank administration; receivership; a composition between the financial institution and its creditors; and a scheme of arrangement.[24] It follows that for banks the most frequent triggering event would be the inclusion of a bank in the Special Resolution Regime of the Banking Act 2009.

c. The liability standard: capped strict liability with defence of reasonable management in line with financial sustainability

With regard to the nature of liability, it is necessary to strike a balance between, on the one hand, the effectiveness of the provision, and, on the other, the need to avoid excessive deterrence. It is submitted that liability in case of financial institution failure ought to be strict but capped at an amount that would be a function of the director's or senior manager's remuneration level, and that defences ought to be available. Of course, ascertaining the appropriate numerical value of the liability cap requires extensive review of relevant empirical evidence, which is not within the scope of this monograph.

Prima facie it appears reasonable to suggest liability to be capped at the total level of remuneration actually received within the five years prior to the failure of

belief, in some cases to this day, that HBOS was a conservative institution when in fact it was the very opposite.' See Parliamentary Commission on Banking Standards, *'An Accident Waiting to Happen': The Failure of HBOS* (2012–13, HL 144, HC 705), para 19.

21 An overview of the board structure of major UK financial services companies, as of April 2017, can be found in Chapter 2, n 128.

22 A brief discussion of the Banking Act 2009 can be found in Chapter 4, section III.

23 Eligibility to be compensated by the Scheme was discussed in Chapter 1, n 80 and accompanying text.

24 See Companies Act 2006, ss 895–901.

the financial institution. This would include components of variable remuneration awarded with respect to earlier performance (indeed up to seven years before the five-year period) which were vested during the relevant period of time. So, liability under the new provision would come on top of any loss suffered by the relevant individuals, due to the failure of the institution with respect to unvested variable remuneration. However, in the case that a firm recovers any variable remuneration components that were vested during the relevant period of time,[25] such amounts ought to be deduced from the total liability under the new provision so that the relevant individual does not repay the relevant sum twice to the institution. With regard to vested remuneration paid in the form of shares, any vested shares held by the executives at the time of failure ought to be valued at the time of failure and not at the time they are vested, so as to prevent a perverse incentive to sell shares immediately after they are vested. This ensures that the civil sanction would be proportionate to the level of reward of each director and senior manager, which means that independent directors would be subject to much lower liability than executives.[26] In addition, if a director has served for less than five years during the five-year period preceding the financial year during which the failure of the financial institution occurred, his or her maximum liability would be reduced accordingly. This also means that if a director or senior manager left the employment of a financial institution at least five years before the year when failure occurred, they would not be liable at all. The five-year time limit is inevitably an arbitrary one, but it reflects the experience gained from the recent major bank failures on the long-term effects of particular business strategies.[27] It is therefore submitted that the level of liability imposed would not be unreasonably onerous.[28]

25 That would be by virtue of the PRA Rulebook, CRR Firms, Remuneration 15.23.

26 This is consistent with the approach taken by the court in *Re Barings*: 'Where there is an issue as to the extent of a director's duties and responsibilities in any particular case, the level of reward which he is entitled to receive or which he may reasonably have expected to receive from the company may be a relevant factor in resolving that issue. It is not that the fitness or otherwise of a respondent depends on how much he is paid. The point is that the higher the level of reward, the greater the responsibilities which may reasonably be expected (prima facie, at least) to go with it.' *Barings plc (No. 5), Re, Secretary of State for Trade and Industry v Baker (No 5)* [1999] 1 BCLC 433, 488 per Parker J.

27 For instance, the FSA considered that the events leading to the failure of RBS covered the last four years before its collapse: 'The Report considers events up to the day RBS first received ELA [Emergency Liquidity Assistance] from the Bank of England – 7 October 2008 – since this was in effect the point of failure. Its coverage (the "Review Period") commences at the beginning of 2005: this reflects a judgement about the timescale that needs to be covered if we are to understand the steady build-up of factors that led to RBS's failure.' See FSA, 'The Failure of the Royal Bank of Scotland: Financial Services Authority Board Report' (2011), para 19 www.fsa.gov.uk/pubs/other/rbs.pdf accessed 1 May 2017.

28 Absent a cap on liability, directors would be held liable for the whole of the damages suffered by a financial institution, which can amount to several billions. That would create an inappropriate disincentive to accept appointments and thus discourage prudent individuals from assuming high positions in financial institutions to the detriment of financial stability. This is why courts are reluctant to hold the directors of large

Making the total potential liability proportionate to the remuneration received by a director or senior manager brings one additional benefit. It reduces the likelihood that the new civil liability will lead to an excessive increase in the remuneration of the relevant persons as compensation for the liability risk, since higher remuneration would lead to higher liability risk. Of course, the proposed provision would still be likely to lead to an increase in the remuneration of financial institution directors and senior managers to compensate them for the increased liability risk. Such an increase would ensure that appropriate candidates can easily be attracted and retained by UK financial institutions and would not be problematic per se, as it would not undermine the incentive created by the new provision, and its overall cost for financial institutions would be likely to be negligible compared to their size and capital.[29]

It is submitted that the above formulation of the statutory liability provision would ensure effective deterrence of excessive risk-taking, while at the same time creating a powerful incentive for individual directors and senior managers to resign and disclose their concerns to the PRA, should they have reasons to suspect that a financial institution is managed in a potentially unsustainable manner. The reversal of the standard of proof means that once a financial institution fails, each director is personally liable unless they are able to prove that the board as a whole managed the financial institution in a way consistent with the objective of financial sustainability.[30] It must be emphasised that under the proposed provision it would not be sufficient for financial institution directors to demonstrate that they followed a reasonable decision-making process and that they seriously considered all the factors listed below, but rather that they had actually been managing the financial institution in a way that did not create any risk to its sustainability.

In particular a director would have to satisfy the court that the board: (a) decided the business strategy of the institution with a view to maintaining the safety and soundness of the institution in the long term, and refrained from approving any transaction or venture that posed a material risk to the safety and soundness of the institution; (b) effectively supervised the discharge of any functions delegated to senior managers, and withheld direct responsibility for approving any transaction or venture that may potentially pose a risk to the safety and soundness of the institution; (c) set the remuneration of senior employees in a way consistent with the objective of maintaining the safety and soundness of the institution in the long term; (d) managed the risks taken by the institution in a way consistent with the

companies liable for breach of their duty of care. On this, see Chapter 2, n 107 and accompanying text.

29 The additional remuneration that a rational, risk-neutral director would demand to compensate for the new liability risk would depend on his estimation of the likelihood that the financial institution will fail within the relevant period of time.

30 The proposed rule has some similarity with the entire fairness review of certain business decisions in Delaware. A discussion of the different standards of judicial review of business decisions in Delaware company law can be found in William Allen, Jack Jacobs and Leo Strine, 'Function over Form: A Reassessment of Standards of Review in Delaware Corporation Law' (2001) 56 *Business Lawyer* 1287.

objective of maintaining the safety and soundness of the institution in the long term; and (e) ensured that all information disclosed to the public, the PRA and the FCA was accurate and provided a fair and true image of the financial position of the institution. This will be very difficult to establish, as the failure of a financial institution indicates strongly that its board has not been effective in setting corporate strategy and remuneration packages prudently, and in moderating risk, unless there is some clear external factor beyond the control of the board that materially contributed to the failure.

Given the different position of senior managers who do not sit on the board, the proposed provision would only require them to establish that – at all relevant times – they had no grounds to believe that the board was not performing the above functions effectively. This will depend on the level of information available to each senior manager, but in many cases, it will be very difficult to prove that the manager had no reason to suspect that the board was not functioning in the requisite manner. In parallel, to avoid liability a senior manager would have to establish that all decisions made or approved by him were consistent with the objective of maintaining the safety and soundness of the institution in the long term.

Furthermore, there should be an additional defence for both directors and senior managers to the following effect. A relevant person should not be held liable if he or she had disclosed his or her concerns about the way the financial institution was run to the PRA and resigned before the forthcoming failure became apparent.[31] So resigning and notifying the PRA before an institution enters into financial difficulties effectively insulates a person from liability in the case where the financial institution fails, thus incentivising directors and senior managers to act as whistle-blowers.[32] For the notification and resignation to be effective in insulating a director from liability, they must be made as soon as the director or senior manager ought to have known that the relevant functions of the board and/or the senior management are not performed appropriately.

The relevant standard of care to determine whether a relevant person's behaviour satisfies the conditions of the two defences ought to reflect the expectation that financial institution directors and senior managers have financial expertise and remain fully informed of the financial position of the institution at all times. It is suggested that the standard of care ought to replicate the one in section 174 of

31 The restriction that the notification of the PRA ought to happen before the point when the financial institution is beyond the point of no return aims to preclude the inappropriate avoidance of liability by directors who – absent the restriction – would be able to notify the PRA and resign *en masse* soon before the failure of a financial institution.

32 There is a rich management studies and psychology literature on the role of whistle blowers which cannot be done justice to here. See e.g. Terry Morehead Dworkin and Melissa Baucus, 'Internal vs. External Whistleblowers: A Comparison of Whistleblowering Processes' (1998) 17 *Journal of Business Ethics* 1281. On the role of auditors as whistle blowers in company law, see David Kershaw, 'Waiting for Enron: The Unstable Equilibrium of Auditor Independence Regulation' (2006) 33 *Journal of Law and Society* 388, 407–419.

the Companies Act with one significant difference: that the objective element ought to refer to a reasonable financial institution director or senior manager and specify that such person ought to: (a) possess relevant financial expertise in proportion to the size and complexity of the institution, and (b) be aware of the main risks faced by the institution and of the true financial position of the institution at all times.

An additional parameter of the implementation of the new statutory liability is its compliance with the Human Rights Act 1998.[33] This requires that the provision does not impose a criminal sanction in the guise of civil liability,[34] as that would infringe the right to a fair trial and the presumption of innocence.[35] The formulation of the proposed provision is intended to emphasise its purely civil nature, which is demonstrated by the compensatory nature of the imposed liability. Indeed, the proposed provision imposes a duty to contribute to the assets of a failed financial institution rather than to pay a fine, and although it aims to deter excessive risk-taking, it does not aim to punish the relevant persons and does not presuppose any finding of dishonesty or culpability. Given the scope of the provision as applying to a particular class of persons only, it is clear that there is no risk that it would be characterised as a criminal provision by the European Court of Human Rights.[36]

33 The Act, which came into force in 2000, incorporated into domestic UK law the European Convention on Human Rights (ECHR). The Ministry of Justice has published a series of relevant handbooks, including one on regulatory authorities. See Ministry of Justice, 'The Human Rights Framework as a Tool for Regulators and Inspectorates' www.equalityhumanrights.com/sites/default/files/moj_guide_regulators_inspectorates.pdf accessed 1 May 2017. An academic analysis of the role of the courts under the Act can be found in Aileen Kavanagh, 'The Elusive Divide between Interpretation and Legislation under the Human Rights Act 1998' (2004) 24 *Oxford Journal of Legal Studies* 259.

34 The terms 'criminal charge' and 'criminal offence' used in ECHR Article 6 have an independent meaning to be determined by the European Court of Human Rights: 'These expressions are to be interpreted as having an autonomous meaning in the context of the Convention and not on the basis of the meaning in domestic law. The legislation of the State concerned is certainly relevant, but it provides no more than a starting-point in ascertaining whether at any time there was a "criminal charge" against [a person] or he was "charged with a criminal offence". The prominent place held in a democratic society by the right to a fair trial favours a "substantive" rather than a "formal", conception of the "charge" referred to by Article 6; it impels the court to look behind the appearances and examine the realities of the procedure in question in order to determine whether there has been a "charge" within the meaning of Article 6.' See *Adolf v Austria* (1982) All EHRR 313, para 30.

35 See ECHR, art 6.

36 'Under the second criterion, the court considers whether or not, under the law concerned, the "offence" is one which applies generally to the public at large or is restricted to a specific group. If the former, then despite its "de-criminalisation" by the national law, it is apt to be regarded as criminal. Further, if a punitive and deterrent penalty is attached, it is likely to be regarded as criminal in character, even in cases where the penalty is in the nature of a fine rather than imprisonment. On the other hand, where the offence is limited to a restricted group, as is generally the case in relation to disciplinary offences, the court is unlikely to classify a charge under the

It follows that the proposed provision would amount to much more than a mere box-ticking exercise resulting in boards producing detailed board minutes and incurring legal costs to ensure that they demonstrate compliance. Indeed, the objective standard of behaviour imposed by the new rule, which would effectively enable the court to review the substantive merits of business decisions made by the boards of failed financial institutions, would be likely to lead to an actual change of behaviour by directors and senior managers and thus substantially enhance financial stability. The list of five parameters of the function of the board reflects existing regulatory requirements on financial firms. However, the importance of incorporating them into the provision is that each individual member of the board potentially becomes personally liable for the failure of the board to perform these functions effectively, irrespective of the individual fault of each director.

The proposed provision reflects the collective nature of the board of directors and resolves the problem of apportioning individual responsibility to each director and senior manager. This emphasises the role of independent directors to deliberate collectively and to assume ultimate responsibility for the management of financial institutions.[37] In particular, a director who did not resign in good time before failure can escape liability only if he can establish that the board *as a whole* has actually been effective in deciding on strategy, setting executive remuneration, moderating risk-taking, monitoring financial disclosures and supervising the discharge of delegated function in a way consistent with the corporate objective of financial stability. This is not a good faith test. The relevant director will have to prove that the way the board functioned was in fact effective with regard to all the above parameters.

Thus, the new provision would create powerful deterrence and would materially alter directors' and senior managers' financial incentives by discouraging risk-taking. In a sense, this would bring back many of the benefits of 19th-century unlimited liability banking,[38] without sacrificing the undeniable economic benefits of limited liability in the financial sector. That being said, it must be kept in mind that there are limitations to the potential of financial incentives to shape behaviour,[39] and that excessive risk-taking can result not only from perverse incentives

applicable disciplinary or regulatory code as criminal, at least unless it involves or may lead to loss of liberty.' See *Han & Yau v Commissioners of Customs and Excise* [2001] EWCA Civ 1048, para 67 per Potter LJ. See also *Engel and others v The Netherlands (No 1)* 1976 1 EHRR 647; *Ozturk v Germany* (1984) EHRR 409; *Bendenoun v France* (1994) 18 EHRR 54; *AP, MP and TP v Switzerland* (1997) 26 EHRR 541; and *Brown v United Kingdom* (1998) 28 EHRR CD 233.

37 CG Code, para A.1 states that: 'Every company should be headed by an effective board which is collectively responsible for the long-term success of the company.'

38 For instance, Turner concludes that: 'The history of British banking [...] teaches that stability can be attained only if bankers are given adequate incentives to not engage in risk shifting. British banking was relatively stable when shareholders and managers faced some form of extended liability.' See John D Turner, *Banking in Crisis; The Rise and Fall of British Banking Stability, 1800 to the Present* (CUP, 2014), 207.

39 Marc T Moore, 'Reconstituting Labour Market Freedom: Corporate Governance and Collective Worker Counterbalance' (2014) 43 *Industrial Law Journal* 398.

but also from cognitive failures.[40] Still, it is submitted that introducing civil liability for financial institution failures along the lines suggested above would not only create a powerful financial incentive to minimise institutions' insolvency risk but would also play a positive role in fostering an appropriate culture in financial institutions. Indeed, research on corporate culture emphasises the importance of setting a clear tone from the top of an organisation, communicating this clearly down all the layers of hierarchy, with appropriate employee participation, and having credible internal enforcement procedures.[41] Evidently, creating appropriate incentives at the top of a complex organisation is likely to facilitate the development of a culture of safe and sound management across all management levels of financial institutions.

d. The enforcement of the new provision: the role of the PRA, shareholders and bondholders

It is worth highlighting that the proposed provision empowers the court to impose liability rather than relying on regulatory enforcement by administrative sanctions. It is submitted that the PRA ought to be under a legal duty to petition the court on each occasion that a financial institution fails, but should be allowed to delay taking action for a reasonable period of time if necessary to protect financial stability. Delaying enforcement can alleviate the risk of undermining confidence in the financial system in a period of investor and depositor panic. In parallel, a failed institution's shareholders and any bondholders whose bonds were converted to equity or who were subject to bail-in[42] ought also to be empowered to petition the court. This would place additional pressure on the PRA to act and ensure that there are multiple avenues of initiating the litigation, thus harnessing the incentives of private actors. Of course, in case an institution is insolvent, shareholders would – in all likelihood – stand to gain nothing from a contribution to its assets by directors and senior managers in their capacity as shareholders, as any contributions would first benefit creditors. However, shareholders may at the same time also hold bonds issued by the failed institution, and in any case failure in this context is broader than balance sheet insolvency, so on some occasions they may still have a direct financial interest in increasing the institution's assets. Consistent with giving the PRA discretion regarding the time of enforcement, if a petition is presented by the shareholders or creditors, the PRA ought to be able to request the court to suspend proceedings for a reasonable period of time.

40 On this, see Arnold Kling, 'The Financial Crisis: Moral Failure or Cognitive Failure?' (2010) 33 *Harvard Journal of Law and Public Policy* 507.

41 Anna P Donovan, 'Systems and Controls in Anti-Bribery and Corruption' in Iris H-Y Chiu (ed), *The Law on Corporate Governance in Banks* (Edward Elgar Publishing, 2015); see also Charles O'Reilly, 'Corporations, Culture and Commitment: Motivation and Social Control in Organizations' (1989) 31 *California Management Review* 12.

42 On contingent convertible bonds and bail-in, see Chapter 4, nn 116–120 and accompanying text.

Granted, regulatory enforcement is generally less expensive and time consuming than the judicial process, and is thus likely to economise on public funds and on the time of courts.[43] In parallel, the availability of the FSMA 2000 appeal mechanism would ensure a degree of protection of defendants. However, it is submitted that judicial enforcement is preferable in the present context on a number of grounds. First, it is the only way to afford the requisite level of protection to defendants who should be entitled to try to defend against liability in front of an impartial court rather than the authority that seeks to impose liability. Second, the publicity attained through the judicial process, but not in the case of regulatory enforcement, would increase public confidence in the financial system and decrease the perception of decision-making behind closed doors. Third, judicial enforcement combined with a legal duty of the authority to petition the court would mitigate the risk that the new provision may be ineffective due to regulatory capture or ineffectiveness. Regulatory effectiveness can generally be undermined by a series of factors, most notably, the presence of perverse incentives and the lack of necessary resources. It is, however, suggested that, in the context of the limited role assigned to the PRA herein, these problems are unlikely to have a serious impact on regulatory effectiveness. To demonstrate this, the issues of regulatory incentives and resources will be examined in turn with a particular focus on financial regulation. Of course, the forthcoming discussion does not purport to tackle the multiple aspects of the problem of regulatory effectiveness, nor to explore in detail the rich literature on the subject,[44] but rather it aims to draw some tentative arguments with regard to regulatory effectiveness to the extent relevant.

Similar to the problem of managerial agency costs in large companies,[45] the individuals heading regulatory authorities do not necessarily have an incentive to do their best to achieve the statutory objectives of the authority. Instead, they may prioritise any of the following: the interests of the government, the interests of the regulated persons, and their own interests. In theory, political pressure by the government can incentivise financial regulators to allow excessive risk-taking, as the latter tends to lead to faster economic growth in the short term.[46] Capture by

43 A general discussion of the merits of regulatory enforcement over litigation, as the most efficient strategy to achieve the social control of business, can be found in Andrei Shleifer, *The Failure of Judges and the Rise of Regulators* (MIT Press, 2012).

44 See e.g. Michael Levine and Jennifer Forrence, 'Regulatory Capture, Public Interest and the Public Agenda: Toward a Synthesis' (1990) 6 *Journal of Law, Economics, and Organization* 167; Michael Moran, 'The Rise of the Regulatory State in Britain' (2001) 54 *Parliamentary Affairs* 19; Giandomenico Majone, 'The Rise of the Regulatory State in Europe' (1994) 17 *West European Politics* 77; Edward Glaeser and Andrei Shleifer, 'The Rise of the Regulatory State' (2003) 41 *Journal of Economic Literature* 401; Julia Black, Martin Lodge and Mark Thatcher (eds), *Regulatory Innovation: A Comparative Analysis* (Edward Elgar, 2005).

45 On this, see Chapter 2, section I.

46 Still, evidence suggests that in European countries, party political pressure on independent authorities is limited. See Mark Thatcher, 'Regulation After Delegation: Independent Regulatory Agencies in Europe' (2002) 9 *Journal of European Public Policy* 954.

the regulated industry[47] can reduce the ability of regulators to impose meaningful constraints on the behaviour of private actors or to detect practices that jeopardise the achievement of the regulatory objectives. Pursuing regulatory self-interest can lead to a proliferation of regulatory rules, guidance and activity to the effect that an unduly complex system arises, as proliferous activity gives regulators the appearance of effectiveness. Indeed, economic evidence suggests that – internationally – the problem of regulatory capture affects banking regulation more severely than most other areas of regulation.[48]

Regarding resources, the successful implementation of the new provision would be facilitated if each financial institution failure were followed by an in-depth inquiry into the causes and circumstances of the failure. Such reviews would also satisfy the public demand for transparency and accountability, and could serve as an opportunity to evaluate the performance of the PRA.[49] It follows that such inquiries ought to be performed by an independent committee. It is therefore submitted that a statutory provision ought to be introduced requiring the Treasury to appoint a special committee to investigate the failure of any institution regulated by the PRA. The committee ought to consist of persons who are not connected with the PRA, the Bank of England, or any financial institution regulated by the PRA. To ensure the effectiveness of the review process, the PRA ought to be required to provide the committee with all relevant information and technical support. The findings of the aforementioned committee would be particularly useful for the court to assess whether the board and management of the failed institution discharged their functions effectively at all times.

II. Complementing the new provision: broader reforms to directors' duties and corporate governance

Having outlined the main parameters of the proposed statutory liability regime for financial institution directors and senior managers, this section examines the legislative context to the new provision looking at directors' duties, insolvency law and remuneration regulation in the financial sector. Several additional legal reforms are thus proposed with a view to complementing and enhancing the effectiveness of the statutory liability regime for financial institution failures which was canvassed in the previous section.

47 Jean-Jacques Laffont and Jean Tirole, 'The Politics of Government Decision-Making: A Theory of Regulatory Capture' (1991) 106 *The Quarterly Journal of Economics* 1089.

48 See Daniel C Hardy, 'Regulatory Capture in Banking' (2006) IMF WP/06/34, esp 4–6 www.imf.org/external/pubs/ft/wp/2006/wp0634.pdf accessed 1 May 2017.

49 On the legal accountability of financial regulators generally, see Dalvinder Singh, *Banking Regulation of the UK and US Financial Markets* (Ashgate Publishing, 2007), 181–210; and Pablo Iglesias-Rodriguez, *The Accountability of Financial Regulators: A European and International Perspective* (Wolters Kluwer, 2013).

a. Reforming the duty of loyalty for financial institution directors

An issue that warrants examination is the relationship between the proposed new provision and the duty of loyalty in section 172 of the Companies Act. Given the aim of the new provision to implement long-term sustainability as the corporate objective of financial institutions, there must not be any ambiguity regarding the prioritisation of financial sustainability over promoting the success of financial institutions for the benefit of their shareholders as a whole.[50] It is therefore submitted that a new subsection ought to be inserted into section 172 to clarify that the section applies in a modified way to financial institutions. Indeed, directors of financial institutions ought to be under a duty to protect the financial sustainability of the institution in advance of the duty to promote its success for the benefits of its members.[51] This would achieve legal certainty and would preclude any ambiguity as to their duties and responsibilities. Doing so would not add much in the context of failure, as then the strict civil liability provision would apply, but would play a role *ex ante* as shareholders would be able to seek permission to bring a derivative claim if they believed that directors were not acting according to the duty. Of course, shareholders who were keen to achieve profit maximisation would have no reason to litigate against directors who put profitability ahead of financial sustainability. Still, any shareholders who may in the future invest in financial institutions relying on the sustainability duty as a safe investment with lower returns and lower risks might be willing to bring litigation.

Furthermore, it is submitted that the holders of contingent convertible bonds and of bonds that are subject to bail-in should also have the right to ask permission to bring a derivative claim for breach of the revised duty of loyalty for financial institution directors. This would give them a meaningful corporate governance function, would complement the role of financial regulators and might also encourage investors to invest in contingent convertible bonds. At the same time the risk of undue interruption of the business affairs of financial institutions by unmeritorious derivative litigation would be minimal given the very restrictive approach courts take with regard to derivative litigation.[52]

b. Amending the wrongful trading and disqualification provisions to reflect the broad notion of financial institution failure

The new civil liability provision ought to be complemented by an amendment to the wrongful trading provision extending the scope of the latter to cover all financial institution failures, in the sense the term was defined with respect to the

50 A discussion of the duty of loyalty can be found in Chapter 2, section IV.

51 Parliamentary Commission on Banking Standards (above n 1), para 124: 'The Commission recommends that the Government consult on a proposal to amend section 172 of the Companies Act 2006 to remove shareholder primacy in respect of banks, requiring directors of banks to ensure the financial safety and soundness of the company ahead of the interests of its members.'

52 On this see Chapter 2, nn 82–83 and accompanying text.

civil liability provision. Ensuring that financial institution directors can be held liable for wrongful trading would still be relevant despite the broader scope of the statutory liability proposed in this chapter. Once a financial institution has no reasonable prospect of avoiding failure, there should be a duty to take all possible steps to minimise losses to creditors. The breach of this duty would lead to additional liability of the errant directors which would not be capped, and could also lead to their disqualification from acting as directors of limited liability companies.[53] Wrongful trading would thus offer an additional accountability device which would incentivise financial institution directors to prioritise the interests of creditors when a financial institution approaches failure, while the proposed new provision would deter excessive risk-taking at all times. It is therefore necessary to insert a new subsection into section 214 of the Insolvency Act 1986 to provide that, for directors of financial institutions, the section applies whenever the institution has failed.[54] The terms 'financial institution' and 'failure' ought to be interpreted in the same manner as for the civil liability provision. In parallel, given that banks and other financial institutions usually do not enter liquidation, the section should be amended so that the PRA can apply to the court for a declaration of liability along with liquidators.

Reforming the wrongful trading provision would bring one additional benefit. If a director of a failed financial institution is found liable on the wrongful trading provision, the court will also be able to disqualify them from being a director of a limited liability company. However, it is submitted that disqualification ought to be more broadly available for directors of failed financial institutions.[55] The most effective way to achieve this would be to amend the Company Directors Disqualification Act 1986 in order to add an additional ground for disqualification: being found liable under the provision imposing liability for financial institution failures proposed herein. Of course, even without any legislative change a director of a failed institution can be precluded by the PRA from being employed in the regulated sector,[56] but would still be able to act as a director of non-financial companies. Disqualification thus can offer additional deterrence as it further reduces the employment prospects of directors of failed institutions, thus strengthening their incentive to safeguard the sustainability of the institution they serve.

c. Regulating the performance metrics used to decide the variable remuneration of financial institution directors

With regard to the performance criteria used to decide the award of variable executive remuneration, it is argued that legislation should enhance the existing

53 Company Directors Disqualification Act 1986, s 10.

54 A similar recommendation was made by Demetra Arsalidou, 'The Banking Crisis: Rethinking and Refining the Accountability of Bank Directors' (2010) *Journal of Business Law* 284, 303–309. See also Demetra Arsalidou, *Rethinking Corporate Governance in Financial Institutions* (Routledge, 2016), 42–43.

55 On the limited relevance of disqualification in case of financial institution failures under the present legal regime, see Chapter 2, section V.

56 A discussion of post-crisis enforcement cases can be found in Chapter 5, section IV (a).

regulatory framework in two respects with a view to removing incentives to increase institutions' insolvency risk. First, financial institutions should be required to use return on risk-weighted assets (RoRWA) rather than total shareholder return (TSR) or earnings per share (EPS). RoRWA is currently used by Barclays as a criterion weighted at 50% to determine pay-outs under its LTIP, while a metric of loan losses is weighted at 20% and a balanced scorecard (non-financial performance) at 30%.[57] Using metrics such as TSR and EPS is especially prone to lead to excessive risk-taking for reasons that are already widely explored and acknowledged by prudential regulators.[58] The major advantage of using RoRWA is that it measures financial performance without being affected by leverage. Return on assets is the same irrespective of the capital structure of a financial institution so that the perverse incentive to increase a financial institution's leverage and hence profits per share is removed. A further advantage of using RoRWA is that it creates a strong incentive to include in an institution's portfolio a higher portion of low-risk assets, as they are weighted with a lower multiplier and, therefore, return on them will be higher.[59]

In addition, as the new corporate objective for financial institutions places financial sustainability above profit maximisation, the PRA rules ought to require financial institutions to use only institutions that are under the same or equivalent rules for their baskets of comparable companies for the purposes of determining variable remuneration payments. For these purposes, the PRA ought to judge whether foreign financial institutions are under an equivalent regime. In this way, there will be no perverse incentive for the senior executives of UK firms to try to emulate the financial performance of non-financial companies or of overseas financial institutions which are governed with the objective of maximising shareholder value.

d. Regulating the remuneration of independent directors to safeguard substantive independence

The level of remuneration received by a (purportedly) independent director compared to his or her overall income should be included as an additional criterion of independence. In recent years, the remuneration of independent directors has increased considerably in all large public companies. In HSBC, for example,

57 Data are taken from the Barclays plc annual reports and accounts 2016.

58 See PRA and FCA Handbook, SYSC 19A.3.24.

59 Compare, for example, the following two scenarios. Bank A owns assets with a real value of 200, all of them risk-weighted at 100%. If its returns are 10, then RoRWA will be 10/200 = 0.05, i.e. 5%. Bank B owns assets with a real value of 200 but 30% of them are risk-weighted at 0%, 25% are weighted at 20% and the remaining 45% at 100%. The risk-weighted assets of Bank B are 100 and therefore if its returns are 10, its RoRWA will be 10/100 = 0.10, i.e. 10%. We observe that Bank B has double RoRWA while the return on assets is the same for both banks. This creates a strong financial incentive for bank executives to structure banks' portfolios of assets including more safe assets.

independent director fees are currently 4.4 times higher than in 1999.[60] This reflects their increased time commitment and responsibilities, and is not necessarily controversial *per se*. The problem is that if an independent director earns a very substantial part of his or her income by appointment on the board of one financial institution, it becomes more difficult for him or her to stand up against the CEO or resign in case he or she disagrees with some important aspects of the financial institution's strategy. Excessive financial dependence on one financial institution can thus undermine the substantive independence of notionally independent directors.[61] This is a real danger in view of the high fees paid, especially when a director acts as chair (or sits on) several board committees and/or has parallel non-executive appointments on the boards of the subsidiaries of the financial institution. In addition, the cap on multiple appointments imposed by CRD IV can further exacerbate the problem of financial dependence of independent directors on the continuation of their appointment.[62]

It is therefore necessary to impose a limit on the remuneration received by independent directors as a percentage of their overall income from all their board appointments and other professional positions. The exact level of the limit ought to be decided after extensive consultation with the relevant parties, but a figure in the area of 25% appears to be reasonable.[63] This would ensure that independent directors can readily afford to be dismissed or resign, while at the same time it is considerably higher than the proportion of their working time that independent directors are expected to devote to their posts, which is typically 13–15%.[64] The CRD IV requirement that bank independent directors should not hold more than four non-executive appointments can render the implementation of the 25% cap difficult, as it would mean that bank independent directors cannot be paid a salary that is higher than the average of their salaries for their other three appointments. However, it must be kept in mind that the CRD IV cap excludes appointments in the not-for-profit sector and empowers national

60 In HSBC, the base fee for non-executive directors in 2017 is £110,000 while in 1999 it was £25,000. The data are derived from the HSBC annual reports and accounts 2016 and 2000, respectively.

61 This is not a problem that is particular to the banking sector but rather affects all independent directors of all large public companies. However, given the increased significance of substantive independence in banks from a public interest perspective, the stringent regulatory response proposed in the context of banks may not be appropriate for other companies.

62 CRD IV, art 91 (3).

63 This would also be compatible with the CRD IV requirement that the same director does not hold more than four parallel non-executive appointments.

64 Assuming that there are 253 working days in a year and 20 days of annual leave, a director's full-time employment is 233 days a year. Bank independent directors are now recommended to spend 30–36 days on their position, i.e. approximately 13% – 15% of their working time. See David Walker, 'A Review of Corporate Governance in UK Banks and Other Financial Industry Entities: Final Recommendations' (2009), para 3.20 www.icaew.com/en/library/subject-gateways/corporate-governance/codes-and-reports/walker-report accessed 1 May 2017.

regulators to allow one additional appointment, which makes the proposed 25% limit workable.

A potential drawback of limiting the remuneration received by financial institution independent directors as a percentage of their aggregate employment income is that it will make it more difficult for individual directors to combine a number of board committee functions and may thus force some financial institutions to increase the size of their boards. Such a side effect, however, does not seriously undermine the potential benefits of the proposed rule, as empirical evidence suggests that larger boards tend to be associated with lower risk-taking and therefore large board size is not inconsistent with the regulatory approach to financial institution corporate governance.

e. Monitoring the expertise of independent directors

Although available evidence from the US does not demonstrate a positive correlation between increased financial expertise in bank boards and lower risk-taking,[65] it is reasonable to assume that under the civil liability framework proposed herein, directorial expertise will contribute to financial institution sustainability. Absent a strong financial incentive to prevent failures, the positive effect of independent director expertise may have been limited or even offset by a potential loss of diversity. However, if independent directors faced a very high risk of liability in case of failure of the financial institution on whose board they serve, they would be incentivised to do everything possible to minimise insolvency risk. Expert directors would no doubt be better placed to do so than non-expert directors, as expertise would enable directors to identify risky decisions and evaluate the business model of a financial institution. In other words, the strong personal incentive would – in all likelihood – reduce the effect of groupthink and improve the cognitive process, as is suggested by relevant psychological studies.[66]

It is therefore crucial that legislation requires the PRA to focus on the financial expertise of proposed financial institution directors and senior managers, which would inevitably entail a broader use of interviews and avoidance of complete reliance on the assessment made by institutions themselves. Of course, the level of expertise required depends on the particular position of each candidate. Executive directors and board chairmen ought to have a very high level of recent financial

65 See Bernadette Minton, Jérôme Taillard and Rohan Williamson, 'Do Independence and Financial Expertise of the Board Matter for Risk Taking and Performance?' (2011) Ohio State University, Fisher College of Business WP 2010-03-014 http://papers.ssrn.com/sol3/papers.cfm?abstract_id=1787126 accessed 1 May 2017. The study was based on a sample of US banks from 2003 to 2008. A potential explanation of the detected *negative* effect of expertise on prudent risk management is the loss of diversity of viewpoints due to independent directors sharing a similar financial sector background.

66 See e.g. Robert Libby and Marlys Gascho Lipe, 'Incentives, Effort, and the Cognitive Processes Involved in Accounting-Related Judgements' (1992) 30 *Journal of Accounting Research* 249, esp 251–255.

sector experience and relevant expertise, whereas independent directors need to have some financial sector management experience or – alternatively – academic qualifications relevant to the financial sector.

f. Mandatory inclusion of CROs on financial institution boards

It has already been explained that major financial institutions are now required by the PRA rules to designate a specific individual as chief risk officer (CRO) and to equip that individual with broad powers relating to risk management.[67] International empirical evidence suggests that bank CROs are more likely to be effective when they report directly to the board as a whole rather than to the CEO,[68] and that having an independent risk management function is correlated with lower risk-taking by banks.[69] Moreover, a recent longitudinal empirical study on the role of CROs in two major (unnamed) UK banks implies that without broader corporate governance changes CROs may still have little effect on decision-making as executives may still engage in excessive risk-taking.[70] It is therefore submitted that legislation ought to prescribe that CROs sit on financial institution boards. Until recently no major UK bank had appointed its CRO on its board.[71] However, since 2014, HSBC and Lloyds have both included their CROs in their boards as a step to emphasise the importance of the risk management function.[72] There are a number of benefits to be gained from appointing CROs on financial institution boards.

First, the elevation of CROs at board level would emphasise their independence from the CEO and would increase the likelihood of them challenging the CEO

67 On this, see Chapter 5, section I.

68 A study of a sample of 573 US banks found that banks whose CRO reported to the board rather than to the CEO in 2006 performed better during the 2007–2009 crisis. See Vincent Aebi, Gabriele Sabato and Markus Schmid, 'Risk Management, Corporate Governance, and Bank Performance in the Financial Crisis' (2011) http://papers.ssrn.com/sol3/papers.cfm?abstract_id=1942896 accessed 1 May 2017.

69 A study of a sample of US banks from 1995 to 2010 suggests that a strong and independent internal risk management function can lead to lower risk-taking. See Andrew Ellul and Vijay Yerramilli, 'Stronger Risk Controls, Lower Risk: Evidence from U.S. Bank Holding Companies' (2013) 68 *The Journal of Finance* 1757.

70 See Matthew Hall, Anette Mikes and Yuval Millo, 'How Do Risk Managers Become Influential? A Field Study in Two Financial Institutions' (2011) Harvard Business School Working Paper No 11–068, 33 www.hbs.edu/faculty/Pages/item.aspx?num=39382 accessed 1 May 2017.

71 Based on the annual reports and accounts for 2012 of Barclays, HSBC, Lloyds, RBS and Standard Chartered. However, CROs were included in the top layer of senior managers in all banks.

72 Data are taken from the HSBC Holdings and Lloyds Banking Group annual reports and accounts for 2014, 2015 and 2016. Interestingly, HSBC stated that: 'The Board has also been strengthened by the appointment of Marc Moses, Group Chief Risk Officer, as an executive Director with effect from 1 January 2014. This reflects the criticality of the Risk function.' See 'HSBC Holdings plc Annual Report and Accounts 2013' (2014), 330 www.hsbc.co.uk/1/PA_esf-ca-app-content/content/pws/content/personal/pdfs/hbeu-2014-ara-final-online.pdf accessed 1 May 2017.

when necessary. The board is the appropriate forum for CROs to express concerns that they have previously discussed privately with the CEO but with no satisfactory outcome. The presence on the board of a majority of independent directors who are likely to support the views of the CRO is a crucial factor that can encourage open discussion and constructive challenge. Second, including the CRO on the board would enable the chairman and independent directors to form a direct opinion with regard to the suitability of the CRO and the approach he or she takes in discharging his or her duties. This is essential for the board to be able independently to assess the performance of the CRO in case the CEO raises a concern. Third, the presence of CROs on boards would enhance information flows to non-executive directors,[73] as CROs are in a unique position to have a global view of the risks faced by a financial institution and of the tools available to manage these risks. Indeed, it should be kept in mind that CROs typically possess substantial technical knowledge which is not shared by other directors and therefore their membership of the board can materially increase the collective expertise of the board and help non-executives perform their function effectively. In parallel, sitting on the board can be beneficial for the CRO, as he or she would be exposed to the concerns of the board, and face the constructive challenge and external viewpoint of independent directors. A related benefit would be the increased publicity of the role of CROs and the higher visibility of CROs to regulators, shareholders and other stakeholders. Finally, including at least three executive directors on financial institution boards would be likely to enhance board effectiveness and hence reduce the risk of excessive risk-taking by mitigating the problems associated with super-majority independent boards.

III. Elements of the corporate law regime that ought not to be reformed: the exclusivity of shareholder voting rights

As explained in Chapter 6, the contractarian theory of the company explains and defends the exclusivity of shareholder voting rights as the probable outcome of a notional bargain between all corporate constituencies, in line with the corporate objective of shareholder wealth maximisation. The adoption of the regulatory paradigm of financial institution corporate governance and of long-term financial sustainability as their corporate objective questions the standard contractarian justification of shareholder voting rights and raises the question of the appropriate attribution of voting rights within the proposed new framework. It is submitted that the existing regulatory approval mechanism for financial institution directors, senior managers and substantial shareholders provides an adequate tool to implement the financial sustainability objective, provided that regulators take a proactive and interventionist approach.[74]

73 This hypothesis is supported by the finding that CROs are more effective when they report directly to the board. See Aebi, Sabato and Schmid (above n 68).

74 A detailed examination of the regulatory regime is provided in Chapter 5, section III.

Preserving shareholder voting rights would maintain the ability of financial institution shareholders to monitor managers with a view to minimising managerial agency costs which affect the shareholders of all widely held companies.[75] Granted, it has been demonstrated in Chapter 1 that the ability of shareholders to monitor financial institution managers effectively is limited, and should not be relied on by prudential regulators. This, however, does not mean that shareholder voting rights are superfluous. Although the actual beneficial effect of shareholder voting on financial institution performance may be limited, the availability of shareholder voting rights is important as they can potentially improve investor confidence and thus facilitate the raising of equity capital by financial institutions.[76] This is beneficial from the perspective of financial stability especially at a time when banks are expected to maintain higher levels of common equity capital and to reduce their overall leverage.

Furthermore, it must be kept in mind that there are situations when the interests of shareholders are not inconsistent with the public interest in financial stability. One example is the approval of the level of remuneration paid to high-end employees. Indeed, in recent years, shareholder opposition to banks' remuneration packages and policies has risen[77] and the same phenomenon has been observed in

75 Nevertheless, shareholder voting rights have recently become the target of academic criticism, especially due to the potential short-termist pressures that they create or encourage. See Marc T Moore and Edward Walker-Arnott, 'A Fresh Look at Stock Market Short-Termism' (2014) 41 *Journal of Law and Society* 416, 437–444. See also Lorraine E Talbot, 'Why Shareholders Shouldn't Vote: A Marxist-progressive Critique of Shareholder Empowerment' (2013) 76 *Modern Law Review* 791, 812–817.

76 Empirical literature on the impact of disproportionate voting rights on shareholder value suggests that multiple voting rights and similar structures reduce the wealth of external investors. This finding implies that shareholder voting is an important mechanism for shareholder value creation. See Renee Adams and Daniel Ferreira, 'One Share-One Vote: The Empirical Evidence' (2008) *12 Review of Finance* 51, 62–72. In parallel, shareholder voting is one of the core mechanisms of investor protection that are necessary for a jurisdiction to achieve developed capital markets. See Rafael La Porta and others, 'Investor Protection and Corporate Valuation' (2002) 57 *Journal of Finance* 1147; Rafael La Porta and others, 'Investor Protection and Corporate Governance' (2000) 58 *Journal of Financial Economics* 3.

77 The Association of British Insurers (ABI) urged the five major UK banks to reform their remuneration policies in December 2011. ABI argued that the balance of rewards between bank managers and shareholders was unacceptable and that the former should not be rewarded for poor performance. ABI thus demanded an overall decrease in bonuses and share options grants, and a closer alignment of remuneration with corporate performance. See Nils Pratley, 'ABI Calls for Root-and-branch Bank Pay Reform – Finally' *The Guardian* (London, 5 December 2011). Indeed, banks faced increased shareholder opposition in their 2011 annual meetings. The most notable case was that of HSBC where 19% of shareholders voted against the directors' remuneration report. In other banks there was lower but significant dissent: 9.7% in Barclays, 8.1% in Lloyds and 7.8% in Standard Chartered. See Gavin Finch, 'HSBC Shareholders Record Biggest Revolt of 2011 on Bank Pay', *Bloomberg* (27 May 2011) www.bloomberg.com/news/2011-05-27/hsbc-chairman-says-it-s-irresponsible-to-ignore-pay-pressure.html accessed 1 May 2017. Shareholder opposition against bank executive pay arrangements was also strong in 2012. In Barclays, for instance, there

large non-financial companies. Excessive levels of remuneration are against the financial interests of shareholders and also potentially dangerous from the perspective of financial stability given that they may weaken the capital of financial institutions and create perverse incentives to take excessive risk. It follows that using shareholder voting to curb excessive remuneration can be beneficial for the financial sustainability of individual financial institutions provided that the broader framework is appropriated, tailored to safeguard financial stability.[78] It is therefore argued that, in view of existing regulatory approval and oversight of senior appointments, and – most crucially – of the civil liability framework in case a financial institution fails proposed herein, short-termist shareholder pressure would not be able to affect materially the decisions of financial institution directors and senior managers. Therefore, it follows that shareholder voting rights would be consistent with the regulatory approach to financial institution corporate governance.

A related issue is the potential attribution of voting rights to some classes of financial institution creditors such as bondholders (who do not benefit from deposit insurance) as a tool to enhance the safety and soundness of financial institutions.[79] Within the corporate objective of financial sustainability, granting voting rights to bondholders is a *prima facie* attractive option as bondholders' utility function is substantially different from that of the shareholders. Rational bondholders have no incentive to support risky business strategies as they stand to lose their investments if the risky strategies fail, but have nothing to gain in case of success.

This, nevertheless, also constitutes the main weakness of creditors as potential direct governance players. As creditors are only interested in securing a modest financial performance which is adequate to minimise the risk of insolvency, they are indifferent as to whether the debtor achieves the best possible performance. Conversely, shareholders are entitled to profit distributions and benefit directly from increases in share prices, so that they are strongly motivated to seek to achieve the highest possible profitability for their investee company. In parallel,

was a dissent of 26.9%. See 'Barclays Stung by Shareholder Pay Revolt' BBC (27 April 2012) www.bbc.co.uk/news/business-17860232 accessed 1 May 2017. The same trend continued in 2013 with most notably the case of HSBC where 11% of the shareholders voted against the remuneration report. See Rupert Neate, 'HSBC Suffers Investor Revolt over Pay' *The Guardian* (London, 24 May 2013). In 2014, it was Standard Chartered that faced the most impressive opposition as more than 40% of its shareholders rejected its remuneration policy. See Sharlene Goff and David Oakley, 'Standard Chartered Investors Revolt over New Pay Structure' *Financial Times* (London, 8 May 2014).

78 An analysis of the CRD IV mandatory rules on the structure of executive remuneration in banks can be found in Chapter 5, section II.

79 Currently, many banks have issued contingent convertible bonds which are converted to shares (with voting rights) if the issuing bank enters serious financial difficulties, before it is insolvent. A discussion of the potential benefits that this approach engenders for financial stability can be found in John Coffee Jr, 'Systemic Risk after Dodd-Frank: Contingent Capital and the Need for Regulatory Strategies beyond Oversight' (2011) 111 *Columbia Law Review* 795.

given the nature of the contractual relationship between bondholders and financial institutions (i.e. that bondholders have contractual rights against issuers), giving bondholders voting rights could potentially allow them to influence managerial decisions to their own benefit, but to the detriment of financial institutions' capital, for example, by issuing further bonds to existing bondholders at a high interest rate. In any case, due to financial institutions' opacity, creditors cannot be relied on to effectively monitor risk-taking. Attributing voting rights to bondholders would therefore not have a significant risk-reduction effect for the same reasons that interest rates paid by banks do not fully reflect their riskiness.

A further concern is that creditors would not be suitable corporate governance actors in times of crisis. Creditors are generally strongly incentivised to wind up immediately a troubled company or part of its business, so as to minimise their losses. Indeed, in the absence of a single large creditor who would take the lead in a rescue process,[80] creditors are likely to wind up a troubled company, even if it is feasible to rescue it, and thus diminish its value, due to severe co-ordination problems. This could lead to increased pressures on financial institution managers to sell problematic assets as soon as creditors realise that an institution is facing financial difficulties. This would be detrimental to financial stability as it could lead to contagion affecting other financial institutions.[81] In addition, liquidation can often be more beneficial to creditors than reorganising an ailing company. In the context of banks, the Special Resolution Regime and the Recovery and Resolution Directive[82] illustrate the public interest aspect of managing a crisis faced by a financial institution, and thus support the argument that direct creditor empowerment would not be consistent with financial stability. Finally, introducing bondholder board representation would be costly and potentially detrimental to sound information flows within financial institution boards. If some directors were appointed by bondholders, the frank exchange of information and views within the board would be impeded, thus weakening boards' monitoring ability.[83]

IV. Conclusions

This chapter proposed a radical reform of financial institution directors' and senior managers' liability via the introduction of a new civil liability provision. The main characteristic of the proposed provision is that directors would be made liable to contribute to the assets of a financial institution that has failed. They could only

80 On corporate rescue generally, see Vanessa Finch, 'Corporate Rescue: A Game of Three Halves' (2012) 32 *Legal Studies* 302.

81 A discussion of contagion in banking can be found in George Kaufman, 'Bank Contagion: A Review of the Theory and Evidence' (1994) 8 *Journal of Financial Services Research* 123.

82 Both are discussed in Chapter 4, section III.

83 Indeed, evidence on the effects of employee representation in Germany confirms that it inhibits the monitoring function of supervisory boards. See Klaus Hopt, 'The German Two-Tier Board: Experience, Theories, Reforms' in Klaus Hopt and others (eds), *Comparative Corporate Governance* (Clarendon Press, 1998), 225.

avoid liability if they had resigned and notified the PRA of their concerns about the way the financial institution was managed before its failure became apparent, or were able to satisfy the court that the board as a whole discharged its strategy setting and risk moderation function effectively with a view to protecting the safety and soundness of the institution. It is submitted that the proposed provision would effectively overhaul the incentive structure for financial institution directors and senior managers, thus mitigating the fundamental danger to financial stability stemming from the nature of most financial institutions as limited liability companies, and especially as public companies with dispersed shareholders. A reform to the duty of loyalty would confirm the priority of financial sustainability over profitability and thus complement the *ex post* imposition of civil liability. Subsidiary reforms would strengthen the accountability of financial institution directors under the wrongful trading and disqualification provisions, mitigate the problem of perverse incentives created by variable remuneration, and enhance the substantial independence of independent directors.

The majority of the reforms proposed herein would not rely on regulatory discretion, but rather would be implemented by legislation to be enforced by the courts. The PRA would have a duty to seek to enforce the civil liability provision, and additional *locus standi* would be given to financial institution shareholders and qualifying creditors. The latter private actors would also be entrusted with the enforcement of the reformed duty of loyalty for financial institution directors. Only the proposed enhanced assessment of the expertise of independent directors would rely entirely on regulatory discretion, and would be added to the existing responsibility of the PRA for assessing the competence of proposed financial institution directors and senior managers. It is therefore submitted that the role assigned to the PRA within the context of the present study would not expand the scope for over-regulation. Overall, the approach proposed herein of amending legislation and relying on the courts rather than on regulators has one major advantage over the current regime: it is much less susceptible to regulatory capture. In parallel, the deterrence effect of a clear strict liability provision and the cultural effect of a reformed duty of loyalty would go beyond what regulatory rules and regulatory enforcement can achieve, thus complementing prudential regulation by enhancing the safety and soundness of systemically important financial institutions, to the ultimate benefit of financial stability.

Conclusions

This book sought to explore the financial stability ramifications of financial institution corporate governance structures, especially of the profit maximisation norm. It began by asking whether a special corporate law regime is necessary for systemically important financial institutions. In short, the answer to this question is positive. The discussion identified the economic grounds for regulating financial institutions' corporate objective and constraining the incentives faced by their directors and senior managers to take risks by mandatory rules with a view to enhancing financial stability. Then, the discussion focused on canvassing the core features of a regulatory approach to financial institution corporate governance with a particular focus on the appropriate corporate objective and on the accountability of directors and senior managers in the context of financial institution failures. The positive and normative outcomes of the present study can be summarised as follows.

First, an extensive review of relevant empirical economic literature, with a particular emphasis on post-crisis studies, demonstrated that running financial institutions with a view to maximising profit involves a level of insolvency risk that is excessive from the point of view of society, as it undermines financial stability. In parallel, private actors such as shareholders, bondholders and depositors cannot be relied on to monitor risk-taking by financial institutions to the requisite extent, due to the combined effect of the misalignment between their own interests and the public interest, and the opacity of financial assets that precludes them from accurately assessing the level of risk taken by individual institutions. It was also demonstrated that the existing UK corporate law framework exacerbates the problem of risk-taking as it insulates company shareholders and directors from the negative consequences of risk-taking.

Second, the book explored the potential effectiveness of existing regulatory measures to mitigate the problems caused by conventional corporate governance structures and the pursuit of profit maximisation in the financial sector. The discussion illustrated the complementarity between, on the one hand, regulating financial institutions' corporate structure and capital adequacy requirements, and on the other, regulating their internal governance. This finding illustrates the need for a paradigm shift regarding the corporate law framework for financial institutions, as a necessary complement to other regulatory measures. In parallel, the doctrinal legal analysis of recent reforms in the UK and EU revealed that the internal corporate governance of banks and other financial institutions has, since the onset of the 2007–2009 financial crisis, been partially transformed due to the introduction of new mandatory rules. Although these changes fall short of effecting a full paradigm shift as advocated in the present volume, they evince the broad recognition of the crucial importance of corporate governance from a financial stability perspective, and suggest that the implementation of the reforms proposed herein does not lie in the sphere of utopia.

Third, it was demonstrated that the broadly accepted contractarian theory of the corporation does not provide unqualified support for a private ordering/facilitative model of corporate law and governance, but rather defends the economic efficiency of a market-driven approach insofar as: (a) equity and debt investors are capable of monitoring the adequacy of governance structures and business strategies; and (b) risk-taking by companies does not lead to negative externalities – or, if it does, these externalities are effectively tackled by other areas of law. It was therefore argued that adopting long-term financial sustainability as the corporate objective of systemically important financial institutions is not only necessary from a public interest perspective but also consistent with law and economics. Such reform necessitates a radical change of the incentives faced by financial institution directors and senior managers. In particular, it was submitted that a new statutory provision should be introduced to the effect of holding directors and senior managers personally liable in case an institution fails. Such liability would be limited to the total remuneration received by the relevant person within five years before the collapse of the bank and would be avoidable in certain circumstances. Other reforms were proposed regarding the duties of financial institution directors, the inclusion of CROs on boards, the way financial performance is assessed for the purposes of variable remuneration, and the expertise and independence of independent directors.

Inevitably, the present study raises a number of questions that can only be explored by future research in the area. Further legal research could explore potential ways to implement similar reforms in other comparable jurisdictions that have adopted a shareholder-centric model of corporate governance, most notably the US and other common law jurisdictions, but also several continental European countries. Furthermore, the discussion highlighted the importance of economic evidence with respect to identifying appropriate board structure and remuneration practices from the perspective of financial stability. Empirical economic or interdisciplinary research can shed additional light on several aspects of this problem and could help evaluate the effectiveness of recent and prospective regulatory reforms. Finally, the inevitable reliance on regulatory supervision and intervention raises issues of regulatory effectiveness, regulatory capture and the appropriate institutional design of regulatory architecture. In view of the interplay between prudential regulation, conduct of business regulation, and regulation of market power, it is submitted that evaluating the regulatory architecture in the financial sector is a formidable task which crosses the boundaries of a number of areas of law, including financial regulation, regulatory theory, corporate governance, and competition law; and of other disciplines, mainly financial, institutional and behavioural economics, management studies and political science.

The intended contribution of the present book to the broader area is the identification of the inherent misalignment between the conventional UK corporate law framework and financial stability, and the exploration of several potential reforms to ensure that corporate governance structures do not create incentives that are inconsistent with the public interest in financial stability but, rather, provide an institutional framework that supports the achievement of regulatory objectives. It is hoped that the normative recommendations put forward herein, apart from provoking academic discussion and debate, may inform current and future regulatory initiatives in the UK and EU. It is therefore lamentable that the UK government did not use the opportunity of the passing of the Banking Reform Act 2013 to implement such reforms, and is currently negative towards the idea of reforming the duties owed by bank directors in favour of financial stability. In view of the forthcoming withdrawal of the UK from the EU, it becomes even more difficult for policy-makers to devote time and effort to issues such as this, which appear to be non-urgent. It is, therefore, only after the UK has successfully navigated the uncharted waters of Brexit that policy space will become again available for reforms such as the ones suggested herein. Even then, however, taking the time to deliberate on and implement policies with a long-term perspective will only be possible if the current political climate which is dominated by constantly responding to crises – real or perceived – is reversed. In the absence of legislative reform, the findings of this book could be taken into account by the courts when shaping the future development of directors' duties in cases involving financial institutions.

In any case, the public debate on the corporate law regime for UK financial institutions and its impact on financial stability will no doubt continue. The reforms proposed in this book will hopefully contribute to this continuing debate and – ultimately – to future legislative reform.

Bibliography

Acharya V and Richardson M, 'Causes of the Financial Crisis' (2009) 21 *Critical Review Journal of Politics and Society* 195

Adams R and Ferreira D, 'One Share-One Vote: The Empirical Evidence' (2008) 12 *Review of Finance* 51

Adams R, Hermalin B and Weisbach M, 'The Role of Boards of Directors in Corporate Governance: A Conceptual Framework and Survey' (2010) 48 *Journal of Economic Literature* 58

Admati A and others, 'Debt Overhang and Capital Regulation' (2012) Stanford University Rock Center for Corporate Governance Working Paper No 114 http://ssrn.com/abstract=2031204 accessed 1 May 2017

Advisory, Conciliation and Arbitration Service, *Code of Practice 1: Disciplinary and Grievance Procedures* (The Stationery Office, 2009)

Aebi V, Sabato G and Schmid M, 'Risk Management, Corporate Governance, and Bank Performance in the Financial Crisis' (2011) http://papers.ssrn.com/sol3/papers.cfm?abstract_id=1942896 accessed 1 May 2017

Agrawal A and Knoeber C, 'Firm Performance and Mechanisms to Control Agency Problems Between Managers and Shareholders' (1996) 31 *Journal of Financial and Quantitative Analysis* 377

Akerlof G, 'The Market for "Lemons": Quality Uncertainty and the Market Mechanism' (1970) 84 *The Quarterly Journal of Economics* 488

Akseli O, 'Was Securitisation the Culprit? Explanation of Legal Processes Behind Creation of Mortgage-backed Sub-Prime Securities' in Gray J and Akseli O (eds), *Financial Regulation in Crisis? The Role of Law and the Failure of Northern Rock* (Edward Elgar Publishing, 2011)

Albertazzi U and Gambacorta L, 'Bank Profitability and the Business Cycle' (2009) 5 *Journal of Financial Stability* 393

Alchian AA and Demsetz H, 'Production, Information Costs, and Economic Organisation' (1972) 62 *American Economic Review* 777

Alcock A, 'An Accidental Change to Director's Duties?' (2009) 30 *The Company Lawyer* 362

Allen F and Santomero A, 'What Do Financial Intermediaries Do?' (2001) 25 *Journal of Banking and Finance* 271

Allen L and Cebenoyan S, 'Bank Acquisitions and Ownership Structure: Theory and Evidence' (1991) 15 *Journal of Banking and Finance* 425

Allen W, 'Our Schizophrenic Conception of the Business Corporation' (1992) 14 *Cardozo Law Review* 261

Allen W, Jacobs J and Strine L, 'Function Over Form: A Reassessment of Standards of Review in Delaware Corporation Law' (2001) 56 *Business Lawyer* 1287

Altunbas Y and Molyneux P, 'Economies of Scale and Scope in European Banking' (1996) 6 *Applied Financial Economics* 367

Andenas M and Chiu IHY, *The Foundations and Future of Financial Regulation: Governance for Responsibility* (Routledge, 2014)

Arcot S and Bruno V, 'In Letter but not in Spirit: An Analysis of Corporate Governance in the UK' (2006) http://papers.ssrn.com/sol3/papers.cfm?abstract_id=819784 accessed 1 May 2017

Arrow K, 'Uncertainty and the Welfare Economics of Medical Care' (1963) 53 *The American Economic Review* 941

Arsalidou D, 'The Banking Crisis: Rethinking and Refining the Accountability of Bank Directors' (2010) *Journal of Business Law* 284

Arsalidou D, *Rethinking Corporate Governance in Financial Institutions* (Routledge, 2016)

Ashcraft A and Bleakley H, 'On the Market Discipline of Informationally Opaque Firms: Evidence from Bank Borrowers in the Federal Funds Market' (2006) Federal Reserve Bank of New York Staff Report 257 www.newyorkfed.org/research/staff_reports/sr257.html accessed 1 May 2017

Ashley-Fenn G, *Corporate Governance – An FSA Perspective* (Building Societies Association Corporate Governance Seminar, London, 2010) www.fsa.gov.uk/pages/Library/Communication/Speeches/2010/0303_gaf.shtml accessed 1 May 2017

Athanasoglou P, Brissimis S and Delis M, 'Bank-specific, Industry-specific and Macroeconomic Determinants of Bank Profitability' (2008) 18 *Journal of International Financial Markets, Institutions and Money* 121

Atkeson A and Simon W, 'The Rising Fear in Bank Stock Prices', *The Wall Street Journal* (New York, 28 November 2011) http://online.wsj.com/news/articles/SB10001424052970204531404577052493270860130 accessed 1 May 2017

Avgouleas E, 'The Global Financial Crisis and the Disclosure Paradigm in European Financial Regulation: The Case for Reform' (2009) 6 *European Company and Financial Law Review* 440

Avgouleas E, 'The Reform of the "Too-Big-To-Fail" Bank: A New Regulatory Model for the Institutional Separation of "Casino" from "Utility" Banking' (2010) https://papers.ssrn.com/sol3/papers.cfm?abstract_id=1552970&rec=1&srcabs=1525670&alg=1&pos=6 accessed 1 May 2017

Avgouleas E, 'What Future for Disclosure as a Regulatory Technique? Lessons from Behavioural Decision Theory and the Global Financial Crisis' in McNeil I and O'Brien J, *The Future of Financial Regulation* (Hart Publishing, 2010)

Avgouleas E and Cullen J, 'Market Discipline and EU Corporate Governance Reform in the Banking Sector: Merits, Fallacies, and Cognitive Boundaries' (2014) 41 *Journal of Law and Society* 28

Avgouleas E and Goodhart C, 'Critical Reflections on Bank Bail-ins' (2015) 1 *Journal of Financial Regulation* 3

Awrey D, Blair W and Kershaw D, 'Between Law and Markets: Is there a Role for Culture and Ethics in Financial Regulation?' (2013) 38 *Delaware Journal of Corporate Law* 191

Ayadi R, Arbak E and De Groen W, 'Executive Compensation and Risk-taking in European Banking' in Barth J, Lin C and Wihlborg C (eds), *Research Handbook on International Banking and Governance* (Edward Elgar Publishing, 2012)

Bahadir A and de los Fayos FG, 'The European Economic Area (EEA), Switzerland and the North' (European Parliament, November 2016) www.europarl.europa.eu/atyourservice/en/displayFtu.html?ftuId=FTU_6.5.3.html accessed 1 May 2017

Bainbridge SM, 'Director Primacy and Shareholder Disempowerment' (2006) 119 *Harvard Law Review* 1735

Bainbridge SM, 'Director Primacy: The Means and Ends of Corporate Governance' (2002–2003) 97 *Northwestern University Law Review* 547

Bainbridge SM and Henderson MT, *Limited Liability: A Legal and Economic Analysis* (Edward Elgar Publishing, 2016)

Ball R, 'The Global Financial Crisis and the Efficient Markets Hypothesis: What Have We Learned?' (2009) 21 *Journal of Applied Corporate Finance* 8

Bank for International Settlements, *International Convergence of Capital Measurement and Capital Standards: A Revised Framework- Comprehensive Version* (Bank for International Settlements Publications, 2006)

Bank of England and Financial Services Authority, 'Instruments of Macroprudential Policy' (December 2011) www.bankofengland.co.uk/publications/Documents/other/financialstability/discussionpaper111220.pdf accessed 1 May 2017

Barker A, Jones C and Sanderson R, 'Brussels and ECB Split on Monte dei Paschi's Capital Proposals', *Financial Times* (London, 23 February 2017)

Barker R, 'Ownership Structure and Shareholder Engagement: Reflections on the Role of Institutional Shareholders in the Financial Crisis' in Sun W, Stewart J and Pollard D (eds), *Corporate Governance and the Global Financial Crisis* (CUP, 2011)

Barnhart S and Rosenstein S, 'Board Composition, Managerial Ownership, and Firm Performance: An Empirical Analysis' (1998) 33 *Financial Review* 1

Barth J, Caprio G and Levine R, 'Bank Regulation and Supervision: What Works Best?' (2004) 13 *Journal of Financial Intermediation* 205

Barth J, Caprio G and Levine R, *Rethinking Bank Regulation: Till Angels Govern* (CUP, 2006)

Barth J, Chen Lin C and Wihlborg C (eds), *Research Handbook on International Banking and Governance* (Edward Elgar Publishing, 2012)

Basel Committee on Banking Supervision, *Basel III: A Global Regulatory Framework for more Resilient Banks and Banking Systems* (rev edn, Bank of International Settlements Publications, 2011)

Basel Committee on Banking Supervision, *Basel III: The Liquidity Coverage Ratio and Liquidity Risk Monitoring Tools* (Bank for International Settlements Publications, 2013)

Basel Committee on Banking Supervision, *Basel III: The Net Stable Funding Ration: Consultative Document* (Bank for International Settlements Publications, 2014)

Basel Committee on Banking Supervision, *Resolution Policies and Frameworks – Progress so far* (Bank of International Settlements Publications, 2011)

Basel Committee on Banking Supervision, *The Joint Forum Report on Special Purpose Entities* (Bank for International Settlements Publications, 2009)

Bebchuk LA, 'Federalism and the Corporation: The Desirable Limits on State Competition in Corporate Law' (1992) 105 *Harvard Law Review* 1435

Bebchuk LA, 'Private Ordering and the Proxy Access Debate' (2010) 65 *Business Lawyer* 329

Bebchuk LA, 'The Case for Increasing Shareholder Power' (2004–2005) 118 *Harvard Law Review* 833

Bebchuk LA, Cohen A and Spamann H, 'The Wages of Failure: Executive Compensation at Bear Stearns and Lehman 2000–2008' (2010) 27 *Yale Journal on Regulation* 257

Bebchuk LA, Fried J and Walker D, 'Managerial Power and Rent Extraction in the Design of Executive Compensation' (2002) 69 *University of Chicago Law Review* 751

Bebchuck LA and Spamann H, 'Regulating Bankers' Pay' (2010) 98 *Georgetown Law Journal* 247

Beltratti A and Stulz R, 'The Credit Crisis Around the Globe: Why Did Some Banks Perform Better?' (2012) 105 *Journal of Financial Economics* 1

Berle A, 'For Whom Corporate Managers are Trustees: A Note' (1932) 45 *Harvard Law Review* 1365

Berle A, *The 20th Century Capitalist Revolution* (Harcourt, Brace & Co, 1954)

Berle A and Means G, *The Modern Corporation and Private Property* (rev edn, Harcourt, Brace & World, 1967)

Bhagat S, 'The Non-Correlation Between Board Independence and Long-Term Firm Performance' (2002) *Journal of Corporation Law* 231

Bhagat S and Black B, 'The Uncertain Relationship Between Board Composition and Firm Performance' (1999) 54 *Business Lawyer* 921

Bhattacharya U and Galpin N, 'The Global Rise of the Value-Weighted Portfolio' (2011) 46 *Journal of Financial and Quantitative Analysis* 737

Bieri DS, 'Regulation and Financial Stability in the Age of Turbulence' in Kolb RW (ed), *Lessons from the Global Financial Crisis* (John Wiley, 2010)

Black B, 'Agents Watching Agents: The Promise of Institutional Investor Voice' (1991–1992) 39 *University of California Los Angeles Law Review* 811

Black J, 'Paradoxes and Failures: "New Governance" Techniques and the Financial Crisis' (2012) 75 *Modern Law Review* 1037

Black J, *Rules and Regulators* (Clarendon Press, 1997)

Black J, 'The Emergence of Risk-based Regulation and the New Public Risk Management in the United Kingdom' (2005) *Public Law* 512

Black J, Hopper M and Band C, 'Making a Success of Principles-based Regulation' (2007) 1 *Law and Financial Markets Review* 191

Black J, Lodge M and Thatcher M (eds), *Regulatory Innovation: A Comparative Analysis* (Edward Elgar Publishing, 2005)

Blair M, *Ownership and Control: Rethinking Corporate Governance for the 21st Century* (Brookings Institute, 1995)

Blair M and others, *Blackstone's Guide to the Bank of England Act 1998* (Blackstone Press Limited, 1998)

Blair M and Stout L, 'A Team Production Theory of Corporate Law' (1999) 24 *Journal of Corporation Law* 751

Bloomfield S, *Theory and Practice of Corporate Governance: An Integrated Approach* (CUP, 2013)

Boyer P and Ponce J, 'Regulatory Capture and Banking Supervision Reform' (2012) 8 *Journal of Financial Stability* 206

Bratton W, 'The New Economic Theory of the Firm: Critical Perspectives from History' (1989) 41 *Stanford Law Review* 1471

Breitenmoser S, 'Sectoral Agreements between the EC and Switzerland: Contents and Context' (2003) 40 *Common Market Law Review* 1137

Brener A, 'No-Man is an Island: UK and EU Banking Regulatory Engagement after "Brexit"' (2016) 27 *European Business Law Review* 1029

Brunner C, *Corporate Governance in the Common-Law World: The Political Foundations of Shareholder Power* (CUP, 2013)

Brunnermeier MK and others, *The Fundamental Principles of Financial Regulation: Geneva Reports on the World Economy* (Center for Economic Policy Research, 2009)

Brunnermeier MK, 'Deciphering the Liquidity and Credit Crunch 2007–2008' (2009) 23 *Journal of Economic Perspectives* 77

Bryer RA, 'The Mercantile Laws Commission of 1854 and the Political Economy of Limited Liability' (1997) 50 *Economic History Review* 37

Bucher C, 'Risk Models-at-risk' (2014) 44 *Journal of Banking & Finance* 72

Burgess S, 'Measuring Financial Sector Output and Its Contribution to UK GDP' (2011) *Bank of England Quarterly Bulletin* 234

Burghardt M, *Retail Investor Sentiment and Behavior* (Gabler Verlag, 2011)

Business, Energy and Industrial Strategy Committee, *Corporate Governance* (HC 2016–2017, 702)

Cadbury A, *Report of the Committee on the Financial Aspects of Corporate Governance* (Gee Professional Publishing, 1992)

Calomiris CW and Herring RJ, 'Why and How to Design a Contingent Convertible Debt Requirement' (2011) https://ssrn.com/abstract=1815406 accessed 1 May 2017

Calomiris CW and Kahn CM, 'The Role of Demandable Debt in Structuring Optimal Banking Arrangements' (1991) 81 *American Economic Review* 497

Campbell A, 'Northern Rock, the Financial Crisis and the Special Resolution Regime' in Gray J and Akseli O (eds), *Financial Regulation in Crisis? The Role of Law and the Failure of Northern Rock* (Edward Elgar Publishing, 2011)

Campbell A and Lastra R, 'Revisiting the Lender of Last Resort – The Role of the Bank of England' in MacNeil I and O'Brien J (eds), *The Future of Financial Regulation* (Hart Publishing, 2010)

Carney WJ, 'Limited Liability Companies: Origins and Antecedents' (1995) 66 *University of Colorado Law Review* 855

Carpenter MA and Sanders WG, 'Top Management Team Compensation: The Missing Link Between CEO Pay and Firm Performance?' (2002) 23 *Strategic Management Journal* 367

Casteuble C, Nus E and Rous P, 'Do Bank Bondholders Price Banks' Ability to Manage Risk/Return' (2015) Université de Limoge Working Paper http://papers.ssrn.com/sol3/papers.cfm?abstract_id=2232889 accessed 1 May 2017

Casu B, Girardone C and Molyneux P, 'Is There a Conflict Between Competition and Financial Stability?' in Barth J, Lin C and Wihlborg C (eds), *Research Handbook on International Banking and Governance* (Edward Elgar Publishing, 2012)

Charny D, 'Hypothetical Bargains: The Normative Structure of Contract Interpretation' (1991) 89 *Michigan Law Review* 1815

Cheffins BR, *Company Law: Theory, Structure and Operation* (OUP, 1997)

Cheffins BR, 'Did Corporate Governance "Fail" During the 2008 Stock Market Meltdown? The Case of the S&P 500' (2009) ECGI Working Paper No 124/2009 http://papers.ssrn.com/sol3/papers.cfm?abstract_id=1396126 accessed 1 May 2017

Cheffins BR, 'The Stewardship's Code Achilles' Heel' (2010) 73 *Modern Law Review* 985

Cheffins BR and Armour J, 'The Rise and Fall (?) of Shareholder Activism by Hedge Funds' (2012) 14 *Journal of Alternative Investments* 17

Cheng M, Dhaliwal D and Neamtiu M, 'Asset Securitization, Securitization Recourse, and Information Uncertainty' (2011) 86 *The Accounting Review* 541

Chiu Iris H-Y, 'Comparing Directors' Duties in the Financial Services Sector with Regulatory Duties under the Senior Persons Regime – Some Critical Observations' (2016) 27 *European Business Law Review* 261

Chiu Iris H-Y, 'Corporate Governance and Risk Management in Banks and Financial Institutions' in Chiu IHY (ed), *The Law on Corporate Governance in Banks* (Edward Elgar Publishing, 2015)

Chiu Iris H-Y, 'Corporate Reporting and the Accountability of Banks and Financial Institutions' in Chiu IHY (ed), *The Law on Corporate Governance in Banks* (Edward Elgar Publishing, 2015)

Chow JTS and Surti J, 'Making Banks Safer: Can Volcker and Vickers do it?' (IMF Working Paper WP/11/236, Nov 2011) https://papers.ssrn.com/sol3/papers.cfm?abstract_id=1945623&rec=1&srcabs=1945621 accessed 1 May 2017

Ciancanelli P and Reyes-Gonzalez J, 'Corporate Governance in Banking: A Conceptual Framework' (European Financial Management Association conference, Athens, June 2000) http://ssrn.com/abstract=253714 accessed 1 May 2017

Cioffi J, *Public Law and Private Power: Corporate Governance Reform in the Age of Finance Capitalism* (Cornell University Press, 2010)

Claessens S, Herring R and Schoenmaker D, *A Safer World Financial System: Improving the Resolution of Systemic Institutions* (Centre for Economic Policy Research, 2010)

Clarke B, '"Corporate Governance" an Oxymoron? The Role of Corporate Governance in the Current Banking Crisis' in Macneil I and O'Brien J (eds), *The Future of Financial Regulation* (Hart Publishing, 2010)

Clarke T, 'Corporate Governance Causes of the Global Financial Crisis' in Sun W, Stewart J and Pollard D (eds), *Corporate Governance and the Global Financial Crisis: International Perspectives* (CUP, 2011)

Clarke T, 'The Stakeholder Corporation: A Business Philosophy for the Information Age' (1998) 31 *Long Range Planning* 182

Coase R, 'The Nature of the Firm' (1937) reprinted in Buckley P and Michie J (eds), *Firms, Organizations and Contracts: A Reader in Industrial Organisation* (OUP, 1996)

Coase R, 'The Problem of Social Cost' (1960) 3 *Journal of Law and Economics* 1

Coffee J, 'Racing Towards the Top?: The Impact of Cross-Listings and Stock Market Competition on International Corporate Governance' (2002) 102 *Columbia Law Review* 1757

Coffee J, 'Systemic Risk after Dodd-Frank: Contingent Capital and the Need for Regulatory Strategies beyond Oversight' (2011) 111 *Columbia Law Review* 795

Commission, 'Corporate Governance in Financial Institutions and Remuneration Policies' *COM* (2010) 284

Commission, 'Proposal for a Regulation of the European Parliament and of the Council on Structural Measures Improving the Resilience of EU Credit Institutions' *COM* (2014) 43

Company Law Review Steering Group, 'Modern Company Law for a Competitive Economy: Developing the Framework' (2000) http://webarchive.nationalarchives.gov.uk/20121029131934/http://www.berr.gov.uk/files/file23245.pdf accessed 1 May 2017

Company Law Review Steering Group, 'Modern Company Law for a Competitive Economy: Final Report' (2001) http://webarchive.nationalarchives.gov.uk/20070603164510/http:/www.dti.gov.uk/cld/final_report/prelims.pdf accessed 1 May 2017

Conn R and others, 'The Impact on UK Acquirers of Domestic, Cross-Border, Public and Private Acquisitions' (2005) 32 *Journal of Business Finance & Accounting* 815

Connelly SJ, 'The Implementation of the EU Bank Recovery and Resolution Directive's Derivative Bail-In Powers in the UK' in Binder JH and Singh D (eds), *Bank Resolution: The European Regime* (OUP, 2016)

Copp S, 'S. 172 of the Companies Act 2006 Fails People and Planet' (2010) *The Company Lawyer* 406

Cornes R and Sandler T, *The Theory of Externalities, Public Goods and Club Goods* (2nd edn, CUP, 1996)

Crawford A, Ezzell J and Miles J, 'Bank CEO Pay-Performance Regulations and the Effects of Deregulation' (1995) 68 *Journal of Business* 231

Crotty J, 'Structural Causes of the Global Financial Crisis: A Critical Assessment of the New Financial Architecture' (2009) 33 *Cambridge Journal of Economics* 563

Datla K and Revesz R, 'Deconstruing Independent Agencies (and Executive Agencies)' (2013) 98 *Cornell Law Review* 769

Davies H and Green D, *Banking on the Future: The Rise and Fall of Central Banking* (Princeton University Press, 2010)

DeAngelo H and Stulz R, 'Liquid-Claim Production, Risk Management, and Bank Capital Structure: Why High Leverage is Optimal for Banks' (2013) Fisher College of Business Working Paper 2013-03-08 http://papers.ssrn.com/sol3/papers.cfm?abstract_id=2254998 accessed 1 May 2017

Dechow P, Myers L and Shakespeare C, 'Fair Value Accounting and Gains from Asset Securitizations: A Convenient Earnings Management Tool with Compensation Side-benefits' (2010) 49 *Journal of Accounting and Economics* 2

Dechow P and Shakespeare C, 'Do Managers Time Securitization Transactions to Obtain Accounting Benefits?' (2006) http://papers.ssrn.com/sol3/papers.cfm?abstract_id=928741 accessed 1 May 2017

Deci EL, 'Effects of Externally Mediated Rewards on Intrinsic Motivation' (1971) 18 *Journal of Personality and Social Psychology* 105

Demb A and Neubauer F, *The Corporate Board: Confronting the Paradoxes* (OUP, 1992)

Department of Business, Innovations and Skills (BIS), 'A Long-Term Focus for Corporate Britain – A Call for Evidence' BIS/10/1225 (2010) www.gov.uk/government/consultations/a-long-term-focus-for-corporate-britain-a-call-for-evidence accessed 1 May 2017

Department of Business, Innovations and Skills (BIS), 'Executive Pay: Shareholder Voting Rights Consultation' (BIS, 14 March 2012) www.bis.gov.uk/assets/biscore/business-law/docs/e/12-639-executive-pay-shareholder-voting-rights-consultation.pdf accessed 1 May 2017

Department of Business, Innovations and Skills (BIS), 'Transparency & Trust: Enhancing the Transparency of UK Company Ownership and Increasing Trust in UK Business: Government Response' (April 2014) www.gov.uk/government/consultations/company-ownership-transparency-and-trust-discussion-paper accessed 1 May 2017

DeYoung R, Peng E and Yan M, 'Executive Compensation and Business Policy Choices at U.S. Commercial Banks' (2013) 48 *Journal of Financial and Quantitative Analysis* 165

Dietrich A and Wanzenried G, 'The Determinants of Commercial Banking Profitability in Low-, Middle-, and High-income Countries' (2014) 54 *The Quarterly Review of Economics and Finance* 337

Dignam A, 'Remuneration and Riots: Rethinking Corporate Governance in the Age of Entitlement' (2013) 66 *Current Legal Problems* 401

Dodd M, 'For Whom are Corporate Managers Trustees' (1932) *Harvard Law Review* 1142

Donaldson T and Preston L, 'The Stakeholder Theory of the Corporation: Concepts, Evidence, Implications' (1995) 20 *Academy Management Review* 65

Donovan AP, 'Systems and Controls in Anti-Bribery and Corruption' in Chiu IHY (ed), *The Law on Corporate Governance in Banks* (Edward Elgar Publishing, 2015)

Dunkley E, 'Lloyds Back in Private Ownership After Government Sells Out', *Financial Times* (London, 17 May 2017)

Dyllick T and Hockerts K, 'Beyond the Business Case for Corporate Sustainability' (2002) 11 *Business Strategy and the Environment* 130

Easterbrook FH, 'Managers' Discretion and Investors' Welfare: Theories and Evidence' (1984) 9 *Delaware Journal of Corporate Law* 540

Easterbrook FH and Fischel DR, 'Mandatory Disclosure and the Protection of Investors' (1984) 70 *Virginia Law Review* 669

Easterbrook FH and Fischel DR, 'The Corporate Contract' (1989) 89 *Columbia Law Review* 1416

Easterbrook FH and Fischel DR, *The Economic Structure of Corporate Law* (Harvard University Press, 1991)

Easterbook FH and Fischel DR, 'Voting in Corporate Law' (1983) 26 *Journal of Law and Economics* 395

Edmans A and Gabaix X, 'Is CEO Pay Really Inefficient? A Survey of New Optimal Contracting Theories' (2009) 15 *European Financial Management* 486

Edwards DO, 'An Unfortunate "Tail": Reconsidering Risk Management Incentives after the Financial Crisis of 2007–2009' (2010) 81 *University of Colorado Law Review* 247

EFTA Court (ed), *The EEA and the EFTA Court* (Oxford, Hart Publishing, 2015)

Eisenberg M, 'The Conception that the Corporation is a Nexus of Contracts and the Dual Nature of the Firm' (1999) 24 *Journal of Corporation Law* 819

Eisner M, 'Private Environmental Governance in Hard Times: Markets for Virtue and the Dynamics of Regulatory Change' (2011) 12 *Theoretical Inquiries in Law* 489

Elhauge E, 'Sacrificing Corporate Profits in the Public Interest' (2005) 80 *New York University Law Review* 733

Ellinger P, Lomnicka E and Hare C, *Ellinger's Modern Banking Law* (5th edn, OUP, 2011)

Ellul A and Yerramilli V, 'Stronger Risk Controls, Lower Risk: Evidence from U.S. Bank Holding Companies' (2013) 68 *The Journal of Finance* 1757

Elton E and others, *Modern Portfolio Theory and Investment Analysis* (8th edn, John Wiley & Sons Inc, 2010)

Erkens D, Hung M and Matos P, 'Corporate Governance in the 2007–2008 Financial Crisis: Evidence from Financial Institutions Worldwide' (2012) 18 *Journal of Corporate Finance* 389

Esho N and others, 'Market Discipline and Subordinated Debt of Australian Banks' (2005) Australian Prudential Regulation Authority Working Paper https://pdfs.semanticscholar.org/cc95/2d0f4b0dbe0289991d33f2fbfa0c65798cb2.pdf accessed 1 May 2017

Eurogroup, 'Statement of 21 February 2012' (2012) www.consilium.europa.eu/uedocs/cms_data/docs/pressdata/en/ecofin/128075.pdf accessed 1 May 2017

European Banking Authority (EBA), 'Consultation on Guidelines on Internal Governance (Revised)' (EBA/CP/2016/16, 2016) www.eba.europa.eu/regulation-and-policy/internal-governance/guidelines-on-internal-governance-revised-/-/regulatory-activity/consultation-paper accessed 1 May 2017

European Banking Authority (EBA), 'Guidelines on the Applicable Notional Discount Rate for Variable Remuneration' (EBA/GL/2014/01, 27 March 2014) www.eba.europa.eu/regulation-and-policy/remuneration/guidelines-on-discount-rate-for-variable-remuneration accessed 1 May 2017

European Banking Authority (EBA), 'Guidelines on Sound Remuneration Policies under Articles 74(3) and 75(2) of Directive 2013/36/EU and Disclosures under Article 450 of Regulation (EU) No 575/2013' (EBA/GL/2015/22, 2015) www.eba.europa.eu/documents/10180/1314839/EBA-GL-2015-22+Guidelines+on+Sound+Remuneration+Policies_EN.pdf accessed 1 May 2017

European Central Bank, 'List of Supervised Entities' (2017) www.bankingsupervision.europa.eu/banking/list/who/html/index.en.html accessed 1 May 2017

European Council, 'Structural Reform of EU Banking Sector: Improving the Resilience of Credit Institutions' (7 April 2016) www.consilium.europa.eu/en/policies/banking-structural-reform/ accessed 1 May 2017

Evans LT and Quigley NC, 'Shareholder Liability Regimes, Principal-agent Relationships, and Banking Industry Performance' (1995) 38 *Journal of Law and Economics* 497

Fahlenbrach R and Stulz R, 'Bank CEO Incentives and the Credit Crisis' (2010) Dice Center Working Paper 2009–2013 www.ssrn.com/abstract=1439859 accessed 1 May 2017

Fama EF, 'Efficient Capital Markets: A Review of Theory and Empirical Work' (1970) 25 *The Journal of Finance* 383

Fama EF, 'Market Efficiency, Long-Run Returns, and Behavioral Finance' (1998) 49 *Journal of Financial Economics* 283

Fassin Y, 'The Stakeholder Model Refined' (2009) 84 *Journal of Business Ethics* 113

Fee EC and Hadlock CJ, 'Management Turnover Across the Corporate Hierarchy' (2004) 37 *Journal of Accounting and Economics* 3

Fein ML, 'The Shadow Banking Charade' (2013) 3–11 https://papers.ssrn.com/sol3/papers.cfm? abstract_id=2218812 accessed 1 May 2017.

Ferran E, 'Examining the UK's Experience in Adopting the Single Financial Regulator Model' (2003) 28 *Brooklyn Journal of International Law* 257

Ferran E, 'The Break-up of the Financial Services Authority' (2011) 31 *Oxford Journal of Legal Studies* 455

Ferran E and Babis V, 'The European Single Supervisory Mechanism' (2013) 13 *Journal of Corporate Law Studies* 255

Ferreira D and others, 'Measuring Management Insulation from Shareholder Pressure' (2016) ECGI Finance Working Paper No 345/2013 http://papers.ssrn.com/sol3/papers.cfm?abstract_id=2170392## accessed 1 May 2017

Financial Conduct Authority, 'Final Notice for Mr Willford' (Reference Number: CXW01232, 11 December 2013) www.fca.org.uk/static/documents/final-notices/christopher-willford.pdf accessed 1 May 2017

Financial Reporting Council, 'The UK Stewardship Code' (2012) www.icaew.com/en/library/subject-gateways/corporate-governance/codes-and-reports/uk-stewardship-code accessed 1 May 2017

Financial Services Authority, 'Effective Corporate Governance (Significant Influence Controlled Functions and the Walker Review)' (FSA Consultation Paper 10/3, 2010) www.fsa.gov.uk/pubs/cp/cp10_03.pdf accessed 1 May 2017

Financial Services Authority, 'FSA Statement on Johnny Cameron' (FSA/PN/081/2010, 2010) www.fsa.gov.uk/pages/Library/Communication/PR/2010/081.shtml accessed 1 May 2017

Financial Services Authority, 'The Failure of the Royal Bank of Scotland: Financial Services Authority Board Report' (2011) www.fsa.gov.uk/pubs/other/rbs.pdf accessed 1 May 2017

Financial Stability Board, 'Key Attributes of Effective Resolution Regimes for Financial Institutions' (2011) www.fsb.org/wp-content/uploads/r_111104cc.pdf accessed 1 May 2017

Financial Stability Board, '2015 Update of Group of Global Systemically Important Banks (G-SIBs)' (2015) www.fsb.org/2015/11/2015-update-of-list-of-global-systemically-important-banks-g-sibs/ accessed 1 April 2017

Finch G, 'HSBC Shareholders Record Biggest Revolt of 2011 on Bank Pay', Bloomberg (27 May 2011) www.bloomberg.com/news/2011-05-27/hsbc-chairman-says-it-s-irresponsible-to-ignore-pay-pressure.html accessed 1 May 2017

Finch V, *Corporate Insolvency Law: Perspectives and Principles* (2nd edn, CUP, 2009)

Finch V, 'Corporate Rescue: A Game of Three Halves' (2012) 32 *Legal Studies* 302

Fischel D, 'The Corporate Governance Movement' (1982) 35 *Vanderbilt Law Review* 1259

Flannery M, Kwan S and Nimalendran M, 'Market Evidence on the Opaqueness of Banking Firms' Assets' (2004) 71 *Journal of Financial Economics* 419

Flannery M, Kwan S and Nimalendran M, 'The 2007–09 Financial Crisis and Bank Opaqueness' (2010) Federal Reserve Bank of San Francisco Working Paper 2010–27 www.frbsf.org/economic-research/files/wp10-27bk.pdf accessed 1 May 2017

Friedman M, *Capitalism and Freedom* (40th anniversary edn, The University of Chicago Press, 2002)

Friedman M, 'The Social Responsibility of Business is to Increase its Profits', *New York Times Magazine* (New York, 13 September 1970)

Freeman E, *Strategic Management: A Stakeholder Approach* (Pitman/Ballinger, 1984)

Future of Banking Commission, 'Final Report' (2010) http://i.telegraph.co.uk/telegraph/multimedia/archive/01656/Bankpdf_1656684a.pdf accessed 1 May 2017

Galbraith JK, *Inequality and Instability: A Study of the World Economy Just Before the Great Crisis* (OUP, 2012)

Gambacorta L and van Rixtel A, *Structural Bank Regulation Initiatives: Approaches and Implications* (BIS Working Paper 412, Bank for International Settlements Publications, 2013)

Gindis D, 'From Fictions and Aggregates to Real Entities in the Theory of the Firm' (2009) 5 *Journal of Institutional Economics* 25

Glaeser E and Shleifer A, 'The Rise of the Regulatory State' (2003) 41 *Journal of Economic Literature* 401

Goergen M, *Corporate Governance and Complexity Theory* (Edward Elgar Publishing, 2010)

Goergen M, Renneboog L and Zhang C, 'Do UK Institutional Shareholders Monitor their Investee Firms?' (2008) 8 *Journal of Corporate Law Studies* 39

Goff S and Oakley D, 'Standard Chartered Investors Revolt over New Pay Structure', *Financial Times* (8 May 2014)

Gonenc R, Maher M and Nicoletti G, 'The Implementation and the Effects of Regulatory Reform: Past Experience and Current Issues' (2000) OECD Working Paper 251 http://papers.ssrn.com/sol3/papers.cfm?abstract_id=238213 accessed 1 May 2017

Goodheart C, *The Evolution of Central Banks* (MIT Press, 1988)

Goodland R, 'The Concept of Environmental Sustainability' (1995) 26 *Annual Review of Ecology and Systematics* 1

Gordon J, 'The Rise of Independent Directors in the United States: Of Shareholder Value and Stock Market Prices' (2007) 59 *Stanford Law Review* 1465

Gordon M, *Finance, Investment and Macroeconomics: The Neoclassical and a Post-Keynesian Solution* (Edward Elgar Publishing, 1994)

Gracie A, 'A Practical Process for Implementing a Bail-in Resolution Power' (British Bankers' Association, London, September 2012) www.bankofengland.co.uk/archive/Documents/historicpubs/speeches/2012/speech600.pdf accessed 1 May 2017

Gray J, 'Financial Regulation before and after Northern Rock' in Gray J and Akseli O (eds), *Financial Regulation in Crisis? The Role of Law and the Failure of Northern Rock* (Edward Elgar Publishing, 2011)

Grossman S and Hart O, 'An Analysis of the Principal-Agent Problem' (1983) 51 *Econometrica* 7

Guest P, Bild M and Runsten M, 'The Effect of Takeovers on the Fundamental Value of Acquirers' (2010) 40 *Accounting and Business Research* 333

Gulinello C, 'The Retail Investor Vote: Mobilizing Rationally Apathetic Shareholders to Preserve or Challenge the Board's Presumption of Authority' (2010) *Utah Law Review* 547

Gunningham N and Johnstone R, *Regulating Workplace Safety: System and Sanctions* (OUP, 1999)

Gup B (ed), *Corporate Governance in Banking: A Global Perspective* (Edward Elgar Publishing, 2007)

Hadjiemmanuil C, *Banking Regulation and the Bank of England* (LLP Publishing, 1996)

Hadjiemmanuil C, 'Special Resolution Regimes for Banking Institutions: Objectives and Limitations' in Ringe G and Huber P (eds), *Legal Challenges in the Global Financial Crisis* (Hart Publishing, 2014)

Hadjiemmanuil C, 'The Bank of England and the Lessons from Barings: UK Banking Regulation under Parliamentary Scrutiny' (1996) 1 *Yearbook of International Financial and Economic Law* 333

Hadjiemmanuil C, 'The Bank Recovery and Resolution Directive in Context' in Binder JH and Singh D (eds), *Bank Resolution: The European Regime* (OUP, 2016)

Haggard S and Howe J, 'Are Banks Opaque?' (2007) University of Southern Mississippi Working Paper www.scribd.com/doc/156507098/Haggard-Stephen-K-John-S-Howe-2007-Are-Banks-Opaque-Jan-11-41-Pp accessed 1 May 2017

Haldane A, 'The Contribution of the Financial Sector: Miracle or Mirage?' (Future of Finance conference, London, 14 July 2010) www.bis.org/review/r100716g.pdf accessed 1 May 2017

Hall M, Mikes A and Millo Y, 'How Do Risk Managers Become Influential? A Field Study in Two Financial Institutions' (2011) Harvard Business School Working Paper No 11-068 www.hbs.edu/faculty/Pages/item.aspx?num=39382 accessed 1 May 2017

Hamermesh LA, 'The Policy Foundations of Delaware Corporate Law' (2006) 106 *Columbia Law Review* 1749

Hamilton J, 'Depositor Protection and Co-insurance after Northern Rock: Less a Case of Moral Hazard and More a Case of Consumer Responsibility?' in Gray J and Akseli O (eds), *Financial Regulation in Crisis? The Role of Law and the Failure of Northern Rock* (Edward Elgar Publishing, 2011)

Hannigan B, 'Drawing Boundaries Between Derivative Claims and Unfairly Prejudicial Petitions' (2009) *Journal of Business Law* 606

Hannigan B, 'Board Failures in the Financial Crisis – Tinkering with Codes and the Need for Wider Corporate Governance Reforms: Part 1' (2011) 32 *The Company Lawyer* 363

Hannigan B, 'Board Failures in the Financial Crisis – Tinkering with Codes and the Need for Wider Corporate Governance Reforms: Part 2' (2012) 33 *The Company Lawyer* 35

Hansen J, 'Insider Dealing after the Market Abuse Directive' in Prentice D and Reisberg A (eds), *Corporate Finance in the UK and EU* (OUP, 2011)

Hansmann H and Kraakman R, 'The Essential Role of Organizational Law' (Harvard Law and Economics Discussion Paper 284, April 2000) http://ssrn.com/abstract=229956 accessed 1 May 2017

Hardjono T and De Klein P, 'Introduction on the European Sustainability Framework (ECSF)' (2004) 55 *Journal of Business Ethics* 99

Hardy D, 'Regulatory Capture in Banking' (2006) IMF WP/06/34, www.imf.org/external/pubs/ft/wp/2006/wp0634.pdf accessed 1 May 2017

Hasan I and Song L, 'Bank Ownership and Performance: A Global Perspective' in Barth J, Chen L and Wihlborg C (eds), *Research Handbook on International Banking and Governance* (Edward Elgar Publishing, 2012)

Hauck A and Neyer U, 'Are Rating Splits a Useful Proxy for Industry Opacity' (2012) http://papers.ssrn.com/sol3/papers.cfm?abstract_id=2103169 accessed 1 May 2017

Health and Safety Executive, 'Write a Health and Safety Policy for your Business' www.hse.gov.uk/simple-health-safety/write.htm accessed 1 May 2017

Heidmann M, 'Current Issues of Directors' Liability – The Scottish View' (2016) 27 *European Business Law Review* 243

Heremans D, 'Corporate Governance Issues for Banks. A Financial Stability Perspective' (2007) University of Leuven Working Paper http://ssrn.com/abstract=1024693 accessed 1 May 2017

Hermalin B and Weisbach M, 'Boards of Directors as an Endogenously Determined Institution: A Survey of the Economic Literature' (2003) 9 *Federal Reserve Bank of New York Economic Policy Review* 7

Hirsch F, 'The Bagehot Problem' (1977) 45 *The Manchester School* 241

HM Treasury Consultation Papers, *A New Approach to Financial Regulation: Building a Stronger System* (2011)

HM Treasury Consultation Papers, *A New Approach to Financial Regulation: Judgement, Focus and Stability* (2010)

HM Treasury, *Annual Report and Accounts 2012–13* (2013–2014, *HC* 34)

HM Treasury, *The Wheatley Review of LIBOR: Final Report* (Government Publications, 2012)

Holmstrom B, 'Moral Hazard in Teams' (1982) 13 *Bell Journal of Economics* 324

Hopt KJ, 'Comparative Company Law' in Reimann M and Zimmermann R (eds), *The Oxford Handbook of Comparative Law* (OUP, 2008)

Hopt KJ, 'Corporate Governance of Banks after the Financial Crisis' in Wymeersch E, Hopt KJ and Ferranini G (eds), *Financial Regulation and Supervision: A Post-crisis Analysis* (OUP, 2012)

Hopt KJ, 'Corporate Governance of Banks and Other Financial Institutions after the Financial Crisis' (2013) 13 *Journal of Corporate Law Studies* 219

Hopt KJ, 'The German Two-Tier Board: Experience, Theories, Reforms' in Hopt KJ and others (eds), *Comparative Corporate Governance* (Clarendon Press, 1998)

Hornuf L, *Regulatory Competition in European Corporate and Capital Market Law: An Empirical Analysis* (Intersentia, 2012)

Hou D and Skeie DR, 'LIBOR: Origins, Economics, Crisis, Scandal, and Reform' (2014) Federal Reserve Bank of New York Staff Report 667 https://papers.ssrn.com/sol3/papers.cfm?abstract_id=2423387 accessed 1 May 2017

Howson N, 'When "Good" Corporate Governance Makes "Bad" (Financial) Firms: The Global Crisis and the Limits of Private Law' (2009) 108 *Michigan Law Review (First Impressions)* 44

Hughes J, 'Cocos and Bail-in Share Common Goal', *Financial Times* (London, 20 February 2011)

Hull J, 'Credit Ratings and the Securitization of Subprime Mortgages' (Up from the Ashes: The Financial System after the Crisis, Atlanta, Georgia, May 2010) https://pdfs.semanticscholar.org/7988/f7d04ea6ca17ecac7cadf7092ab1e877a207.pdf accessed 1 May 2017

Hunt B, *The Development of the Business Corporation in England 1800–1867* (Harvard University Press, 1936)

Hunt J, 'Credit Rating Agencies and the "Worldwide Credit Crisis": The Limits of Reputation, the Insufficiency of Reform, and a Proposal for Improvement' (2009) *Columbia Business Law Review* 109

Iannotta G, 'Testing for Opaqueness in the European Banking Industry: Evidence from Bond Credit Ratings' (2006) 30 *Journal of Financial Services Research* 287

Iannotta G and Navone M, 'Crashes and Bank Opaqueness' (2009) Universita Luigi Bocconi CAREFIN Research Paper No 20/09 http://papers.ssrn.com/sol3/papers.cfm?abstract_id=1600190 accessed 1 May 2017

Iannotta G, Nocera G and Sironi A, 'Ownership Structure, Risk and Performance in the European Banking Industry' (2007) 31 *Journal of Banking and Finance* 2127

Iglesias-Rodriguez P, *The Accountability of Financial Regulators: A European and International Perspective* (Wolters Kluwer, 2013)

Independent Commission on Banking, *Final Report: Recommendations* (Domarn Group, 2011)

International Labour Organisation, 'ILO Declaration on Fundamental Principles and Rights at Work' (18 June 1999) www.ilo.org/declaration/thedeclaration/textdeclaration/lang–en/index.htm accessed 1 May 2017

Ireland P, 'The Myth of Shareholder Ownership' (1999) 62 *Modern Law Review* 32

Iwai K, 'Persons, Things, and Corporations: The Corporate Personality Controversy and Comparative Corporate Governance' (1999) 47 *American Journal of Comparative Law* 583

Jensen MC, 'Value Maximization, Stakeholder Theory, and the Corporate Objective Function' (2001) 14 *Journal of Applied Corporate Finance* 8

Jensen MC and Meckling W, 'Theory of the Firm: Managerial Behavior, Agency Costs and Ownership Structure' (1976) 3 *Journal of Financial Economics* 305

Jensen MC and Murphy K, 'CEO Incentives – It's Not How Much You Pay, But How' (1990) *Harvard Business Review* 138

Johnston A, *EC Regulation of Corporate Governance* (CUP, 2009)

Johnston A, 'Preventing the Next Financial Crisis? Regulating Bankers' Pay in Europe' (2014) 41 *Journal of Law and Society* 6

Jones J, Lee W and Yeager T, 'Opaque Banks, Price Discovery, and Financial Instability' (2012) 21 *Journal of Financial Intermediation* 383

Jones J, Lee W and Yeager T, 'Valuation and Systemic Risk Consequences of Bank Opacity' (2013) 37 *Journal of Banking and Finance* 693

Kahan M and Rock E, 'Embattled CEOs' (2010) 88 *Texas Law Review* 987

Kaplan SN and Minton BA, 'How Has CEO Turnover Changed?' (2012) 12 *International Review of Finance* 57

Kaplow L and Shavell S, 'Why the Legal System is Less Efficient than the Income Tax in Redistributing Income' (1994) 23 *Journal of Legal Studies* 667

Kaufman G, 'Bank Contagion: A Review of the Theory and Evidence' (1994) 8 *Journal of Financial Services Research* 123

Kavanagh A, 'The Elusive Divide between Interpretation and Legislation under the Human Rights Act 1998' (2004) 24 *Oxford Journal of Legal Studies* 259

Kay J, 'Narrow Banking: The Reform of Banking Regulation' (2009) www.johnkay.com/2009/09/15/narrow-banking/ accessed 1 May 2017

Kay J, 'The Kay Review of UK Equity Markets and Long-Term Decision Making – Final Report' BIS/12/917 (2012) www.gov.uk/government/consultations/the-kay-review-of-uk-equity-markets-and-long-term-decision-making accessed 1 May 2017

Keay A, 'A Theoretical Analysis of the Director's Duty to Consider Creditor Interests: The Progressive School's Approach' (2004) 4 *Journal of Corporate Law Studies* 307

Keay A, 'Ascertaining the Corporate Objective: An Entity Maximisation and Sustainability Model' (2008) 71 *Modern Law Review* 663
Keay A, 'Company Directors Behaving Poorly: Disciplinary Options for Shareholders' (2007) *Journal of Business Law* 656
Keay A, 'Directors' Duties to Creditors: Contractarian Concerns Relating to Efficiency and Over-Protection of Creditors' (2003) 66 *Modern Law Review* 665
Keay A, 'Stakeholder Theory in Corporate Law: Has it Got What it Takes?' (2010) 9 *Richmond Journal of Global Law & Business* 240
Keay A, *The Corporate Objective* (Edward Elgar Publishing, 2011)
Keay A, *The Enlightened Shareholder Value Principle and Corporate Governance* (Routledge, 2013)
Keay A, 'The Ultimate Objective of the Public Company and the Enforcement of the Entity Maximisation and Sustainability Model' (2010) 10 *Journal of Corporate Law Studies* 35
Kelly G and Parkinson J, 'The Conceptual Foundations of the Company: A Pluralist Approach' in Parkinson J, Kelly G and Gamble A (eds), *The Political Economy of the Company* (Hart Publishing, 2000)
Kershaw D, 'Waiting for Enron: The Unstable Equilibrium of Auditor Independence Regulation' (2006) 33 *Journal of Law and Society* 388
King M, 'The Cost of Equity for Global Banks: A CAPM Perspective from 1990 to 2009' (2009) *BIS Quarterly Review* 56
King THD and Wen MM, 'Shareholder Governance, Bondholder Governance and Managerial Risk-taking' (2011) 35 *Journal of Banking and Finance* 512
Kirkpatrick G, 'The Corporate Governance Lessons from the Financial Crisis' (2009) *OECD Journal: Financial Market Trends* 61
Kleinman M, 'Bank Watchdog Steps Up Bonus Cap Opposition' Sky News (London, 23 September 2013) http://news.sky.com/story/1145453/bank-watchdog-steps-up-bonus-cap-opposition accessed 1 May 2017
Kling A, 'The Financial Crisis: Moral Failure or Cognitive Failure?' (2010) 33 *Harvard Journal of Law and Public Policy* 507
Knight F, *Risk, Uncertainty and Profit* (Houghton Mifflin Co, 1967, first printed in 1921)
Kokkinis A, 'A Primer on Corporate Governance in Banks and Financial Institutions – Are Banks Special?' in Chiu IHY (ed), *The Law on Corporate Governance in Banks* (Edward Elgar Publishing, 2015)
Kokkinis A, 'Shareholder Short-Termism in the UK: The Kay Review and the Potential Role of Corporate Law' (2014) 11 *Corporate Ownership and Control* 166
Kokkinis A, 'The Financial Services Act 2012: The Recent Overhaul of the United Kingdom's Financial Regulatory Structure' (2013) *International Company and Commercial Law Review* 325
Kokkinis A, 'The Impact of Brexit on the Legal Framework for Cross-border Corporate Activity' (2016) 27 *European Business Law Review* 959
Kokkinis A, 'The Reformed "Fit and Proper" Test: A Call for a Broader Rethink of Bank Corporate Governance?' (2012) 9 *International Corporate Rescue* 5
KPMG, 'Road to Recovery? What the Future Holds for UK Banks: Half Year Results 2013' (2013) www.criticaleye.com/insights-servfile.cfm?id=3740 accessed 1 May 2017
Kraakman R and others, *The Anatomy of Corporate Law: A Comparative and Functional Approach* (3rd edn, OUP, 2017)
Kynaston D, *The City of London – Volume IV: A Club No More, 1945–2000* (Pimlico Publications, 2002)

La Porta R and others, 'Investor Protection and Corporate Governance' (2000) 58 *Journal of Financial Economics* 3

La Porta R and others, 'Investor Protection and Corporate Valuation' (2002) 57 *Journal of Finance* 1147

LaBrosse JR and Walker DK, 'The Role of Deposit Insurance Post Implementation of the EU Recovery, Resolution and Deposit Guarantee Directives' in Binder JH and Singh D (eds), *Bank Resolution: The European Regime* (OUP, 2016)

Laffont J and Tirole J, 'The Politics of Government Decision-Making: A Theory of Regulatory Capture' (1991) 106 *The Quarterly Journal of Economics* 1089

Langevoort D, 'The Human Nature of Corporate Boards: Law, Norms, and the Unintended Consequences of Independence and Accountability' (2001) 89 *Georgetown Law Journal* 797

Laux V, 'Board Independence and CEO Turnover' (2008) 46 *Journal of Accounting Research* 137

Law Commission, *Company Directors: Regulating Conflicts of Interests and Formulating a Statement of Duties* (Law Com No 261, 1999)

Lazonick W, 'From Innovation to Financialization: How Shareholder Value Ideology is Destroying the US Economy' in Wolfson MH and Epstein GA (eds), *The Handbook of the Political Economy of Financial Crises* (OUP, 2013)

Le Mire S and Gilligan G, 'Independence and Independent Company Directors' (2013) 13 *Journal of Corporate Law Studies* 443

Lee IB, 'Efficiency and Ethics in the Debate about Shareholder Primacy' (2006) 31 *Delaware Journal of Corporate Law* 533

Levine M and Forrence J, 'Regulatory Capture, Public Interest and the Public Agenda: Toward a Synthesis' (1990) 6 *Journal of Law, Economics, and Organization* 167

Levine R, 'The Corporate Governance of Banks: A Concise Discussion of Concepts and Evidence' (2004) World Bank Policy Research Working Paper 3404 http://elibrary.worldbank.org/doi/book/10.1596/1813-9450-3404 accessed 1 May 2017

Libby R and Lipe M, 'Incentives, Effort, and the Cognitive Processes Involved in Accounting-Related Judgements' (1992) 30 *Journal of Accounting Research* 249

Liebenberg A and Hoyt R, 'The Determinants of Enterprise Risk Management: Evidence from the Appointment of Chief Risk Officers' (2003) 6 *Risk Management & Insurance Review* 37

Liikanen E, 'High-level Expert Group on Reforming the Structure of the EU Banking Sector: Final Report' (2012) http://ec.europa.eu/internal_market/bank/docs/high-level_expert_group/report_en.pdf accessed 1 May 2017

Llewellyn D, 'The Economic Rationale for Financial Regulation' (FSA Occasional Paper Series 1, April 1999) www.fsa.gov.uk/pubs/occpapers/op01.pdf accessed 1 May 2017

Lowry J, 'The Irreducible Core of the Duty of Care, Skill and Diligence of Company Directors' (2012) 75 *Modern Law Review* 249

Lowry J and Edmunds R, 'Directors Duties and Liabilities: Disqualifying "Unfit" Directors at Banks? Political Rhetoric and the Directors' Disqualification Regime' in Chiu IHY (ed), *The Law on Corporate Governance in Banks* (Edward Elgar Publishing, 2015)

Lowry J and Reisberg A, *Pettet's Company Law: Company Law & Corporate Finance* (4th edn, Pearson, 2012)

Lu L, 'The End of Bankers' Bonus Cap: How Will the UK Regulate Bankers' (2016) 27 *European Business Law Review* 1091

Lupold M and Schnyder G, 'Horse, Cow, Sheep, or "Thing-in-itself"? The Cognitive Origins of Corporate Governance in Switzerland, Germany, and the US, 1910s-1930s' (28 February 2008) http://ssrn.com/abstract=1018413 accessed 1 May 2017

Macey J and O'Hara M, 'The Corporate Governance of Banks' (2003) 9 *Federal Reserve Bank of New York Economic Policy Review* 91

MacNeil I and O'Brien J, *The Future of Financial Regulation* (Hart Publishing, 2010)

Majone G, 'The Rise of the Regulatory State in Europe' (1994) 17 *West European Politics* 77

Malkiel BG, 'The Efficient Market Hypothesis and Its Critics' (2003) 17 *The Journal of Economic Perspectives* 59

Mallin C, 'The Co-Operative Bank – What Went Wrong?' in Mallin C (ed), *Handbook on Corporate Governance in Financial Institutions* (Edward Elgar Publishing, 2016)

Manne H, 'Mergers and the Market for Corporate Control' (1965) 73 *The Journal of Political Economy* 110

Markowitz H, 'Portfolio Selection' (1952) 7 *The Journal of Finance* 77

Maurice E, 'EU and Switzerland Agree on Free Movement' *Eurobserver* (22 December 2016) https://euobserver.com/justice/136398 accessed 1 May 2017

McVea H, 'Financial Services Regulation under the Financial Services Authority: A Reassertion of the Market Failure Thesis?' (2005) 64 *Cambridge Law Journal* 413

Meeks R, Nelson B and Alessandri P, 'Shadow Banks and Macroeconomic Instability' (2014) Bank of England Working Paper No 487 www.bankofengland.co.uk/research/Pages/workingpapers/2014/wp487.aspx accessed 1 May 2017

Milgram S, *Obedience to Authority* (Harper and Row, 1974)

Miller E, 'Risk, Uncertainty and Divergence of Opinion' (1977) 32 *The Journal of Finance* 1151

Millon D, 'Theories of the Corporation' (1990) 39 *Duke Law Journal* 201

Ministry of Justice, 'The Human Rights Framework as a Tool for Regulators and Inspectorates' www.equalityhumanrights.com/sites/default/files/moj_guide_regulators_inspectorates.pdf accessed 1 May 2017

Minton B, Taillard J and Williamson R, 'Do Independence and Financial Expertise of the Board Matter for Risk Taking and Performance?' (2011) Ohio State University, Fisher College of Business WP 2010-03-014 http://papers.ssrn.com/sol3/papers.cfm?abstract_id=1787126 accessed 1 May 2017

Mitchell L, *Corporate Irresponsibility* (Yale University Press, 2001)

Mitchell L, *Progressive Corporate Law* (Westview Press, 1995)

Modigliani F and Miller M, 'The Cost of Capital, Corporation Finance and the Theory of Investment' (1959) 48 *American Economic Review* 261

Monks R, 'A Review of Corporate Governance in UK Banks and Other Financial Industry Entities: The Role of Institutional Shareholders' in Sun W, Stewart J and Pollard D (eds), *Corporate Governance and the Global Financial Crisis: International Perspectives* (CUP, 2011)

Monteiro D, *The Flow of Credit in the UK Economy and the Availability of Financing to the Corporate Sector* (Economic Papers 509, EU 2013) http://ec.europa.eu/economy_finance/publications/economic_paper/2013/pdf/ecp509_en.pdf accessed 1 May 2017

Moore MT, *Corporate Governance in the Shadow of the State* (Hart Publishing, 2013)

Moore MT, 'Corporate Governance, Pay Equity, and the Limitations of Agency Theory' (2015) 68 *Current Legal Problems* 431

Moore MT, 'Design and Control of Remuneration in UK Banks' in Chiu IHY (ed), *The Law on Corporate Governance in Banks* (Edward Elgar Publishing, 2015)

Moore MT, 'Private Ordering and Public Policy: The Paradoxical Foundations of Corporate Contractarianism' (2014) 34 *Oxford Journal of Legal Studies* 693

Moore MT, 'Reconstituting Labour Market Freedom: Corporate Governance and Collective Worker Counterbalance' (2014) 43 *Industrial Law Journal* 398

Moore MT, 'The Evolving Contours of the Board's Risk Management Function in UK Corporate Governance' (2010) 10 *Journal Corporate Law Studies* 279

Moore MT and Walker-Arnott E, 'A Fresh Look at Stock Market Short-termism' (2014) 41 *Journal of Law and Society* 416

Moorehead Dworkin T and Baucus M, 'Internal vs. External Whistleblowers: A Comparison of Whistleblowering Processes' (1998) 17 *Journal of Business Ethics* 1281

Moran M, 'The Rise of the Regulatory State in Britain' (2001) 54 *Parliamentary Affairs* 19

Morck R, 'Behavioral Finance in Corporate Governance – Independent Directors, Non-Executive Chairs, and the Importance of the Devil's Advocate' (2004) 12 *Journal of Management and Governance* 179

Morgan B and Yeung K, *An Introduction to Law and Regulation: Text and Materials* (CUP, 2007)

Morgan D and Stiroh K, 'Bond Market Discipline of Banks: The Asset Test' (2001) 20 *Journal of Financial Services Research* 195

Morgan D, 'Rating Banks: Risk and Uncertainty in an Opaque Industry' (2002) 92 *American Economic Review* 874

Mulbert PO, 'Corporate Governance of Banks after the Financial Crisis – Theory, Evidence, Reforms' (2010) ECGI Working Paper No 151/2010 http://papers.ssrn.com/sol3/papers.cfm?abstract_id=1448118 accessed 1 May 2017

Murphy KJ, 'Regulating Banking Bonuses in the European Union: A Case Study in Unintended Consequences' (2013) 19 *European Financial Management* 631

Neate R, 'HSBC Suffers Investor Revolt over Pay', *The Guardian* (London, 24 May 2013)

Newton LA, 'The Birth of Joint-stock Banking: England and New England Compared' (2010) 84 *Business History Review* 27

O'Reilly C, 'Corporations, Culture and Commitment: Motivation and Social Control in Organizations' (1989) 31 *California Management Review* 12

Office for National Statistics, 'Ownership of UK Quoted Shares: 2014' (2015) www.ons.gov.uk/economy/investmentspensionsandtrusts/bulletins/ownershipofukquotedshares/2015-09-02 accessed 1 May 2017

Organisation for Economic Co-operation and Development, 'G20/OECD Principles of Corporate Governance' (2004) www.oecd.org/corporate/oecdprinciplesofcorporategovernance.htm accessed 1 May 2017

Organisation for Economic Co-operation and Development, *OECD Guidelines for Multinational Enterprises* (OECD Publishing, 2011)

Osili U and Paulson A, 'Bank Crises and Investor Confidence: An Empirical Investigation' (2009) Federal Reserve Bank of Chicago Working Paper No 2008–2017 www.chicagofed.org/webpages/publications/policy_discussion_papers/2009/pdp_9.cfm accessed 1 May 2017

Pacces A (ed), *The Law and Economics of Corporate Governance: Changing Perspectives* (Edward Elgar Publishing, 2010)

Panel on Takeovers and Mergers, *The City Code on Takeovers and Mergers* (11th edn, RR Donnelley, 2013)

Parkinson J, *Corporate Power and Responsibility: Issues in the Theory of Company Law* (Oxford Clarendon Press, 1993)

Parkinson J, 'Disclosure and Corporate Social and Environmental Performance: Competitiveness and Enterprise in a Broader Social Frame' (2003) 3 *Journal of Corporate Law Studies* 3

Parliamentary Commission on Banking Standards, *'An Accident Waiting to Happen': The Failure of HBOS* (2012–2013, *HL*144, *HC* 705)

Parliamentary Commission on Banking Standards, *Changing Banking for Good* (2013–2014, *HL*27-II, *HC*175-II)

Pasiouras F and Kosmidou K, 'Factors Influencing the Profitability of Domestic and Foreign Commercial Banks in the European Union' (2007) 21 *Research in International Business and Finance* 222

Pauly M, 'The Economics of Moral Hazard: Comment' (1968) 58 *The American Economic Review* 531

Penn G, *Banking Supervision: Regulation of the UK Banking Sector under the Banking Act 1987* (Butterworths, 1989)

Perez O, 'Private Environmental Governance as Ensemble Regulation: A Critical Exploration of Sustainability Indexes and the New Ensemble Politics' (2011) 12 *Theoretical Inquiries in Law* 543

Peters FS and Wagner AF, 'The Executive Turnover Risk Premium' (2014) 69 *Journal of Finance* 1529

Picciotto S, *Regulating Global Corporate Capitalism* (CUP, 2011)

Policy Exchange, *Ringfencing UK Banks: More of a Problem than a Solution*, James Barty ed (Heron, Dawson and Sawyer, 2013)

Polo A, 'Corporate Governance of Banks: The Current State of the Debate' (2007) http://ssrn.com/abstract=958796 accessed 1 May 2017

Posner R, *Economic Analysis of Law* (8th edn, Wolters Kluwer, 2011)

Posner R and Scott KE, *Economics of Corporation Law and Securities Regulation* (Little, Brown and Company, 1980)

Power M, *Organized Uncertainty: Designing a World of Risk Management* (OUP, 2007)

Prabha A, Wihlborg C and Willett T, 'Market Discipline for Financial Institutions and Markets for Information' in Barth J, Lin C and Wihlborg C (eds), *Research Handbook on International Banking and Governance* (Edward Elgar Publishing, 2012)

Pratley N, 'ABI Calls for Root-and-branch Bank Pay Reform – Finally', *The Guardian* (London, 5 December 2011)

Prentice D, 'Creditors' Interests and Director's Duties' (1990) 10 *Oxford Journal of Legal Studies* 265

Prowse S, 'Alternative Methods of Corporate Control in Commercial Banks' (1995) *Federal Reserve Bank of Dallas Economic and Financial Policy Review* 3

Prudential Regulation Authority, 'Capital Requirements for Major UK Banks and Building Societies' (Supervisory Statement SS3/13, November 2013) www.bankofengland.co.uk/pra/Pages/publications/ss/2015/ss313update.aspx accessed 1 May 2017

Prudential Regulation Authority, 'Designation of Investment Firms for Prudential Supervision by the Prudential Regulation Authority' (Statement of Policy, March 2013) www.bankofengland.co.uk/publications/Documents/other/pra/designationofinvestmentfirms.pdf accessed 1 May 2017

Prudential Regulation Authority, 'Final Notice for Mr Alderson' (Reference Number: KBA01005, 14 January 2016) www.bankofengland.co.uk/publications/Pages/news/2016/022.aspx accessed on 1 May 2017

Prudential Regulation Authority, 'Final Notice for Mr Tootell' (Reference Number: BXT01184, 14 January 2016) www.bankofengland.co.uk/publications/Pages/news/2016/022.aspx accessed on 1 May 2017

Prudential Regulation Authority, 'Implementing the Bank Recovery and Resolution Directive' (Policy Statement PS1/15, January 2015) www.bankofengland.co.uk/pra/Pages/publications/ps/2015/recoveryresolutionupdate.aspx accessed 1 May 2017

Prudential Regulation Authority, 'Strengthening Capital Standards: Implementing CRD IV, Feedback and Final Rules' (Policy Statement PS 7/13, 13 June 2013) www.bankofengland.co.uk/pra/Pages/publications/implemcrdiv.aspx accessed 1 May 2017

Prudential Regulation Authority, 'Strengthening the Alignment of Risk and Reward: New Remuneration Rules' (PRA PS12/15, 2015) www.bankofengland.co.uk/pra/Pages/publications/ps/2015/ps1215.aspx accessed 1 May 2017

Prudential Regulation Authority, 'The PRA's Approach to Banking Supervision' (2012) www.bankofengland.co.uk/pra/Pages/publications/bankingappr1210.aspx accessed 1 May 2017

Prudential Regulation Authority, 'The PRA's Approach to Insurance Supervision' (2012) www.fsa.gov.uk/about/what/reg_reform/pra accessed 1 May 2017

Rabin M and Thaler RH, 'Anomalies: Risk Aversion' (2001) 15 *The Journal of Economic Perspectives* 219

Rathenau W, *Von kommenden Dingen* (Berlin, S Fischer, 1917)

Rawlings P, 'Bank Reform in the UK: Part II- Return to the Dark Ages?' (2011) 8 *International Corporate Rescue* 55

Reid M, *The Secondary Banking Crisis, 1973–75: Its Causes and Course* (Macmillan Publishers, 1982)

Reisberg A, *Derivative Actions and Corporate Governance* (OUP, 2007)

Reisberg A, 'Shadows of the Past and Back to the Future: Part 11 of the UK Companies Act 2006 (In)Action' (2009) 6 *European Company and Financial Law Review* 219

Reisberg A, 'The Notion of Stewardship from a Company Law Perspective' (2011) 18 *Journal of Financial Crime* 126

Reisberg A, 'The Role of Institutional Shareholders: Stewardship and the Long/Short Term Debate' in Chiu IHY (ed), *The Law on Corporate Governance in Banks* (Edward Elgar Publishing, 2015)

Riley W and Chow V, 'Asset Allocation and Individual Risk Aversion' (1992) 48 *Financial Analysts Journal* 32

Rock EB, 'Adapting to the New Shareholder-Centric Reality' (2013) 161 *University of Pennsylvania Law Review* 1907

Roe MJ, 'Corporate Short-termism – In the Boardroom and in the Courtroom' (2013) 68 *Business Lawyer* 981

Rogowski R, *Reflexive Labour Law in the World Society* (Edward Elgar Publishing, 2013)

Rosenblum L, 'The Failure of the City of Glasgow Bank' (1933) 8 *The Accounting Review* 285

Ryan C, 'Transfer of Banking Supervision to the Financial Services Authority' in Blair M and others (eds), *Blackstone's Guide to the Bank of England Act 1998* (Blackstone Press, 1998)

Sabato G, 'Financial Crisis: Where Did Risk Management Fail?' (2010) 2 *International Review of Applied Financial Issues and Economics* 315

Samuelson P, 'The Pure Theory of Public Expenditure' (1954) 36 *Review of Economics and Statistics* 387

Santos J, 'Bank Capital Regulation in Contemporary Banking Theory: A Review of the Literature' (2001) 10 *Financial Markets, Institutions & Instruments* 41

Saunders A, Strock E and Travlos N, 'Ownership Structure, Deregulation and Bank Risk Taking' (1990) 45 *The Journal of Finance* 643

Schrader D, 'The Corporation and Profits' (1987) 6 *Journal of Business Ethics* 589

Schwarcz SL, 'Information Asymmetry and Information Failure: Disclosure Problems in Complex Financial Markets' in Sun W, Stewart J and Pollard D (eds), *Corporate Governance and the Global Financial Crisis: International Perspectives* (CUP, 2011)

Schwarcz SL, 'Systemic Risk' (2008) 97 *Georgetown Law Journal* 193

Schwarcz SL and Chang L, 'The Custom to Failure Cycle' (2012) 62 *Duke Law Journal* 767

Shavell S, 'Criminal Law and the Optimal Use of Non-Monetary Sanctions as Deterrants' (1985) *Columbia Law Review* 1232

Shleifer A, *The Failure of Judges and the Rise of Regulators* (MIT Press, 2012)

Shleifer A and Vishny R, 'A Survey of Corporate Governance' (1997) 52 *The Journal of Finance* 737

Simonsohn U, 'Direct Risk Aversion: Evidence from Risky Projects Valued Below Their Worst Outcome' (2009) 20 *Psychological Science* 686

Singh D, *Banking Regulation of the UK and US Financial Markets* (Ashgate, 2007)

Singh D, 'Recovery and Resolution Planning: Reconfiguring Financial Regulation and Supervision' in Binder JH and Singh D (eds), *Bank Resolution: The European Regime* (OUP, 2016)

Sjoberg G, 'Banking Special Resolution Regimes as a Governance Tool' in Ringe WG and Huber P (eds), *Legal Challenges in the Global Financial Crisis* (Hart Publishing, 2014)

Smith A, *An Inquiry into the Nature and Causes of the Wealth of Nations* (Strahan and Cadell, 1776)

Spina J, 'The Failure of Lehman Brothers' (2013) http://papers.ssrn.com/sol3/papers.cfm?abstract_id=2337124 accessed 1 May 2017

Spong K, *Banking Regulation: Its Purposes, Implementation and Effects* (5th edn, Federal Reserve Bank of Kansas City Publication, 2000)

Spong K and Sullivan R, 'Bank Ownership and Risk Taking: Improving Corporate Governance in Banking after the Crisis' in Barth J, Chen Lin C and Wihlborg C (eds), *Research Handbook on International Banking and Governance* (Edward Elgar Publishing, 2012)

Stefanescu C, 'Does a Strong Governance Mechanism Improve Efficiency in Banking System?' (2014) 20 *International Advances in Economic Research* 117

Steward R, 'A New Generation of Environmental Regulation?' (2001–2002) 29 *Capital University Law Review* 21

Stiglitz J, 'Principal and Agent' in Eatwell J, Milgate M and Newmann P (eds), *The New Palgrave Dictionary of Economics, Vol. 3* (Macmillan, 1987)

Stout L, 'Bad and Not-so-Bad Arguments for Shareholder Primacy' (2001–2002) 75 *Southern California Law Review* 1189

Stout L, 'The Mechanisms of Market Inefficiency' (2003) 28 *Journal of Corporation Law* 635

Stout L, 'The Shareholder as Ulysses: Some Empirical Evidence on Why Investors in Public Corporations Tolerate Board Governance' (2003–2004) 152 *University of Pennsylvania Law Review* 667

Talbot LE, 'Critical Corporate Governance and the Demise of the Ultra Vires Doctrine' (2009) 38 *Common Law World Review* 170

Talbot LE, 'Keeping Bad Company: Building Societies a Case Study' (2009) 60 *Northern Ireland Legal Quarterly* 443

Talbot LE, *Progressive Corporate Governance for the 21st Century* (Routledge, 2013)

Talbot LE, 'Why Shareholders Shouldn't Vote: A Marxist-progressive Critique of Shareholder Empowerment' (2013) 76 *Modern Law Review* 791

Tanna S, Pasiouras F and Nnadi M, 'The Effect of Board Size and Composition on the Efficiency of UK Banks' (2011) 18 *International Journal of the Economics of Business* 441

Teubner G, 'Enterprise Corporatism: New Industrial Policy and the "Essence" of the Legal Person' (1988) 36 *American Journal of Comparative Law* 130

Teubner G, *Law as an Autopoietic System*, Bankowska A and Adler R trs, Bankowski Z ed (Blackwell, 1993)

Thanassoulis J, 'The Case for Intervening in Bankers' Pay' (2012) 67 *The Journal of Finance* 849

Thatcher M, 'Regulation after Delegation: Independent Regulatory Agencies in Europe' (2002) 9 *Journal of European Public Policy* 954

Tomasic R, 'Beyond "Light Touch" Regulation of British Banks after the Financial Crisis' in MacNeil I and O'Brien J (eds), *The Future of Financial Regulation* (Hart Publishing, 2010)

Tomasic R, 'Corporate Rescue, Governance and Risk Taking in Northern Rock: Part 2' (2008) 29 *The Company Lawyer* 330

Tomasic R, 'The Failure of Corporate Governance and the Limits of Law: British Banks and the Global Financial Crisis' in Sun W, Stewart J and Pollard D (eds), *Corporate Governance and the Global Financial Crisis: International Perspectives* (CUP, 2011)

Treasury Committee, *Competition and Choice in Retail Banking* (*HC*2010–2011, 612-I)

Treasury Committee, *The Run on the Rock* (*HC*2007–2008, 56-I)

Trubek D and Trubek L, 'New Governance & Legal Regulation: Complementarity, Rivalry, and Transformation' (2006–2007) 13 *Columbia Journal of European Law* 539

Tsagas G, 'The Market for Corporate Control in the Banking Industry' in Chiu IHY (ed), *The Law on Corporate Governance in Banks* (Edward Elgar Publishing, 2015)

Turner JD, *Banking in Crisis: The Rise and Fall of British Banking Stability, 1800 to the Present* (CUP, 2014)

Tversky A and Kahneman D, 'Advances in Prospect Theory: Cumulative Representation of Uncertainty' (1992) 5 *Journal of Risk and Uncertainty* 297

Ungureanu MC, 'Banks: Regulation and Corporate Governance Framework' (2008) 5 *Corporate Ownership and Control* 449

Vafeas N and Theodorou E, 'The Relationship between Board Structure and Firm Performance in the UK' (1998) 30 *British Accounting Review* 383

Valdez S and Molyneux P, *An Introduction to Global Financial Markets* (6th edn, Palgrave Macmillan, 2010)

Valnek T, 'The Comparative Performance of Mutual Building Societies and Stock Retail Banks' (1999) 23 *Journal of Banking and Finance* 925

Veblen T, *Absentee Ownership and Business in Recent Times* (Viking Adult, 1923)

Vitols S, 'Varieties of Corporate Governance: Comparing Germany and the UK' in Hall P and Soskice D (eds), *Varieties of Capitalism: The Institutional Foundations of Comparative Advantage* (OUP, 2001)

Walker D, 'A Review of Corporate Governance in UK Banks and Other Financial Industry Entities: Final Recommendations' (2009) www.icaew.com/en/library/subject-gateways/corporate-governance/codes-and-reports/walker-report accessed 1 May 2017

Walker-Arnott E, 'Company Law, Corporate Governance and the Banking Crisis' (2010) 7 *International Corporate Rescue* 19

Walker-Arnott E, 'Corporate Governance and Banks – The Role and Composition of the Board Corporate Governance' in Chiu IHY (ed), *The Law on Corporate Governance in Banks* (Edward Elgar Publishing, 2015)

Wallison P, 'Did the "Repeal" of the Glass-Steagall Have any Role in the Financial Crisis? Not Even Close' (2009) 106 *Public Lawyer* 102

Weinstein N and Klein W, 'Unrealistic Optimism: Present and Future' (1996) 15 *Journal of Social and Clinical Psychology* 1

Weir C, Laing D and McKnight P, 'Internal and External Governance Mechanisms: Their Impact on the Performance of Large UK Public Companies' (2002) 29 *Journal of Business Finance and Accounting* 579

Weisbach MS, 'Outside Directors and CEO Turnover' (1988) 20 *Journal of Financial Economics* 431

Wells H, 'The Cycles of Corporate Social Responsibility: An Historical Retrospective for the Twenty-first Century' (2002–2003) 51 *Kansas Law Review* 77

White L, 'Corporate Governance and Prudential Regulation of Banks: Is There any Connection?' in Barth J, Lin C and Wihlborg C (eds), *Research Handbook on International Banking and Governance* (Edward Elgar Publishing, 2012)

Williams R, 'Disqualifying Directors: A Remedy Worse than the Disease?' (2007) 7 *Journal of Corporate Law Studies* 213

Williamson O, *The Mechanisms of Governance* (OUP, 1996)

Winter J, 'The Financial Crisis: Does Good Corporate Governance Matter and how to Achieve it?' in Wymeersch E, Hopt KJ and Ferranini G (eds), *Financial Regulation and Supervision: A Post-crisis Analysis* (OUP, 2012)

Winter R, 'State Law, Shareholder Protection and the Theory of the Corporation' (1977) 6 *Journal of Legal Studies* 251

Working Group on Corporate Governance of the Basel Committee, *Principles for Enhancing Corporate Governance*, Nouy D and others (Bank of International Settlements Publications, 2010)

Yermack D, 'Higher Market Valuation of Companies with a Small Board of Directors' (1996) 40 *Journal of Financial Economics* 185

Yoshimori M, 'Whose Company is it? The Concept of Corporations in Japan and the West' (1995) 28 *Long Range Planning* 33

Zingales L, *Capitalism for the People: Recapturing the Lost Genius of American Capitalism* (Basic Books, 2012)

Index

www.ingramcontent.com/pod-product-compliance
Ingram Content Group UK Ltd.
Pitfield, Milton Keynes, MK11 3LW, UK
UKHW011004180926
475701UK00004B/550
* 9 7 8 0 3 6 7 8 8 6 4 1 7 *